ST. MARY'S COLLEGE OF MARYLAND
ST. MARY'S CITY, MARYLAND

47316

NEWS EDITING AND DISPLAY

News Editing and Display

By CHARLES H. BROWN

THE PENNSYLVANIA STATE COLLEGE

GREENWOOD PRESS, PUBLISHERS
WESTPORT, CONNECTICUT

Copyright 1952 by Harper & Row, Publishers

Reprinted with the permission
of Harper & Row, Publishers, New York

First Greenwood Reprinting 1970

Library of Congress Catalogue Card Number 74-109285

SBN 8371-3828-0

Printed in the United States of America

CONTENTS

Foreword by Fayette Copeland ix

Preface xi

1. CONTROL POINT FOR THE NEWS 1
   When a Big Story Breaks. The Need for Copyreaders. Duties of the Copyreader. Copyreading—Art and Science

2. PREPARING COPY FOR THE PRINTER 10
   Copyreading Symbols. Instructions to the Printer. Marking Wire Copy. Keeping Track of Stories. Handling Story Revisions. Marking Proofs. Faults of Copyreaders

3. THE GUARDIAN OF CORRECT USAGE 29
   The Office Stylesheet. Typographical Errors. Spotting Misspelled Words. Errors in Punctuation. Wrong Use of Words. Common Grammatical Errors

4. SHAPING THE STORY TO THE NEWS 46
   Developing a Formula. Applying the Formula

5. EXPLANATION AND AUTHORITY IN THE NEWS 56
   Need for Explanatory Background. Identification of Persons. Identification of Organizations. Identification of Places. Identification of Events. Identification of Words. How the Explanation Should Be Presented. Indicating Sources of Information. Editing Speech Reports. Use of Speech Tags

CONTENTS

6. MAKING ROOM FOR ALL THE NEWS 70

   The Need for Trimming Stories. Unnecessary Words. Wordy Phrases. Wordy Clauses. Unnecessary Transitions. Unnecessary Attributions. Eliminating Trivial Details. Unnecessary Repetition. Opinion and Interpretation. Space-Stealing Reporters

7. ON GUARD AGAINST MISTAKES 82

   The Omniscient Copyreader. Knowing the Reporters. The Nature of Newspaper Error. The Ability to Find Errors. Ambiguities and Hidden Meanings. False Emphasis and Exaggeration

8. READABILITY AND UNDERSTANDING 91

   News and Literary Style. Measuring Readability. Making Sentences Readable. The Short Paragraph. Personal Words and Sentences. Words That People Know. Semantics for the Copyreader

9. PRESS ASSOCIATION NEWS 110

   World-Wide News Networks. AP, INS, UP. The Wire Report. Assembling the Stories. News by Perforated Tape. Copyreading Wire Stories

10. HEADLINE FUNDAMENTALS 132

    How Headlines Evolved. Functions of Headlines. Headline Patterns and Terminology. Counting Out Heads. Headline Schedules

11. RULES FOR WRITING HEADLINES 142

    Headline Appearance. Action in Headlines. Omission of Words. Split Headlines. Blind First Lines. Identifications in Heads. Abbreviations. Headline Style. The Diction of Headlines. The Ethics of Headlines

12. COMPOSING THE HEADLINE 158

    Getting Started. Exercise in Condensation. Choosing the "Must" Elements. Heads with More Than One Deck. Hangers for Spread Heads. Jump Heads. Subheads Within Stories. Heads for Follow-Up Stories. Feature Head Techniques. Headlines for Nonnews Features

CONTENTS

13. TYPOGRAPHY FOR THE DESKMAN ... 178
    Composing Room Machinery. Measurement of Type. Classification of Type by Design. Leading, Rules, and Dashes

14. NEWSPAPER USE OF TYPE ... 199
    Trend Toward Larger Body Type. Headline Type Faces. Headline Patterns. Headline Type Sizes. Typographical Brighteners. Principles of Good Typography

15. PRINCIPLES OF MAKE-UP ... 218
    Position and Rank of Pages. Types of Front-Page Make-Up. Rules for Make-Up. Inside-Page Make-Up. Make-Up of Tabloids

16. MAKE-UP PROCEDURES AND PROBLEMS ... 247
    Complexities of Make-Up. Determining Space. Keeping the Record. The Page Dummy. Checking for Make-Up Errors. Some Front-Page Problems. Major News Display. Make-Up with Pictures. Inside-Page Problems

17. DECIDING THE PAPER'S CONTENT ... 271
    The Problem of the News. Judging the News. News and Newspaper Economics. Popularity Polls and Surveys. How Much Entertainment? Publication Conditions

18. PUBLICITY AND PROPAGANDA ... 287
    Handouts Swamp the Desk. Some Guiding Principles. Some Specific Problems. The Prime Evil of Publicity. From Products to Ideas. Techniques of Propaganda. Combating the Propagandist

19. ETHICAL PROBLEMS OF THE NEWS ... 302
    Violations of Personal Privacy. The Obligation of Fair Play. News Suppression. News About Minorities. Maintaining the Proprieties

20. PRESS LAW AND THE COPY DESK ... 320
    Curbs on the Press. On Guard Against Libel. The Copyreader's Problem. Contempt of Court. Miscellaneous Restrictions. Property Rights in News

CONTENTS

21. PICTURES AND THE NEWS — 339
The Place of Pictorial Journalism. Sources of Newspaper Pictures. What Pictures to Publish. Editing the Picture. Determining the Size of the Cut. Ordering Engravings. Writing Cutlines

22. TRADE AREA NEWS — 365
A Gap in News Coverage. Handling State Correspondents. Some State Desk Problems. Coverage by Staff Members. Display of Area News. Country Correspondence. Selecting Correspondents. Editing and Display

23. THE SPORTS SECTION — 379
A High-Pressure Job. Space and Coverage. News About Participant Sports. Sports—Racket or Recreation. College Publicity Handouts. The Strange World of Sports. The Deskman at Work

24. BUSINESS AND FINANCIAL NEWS — 397
Room for Improvement. The Business Page Editor. Local Business News. The Wire News Report. Financial Page Jargon

25. THE WOMEN'S DEPARTMENT — 410
New Styles in Women's Pages. The Editor's Qualifications. Who Is Society? Social News Problems. Feature Articles for Women. Women's Page Make-Up

Appendix A. Stylesheet — 429

Appendix B. Words Frequently Misused — 438

Appendix C. Newspaper Terms — 441

Index — 449

FOREWORD

Today's newspaper is a product of continuing change. The issue we buy at the newsstand or pick up from our doorstep may appear exactly like yesterday's. But improvements which began with the first colonial publications still are going on. They affect the concept of the newspaper's relationship to its readers, as well as its readability, illustration, typography, and make-up.

Thus, the teacher of journalism must go into the classroom with a newspaper in one hand and a textbook in the other. The newspaper serves as a factual report of how the job is done today; the text should explain and emphasize principles of procedure.

Instruction in a course in news editing must include teaching and practice in preparation of copy for the printer, in headline writing, in make-up. Along with this training and drill in craftsmanship, the teacher must instill a wholesome respect for detail, an understanding of news values, and a knowledge of the ethics and laws involved in the publication of news.

The student must learn how to guard against mistakes, how to trim a story to meet space requirements, how to select and edit pictures, and how to handle highly specialized kinds of news copy.

Textbooks may be merely points of departure for a study of current trends and practices, or they can be of great value to both teacher and student as storehouses of information and fact.

Authors of journalism texts face a particular dilemma. They must select from today's changing panorama of news enough significant examples to emphasize the "here's how it's done." They must do this without letting the student lose sight of the all-important "here's why."

Charles H. Brown's text on news editing results from years of experience in writing and editing news copy, and even more years of careful study of newsroom practices and problems. He has emphasized the new concept of the editor's essential task of intelligent news presentation, and has transmitted to the student his own fresh viewpoint which has made him an outstanding teacher.

This text sets the pattern for editing which should fit both small and large newspapers. It should be of great value to the student in the classroom and to the editor who faces the never-ending flow of copy across his desk.

Fayette Copeland
Director, School of Journalism
University of Oklahoma

PREFACE

Conventions rather than independent judgments as to news and its display—what Walter Lippmann has labeled stereotypes—have in the past been the pragmatic bases of daily journalism. Especially has this been true of desk work in which large masses of material must with great speed be sorted out, checked, given headlines, and designated for places in the newspaper.

Such robot editing, although it sufficed when the newspaper was looked upon as a "daily miracle," is out of place today. The copyreader must be able speedily and efficiently to process material for the printers, but his job calls also for an understanding of the social responsibilities of the newspaper and the ethical and legal problems that arise daily. The stories he edits and the headlines he writes have an independent life of their own after they leave his desk—in the minds of the newspaper's readers. They may clarify or becloud the understanding of an important issue, they may reinforce prejudices or remove them, they may influence opinion, and they may move to action.

This textbook, in consequence, goes beyond the concept of the desk man's job as that of a corrector of errors, a trimmer of stories to space, and a writer of headlines. These tasks require expert technical ability, what critics of schools of journalism have condemned as merely "tricks of the trade." It is important that the journalism student learn these techniques, but he must also be able to judge news for its value in engaging and enlightening readers and to estimate its possible impact on their minds.

The first chapters explain the routine procedures of preparing copy for the printers. These are followed by chapters on headline writing and make-up. Then come chapters on fundamental policies and problems, presented not as absolute rules to follow—for there are none upon which all editors agree—but rather as bases for classroom discussion. Descriptions of the jobs of departmental editors comprise the final chapters.

This arrangement has been followed because it seems adapted to instructional plans in many schools and departments of journalism, regardless of whether the copyreading and editing course is of one or two semesters. It is important that the students start editing copy and writing headlines as early as possible in order to master the techniques demanded by their prospective employers. The discussion of general principles can come later, though of course these principles enter into each operation on the copy desk. Specialized news and departmental editing ordinarily should be taken up toward the end of the course.

Throughout the text the author has sought to distinguish between practices of metropolitan and of small-city newspapers. If there is a bias, it is toward training for work on smaller publications, where most students will get jobs on graduation. For example, questions of policy may be only academic for a long time to graduates who begin their careers on big-city newspapers; they are immediate realities to those who start as deskmen or departmental editors on small-city publications. For the same reason, the author has stressed the importance of an acquaintance with print-shop practices. Except for the make-up editor, editorial room employees of metropolitan newspapers have few contacts with compositors and printers. Deskmen on small publications must deal with them constantly.

This textbook embodies a statement of rules and a description of practices derived from a study of those generally followed by newspapers. Such a codification is essential for instructional purposes, but the student should not consider it as ultimate and unalterable. The author frequently gives reasons for stated practices and traces their origin and development. Even though sometimes he has not found much sense in them, he presents them because that's the way things are done. He would consider his book a failure, however, if students got the idea there are no other and better methods. The newspaper must change with changing conditions and changing needs of readers. Journalism's qualified editors of the future will be those now beginning their careers who are not afraid to break the rules and who do not fear to try new ways of doing things.

CHARLES H. BROWN

NEWS EDITING AND DISPLAY

CHAPTER 1

Control Point for the News

WHEN A BIG STORY BREAKS

At 5:40 P.M. on Thursday, April 12, 1945, Stephen Early, secretary to President Franklin D. Roosevelt, began placing calls from the White House to the three major press association bureaus in Washington.

The White House, staff members of the bureaus were told, wanted to dictate an announcement. They were told to "hang on" while the circuit for the round-robin call was completed.

After a delay of almost ten minutes, the voice of Mr. Early came over the wire to the waiting rewrite men sitting at their typewriters with earphones adjusted. "Here is a flash," he said. "The president died suddenly this afternoon. . . ."

Seconds later a single sentence topped by the word "flash" was ripped from typewriters and handed to trunk-wire teletype punchers. They interrupted the dispatches they were sending and tapped a key which started bells to ringing on receiving teletypes in press association bureaus and newspaper offices all over the United States—the signal for news of transcendent importance.

Machines of the International News Service were starting a story from Rome: "An Italian government spokesman revealed today . . ." The bells rang. There was a short pause. Then:

FLASH
WASHN—FDR DEAD.

In the Associated Press bureau the operator of the Washington wire was tapping out a correction: "In night lead food delete 5th, 6th and 7th graphs beginning . . ." He interrupted the message with the following:

FLASH
WASHINGTON—PRESIDENT ROOSEVELT DIED SUDDENLY THIS AFTERNOON.

The Washington teletype puncher for the United Press had finished a "book" and was ready to start the second "take" of an item about black markets in the capital. But instead he rapped out this urgent message:

FLASH
WASHINGTON—PRESIDENT DIED THIS AFTERNOON.

The flash caught newspapers unprepared, many of them with skeletonized staffs. In the Eastern and Central time zones the afternoon papers were running off their last editions, and morning paper deskmen were leisurely editing early copy for their bulldog editions. In the Mountain and Pacific time zones the situation was about the same, with the wires of the afternoon papers still open and the morning paper wires not due to start.

The news flash—sudden and jolting—galvanized staffs into immediate activity. Executives were notified, and newspapers began organizing to get out extras in spite of the fact that the radio would inform the nation of the death of its president before the papers could reach the street. Mechanical superintendents were told to prepare for a rush job. Circulation managers were told to arrange for quick distribution of the papers.

Meanwhile, the news wires carried bulletins and "adds" giving more details of the president's death. In a few minutes a lead from Warm Springs, Georgia, gave first-hand descriptions of the tragedy from the press association staff men and correspondents. In Washington reporters were out after related stories—the reactions of political and governmental leaders and the arrangements for swearing in the successor to the presidency, Harry S. Truman.

Newspaper city editors, too, were on the job, assigning reporters to get the reactions of local citizens—the "little men and women"—as well as the prominent and the important.

In the center of this far-flung and multifarious activity deskmen and copyreaders with unhurried speed were at their task of assembling into coherent articles the stories coming to them in "takes," often single paragraphs of 15 to 25 words; correcting errors made by writers pressed for time; marking the copy to conform to their newspaper's stylesheet; penciling in instructions as to the size of type the material should be set in; and framing headlines to convey the news succinctly and clearly.

In such moments of high drama—when all the world is waiting for details of happenings that only the newspaper can give—deskmen form an important link between the event and the account of it that newspaper subscribers read. Reporters play their roles out in front, seeing the important actors; deskmen do their work behind the scenes. But the final production is determined by the deskmen. They combine, condense, reshape the news before it goes through a mechanical process to reach the readers.

THE NEED FOR COPYREADERS

No job on a newspaper is more important than the desk worker's. At times it is a job of tingling excitement, as in the handling of a story of the magnitude of President Roosevelt's death. At times it is dull, as in the routine editing of stock market and commodity market quotations or material for the vital statistics column. But usually it is at least interesting, for news of all the world comes to the copyreader to be considered by him and judged by him as to what and how much is to be passed along to the reader.

A newspaper as a physical object is not much—six, ten, twenty, fifty or so pages of printed matter on cheap paper; something to occupy its buyer's time for a half-hour or an hour; then something to be left on a subway train, dropped in a trash can, or used to wrap bundles or line a shelf.

Yet, though it sells for only a few cents, it is an expensive object—the work of thousands of men and women all over the world, the result of fabulous expenditures of money for talent and equipment. And though it is something to be thrown away after a short time, it is almost as indispensable an item of living as food, clothing, and shelter.

It is, in a way, a projection of ourselves. Where we cannot go to listen, it is our ears; where we cannot go to feel, it is our sense of touch; where we cannot go to see, it is our eyes. If we lived in a small community, isolated from other small communities, we could get along without the newspaper. But we do not. Our lives are intertwined not only with those of our families and our neighbors in the area where we live but with people's lives in every other part of the world.

Thus an event like the death of President Roosevelt touches our lives, as do the reports of a multitude of other events funneled to a newspaper copy desk, there to be sorted out and put into a form in which we can comprehend them.

Sitting in the seat of last judgment before news goes to the readers, deskmen and copyreaders are charged with great responsibility. It is of course a responsibility they share with other newspaper workers and with workers in other media of communication: radio, television, magazines, books, and motion pictures. But the "desk" is of unique importance, because the newspaper, of the several agencies of communication, is the one whose principal function is journalistic; that is, its main job is that of collecting and disseminating current information and evaluating or interpreting that information. In the material that comes daily to the desk, editors and copyreaders receive so great a variety and quantity that they could produce several publications bearing little resemblance in content and emphasis. What they choose to print and their treatment of it determine the character of the newspaper. They can make a newspaper an organ of accurate information and enlightenment about the world, or they can turn out a product that gives a shabby, distorted picture of the world.

Deskmen, however, do not make the original and fundamental decision about how the world is to be reported and portrayed. That decision is made largely by the newspaper owner; the deskmen are merely his agents who see that his policies are put into effect. That is their first duty: to process the raw material of news that comes from reporters, correspondents, press services, and syndicates into a product shaped and colored by the desires of the owner.

Fortunately, most American publishers are pretty much of the same mind as to what kind of newspaper they want. They want one that presents the news objectively in accordance with its significance and interest for the largest possible number of readers; that contains a sufficient amount of entertainment matter in the form of features, pictures, and comics to attract and hold readers; and that presents both types of material in as attractive and easy-to-read package as possible.

The primary aim of the newspaper is to achieve reader acceptance by the public or that portion of it to which the paper directs its appeal. There is but one sound measurement of reader acceptance—circulation. A newspaper with a falling circulation may coast along for years, but eventually it will reach a point where the owners will be forced to abandon it.

The task of the newspaper deskmen is therefore to exert incessant effort to maintain and build circulation, that is, to get out a publication that people want to read. Deskmen judge news and features and display them in accordance with their estimates of what, consistent with the standards of good journalism, will appeal to the greatest number of persons. A good editor—like a successful politician—must know people and what interests them and how they react to material presented for their information and entertainment.

While newspapermen contribute to the building of public opinion, they

CONTROL POINT FOR THE NEWS

also react to it. In the past, successful editors gauged public opinion as demonstrated in readership by subjective standards which often were remarkably astute. Nowadays, statistical science has come to the editor's aid with public opinion sampling and readership surveys. These are immensely useful tools which the desk can use in its task of evaluating material in response to the reader's acceptance of what has previously been offered him.

DUTIES OF THE COPYREADER

Evaluating the news in conformance with the character of the newspaper as determined by the owner and by reader acceptance involves such matters as deciding what to print (for a newspaper does not have space to publish everything), how long a story should be, and how much prominence it should be given. Evaluation is the first step in editing.

On a metropolitan newspaper the major judgments regarding a story

Fig. 1. Jerome Weinstein, editor of the *Centre Times*, State College, Pennsylvania, typifies the small-city editor, his job being to edit all general local and wire news. The teletype machines for wire news are only a step or two away from his desk. (Photo by Richard O. Byers.)

may be made after a conference of several editors—the city editor, the news editor, the telegraph editor, the make-up editor, the managing editor. These persons determine in particular what stories should go on the first page and what kind of headline they are worth. But the majority of decisions about stories is made by the head of the desk or chief copyreader. He decides what he wants done with a story and hands it to a copyreader to edit.

On the small-city newspaper these decisions are ordinarily the responsibility of a single individual. Usually given the title of city editor or news editor, he does work which is divided among several persons on a metropolitan publication. His task is difficult and sometimes dangerous, for seldom can he consult anyone for advice and there is no one to check him if he is in error.

The job of the copyreader—be he one of several around the rim of a metropolitan copy desk or a single person on a small newspaper—includes the following:

1. If the story is too long, he trims it to fit the space allotted it in the newspaper.

2. He checks the story carefully for errors—typographical, grammatical, structural, and factual.

3. He strives to perfect the story by deleting verbiage, clarifying ambiguities, improving sentence structure, changing inappropriate words and expressions, and toning down or playing up material wrongly treated by the reporter.

4. He makes the story conform to the newspaper's style in punctuation, spelling, abbreviations, and capitalization.

5. He removes from the story material that is potentially libelous, that is in bad taste, that would unfairly harm the individuals mentioned, or that would needlessly be offensive to readers.

6. He writes a headline that accurately sums up the content of the story and that may be so sparkling and interesting in itself that the reader will feel impelled to read the story.

The copyreader's job is an editing job, not a rewrite job. Occasionally he may find it necessary to recast a lead or write a paragraph for insertion in the story, but the expert copyreader can usually achieve his goals with the major tool of his trade—an editing pencil.

The basic reason for the copyreader's job is that news stories—whether they come from a paper's own reporters, from a press association or syndicate, or from a publicity office—are not ready for publication when they reach editorial rooms.

CONTROL POINT FOR THE NEWS

When this flood of material arrives at the copy desk, it is possible for the first time to judge each item not on its intrinsic merits but on its value as compared with other items. A selection has to be made.

Although reporters are able to judge the worth of the articles they write, they can give only a partial verdict, for all news values are relative, fluctuating with the volume and quality of other news available. And press association stories are written and edited for hundreds of different newspapers. What may be suitable for one paper may not be exactly what another one wants or needs.

No reporter, however brilliant, persistent, and painstaking, is perfect. In the stress of gathering information, writing it up, and transmitting his story to the office, he is subject to all sorts of errors. The copyreader often finds mistakes even in the best-written stories. What is clear and obvious to the reporter, because he knows his material intimately, may be obscure to a reader without the reporter's background. The copyreader can clarify the story. The reporter in his haste may write a clumsy sentence or choose a word that conveys an idea he did not intend. The copyreader can straighten out the sentence and substitute another word for the ambiguous one. The reporter may emphasize in his lead a factor whose significance is not borne out by the remainder of the article. The copyreader can correct the wrong impression that the reader would get if the opening paragraph were allowed to stand.

Wire stories, too, contain faults, even though the stories have been carefully edited before they are transmitted to newspaper offices. Moreover, even if free from errors, they must be processed by each newspaper receiving them. They come over the teletype in all-capitals, and the press association may use an abbreviation where the newspaper spells out a word or omit a title where the paper's style requires one. All telegraph copy must be edited for style before being sent to the composing room. Since press associations serve hundreds of newspapers with differing deadlines, they are constantly revising stories to bring them up to date with the latest details. A fast-developing story may, in the course of two or three hours, have a half dozen new leads with pickups from previous dispatches and insertions and additions incorporating corrections and later developments. This hodgepodge of material must be assembled on the copy desk into a coherent article.

These editing processes lead to the most important work of the copy desk—the preparation of material for display. This includes trimming the story to space, writing headlines, instructing the composing room about the size of type and the width of column to be used, and scheduling stories on pages.

Make-up is more important today than ever before. The newspaper must present its information in an attractive and easy-to-read format. Before the advent of radio, news magazines, and television, people had to read a newspaper if they wanted to find out what was going on in the world. Now they can quickly and easily tune in a news program, either radio or television, or for a few cents they can purchase a magazine which gives them a departmentalized summary in crisp prose.

COPYREADING—ART AND SCIENCE

Newspaper copyreading and desk work have not received the attention of novelists and movie-makers. The reporter, tracking down criminals or wisecracking his way through a series of improbable incidents, and the foreign correspondent, risking his life to describe a battle or defying an international spy ring, are the glamorous workers in the newspaper profession.

Nor when the laurel wreaths for journalistic achievement are handed around do any of them rest on the brow of the man with the green eyeshade. The Pulitzer Prizes, the Heywood Broun Awards, and the Headliners Club citations go to the reporters.

"The newspaper copyreader," wrote Stanley Walker, "doubtless deserves better from fate than he has received. This workman, who edits, corrects and manicures the copy which flows across the desk from the reporters, rewrite men, correspondents and news services, and then writes headlines, is the unsung hero of the Fourth Estate."[1]

Yet copyreading is a job that has its rewards. Generally it pays a better salary than straight reporting, and it is a stepping stone to executive positions on the newspaper. It has, moreover, its own drama—those not infrequent times when "all hell breaks loose" just as the front-page form is being locked up and the press is ready to roar. Quick decisions and fast action—not of body but of mind—are demanded of deskmen, not infrequently but almost continuously throughout their day's work.

Formerly copyreading was a job for the aging members of a newspaper staff, perhaps the last refuge before retirement. It is still true that maturity of judgment and experience are sound qualifications for newspaper desk work, but younger men and women with the necessary qualifications are now being sought by editors and publishers.

Old routines and old patterns of news handling are on their way out.

[1] Stanley Walker, *City Editor*, Frederick A. Stokes Company, 1934, p. 88.

CONTROL POINT FOR THE NEWS

Newspapers must compete with new communication instruments for the public's time, and revolutionary methods for printing the newspaper itself are in the offing. Young, alert, adaptable persons are needed on editing desks to keep the newspaper in step with our changing times.

The qualifications for copyreading are many. Neil MacNeil, assistant night managing editor of the New York *Times*, describes them:

> Copyreading is both an art and a science; both critical and creative. The copyreader must have a fine feeling for the drama and color of the news and a high sense of public responsibility. He must have the background of information and the experience and judgment against which to measure the value of the news story, so he may emphasize the important, eliminate the trivial, and provide adequate coverage. Above all he must know the meaning of words, so that each does the job required of it and an understanding of the newspaper's mechanics and capacity, including its type style and dress. Finally he must be master of the art of headline writing, one of the most difficult of the arts, and the least acclaimed and appreciated, even in newspaper offices.[2]

The world seems increasingly to be a world of turmoil and of conflict. The present generation has almost become inured to crisis, so frequently do situations develop and so often do changes occur. In electronics a transformer is a device that changes a current from a higher to a lower voltage or from alternating to continuous. The deskman in his intermediate spot between news gatherer and news reader performs somewhat the same function. His reactions to the forces of the times to a great extent determine the reactions of the reading public. He must, moreover, be an extremely sensitive instrument, as able to see a misplaced comma or a wrongly capitalized word as to perceive the importance of the death of a world leader like President Franklin D. Roosevelt.

[2] Members of the Staff of the New York *Times, The Newspaper: Its Making and Its Meaning,* Charles Scribner's Sons, 1945, p. 134.

CHAPTER 2

Preparing Copy for the Printer

COPYREADING SYMBOLS

The preparation of copy for the printer involves the use of accepted symbols and abbreviations that constitute a kind of shorthand method of communication between the editorial room and the composing room. The origins of these marks go back to the days before there were typewriters and mechanical typesetting machines. Some of them necessary when printers worked from the longhand scribblings of editors and reporters have little utility now, but most of them continue to be used in these times of almost universally typewritten copy.

The symbols have precise meanings for the printer, and the deskman must employ them correctly and—it should be emphasized—only when needed. By the time the reporter has made his own corrections and the city editor and the chief copyreader have made a few more changes, the copy is likely to be fairly well marked up when it reaches the man on the rim. The danger of errors is increased if by needless and careless marking the copyreader makes the story hard for the operator to read. The copyreader must do his work neatly and precisely with legibility as his chief aim.

The commonly used marks are shown in Fig. 2. In addition to these symbols, an unusual spelling or grammatical mistake that should be set as it is in copy may be indicated by writing above it the word "correct" (often shortened to "CQ") or "Follow copy" (often shortened to "Folo copy"). Periods inserted on copy may be circled for clarity, or they may be written as small x's.

A frequent mistake of beginning copyreading students is overconscientiousness in using the symbols. For example, a few students in each class

The mayor announced today...	Indent for paragraph.
at the meeting. Delegates...	Start new paragraph.
man was uninjured. Police said the accident...	Run in; no paragraph.
The meeting will be held at Chicago in May.	Insert matter.
The election was held Monday.	Separate words.
No o ne was injure d seriously.	Close up.
The four ~~worried~~ defendants...	Delete.
He said he only wished that...	Transpose words.
Hearings will strat Monday.	Transpose letters.
Two men were ~~critically~~ hurt. (Stet)	Don't make correction.
He was born in New York city.	Capitalize word.
The Ohio River was at flood stage.	Lower-case word.
The ②　men were sentenced Friday.	Spell out number.
He scored fourteen points.	Use Arabic figure.
Colonel John M. Witherspoon.	Abbreviate word.
He lived at 100 E. First St.	Spell out abbreviation.
# or 30	End of item.

Fig. 2.

painstakingly put three underscorings beneath the capital letters in a typewritten piece of copy, or draw circles around all the periods. Such markings are superfluous when the copy is correct. The paragraph symbol is not actually needed when the line is indented but is so universally used that it may be routinely inserted.

INSTRUCTIONS TO THE PRINTER

In addition to the conventional copyreading symbols for making changes and corrections, the deskman must know how to mark copy for special typographical arrangement or for type size or column width other than that used regularly. These special instructions are usually circled to indicate that they are not to be set in type.

Most editorial copy is set up as straight matter. This straight matter generally consists of body type of 7, 7½, or 8 points set on slugs 12, 12½,

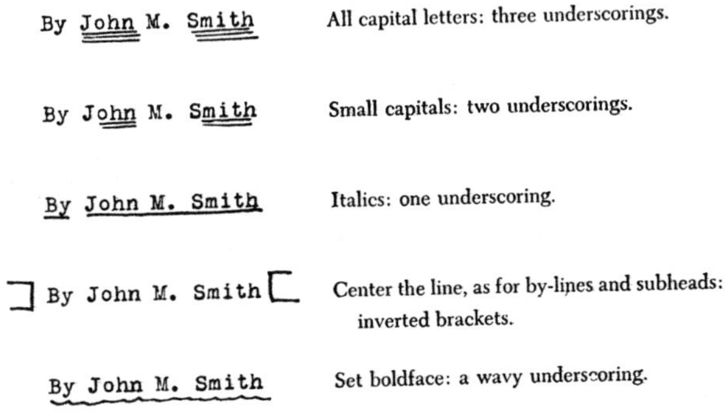

By John M. Smith	All capital letters: three underscorings.
By John M. Smith	Small capitals: two underscorings.
By John M. Smith	Italics: one underscoring.
⌐ By John M. Smith ⌐	Center the line, as for by-lines and subheads: inverted brackets.
By John M. Smith	Set boldface: a wavy underscoring.

Fig. 3.

or 13 picas long. (A point is the unit of type measurement; it is about $1/72$ of an inch. A pica is 12 points, or about $1/6$ of an inch.) Unless otherwise instructed, the composing machine operator sets all stories in the regularly used type size and column width. If the matter is to be set in larger or smaller type, or to a wider or narrower measure, or in a different face or family of type, the deskman must so instruct the compositor on the copy he sends to the composing room. These instructions should be written to the left and at the top of the copy, so that the compositor will be sure to see them before he begins to set the type.

Several copyreading symbols are used to indicate a variation in the face or style of type when only a word or a single line is involved. These are shown in Fig. 3.

If it is not convenient to use these markings, as when a long passage is

PREPARING COPY FOR THE PRINTER 13

involved, the usual method is to write the instructions in the margin at the left and to indicate definitely exactly how much of the copy is to be set in this way. Thus, if a paragraph is to be set in boldface, the copyreader may write to the left of it: "Bf" or "Ff," meaning "Set boldface" or "Set fullface" in capitals and lower-case letters. A variation of this is "Bf c & lc," which means "Set boldface, capitals and lower case." If the matter is to be set in all-capitals, as in a headline, the proper designation is "Bfc" or "Bf caps." Similarly, the abbreviation "Ital." in the left margin tells the compositor to set the copy in italics.

The size of type and the column width are also indicated by top or left-hand marginal instructions. If the matter should be set two columns wide in 10-point type, as for lead paragraphs, the instruction would be: "2-10 pt." or "2 col., 10 pt." The exact pica width may be given when the measurement cannot be conveniently indicated by columns. Thus: "Set 17 picas wide."

At times the copyreader may find it necessary to instruct the printer regarding leading (the space between lines). On mechanical typesetting machines the space between lines is determined by the width of the metal slug on which the letters appear. The instruction, "Set 10 on 12," tells the operator to use type 10 points high on a slug that is 2 points thicker.

Other than regular type sizes are used for different kinds of copy. Anything set wide measure—that is, more than one column—is usually set in 10 point. Two-column leads and editorials are set in 10-point type on many newspapers. Smaller type than regular body type is used to save space in box scores of sports events, musical programs, lists of names, market quotations, and so forth. For example, the copyreader may wish to save space on a list of high-school or college graduates by setting the names in two columns of small type. The instruction to the printer will be, "Set in agate half measure." (Agate is 5½-point type.)

The inverted brackets used for centering lines are also employed as a symbol for indention. A paragraph to be set boldface and indented on both sides is indicated as shown in Fig. 4. The amount of the indention may be written in the left-hand margin: "Indent 1 pica."

When thumbnail or 6-pica cuts are to be used in a story, the copyreader writes in the margin: "Set 16 lines 6 picas for cut," if 16 lines will be required for insertion of the cut. He may also indicate the depth of the cut in inches. Oversize initial letters at the start of an article or at a division point in it must also be indicated on copy. This is done by draw-

14   NEWS EDITING AND DISPLAY

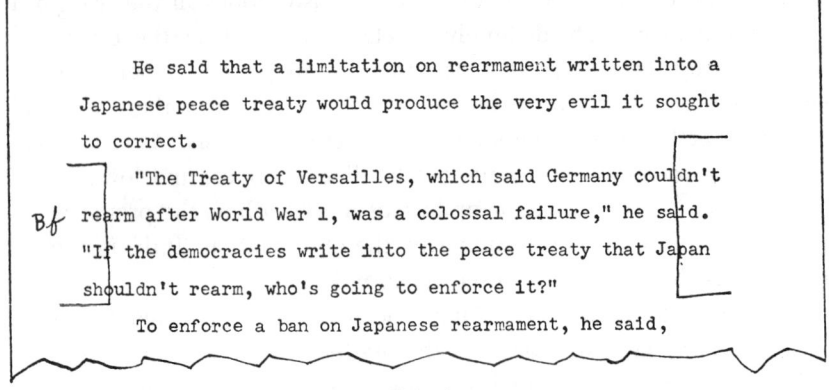

Fig. 4.

ing a square around the letter and writing in the margin the size of type to be used.

MARKING WIRE COPY

Copy received over the teletype machines of the Associated Press, International News Service, and United Press appears in all-capitals. It is edited as though it were in lower case, and the first letter of all words

```
          ⌊VIENNA, AUSTRIA, FEB. 1-(AP)-A SHORTAGE OF ELEPHANTS
IN VIENNA HAS CAUSED A RESTAURANT TO CLOSE.
          ⌊VIENNA'S "GOLDEN OWL" RESTAURANT SPECIALIZED IN
ELEPHANT GOULASH AND SCHNITZEL AFTER ITS OWNER PURCHASED
A CIRCUS MAMMOTH LAST YEAR.
          ⌊THE MEAT LASTED A LONG TIME AND DREW A LOT OF CUSTOMERS.
BUT SAID OWNER RUDOLF SCHIENER TODAY:
          ⌊"TAXES TOOK ALL MY PROFITS AND THERE ARE NO MORE ELE-
PHANTS TO BE HAD."
```

Fig. 5. A wire story showing marking of words that should be capitalized.

that should be capitalized in print is underscored. To save time, some copy desks use a single underscoring instead of the regulation three. Hurried copyreaders sometimes turn the three underscorings into a character resembling a *z*. The proper marking of telegraph copy is shown in Fig. 5.

PREPARING COPY FOR THE PRINTER

KEEPING TRACK OF STORIES

Before a story is seen by the newspaper reader, it passes through the hands of several persons in the complicated operations of being written, prepared for the composing room, set in type, and ultimately appearing in print. Since each day's newspaper contains scores of stories representing thousands of words, editorial and shop workers have developed systems of keeping track of individual items to be sure that they reach their designated place in the paper.

All the systems consist essentially of the use of guidelines or catchlines by which a story can be identified at a glance. The system varies from one newspaper office to another. The one adopted by larger papers is more complicated than that used by smaller ones. The first task of a new man on a copy desk is to learn the newspaper's system of guidelines.

The information required in a guideline includes one or more of the following:

1. An identifying label for the story. The subject matter of a story is indicated by a word or phrase given it usually by the city editor. Typical slugs or labels are: *Weather, Congress, City Council, Hotel Fire.*

2. A headline designation. Frequently used headline styles are indicated by numbers or letters. Thus, a headline customarily placed over stories at the top of a column may be numbered 1. This figure is put beside the identifying label as a necessary part of the guideline. Headlines not keyed to a numbering or lettering system must be indicated by the column width and the size and face of type. Thus "2-30 Bodoni" means a headline two columns wide set in 30-point Bodoni type.

3. An indication of the page, section, or edition for placement of the story. All stories to go on the sports page are designated "Sports" or "Spts"; those on the society page, "Society" or "Soc"; and those for only the state edition, "State."

The use of the guideline or slug on a metropolitan newspaper may be illustrated by the history of a story from the time it appears on the city editor's assignment sheet through editing, being set in type, proofread, placed in the make-up forms, and printed.

The police reporter for the *Morning Sun* telephones the city editor about the robbery of a prominent local woman by a man who took jewels valued at $5000. The city editor switches the reporter to a rewrite man. Beside the reporter's name on the assignment sheet the city editor writes the words "jewel rob," which will be the identifying label for the story not only on his record but also on the copy desk, in the make-up editor's dummy, and on the way through the composing room.

When the rewrite man turns in the story, the city editor slugs it with the proper label and other needed information. The top of the first page of the story appears as in Fig. 6.

```
           1      2
        Johnston--Smith
           3      4        5
         #1  Jewel rob  P1

         Mrs. Randall R. Jones, wife of the president of the
                              (in jewels)
         First National Bank, lost $5,000 to a  robber who held her

         up at gun point last night after she had driven her car into

         the garage of her home at 1500 N. Grand Drive.

              Mrs. Jones told police the robber was waiting at the

         side or behind the garage when she drove the car in.  He
```

Fig. 6. Top of a page of copy showing guideline information. *1.* Rewriteman's name. *2.* Name of reporter who supplied the facts. (Copyreader marks out both, since they do not form part of the guideline.) *3.* Headline number. *4.* Designating label for story. *5.* Instruction to put story on page 1.

Two devices are used to let compositors know there is more than one page to a story. The more common is to write the word "More" at the bottom of each sheet. The other is to write at the bottom, "Rule for add one" or "Turn rule for first add." (A turned rule is a type slug turned face side down so that it appears as a heavy black line on proofs.) The story's identifying label—but not the headline size, page, or other information—is repeated at the top of each succeeding page of copy: "Add 1 jewel rob," "Add 2 jewel rob," and so forth, until the final page, which is headed "Last add jewel rob." Instead of "Add 1," many desks use "First add," "Second add," and so on.

The city editor sends the story to the chief copyreader, who, after glancing over it, hands it to one of the rim men for careful editing to remove errors and polish the writing. The copyreader usually gives it a quick first reading to get the whole story in mind. Then he goes over it word by word, making the changes necessary to correct inaccuracies or

PREPARING COPY FOR THE PRINTER 17

~~Smith~~
#/ Robbery P/

Set lead 2-10pt

B+C] By John M. Smith L

A shaky, 6-foot gunman ro*b*bed a crowded eastside supermarket of $1,000 late yesterday afternoon and matched wits with pursuing police for an hour after making good his escape.

In the ~~xxxx~~ aftermath of the stickup, a patrolman was seriously injured, and the bandit, ~~xxbxklyxlfxhxhxlxxxjkixx~~ abandoned one car, was shot at twice in commandeering a second, and eluded police only by driving without lights after darkness fell.

Police, witnesses, and victims put the story together in this way:

The gunman entere*d* the Eastside Plaza Plaza Supermarket at 5:30 P. M. and approached Albert L. Madison, 46, of 3224 Armstrong Avenue, chief auditor for the company, who was in a small enclosure used as an office in the front of the store.

"Open that safe, or I'll blow your brains out," the stickup man ordered ~~him~~ *Madison,* pointing a revolve*r* at him with a shaking hand.

Sh ———— Loots Cash Registers

After Madison opened the safe, the holdup man forced him to go with him as he looted the store*'s* five cash registers. Miss Mary Adams, 880 E. First (St), was the only cashier on duty.

The robbery lasted approximately (fifteen) minutes. More than 30 ~~people~~ *persons* were in the store. *Several,* ~~A number of those present~~ saw the gunman's revolver and stood by while he carried out his crime.

(More)

Fig. 7. Page 1 of an edited story with instructions to the compositor.

improve the writing. He crosses out the names of the rewrite man and the reporter, since these are not needed in the catchline for the composing room. After he edits the story, he composes the headline. The guideline for the story is also put on the headline copy. In checking the story,

Add 1 robbery

The gunman, with the loot in bills in his jacket pocket, fled to a car parked on Grand boulevard.

About 15 minutes later, Patrolmen Robert Dolman and Arthur Martin spotted a car answering the description of that belonging to the gunman.

With siren going, the officers pursued the car at high speed for a short distance. They gave up the chase when their cruiser sideswiped a truck at Eighteenth street and Elm avenue. Policeman Is Injured Dolman was thrown from the car by the impact. He was taken to Samaritan hospital.

The getaway car was next seen on Parsons avenue near the stockyards by Patrolmen Stanton Warren and Alexander A. Markheim. They radioed the position to police headquarters and took up the chase.

Trapped by police cruisers near Farmsworth avenue and Tenth street, the robber abandoned his car and ran toward Edgeworth drive.

He then doubled back to enter the home of Peter B. Plummer, 821 Fairview avenue. At gun point he forced Plummer to hand over the keys to his automobile. Plummer said he fired at the gunman twice with a .22 rifle as he drove off, and said he believed he hit the car.

Plummer told police the bandit sped south on Fairview avenue, driving without lights.

Fig. 8. The second and last page of an edited story.

the rim man makes sure that the word "more" or the "turn rule" notation appears at the end of each page of copy, that the guideline is at the top of each page, and that an end mark appears after the last paragraph.

Before the story is sent to the composing room, the guideline, the length of the story, and the headline size are recorded. On some newspapers this record is kept by the chief copyreader; on others the story is routed to the make-up editor before going to the composing room.

The story's first stop in the composing room is at the copy cutter's desk.

PREPARING COPY FOR THE PRINTER

His job is to apportion the copy among the typesetting machine operators. The headlines, which in most newspaper offices are written on separate sheets from the stories, go to operators of machines equipped for setting large display type. The stories go to operators of machines which set only straight matter. Hence the necessity for the guideline on the headline copy as well as on the story.

Early in the workday a complete story usually is handed to one operator, since there is no rush for the type. Later, as speed in getting material set becomes essential, the copy cutter may divide a single story into separate pieces, or "takes," that he gives to several operators. A story which would take one operator thirty minutes to set can be completed in five or ten minutes when distributed among several operators. Near deadline, the takes may be as short as a single paragraph. The fact that several operators may be given separate pages of copy of the same story explains the newsroom rule that a page should always end with a completed paragraph.

The typesetting machine operator who receives the first page of the story sets the newsroom slug as a separate line of type. Leaders (a series of dots) may be used to fill the line. To make the guideline stand out from the rest of the type, some shops set it in all-capitals. Others require that it be followed by a turned rule.

After the story or take is in type, the operator carries it to the bank (a table on which type is kept in galleys), where a printer assembles the parts of the story in the proper order. At this point we see the value of using slugs, numbering the pages at the top, and having the "more" or "turn rule" notation at the bottom. These cues in straight-matter material alert the printer to look for the separate parts of the story. In some shops the printer does not pull a galley proof of a story until he sees the end mark or 30-dash. If the deskman fails to indicate one on copy, the story may remain forgotten on the assembly bank until it is time to put the type in the forms and the make-up man calls for it. The result: a hunt through perhaps scores of galleys of type for the missing story, with the deadline coming closer.

Using the word "more" and the end mark and the other copyreading symbols may seem trivial to a beginning copyreader. Only when he sees how their omission may block the proper dovetailing of operations in the shop does he realize that strict adherence to standard procedures is vital.

The guideline's usefulness does not end when the parts of a story are set in type and assembled. The floorman uses it in assembling the headline with the story and in grouping the galleys of type for the various pages and departments—page one, sports, society, financial. It is used by the printer whose job is to make up the forms according to the make-up editor's dummy. When the bankman needs to locate a story for the insertion of corrected lines after galley proofs have been read and lines with mistakes reset, he has only to hunt for the guideline.

The guideline system outlined here is used primarily by large metropolitan newspapers. The majority of papers throughout the country use a simplified system. When only one or two persons handle copy in a newsroom, the key-word label may be dropped. The first two words of the headline are used to identify the story in the back shop and on the page dummy. This procedure does away with the need for setting a separate guideline for identifying the headline.

Another modification of the system involves pasting together at the copy desk all stories of more than one page. In this case reporters and copyreaders need not follow the rule that a completed paragraph must end each page. In some newspaper offices headlines are written at the top of the copy instead of on a separate sheet. The copy goes first to the headline typesetter; when the headline is in type, the copy cutter gives it and the story to the operator who sets the straight matter.

HANDLING STORY REVISIONS

Newspaper reporters are historians who record events while they are still happening. Very often, to meet an edition deadline, they must get a story written before they have all the facts or before the event has reached a climax or culmination. Metropolitan newspapers which issue several editions during the day and press associations which have a deadline every minute for their client publications across the land must keep step with the onward march of events. To get in the latest developments and to correct or amplify the sketchy first reports, news stories must be constantly revised, with new leads and insertions of new or corrected information after the story is already in type or has been printed in an early edition.

New Leads. When the copyreader receives a new lead reporting significant developments that must be incorporated in an article already in type, he must slug the new copy and also obtain a proof or clip the article from an early edition and properly mark it so that the printer can make the changes without resetting the entire story.

The guideline for the original story is incorporated in the slug for the

PREPARING COPY FOR THE PRINTER 21

new material. For example, a new lead might be slugged: "New lead p. 1 #1 robbery." If the new material takes up more than one page or is to go to the composing room in takes, each succeeding page is slugged: "Add 1 new lead robbery," and so forth; the last page is slugged: "Last add new lead robbery." At the end of the story is written: "End new lead robbery. Turn rule for pickup."

When the changes and developments are such that the new story bears little resemblance to the earlier story, the old account may be killed entirely. The usual practice is to use the slug, "Sub robbery." This tells the

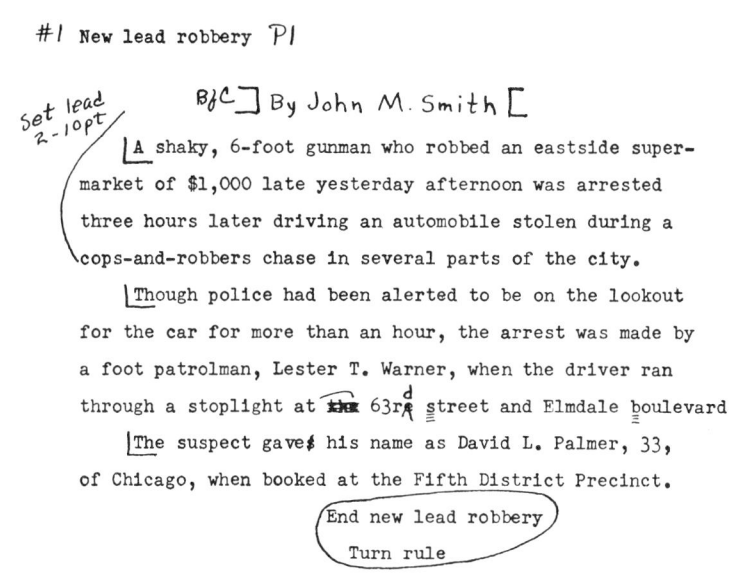

Fig. 9. A new lead ready for the composing room.

print shop to kill the story slugged "robbery" and substitute the new version.

Inserts. Material inserted in a story to bring it up to date or to correct inaccuracies is handled in the same manner as new leads. The insert is slugged: "Insert A robbery." A second page or a take carries the slug: "Add 1 insert A robbery," and so forth until the last page, which carries the notation: "End insert A robbery. Turn rule." If there are additional inserts, they are labeled alphabetically in order "B," "C," "D," and so on. The copyreader marks the place of insert on the proof by an arrow and the notation in the margin: "Turn rule for insert A."

~~Smith~~

(Insert A robbery)

|In the bandit's own car police found $400 in the glove compartment, a high-powered rifle and s͡cope, a suitcase full of tailor-made clothes, and a sock containing $10 in nickels tucked in a shoe.

|There was also a medicine   bottle bearing a prescription made out to David L. Palmer. The prescription had been filled by a Chicago drug store.

(End insert A
Turn rule)

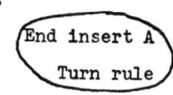

Fig. 10. An insert ready for the composing room.

Bulletins and Precedes. A last-minute dispatch received when there is no time to revise the entire story is handled by a bulletin at the top of the earlier story. The bulletin may be slugged: "Lead all robbery," "Bulletin precede robbery," or "Bulletin lead robbery," according to the practice of the newspaper. At the end of the dispatch the copyreader writes: "End lead all robbery." Most newspapers set bulletins in blacker or larger type than regular body type.

Lead to Come. Many news stories are written in reverse order, the body of the article being prepared in advance of the lead pending final developments. A sports writer may send a running account of a game to the office before the final score is in. A courthouse reporter may describe the opening stages of a trial in chronological order. An obituary of a prominent person may come from the newspaper morgue to the desk before the death story itself is written. To save time, the desk sends this material to the composing room immediately to be set in type.

Editorial room handling of these reverse-order stories varies. On some the slug is: "Lead to come trial," "Add 1 lead to come trial," and so forth. When the lead reaches the desk, it is slugged, "Lead trial," "Add 1 lead trial," and so on. On other newspapers the early material is designated by the label "Letter A" or "A matter." Typical slugs are: "Letter A—trial," "Add 1 letter A—trial," or "A matter—trial," "Add 1 A matter—trial," and so forth. A different letter of the alphabet is used for other stories being handled in this fashion.

PREPARING COPY FOR THE PRINTER

Related Stories. When several stories deal with different angles of the same event, the same identification slug may be used for all, with an additional designation to distinguish the side or related stories. A lead story might be labeled "Hotel fire." Related stories might have the following slugs: "Hotel fire—casualties," "Hotel fire—eyewitnesses," "Hotel fire—rescue."

Markups and Fixes. When a story is changed by a new lead or in-

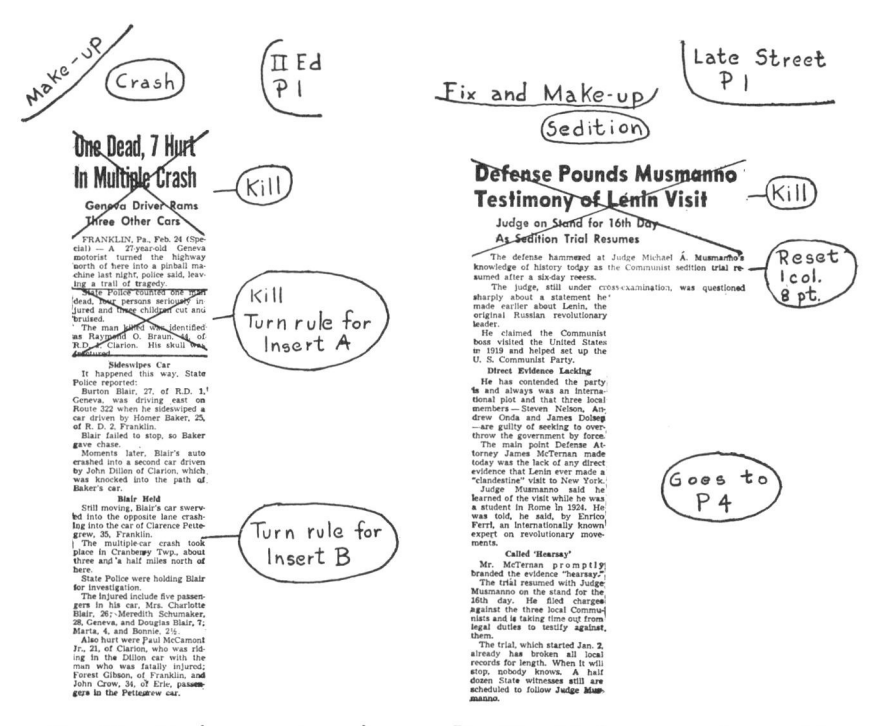

Fig. 11. Marker goes to make-up department only.

Fig. 12. Marker goes to machine, then to make-up.

sertions, it is necessary, as was said above, to mark the changes on a proof or on a copy of the story clipped from the newspaper. Such a markup or marker is also required when any typographical change is made in the earlier version, as when a story under a two-column heading with a two-column lead is knocked down to one column.

One type of marker is labeled "Fix" and is used for stories that require typesetting. On it the copyreader indicates all the changes that involve setting type.

Another type of marker is labeled "Make-up." This is used when the changes require no machine work; it serves as a guide to the printer in making up the page.

A third type, labeled "Fix and Make-up," contains changes that require typesetting and directions for the printer in making up the page.

Markers must give explicit information regarding the type that is to be reset and the kills, transpositions, inserts, and new leads. In addition, they must carry the identifying slug, the page number on which the story appears, the edition, and the new location if the story is to be put on another page.

MARKING PROOFS

The reading of proof for typographical errors is the duty of proofreaders, but every editorial worker at times will have occasion to check and mark proof. The copyreader must do this in marking galleys for revises of stories and in checking proofs for errors that may have been overlooked by the regular proofreaders.

Proofreaders on large newspapers are employees of the mechanical department and occupy a cubicle near the composing room. As soon as the type is set, the copy and galley proofs are taken to them. They work in pairs, one reading the copy aloud and the other following the words on the proof. They look for typographical errors such as transpositions, misspellings, and omitted letters and words; for wrong-font letters and defective type; for incorrect division of words at the end of the line; for faulty alignment and indentions; and for mistakes involving the size or style of type.

Proofreading on smaller newspapers is less meticulous, with one person looking for errors; he has no copyholder to read the copy to him. Under these circumstances, the proofreader seldom compares the proof with the copy except to verify names, figures, and tabular matter.

The proofreader marks all corrections in the margin of the proof. In one method, called the book system, a line is drawn through the incorrect letter or word and the change to be made is indicated in the margin by the appropriate symbol. In the other method, the guideline system, a line is drawn from the error to the nearest margin and the correction is placed there. The guideline method is used in most newspaper offices.

The proofreader's marks that the deskman ordinarily needs to know are shown in Fig. 13.

Symbol	Meaning	Symbol	Meaning
⌄	Insert comma.	=	Align letters.
⌄	Insert apostrophe.	#	Insert space.
⌄⌄	Insert quotation marks.	⌄	Push down space.
⊙	Insert period.	[	Move to left.
⊙	Insert colon.	]	Move to right.
⌄	Insert semicolon.	⊓	Move up.
?/	Insert question mark.	⊔	Move down.
=/	Insert hyphen.	✓✓✓	Correct uneven spacing.
$\frac{1}{M}$	One-em dash.	×	Broken letter.
$\frac{2}{M}$	Two-em dash.	wf	Wrong font.
en	En dash.	bf	Set in boldface type.
⌿	Delete.	Rom.	Set in roman type.
⌒	Close up.	Ital	Set in italic type.
9	Upside down; reverse.	SC	Small capitals.
∧	Insert (caret).	Caps	Capitals.
¶	Paragraph.	lc	Lower-case type.
No ¶	No paragraph; run in.	Stet	Let it stand.
tr	Transpose.	Out See Copy	Omission; check with copy.

Fig. 13.

Fig. 14. The guideline system of marking corrections on galley proof.

FAULTS OF COPYREADERS

The copyreader, working anonymously at his chore of checking names, verifying facts, trimming verbiage, and capsuling the news in headlines, is the guardian of the newspaper's content. He is credited with a sharp eye for detail and meticulousness in writing and editing.

But how well do copy desks prepare material for printing? Not very well, according to a survey of mechanical superintendents—the persons best qualified to judge. Here are the charges made by shopmen against deskmen:

1. The copy that goes to the composing room is illegible; deletions are carelessly indicated, and handwritten insertions are unreadable.

2. Copyreaders don't know the newspaper's style rules for capitalization, punctuation, abbreviations.

3. Stories leaving the copy desk still contain errors in grammar, punctuation, and especially spelling.

4. Too much of the editing job is left up to the proofreaders, necessitating costly and time-consuming correction lines.

5. Instructions as to how the matter should be set—indentions, type size, type face—are incomplete or inaccurate.

6. Headlines are miscounted; too many are too long.

7. Copyreaders are ignorant of mechanical processes; this ignorance often causes needless mixups and delays in getting out the paper.

The mechanical superintendents of two of the nation's best-edited papers with a big corps of copyreaders stated their chief complaints about copyreaders in almost the same words: "Illegible copy," said the New York *Times* superintendent. "Illegibility, poor English, poor grammar," said the New York *Herald Tribune* superintendent.

Similar criticisms were made by the superintendents of newspaper plants throughout the country. Some typical comments were:

Kansas City *Star*: Too fast editing, particularly on telegraph copy. Teletype printer copy, which is in all caps, needs good editing from a style standpoint. It is the tendency of copy desks to edit it hurriedly and not too carefully. This makes for delay in the composing room and thereby increases column costs.

Los Angeles *Times*: The chief faults in copy sent to composing room are crowded copy, narrow margins, poorly written copy, particularly when hard pencils are used and copy is subject to much handling before being set.

Memphis *Commercial Appeal* and *Press-Scimitar*: Lack of copyreaders to properly edit and prepare copy. They depend too much on poorly qualified proofreaders. Proofrooms should not require dictionaries, telephone directories,

PREPARING COPY FOR THE PRINTER 27

or city directories. All potential errors should be checked by copyreaders. Proofreaders should look only for typographical errors.

Minneapolis *Star* and *Tribune*: Illegible interlineations.

Philadelphia *Bulletin*: Poor preparation of copy—ambiguities, construction, etc. Unknown sources—time wasted in trying to find out who edited copy to correct glaring errors in fact.

Roanoke (Va.) *Times* and *World-News*: Insufficiently marked as to style; insufficient indication as to size of indention; illegibility, particularly in handwritten corrections.

St. Paul *Dispatch*: Illegible copy as result of "boiling" at copy desk.

St. Louis *Post-Dispatch*: Failure to carry through capitalization, style, and other marks to the end, forgetting that the copycutter may cut the story into a dozen takes for different operators who may or may not be good guessers. Also the failure to follow the simple expedient of putting the word "folo" over an unusual spelling of a word or name.

St. Louis *Star-Times*: Inconsistency of markings.

Cleveland *Plain Dealer*: Illegible handwriting on the part of copyreaders. Too many times a piece of copy 1½ to 2 feet long is edited down to 10 lines, causing the operator to lose much time in trying to pick out what the editor wants set.

Cincinnati *Enquirer*: The greatest faults are the different systems or styles used by copyreaders. Some mark certain things, others mark very little, and some mark nearly every word to prove they are literary experts.

Chicago *Tribune*: Illegible longhand writing; smudged carbon copies; stories so marked with inserts and deletions that operator cannot easily translate them.

Washington *Star*: Careless and inconsistent marking; overediting of copy; and indistinct markings which might occur either from poor penmanship or a soft pencil with a blunt point.

The foregoing complaints make it clear that copyreaders are guilty of easily remediable faults. These may appear minor, but in the aggregate they are of major seriousness. They result in errors that should not have been made, they cause confusion and delay, they are exasperating to the printers, and they cost the newspaper money.

Careful attention to the following rules will help eliminate many of the faults found by mechanical superintendents:

1. Give the story a first reading before making any changes. This will give you an idea of the overall corrections that need to be made, and you will not find yourself striking out matter that you decide later should be restored.

2. Make no unnecessary changes in copy. Think before you make a change. Ask yourself: Is this change actually correcting an error? Is this change actually improving the story?

3. Do not use any unnecessary marks. The copy that reaches the com-

posing machine operator is messy enough with needed changes and instructions, without being further complicated by a copyreader's useless doodlings.

4. Don't forget to give the compositor needed instructions. He may know that the newspaper's style is to set box scores in 6 point, but nevertheless put in the type size on copy. The operator is not supposed to edit copy as he sets it. His instructions are to "follow copy" even if he knows the deskman has overlooked an error.

5. The copyreader's worst crime is to edit errors into copy. A person can be forgiven for overlooking an error, but there is no excuse for writing in a mistake on copy that is correct.

6. Do not make the copyreading symbols too large. The right-angled lines for paragraphs should not, for example, stretch halfway across the page.

7. Do not use proofreading symbols for copyreading symbols. Some of them are the same, but they cannot be used interchangeably.

8. Use a soft well-sharpened pencil. A hard pencil does not make a distinct enough mark on the soft paper used in editorial rooms. The copy is likely to be smudged by the inky fingers of printers; hence very black penciled corrections are necessary if they are to be seen and read easily. Do not use ink unless you are perfect. If you make a mistake in ink, you can't erase it.

9. It is better to use block letters or print for corrections than to use script. If you write in script, underscore the letters a, u, and w, and overscore o, n, and m.

10. To tell the operator that an unusual spelling is not an oversight or a mistake, write and encircle one of the following above it: "Correct," "CQ," or "Folo copy."

11. Put in all corrections and changes on copy horizontally. The operator should not have to turn the sheet sideways or twist his neck to read what you have written.

12. When you have a long insertion—a long sentence or a paragraph—type it on a separate sheet rather than squeeze it in in tiny handwriting.

13. Remember that you are likely to be blamed if mistakes get into the paper. Your job is to catch errors that other persons may have overlooked. You are not, of course, responsible for typographical errors made in the composing room. The responsibility for those lies with the proofreaders. But you should check the stories you edited on page proof or in the first copies of the paper that reach the desk, watching out for typographical as well as for other errors.

CHAPTER 3

The Guardian of Correct Usage

THE OFFICE STYLESHEET

Horace Greeley is celebrated in the history of journalism as a great molder of public opinion through his editorials. But he is also distinguished for the fact that his New York *Tribune* was a highly literate newspaper. Credit for this is due partly to the *Tribune's* literary editor, George Ripley, who was a watchdog for imprecise language and incorrect usage.

Then as today, copyreaders on the *Tribune* were responsible for grammatically correct stories and articles. When they let a mistake get by, they were immediately called to account. In *News Hunting on Three Continents* a contemporary, Julius Chambers, said of Ripley's rhetorical autocracy: "The index of forbidden words was very lengthy, and the use of them, when they escaped the keen eye of a copyreader and got into print, was punishable by suspension without pay for a week, or immediate discharge. It was a rigid system, rigidly enforced."

Such extreme punishment is not meted out to nodding copyreaders today. They are permitted an occasional slip. But a deskman who habitually fails to correct errors in grammar and choice of words will soon find himself looking for another job.

The goal in newspaper writing today is generally accepted correct English. But the beginner in a newspaper office will not be around long before he hears the word "style." In newspaper offices it does not mean the same thing as it does in literary circles. Style to the literary critic is the author's characteristic way of writing—the tone, the flavor, the personality in his mode of expression. In the editorial rooms style means the rules for capitalization, abbreviation, and punctuation, and the usages which the newspaper has adopted. These are set forth in a manual called a stylebook or stylesheet.

The English language is governed by few absolute rules. Grammars and dictionaries, upon which we customarily rely as ultimate authorities, often vary in their recommended usages. It is just as correct to use the Arabic figure "10" as it is to spell out the number. It is just as correct to write the word "trans-Atlantic" as "transatlantic." It is just as correct to use the abbreviation "Lt." as "Lieut." It is just as correct to write "Ohio River" as "Ohio river."

How does the deskman decide when he is editing copy? He doesn't. He follows the rules adopted by his newspaper. If all the usages are equally correct, why isn't the individual reporter or deskman permitted to choose the ones he prefers? Primarily, for the sake of uniformity and consistency. It is an indication of sloppy and careless work if such differences as "200 E. 10th St." and "200 East Tenth Street" are found in adjoining columns.

Although it is probably impossible to determine the editor who first adopted a style guide, a likely candidate is William Cullen Bryant. As a contributor to the development of the stylebook, Bryant is known for his *index expurgatorius*, a list of 86 words and phrases that he barred from the New York *Evening Post*.

Stanley Walker in *City Editor* cited the younger James Gordon Bennett as a stickler for rules of style, and he listed several pages of Bennett's "don'ts." Some of the usages that Bennett objected to, Walker said, later became accepted as proper. But although rules of good grammar and diction change, many of Bennett's orders regarding style had come down through the years, according to Walker. Some were founded on ordinary tenets of usage and some were the result of the gradual evolution of judgment about what is good newspaper practice and what is bad. Walker added that there were good reasons for most of the commandments.

In the preface to its manual, the Toledo *Blade* writes as follows regarding the use of stylebooks:

Style means uniformity and simplicity.

Without a uniform style, a newspaper lacks good appearance and taste. Abbreviations, capitalizations, and general structure must conform.

It is the duty of every member of the editorial department to become acquainted with the stylebook. This will speed copy and make it neater and easier to handle.

Copyreaders who have journeyed the country will tell you it is not uncommon to get the following answer to style:

"Oh, there are as many styles here as there are linotype operators."

Hence this stylebook—to avoid having as many styles as there are linotype operators, or better still, to avoid having as many styles as there are members of the staff.

Most newspaper stylebooks confine themselves to matters in which there is a choice of usage—spelling, abbreviations, punctuation, capitalization, use of titles—and to the *typographical* style in which material is set. The newspaperman who hasn't learned the rudiments of grammar and the meanings of words can't depend upon a stylebook to give him the education he has missed. As the San Francisco *Chronicle* says about its manual: "This is not a handbook on writing. Questions of accuracy, good taste and good sense, technique, and diction are left to writers and editors."

Most newspapers also do not look upon a stylebook as containing infallible rules. The St. Louis *Post-Dispatch* says that its manual "is not a rule book. It is a guide statement of preferred practices." And the Gannett newspapers: "This is a guide, not a law book. It is a foundation garment, meant to control, not constrict." Nevertheless, the stylebook preferences are mandatory for the most part. The copyreader must know them and make the stories conform.

In general, newspaper grammar and usage correspond to what is correct in other kinds of writing. Certain practices, however, many of them designed to save time in the composing room and space in the paper, have become more characteristic of newspaper writing than of general writing. Since style varies with the newspaper, only a few hints can be given regarding prevailing practices.

Many preferred usages reflect the idiosyncrasies of the editor or publisher. William Rockhill Nelson is said to have barred the word "snake" from his Kansas City *Star* because he thought readers would find it offensive; O. K. Bovard, famed managing editor of the St. Louis *Post-Dispatch*, banned "hit-and-run driver" on the grounds that it was bad taste to refer to a traffic tragedy in sporting terms; and a Kentucky editor said he didn't care a damn about style so long as the word was spelled "whiskey."

A whim of Robert R. McCormick of the Chicago *Tribune* is the use of simplified spelling. The *Tribune* stylebook contains a list of 42 words that "must" be spelled as shown. Among them: *burocracy, criscross, genuinly, tho, thoro, thru*. The Sacramento *Bee* manual insists that *couple, group, trio,* and *duo* are plural—not singular, the preference of most newspapers.

These unusual preferences may be infrequent, but it is important for the copyreader to learn them. They generally indicate an editor's strong belief, if not a mania or phobia.

One of the widest differences between newspaper and ordinary usage is in capitalization. Many newspapers reduce the use of capital letters. This practice originated in the days of handset type. Capital letters were kept in an upper drawer of a type case or cabinet, and small letters in the lower drawers. Even then, before time-and-motion studies, it was obvious that typesetting was slowed if the compositor had to break his rhythm every once in a while to reach into the upper drawer for a capital letter. Hence, newspapers capitalized only when absolutely necessary; that is, they confined the use of capitals to proper nouns. The practice has continued today, because even the operator of a mechanical typesetting machine has to use an extra motion to set a capital letter.

In capitalization, there are *downstyle* and *upstyle* papers. Downstyle papers—those which use capitals sparingly—are inclined to capitalize only proper nouns and words derived from them and only the distinguishing parts of the names of streets, rivers, banks, buildings, and so forth. The generic words—*street, river, bank*—are written in small letters unless they precede the distinguishing or identifying word. Thus the style is: *First street, Red river, First National bank, Geology building.* Downstyle papers do not capitalize geographical divisions like the south or the north; divisions of government like state, county, senate, or congress; names of boards, commissions, or committees like federal trade commission, labor relations board, or senate foreign relations committee; titles of bills and laws; or the seasons. Most downstyle papers are found in the Midwest and the Far West.

Upstyle papers tend to be more conservative than downstyle papers in other usages, more like books and magazines. Upstyle papers spell out words rather than use abbreviations, spell out numbers rather than use figures, quote names of newspapers and magazines rather than print them without quotes, use commas when not absolutely needed for clarity, as before "and" in a series.

The deskman should keep these points in mind, for an understanding of the paper's general policy or trend makes easier the task of learning a new stylebook. No stylebook, of course, answers all the questions that come up regarding usage. On points not covered in the manual the deskman can follow the paper's general trend in deciding whether to capitalize or not and whether to abbreviate or not. The rule of analogy will answer most of his questions.

The deskman will also find it easier to master a stylebook if he ignores the rules that coincide with his own practices. He does not need to memorize what he already knows; he should concentrate on the rules that are new to him or different from the ones he has been accustomed to following.

TYPOGRAPHICAL ERRORS

The spotting of typographical errors is routine for expert copyreaders. Beginners not trained to see mistakes—dropped letters, transposed letters, and wrong letters made when the reporter didn't hit the right typewriter key—often miss them. In the first place, they are in the habit of reading for sense, and their eyes take in phrases and clauses rather than individual words. In the second place, a simple psychological principle operates to make them fail to see that a word is misspelled. The eyes see "for men were hurt"; the mind subconsciously supplies the missing letter so that the word appears as "four." Similarly, in "He placed the paper his brief case," the sense is obviously "in his brief case," and the mind supplies the missing preposition. Proofreaders concentrate on the appearance rather than the meaning of a word; they use a card or ruler under the line as an aid in finding minute errors. Deskmen find this cumbersome, but most of them train themselves to be eagle-eyed in perceiving typographical mistakes.

SPOTTING MISSPELLED WORDS

One of the chief faults editors find with graduates of schools of journalism is that they don't know how to spell. In fact, in some surveys this deficiency tops the list of editors' grievances.

In checking spelling, the copyreader will find that the most frequent errors occur because reporters don't know a relatively few spellings. Most misspelled words are found in the following classifications:

1. Words ending in *-ise* or *-ize*:

    advertise   criticize
    compromise   legalize
    surprise   realize

2. Words ending in *-ence, -ense,* or *-ance*:

    innocence   defense   allowance
    obsolescence   offense   assistance
    presence   pretense   resistance

3. Words ending in *-ent* or *-ant*:

    dependent   ascendant
    persistent   defendant
    transcendent   repentant

4. Words ending in -er or -or:

adviser	bachelor
jailer	distributor
propeller	depositor

5. Words ending in -ible or -able:

admissible	dependable
deductible	impassable
permissible	indispensable

6. Words accented on the last syllable in which the final consonant is doubled before a suffix:

allotted	allotting
controlled	controlling
omitted	omitting

But:

equaled	equaling
kidnaped	kidnaping
traveled	traveling

7. Words in which the final silent e is dropped before a suffix, except when it is needed to preserve the soft c or g:

judgment	salable
likable	sizable
linage	staring

But:

changeable	noticeable
courageous	peaceable
manageable	traceable

8. The plurals of words ending in y, ey, or o:

attorney	attorneys
family	families
money	moneys
potato	potatoes
albino	albinos

9. Transposition of the letters ei and ie:

receive	niece
seize	wield
weird	yield

THE GUARDIAN OF CORRECT USAGE 35

10. Certain expressions that should be two words but are written as one:

>   all right   (alright)
>   en route   (enroute)

11. Combinations that should be one word but are written as two:

>   cannot   somebody
>   airplane   something
>   nowhere   somehow

12. Confusing two words of the same or similar pronunciation:

>   better   bettor
>   canvas   canvass
>   capital   capitol

Most stylebooks contain lists of words frequently misspelled. The following list of frequently used words likely to cause trouble was compiled from a number of stylebooks:

accommodate	harass	phony
acoustics	hemorrhage	practice
align	inflammable	precede
appalled	innocuous	procedure
apropos	inoculate	proceed
arctic	judgeship	questionnaire
battalion	legionnaire	recommend
calendar	liaison	reconnaissance
Caribbean	likelihood	renaissance
cemetery	livelihood	reservoir
clientele	maneuver	saxophone
colossal	Manila	separate
consensus	marijuana	sergeant
diphtheria	marshal	sheriff
ecstasy	matériel	skillful
embarrass	nickel	supersede
foresee	oneself	supersedeas
forty	parallel	tariff
fulfill	pari-mutuel	villain
fullness	partisan	willful
gauge	penicillin	
guerrilla	Philippines	

One of the principal sources of spelling errors—and a major headache to copyreaders—is the writing of word combinations. Most stylebooks say that the dictionary should be followed, but many also give a list of combinations that should be written as one word, prefixes and suffixes that require a hyphen, and expressions that should be written as two words. If there is a general newspaper tendency, it is to avoid the hyphen and write as one word.

The hyphen, however, is usually required for joint adjective modifiers, as in *English-speaking peoples.* It is not used with adverbial modifiers ending in *-ly,* as *badly chosen words.* The hyphen is also required in compounds of different occupations, as *soldier-statesman,* and for compounds of *fellow, master, counter, ill, near, all,* and *self,* as *fellow-servant, master-control, counter-appeal, ill-advised, near-riot, all-American,* and *self-control.* The prefixes *anti-, bi-, by-, centi-, inter-, post-, pre-, semi-,* and so forth usually do not take a hyphen unless the prefix ends and the word begins with the same vowel, as *co-operate, re-elect.* Compounds formed with the suffixes *-like, -wide,* and *-ful* are usually written without the hyphen. In sports copy the hyphen is usually not used in such expressions as *rightfield, leftguard, heavyweight,* and *basketball.*

The tendency in English to form new words by combinations is exemplified in such terms as *deathbed, sideboard, textbook, northbound, bookcase, weekend, cornfield, background, theatergoer, officeholder, courthouse, boatload, newspaperman, courtroom, printshop, snowstorm,* and *byword.*

The copyreader, however, should make a distinction between the use of a word combination as a noun and as a verb. "*Tryouts* will be held" is correct, but not "Students will *tryout* for parts in the play." If *tryout* were used as a verb, the past tense would have to be *tryoutted.* Other examples are the nouns *holdup, lineup,* and *makeup,* and the verbs *hold up, line up,* and *make up.*

Another characteristic of newspaper usage is the stylebook preference for a few simplified spelling forms. Thus many newspapers write *theater* rather than *theatre; catalog* rather than *catalogue; cigaret* rather than *cigarette; glamor* rather than *glamour;* and *employe* rather than *employee.* They also usually prefer the English plurals of Latin words: *indexes* rather than *indices; stadiums* rather than *stadia; gymnasiums* rather than *gymnasia.*

One of the best-known newspaper coöperative promotions is the annual spelling bee for school children. Perhaps this contest misses the mark. It might do more good if it were held for newspaper reporters and copyreaders.

ERRORS IN PUNCTUATION

Many newspaper stylebooks warn against excessive punctuation, saying

THE GUARDIAN OF CORRECT USAGE

that clarity should be the chief end sought. According to the stylebook of the Louisville *Courier-Journal*:

> Punctuation is probably the most erratic and undistinguished feature of most news copy. Yet the fundamentals of punctuation are easily mastered, and small handbooks on the subject can readily be obtained. This style guide cannot undertake even a synthesis of the basic rules. A few things worth remembering are that short sentences require less punctuation and are attractive and forceful; that a misplaced or superfluous punctuation mark can muddy a sentence as badly as an essential mark left out; that the comma should not be used wherever possible, but rather its use should be avoided wherever possible.

Some examples of newspaper preference in avoiding commas are:

1. Do not use a comma before *of* indicating place or position: *George H. Smith of Chicago, T. B. Morgan of the Acme Printing Co.*

2. Omit commas in ages, time, distances, measurements: *3 years 9 months old, 2 hours 15 minutes, 12 feet 5 inches.*

3. Omit commas when *by* is used to indicate authorship: Adam Bede *by George Eliot,* Bleak House *by Charles Dickens.*

4. Do not use a comma between two nouns, one of which identifies the other: *Hemingway's book* The Sun Also Rises, *the painter Van Gogh, the Cunard liner Queen Mary.*

5. The comma is not needed after the name of a school in giving scores: *Penn State 21, Temple 7.*

6. Do not use commas between contrasting phrases separated by *but, if, though: It is a common but useful practice.*

The copyreader should be on guard against the following frequent errors in punctuation:

1. Omission of the second comma in setting off appositional phrases and clauses: *Dr. John Smith, head of the department of psychology, was chosen chairman.*

2. Confusion between restrictive and nonrestrictive phrases and clauses: *The students who signed the petition were expelled.* (The dependent clause is necessary to the meaning of the sentence; it limits the persons expelled to those students who signed the petition.) *The students, who were rowdy and boisterous, gathered in the square to celebrate the victory.* (Here the clause is not necessary to the meaning of the sentence; it is thrown in parenthetically to describe the attitude of the group.)

3. Failure to use a semicolon in a series made up of items which themselves contain commas: *The injured were James Jones, 24, Middletown,*

broken left arm; Robert Smith, 18, Centre City, cuts and bruises about the face; and Thomas Smith, 23, Centre City, broken finger.

4. Use of an unnecessary colon after a verb to introduce a short series: *Officers elected were: James Smith, president; Mary Jones, vice president; and Alice Roberts, secretary.* (The colon after *were* is not needed; newspaper preference is to use a colon only when the material that follows begins a new paragraph.)

5. Violation of the arbitrary rule that commas and periods are placed inside quotation marks and that semicolons are placed outside: *Speakers and their topics are John Smith, "Whither Education?"; Robert Jones, "Our Changing Times"; and T. P. Roberts, "Education for Democracy."*

6. Omission of quotation marks at the end of a quotation and at the beginning of each paragraph when quoted material runs to more than one paragraph.

7. Misuse of the apostrophe in indicating possession and in contractions. Wrong: *Smiths' vote; womens' hats; member's votes. It's* is a contraction of *it is; its* is the possessive of *it.* (Some organizations drop the apostrophe in writing their names: *Veterans Administration; Lions Club; United Steel Workers Union.* Others retain it: *Reader's Digest; the Builders' Supply Company.* Most newspapers recommend following the organization's usage.)

WRONG USE OF WORDS

Since William Cullen Bryant issued his famous *index expurgatorius* of incorrect words, newspapers have sought to teach reporters and copyreaders proper diction. Almost every stylebook contains a list of words frequently misused and confused.

Some of the words and expressions which Bryant condemned are now accepted: *aspirant; beat* for *defeat; bogus; collided; compete; donate; employee; en route; humbug; jeopardize; official* (as a noun); *reliable* (for trustworthy); *retire* (as an active verb); *role; standpoint; debut.*

Many of the words in his *index*, however, are frowned upon in today's stylebooks. For example: *above* and *over* for *more than; artiste* for *artist; balance* for *remainder; banquet* for *dinner* or *supper; casket* for *coffin; claimed* for *asserted; commence* for *begin; decease; devouring element* for *fire; endorse* for *approve; graduate* for *is graduated; inaugurate* for *begin; last* for *latest; lengthy* for *long; loan* or *loaned* for *lend* or *lent; located* for *situated; mutual* for *common; parties* for *persons; partially* for *partly; past two weeks* for *last two weeks; portion* for *part; posted* for

THE GUARDIAN OF CORRECT USAGE

informed; *realized* for *obtained*; *rendition* for *performance*; *repudiate* for *reject*; *Rev.* for *the Rev.*; *state* for *say*.

Stanley Walker in *City Editor* cited expressions abominated by the younger James Gordon Bennett that have come into almost universal use. Bennett barred from the New York *Herald*: *show* for *theatrical performance*; *schedule* applied to the movement of persons, as, "He is scheduled to leave Friday"; *New Yorker*; *week end*; *guest of honor* and *maid of honor*; *gang* and *gangster*; *diplomat* for *diplomatist*; *plan* as a verb; *house guest, house party,* and *reception guest*; *patron* and *guest* for persons staying at a hotel.

Despite the efforts of grammarians, schoolteachers, and editors, the people eventually decide what is correct. A few years ago *contact* as a verb was considered barbarous; today it is accepted by many publications. Despite its ban in stylebooks, the use of *loan* as a verb is listed in dictionaries as a correct Americanism. Copyreaders tend to be slow in admitting new usages into the sanctified society of correct expression. In this deskmen are often more reactionary than college English professors, for the latter understand better that language is not static, that the will of the people usually prevails.

Although the copyreader need not be a 100 percent purist, he should be on the watch for serious violations of good usage, especially for words commonly confused because of similarity in spelling and meaning. These include such words as *principle* and *principal*; *affect* and *effect*; *hailed* and *haled*; *infer* and *imply*; *majority* and *plurality*. A list of these troublesome words chosen from newspaper stylebooks appears in Appendix B.

COMMON GRAMMATICAL ERRORS

Bad grammar in news stories is as often due to the speed and pressure under which reporters work as to ignorance of correct usage. Most of the slips fall into a few categories. Knowing what mistakes the reporter is most likely to make, the copyreader can more quickly spot and correct them. Among frequently made errors are the following:

1. Disagreement of the subject and verb in number.

When the subject is separated from its verb by intervening phrases or a clause, it is easy for the reporter to fall into error, as: *The witness said that every line of the affidavits she and her sister signed were false.* The subject of the verb in the dependent clause is *line*, not *affidavits*. Hence the verb should be *was*.

Another common error occurs in sentences like the following: *The president with his bodyguard were escorted to the auditorium.* The singular verb *was escorted* is correct. *With his bodyguard* is a prepositional phrase modifying *president*.

Sometimes the disagreement in number is due to using a singular verb with a compound and therefore plural subject: *The jury which heard the case and the judge who tried it was obviously weary after the weeks of testimony.*

Collective nouns are frequent problems because of American copy desk insistence that they take a singular verb. The copyreader must be on the alert for such locutions as *none are, the couple are,* and *the minority were.* Copyreaders are perhaps chiefly responsible for the perpetuation of the rule that such words require a singular verb, when spoken usage has almost nullified it. The concept of group action results in such awkward expressions as *The committee seated itself around the table* and *The team was overconfident, and they played badly during the first half.* When a group acts as a unit, the singular verb or pronoun is logically correct; when the persons composing the group act as individuals, the plural is logically correct: *The committee submits its report.* But: *The committee are debating the report.* The British are less frightened by the use of a plural verb with a collective noun than are we Americans. Winston Churchill writes without compunction: *The government are . . .*

2. Overuse of variants for a name or pronoun.

One critic of newspaper writing, Wilson Follett, said in an article in the *Bookman* that he was mystified by the frequent use in news articles of variants for a name, instead of pronouns where the antecedents were unmistakable. He cited this example: *Twelve-year-old Charles Walker sent to King George, convalescing at Bognor, a fish the boy had caught at Brighton.* Follett commented:

> The mind lapsing into its comfortable little bath of gratified curiosity is all at once chilled and dazed by the introduction of a fresh problem of the utmost irrelevance in this instance, *Who was "the boy"?*
>
> Probably no one will ever solve the mystery of where newspaper reporters get the extra personae upon whom they call for performance of the simplest actions. Hardly any other kind of writer was ever able to produce them out of his sleeve at will, making the innocent paper bristle with four or five actors where the niggardly event itself disclosed but one or two.

Other examples cited by Follett are: *The president is reported to have declared at the conference . . . which the chief executive called . . .* and *Zane Grey announced yesterday that the famous author plans to . . .*

A partial explanation of this practice is that reporters frequently find

THE GUARDIAN OF CORRECT USAGE

it a way of unobtrusively supplying extra descriptive and identifying details, and also that some writers are addicted to the vice of "elegant variation" to avoid repetition. Copyreaders should not hesitate to replace the variants with a proper name or a pronoun.

3. Errors in the use of relative pronouns.

Sometimes a relative clause is employed without a definite antecedent: *The governor refused to sign the bill, which furnished ammunition for his enemies in the next election.* The sentence should be recast to: *The governor's refusal to sign the bill furnished ammunition for his enemies in the next election.*

The *and which* error occurs frequently in newspaper copy: *The books locked in the treasure room of the library and which are seen only by special permission . . .* There would have to be two *which's* in the sentence for *and* to be correct.

An error increasing in frequency arises from failure to observe the rule that the number of the noun to which the relative pronoun refers governs the number of the verb. The verb in the relative clause in the following sentence is wrong: *The column represents one of the most forward techniques that has been introduced in the modern newspaper.* The antecedent of *that* is *techniques*, not *one*, and the verb should be *have* rather than *has*.

The interpolation of a parenthetical expression, often not set off by commas, between the relative pronoun and its verb often results in an error in the misuse of *whom* for *who*: *The person whom they thought was responsible was cleared by police.* The correct form is *who*.

4. Improper sequence of tenses.

One of the most difficult tasks of the newspaper writer and deskman is determining the correct tense of the verb in a subordinate clause introduced by a statement of saying, knowing, or thinking.

The general rule is that the tense of the verb in the main clause determines the tense of the verb in the subordinate clause. If the tense in the main clause is present, the tense in the secondary clause must be present or future: *He says he will go tomorrow.* If the tense in the main clause is past, the verb in the clause that follows is also past: *He said he would go tomorrow.*

But there is an exception to this rule, and it causes trouble. The present tense is correct for a verb in the subordinate clause when it expresses a permanent fact or a continuing action. Thus the following sentence is correct: *The ancients did not know that the world is round.* Presumably, the roundness of the world is a permanent fact. Similarly, the following sentence expressing a continuing action is correct: *The governor said he expects the measure to pass the legislature.* The action expected, of course, is still in the future, and presumably the governor's expectation will continue to be true. In fact, the present tense can be used if the fact is true when the newspaper goes to press: *He said that there is no known cure for the common cold.*

Since much newspaper copy is material reporting what someone said, determination of the proper tense sequence is a serious matter. Unless care is taken, such an incongruity as the following from a press association dispatch is likely to be perpetrated: *Dr. Stone said there were three major reasons why people married, and the most important of them is companionship.*

Consider the problem of keeping the tenses straight in the following:

The governor said he would not object if the senate voted to amend the measure. He declared that he thinks some sort of regulation is needed, even if it does not conform exactly to that asked in the original bill.

Senate majority leader John Smith, however, said he thinks the senate will finally adopt the original version of the bill. He said that he believes the governor's supporters can muster enough votes to defeat the proposed amendment.

He said he understood some of the governor's supporters were urging him not to force a vote on the question. One of the latter said he had little liking for the language of the resolution, because it would give the governor too much power, though he granted that the governor lacks adequate authority now.

Questions also arise over the use of *will* and *would.* Generally, *will* is correct when there is no question of uncertainty: *He said the sun will rise tomorrow.* When there is uncertainty, *would* is proper: *He said the law would likely harm business.* In writing about legislative action, the following is correct when a measure is under consideration: *Under the terms of the bill introduced today merchants would be subject to increased taxes.* If the measure becomes law, the following is correct: *Under the terms of the bill signed by the governor, merchants will be subject to increased taxes.*

The tense of the original is preserved in passages of indirect quotation or discourse in which the attribution is thrown in parenthetically: *When the legislature reconvenes, he said, a housing bill will be submitted.*

5. Faulty participial constructions.

Participial constructions are pitfalls for unwary reporters. The dangling participle is frequently found: *Driving at 50 miles an hour, the car failed to make a curve and ran off the highway into a ditch.* The most prevalent participial error is a *non sequitur* statement following a past participle. Almost no obituary is written without the following type of horror: *Born*

THE GUARDIAN OF CORRECT USAGE 43

in Missouri, he attended the University of California, or *Born in Chicago in 1910, he married Anna Smith in New York in 1940.* The circumstance of being born in Missouri has no bearing on attending the University of California, and the circumstance of being born in Chicago has no relevancy to being married in New York. The sentences should be: *He was born in Missouri, and he attended the University of California.* And: *He*

Fig. 15. "What does the younger generation know about past participles?" (Cartoon by W. P. Trent; reproduced by permission of *Editor & Publisher.*)

was born in Chicago in 1910. He married Anna Smith in New York in 1940. The correct use of the past participle is shown in the following: *Hit on the head with a brick, he suffered a severe headache.*

6. Misuse of prepositions and conjunctions.

The San Francisco *Chronicle* stylebook condemns a common grammatical error under the heading: "Special Section with a Prayer Attached." The error calling for this extra attention is the use of *like* as a conjunction. *Like* of course is a preposition and should be followed by a noun as an object, never by a noun used as the subject of a verb. The following is wrong: *He babbled like he was crazy.* Correct versions are: *He babbled like a crazy man* and *He babbled as if he were crazy.*

Other common mistakes in using connectives include the following:

A person dies *of* a disease, not *from.*

According to means primarily in harmony or in agreement with; it is preferably not used as a substitute for a verb such as *say, state,* or *declare.*

The correct expression is *different from,* not *different than.*

A person is hit *on* the head, not *over* it.

7. Failure to maintain a parallel construction.

A series of ideas expressed in the same sentence requires the same grammatical construction throughout. The following is awkward:

Action of the City Council last night included the following:
1. Acceptance of sealed bids for construction of a new warehouse.
2. Voted to reconsider a resolution establishing Fifth Street as a one-way thoroughfare.
3. Refusal to approve a petition for rezoning two districts for business establishments.

The second item begins with a verb, the first and third with substantives. All three should have the same grammatical construction.

Another typical example of failure to maintain parallel construction is: *He was capable, ambitious, and received many honors in college.* To be correct, the sentence requires the insertion of *and* between *capable* and *ambitious.*

Another example: *The stolen jewelry included a diamond ring valued at $1000, a wrist watch worth $200, and a $250 diamond pin.*

8. The split infinitive.

Anathema to most copyreaders is the split infinitive, despite the fact that many grammarians now recognize that it is correct—or at least not necessarily incorrect. Nevertheless, deskmen almost automatically persist in placing the adverb ahead of the infinitive no matter how awkward the result. Their reflex action in changing copy to avoid splitting infinitives has resulted in another newspaper idiosyncrasy which Kittredge Wheeler condemned in an article in the *American Mercury:*

From the war on the split infinitive was evolved the most dubious of all the rules of newspaper English: that against separation of the component parts of a compound verb. It explains why newspaper readers often encounter such miserably awkward passages as these:

Agitation against governmental decreases in salary appeared virtually to have subsided.

THE GUARDIAN OF CORRECT USAGE 45

Even police reserves hardly could take care of the crowd.

It would gravely have endangered their chances.

Copyreaders sometimes believe that they were taught this construction in grammar school, but the fact is that they learned it in newspaper offices, where it is now safely intrenched. The practice has been carried so far that there is even a tendency to keep a verb and a predicate adjective together, as in "John also is deaf," when the thought intended is that John is also deaf.

Instead of regarding the split infinitive as absolutely wrong, the best course for copyreaders probably is to consider clarity and smoothness in deciding about whether to let a divided phrase get by. Certainly there is no excuse for wrenching the language out of joint as was done in the sentences cited by Wheeler.

CHAPTER 4

Shaping the Story to the News

DEVELOPING A FORMULA

Since a few years after the Civil War, cub reporters have been given a simple formula for writing a news story. Somewhere along the line the proper structure for a news story was tagged an "inverted pyramid." That is the name given in textbooks, which show pictures of an upside-down triangle superimposed on a story to illustrate how it should be written.

The textbook discussions have gone little beyond the advice given by Samuel Bowles of the Springfield *Republican* on how to write a story. In "Training for Journalism," an article published in the *Youth's Companion* in 1893, Bowles said:

For newspaper writing that style is best that is most direct. The spoken style of plain minds is a good model.

How does William tell neighbor John that neighbor Thomas's house was burned? Why, he cries out, "Tom's house was burned up last night!" That is the whole story; and the vital points of the story occur in the actual order of their importance. First, it was Tom's house; second, it was burned up; third, it was last night.

How does a badly trained reporter write the story? Like this: "Shortly after midnight last night, a fire was discovered in the house of Mr. Thomas Blank, and before the flames could be extinguished the unfortunate structure was burned to the ground." That is the same story, wrong end foremost.

A good news report never begins with "yesterday," or with any words expressing date or time, or with any subordinate detail or statement; and the best news reports usually give the pith of their story in the first ten lines.

Beyond a few hints like these there is not much that can profitably be said on the subject of newspaper style.

Oftentimes the trouble with a theory—even a practical one like that

SHAPING THE STORY TO THE NEWS

dealing with the proper way to report an event for a newspaper—is not the theory itself but the elaboration upon it.

For example, the theory said that the gist of a news story should be given in the first few lines. The elaboration was that the opening—the *lead*—should answer the questions who, what, when, where, why, and how. The result was that many news articles began with an omnibus sentence that had to be read two or three times before it made sense.

Another theory—the story should not begin with an unimportant detail. Some newspapers followed this rule right out the window and barred any lead that began with "the."

Still another theory held that information and details should be presented in the order of diminishing importance or interest. To obey this, reporters skipped from topic to topic and scrambled chronology in such a way that comprehending a news report was a lot like solving a puzzle.

There are good reasons for the inverted-pyramid structure for news stories. It makes it easier to display the news. Stories flood the copy desk. They have to be assessed quickly as to news value and edited quickly as to length for the space available. On a daily newspaper it would be difficult to handle the big bulk of news if articles were written to build up to a high point of interest. The desk needs to know immediately what a story is about to judge its importance, and the structure must be one that can be easily changed if the story has to be shortened to meet space requirements.

Another good reason for this structure is that it helps the reader select the stories he wants to read. Few people have time to spend hours informing themselves of the day's events. Their reading of the news is sporadic—a headline here, the first two or three paragraphs of a story there, perhaps a complete article now and then if their interest is engaged.

And, as Samuel Bowles said in 1893, the inverted pyramid is the natural way of telling about an event. When we are the bearer of news, we come immediately to the point: "The Yankees won." "The strike's over." "The bank's been robbed." News-telling and storytelling require different techniques.

But recent critics of the inverted pyramid who complain that it makes for bad writing and dull reading have important points in their favor. New communication agencies—radio in particular—have killed the effectiveness of the newspaper as a means of breaking the news. If an event is important, people will have heard about it before they read the newspaper. Big headlines and the-lead-that-tells-all won't bowl them over. They know in general what happened. They want the details that the radio bulletin didn't give, and they want an explanation of why the event happened and what it means. Hence many stories can best be told by the narrative method, in chronological sequence, or in cause-and-effect sequence rather than in the order of diminishing news value.

Despite the occasional awkwardness of the inverted-pyramid pattern of writing and despite the fact that weekly news magazines have developed a readable style for reporting current events, the newspaper's method is functionally successful. It is a method evolved from the exigencies of daily journalism and from the reading needs of subscribers. A special issue (April, 1950) of *Nieman Reports* devoted to the problems of newswriting said about the inverted-pyramid pattern:

> We have heard of no better way to tell [news of urgent interest] than to tell it forthwith, and put all the most urgently interesting facts in a conspicuous position. When a passenger plane catches fire in mid-air and crashes in a city street, it may be effective for a news magazine, days later, to start its account with a takeoff of the plane and describe what happened as a connected narrative. But the daily paper's function is to report the news in a form that enables the reader to see immediately what happened. When the senate votes on an important bill, there may be scores of afternoon papers that barely have time to rush one paragraph into the next edition. It would be inconvenient if that paragraph omitted to say whether the bill was approved. And even a morning paper, which does not go to press until several hours later, assumes that its readers still want a clear, quick picture of the event. The assumption is correct. Very few subscribers at their breakfast tables the next morning would wish to read a thousand words about the senate debate, even though well written, before arriving at the outcome of the vote. Their reading habits are not geared to that sort of thing, and anyhow most of them lack the time. They would rather read first about the outcome and what it will mean to the country, and if possible to *them*. At that point they will decide whether to read the details.

APPLYING THE FORMULA

One of the tasks of the copyreader, then, is to check stories for news value and for presentation of information on the basis of decreasing importance or interest. If the reporter buries the most significant fact in the body of the story or ends with vital information that may be lopped off in make-up, the copyreader must rearrange the story. Sometimes this may involve writing a new lead. Often it means switching the parts of the story—not difficult to do because short, block paragraphs are conventional in newspaper writing. It should not mean rewriting the entire story. If a story needs to be rewritten, it should be returned to the city editor or the reporter.

SHAPING THE STORY TO THE NEWS

In checking for news value and form, the deskman should examine the story for the following:

1. Is the opening paragraph or sentence so long and crowded with details that the reader cannot understand it at the first reading?

On many newspapers today the old-fashioned lead that answered the five W's and the H and indicated the source of or authority for the news has been abolished. Instead, today's lead should be a single short sentence —15 to 30 words—that summarizes the story.

To simplify an opening sentence so that it quickly attracts the reader's attention and tells him what he wants to know, the copyreader can:

a. Defer until the second paragraph names and identifications of persons who are not well known.

James B. Smith, 48, general manager of the Economy Department Store, and Paul T. Thomas, 43, treasurer of the firm, received minor injuries in an automobile accident early today when the car in which they were riding collided with one driven by Peter J. Jones, 33, of 228 E. First Street, at the intersection of N. Second Street and W. Palmer Avenue, during a heavy rainstorm.

The foregoing tells almost everything that a person might want to know about the accident, but it is hard to read. Newspapers today avoid this type of tell-it-all opening. The beginning should be simplified:

Two city businessmen were slightly injured early today in an automobile collision during a heavy rainstorm.

The full names, identifications, and other details can be given in the second paragraph. In fact, the name of a person not already known to newspaper readers seldom belongs in the opening paragraph of the story.

b. Change complex sentences with their ganglia of subordinate clauses to simple sentences.

Because their nominating petitions did not contain the required number of names of qualified electors, two candidates for alderman, James B. Smith, Fifth Ward, and Michael Connolly, Fourth Ward, will not have their names on the ballot in the coming spring election, City Clerk P. T. Jones announced today.

This can be simplified to:

Two candidates for alderman failed to have the required number of names of qualified electors on their nominating petitions to get on the ballot for the spring election.

City Clerk P. T. Jones said that the two are James B. Smith, First Ward, and Michael Connolly, Fourth Ward.

c. Omit minor details or defer them until later in the story.

Comic books are teaching children the methods of crooks and hoodlums, Dr. Philip P. Smith, professor of psychology at Central College, told the Parent-Teacher Association of Middletown High School at its monthly meeting at 8 p. m. yesterday in the high school auditorium.

The phrase, "at its monthly meeting at 8 p. m. yesterday in the high school auditorium," is superfluous. It can be replaced by two words, "last night." After a meeting is over, no one cares about the exact time and place or whether it is a monthly meeting.

2. Is the essential point of the story or the most important or most interesting factor buried in the body of the story?

The accepted principle of newspaper writing is that the opening must attract the reader's attention and enable him to decide if a story is worth reading. The lead must emphasize the feature. If it does not, it is defective and must be recast.

Sometimes emphasizing the feature involves merely shifting subordinate details from the beginning of the opening sentence to the end. Country correspondence and stories by cub reporters frequently begin with such minor information as the time and place:

At its monthly meeting last night the Board of Education voted to build a new $250,000 grade school building in the Highland Park Addition.

The task of the copyreader here is easy. He merely transposes the phrase, "at its monthly meeting last night," to the end of the sentence.

Stories about automobile accidents, minor crimes, meetings, and other routine happenings are so numerous that they all sound much alike. Often the only factor that makes one different from another is the names of the persons involved. The copyreader should examine the story to see that the reporter has not played down a fact that makes the account of an event different from all other similar events.

An unimaginative police reporter turned in the following routine story:

Arthur T. Andrews, 38, of 2400 N. Maple Avenue, was fined $20 in Police Court yesterday for failure to yield the right of way.

His automobile was involved in a collision with a car driven by Wilber P. Roberts, 42, of 2301 E. Tenth Street.

Andrews told Police Judge Thomas Obrien that his car had stalled at an intersection. Neither driver was hurt.

Baked beans which Roberts was carrying to a picnic were plastered over the inside of his car. "Sure I was driving carefully," Roberts told Judge Obrien. "I had to; I was carrying five pans of baked beans to a picnic."

On the copy desk the story was changed to the following readable item:

SHAPING THE STORY TO THE NEWS

"Sure I was driving carefully," Wilber P. Roberts told Police Judge Thomas Obrien in Police Court yesterday. "I had to; I was carrying five pans of baked beans to a picnic."

Roberts, 42, of 2301 E. Tenth Street, was involved in a collision with a car driven by Arthur T. Andrews, 38, of 2400 N. Maple Avenue.

Neither driver was hurt, but baked beans were plastered over the inside of Roberts' car.

Andrews was fined $20 for failure to yield the right of way. He told Judge Obrien his car had stalled at the intersection.

When the reporter buries the feature, it often happens that the story cannot be changed to bring the most interesting element to the fore without rewriting. If time does not permit rewriting, the desk can redeem the story by getting the headline not from the lead—the customary place—but from the body of the story.

Cub reporters and correspondents are not the only offenders in burying the core of the story in the body of it. The nature of press association work often results in the real news being concealed under new developments that are of minor importance. This fault was pointed up in a criticism by the Continuing Study Committee of the Associated Press Managing Editors Association: "Too often AP assumes the reader knows all about the main story and, in trying for a fresh lead on a second-day story, fastens upon some minor angle."

For example, suppose the president makes an important announcement that appears in the afternoon newspapers. The lead for the morning newspapers will develop a new angle—most likely an attack on the statement by members of the opposing party. The follow-up gives too much emphasis to what is likely a minor and surely an inevitable development. The real news is still the president's announcement. The latest story is not always the best one from a reader's point of view.

3. Is the lead an inadequate summary of the story?

Though the lead should emphasize a factor that attracts the reader by its novelty, its general significance, or its personal importance to him, it nevertheless should contain the main elements of the event in capsule form. It should be a base upon which amplifying details and related developments can be constructed.

One type of lead that violates this architectural principle plays up a startling statement or a sensational aspect merely for the effect on the reader. The reporter may write:

Violence flared on the picket lines of the strike-bound Acme Manufacturing Company today as negotiations for settlement of the three-day work stoppage bogged down.

The reader, expecting a story about the beating of strikebreakers, the hurling of brickbats, and bloody scuffles at the plant gates, finds instead that it is concerned mostly with the failure of the workers and management to agree on strike settlement terms. The "violence" is mentioned far down in the story; it consisted of the arrest of one picket for using obscene language.

Anything chosen for mention in the lead must justify its position of emphasis by being capable of expansion by the addition of details in the body of the story.

Because of the present trend toward short leads of from 15 to 30 words, the beginning that says nothing explicit is common. Rudolf Flesch, readability consultant for the Associated Press, labeled them "empty leads." He cited as examples:

BELGRADE, Yugoslavia, Feb. 19—(AP)—Mrs. Emma Dobeljak, a native of the United States, went on trial today.

CINCINNATI, Feb. 12—(AP)—Ohio river men still had their fingers crossed today.

WASHINGTON, Feb. 4—(AP)—Politics had a different look in congress today.

"These are not leads but sounds of someone clearing his throat," Mr. Flesch commented. The empty lead should be rewritten on the copy desk into a sentence carrying some meaning.

4. Is the story coherent, with the information developed in a comprehensible sequence and the parts tied together to give unity to the whole?

One of the results of telling news in the order of dwindling importance or interest is that the story doesn't hang together. Almost any long story covering several angles of an event will be disorganized and hard to follow.

Herbert Brucker in his book *The Changing American Newspaper* cites as an example the following lead from the New York *Times*:

WILLIAMSTOWN, Mass., Oct. 12—The Mark Hopkins Centenary at Williams College ended today with a colorful academic procession, the award of nine honorary degrees and an address by President Tyler Dennett in which he announced bequests totaling $2,400,000 from Samuel Hopkins, New York cotton merchant and cousin of Mark Hopkins, who died in New York City in June.

Aside from the ambiguity as to who died in June, the opening paragraph is a wordy, omnibus-type lead that adequately summarizes the celebration but is hard to read. Its principal topics are: (1) the academic proces-

SHAPING THE STORY TO THE NEWS

sion, (2) the award of honorary degrees, (3) President Dennett's address, and (4) the bequests to the college. After the lead, the story gave amplifying details in the following order: bequests, the president's address, the honorary degrees, a luncheon (not mentioned in the lead), the procession, the president's address again, and the bequests again.

The skipping from topic to topic and back again is not unusual in newspaper stories. In fact, it is commonplace for long and involved stories such as reports about a day in the legislature, a convention, a session of the city council, a major disaster, a violent and sensational crime.

Methods of imposing order on these chaotic stories include the following:

a. Tell the story in chronological sequence, like a narrative. The New York *Herald Tribune* organized its account of the sentencing of Alger Hiss, former State Department official, for perjury as follows: The first few paragraphs gave summarizing facts such as the sentence, the appeal, and background material about the trial and Hiss. The next 23 paragraphs told what happened in chronological order from the moment Mr. and Mrs. Hiss entered the courtroom until they got in a taxicab two hours later. The story ended with a few paragraphs on future legal procedure. It was the natural way to tell it.

b. Keep together in the story all the separate bits of information relating to one topic. In the New York *Times* story about the Williams College centenary, all the details of the president's address could have comprised one block of information. There was no good reason for dropping the address in the middle of the report and picking it up again at the end. Often all the copyreader has to do to reorganize such a story is to cut apart the roaming paragraphs and paste them next to the paragraphs they should follow.

c. Emphasize the major topics in a story by numbering them or giving them a name tag. Either device fixes the main points in the reader's mind, and he can easily follow this outline when he reads the details developed in the body of the story.

For example, suppose the city council transacts several pieces of important business. After a brief summary lead, they can be listed separately with such details as are necessary for understanding. The remainder of the story can then take up each numbered point, giving additional details, the background, the discussion at the council session, and so forth.

The name-tag method can be illustrated with the account of a busy session of a legislature. The opening paragraph may give a summary of the day's work or the most newsworthy action. Instead of the items of business being numbered, they may be categorized under such headings as taxes, appropriations, and public health.

Press associations customarily employ the tag device in "wrap-up" stories about congress, the United Nations, or news originating from different points. It should be used more often in local news stories.

    d. Tie the parts of the story together with necessary transitions and connectives.

The tendency on the copy desk is to delete the transitional words and phrases to save space. Theodore Morrison, Harvard English professor, condemned the practice in an article in the special issue of *Nieman Reports* on newspaper writing. He said:

> A good prose writer can be defined as one who has learned skill enough to get along with a minimum of formal or conspicuous transitional sentences or phrases. But the minimum is indispensable. Good expository writing is a tissue of general and particular, principle and fact, thesis and illustration. A skillful and needed transition is not mere formality. It distributes emphasis, makes a distinction, sets relative importance in order, puts a rib in the skeleton, or generalizes the particulars and illustrations. In a good deal of newspaper writing, transitional sentences seem to be forbidden.

A unified story in which the parts dovetail into one another requires that the reader be helped to bridge the shifts in subject matter and time and be shown the relationship of cause and effect by connectives: *meanwhile, earlier today, therefore, because, but, next, later, however.*

In short articles the connectives may only take up space; but in longer articles they may be needed to carry the reader along without jerks and bumps. The copyreader should not delete them merely for reasons of condensation. When a reporter has omitted needed ones, the copyreader should supply them.

5. Has the reporter prepared for cutting the story in make-up?

A humorous type of filler material used by *The New Yorker* magazine is the following printed under the heading, "Most Fascinating News Story of the Week":

> [*The following item, reprinted in its entirety, is from the Dayton (O.) Herald*]
> CHAMPAIGN, ILL.—(UP)—The little round rings of heavy paper left over when holes are punched in ledger sheets generally are considered useless. But not by Champaign sewer investigators.

The New Yorker finds these tidbits among short, suspended-interest stories

SHAPING THE STORY TO THE NEWS

that have become meaningless or funny because the last paragraph was dropped in making up the newspaper.

Copyreaders must edit stories to prepare for this emergency. The last paragraph should not hinge for its meaning upon the one preceding it. A quotation extending over several paragraphs should not come at the end of a story, for if the last paragraph is dropped in make-up the quotation will be incomplete. The copyreader should guard also against a concluding paragraph that answers a question in the preceding one or is introduced by a colon. And of course any story in which information necessary to understanding it appears at the end is improperly written.

CHAPTER 5

Explanation and Authority in the News

NEED FOR EXPLANATORY BACKGROUND

An editorial room axiom, seemingly more often ignored than heeded, is that newspapermen tend to underestimate people's intelligence and to overestimate their stock of information. Anyone wanting proof that the American people are not well informed need only consult any recent public opinion poll. The lack of knowledge about persons, places, and events indicates either that newspapers are not doing a good job or that the public is disinclined to find out about the important things going on. Both are probably true, in part. But even if the second is the chief reason, newspapers nevertheless as a principal medium of information have the responsibility of correcting the situation—of trying to get the people to know more about current affairs.

What is too often wrong with the newspaper presentation of news was rather well summarized in an editorial published in the *American Mercury* some years ago. Some improvement has been made since the editorial appeared, but the criticism is still valid.

> One of the most curious assumptions of American journalism is that the average newspaper reader is conversant with every fact, date, event and malpractice in recorded history, from the first flinty drawings of Neanderthal man to the esoteric charts of today's astrologists. Not only is this evident of the baseball writer who assumes that his reader recalls Babe Ruth's batting averages all the way back to the 1912 days in Baltimore, and the financial expert who assumes that his reader recalls each one point rise of General Motors in 1929, and the music critic who assumes that his reader recalls every opus in the Beethoven catalogue, but it is particularly evident of the general news reporter, who assumes that *his* reader recalls every detail of a speakeasy murder case, a New Deal feud, a canebrake African war, a Balkan cabinet crisis—and writes

his story accordingly. Hence, since a fourth of any day's news consists of "follow" stories, i.e., stories dealing with matters previously aired in print, the perusal of the daily newspaper becomes a maddening and goading task; one reads facts only half-understood, encounters personalities only half-identified, views pictures of events only half-described.

What these newspaper stories lack is adequate identification of persons and places and sufficient explanation of events for full understanding. The fault lies partly with reporters who, because they are thoroughly familiar with the persons they write about and the background of the events described, assume that readers are equally well informed. The reporter remembers the details of a story he wrote yesterday or the week before, and thinks it unnecessary to repeat them in telling about a new development. He is wrong. His reader has a short memory for things that don't concern him directly. The fault is also partly the copyreader's. Faced with the task of trimming a story, the deskman finds that the easiest and quickest method is to delete background information and explanation. Because they know explanatory details are likely to be removed at the copy desk, many reporters finally leave out such matter altogether except for essential tiebacks.

A movement to get background and explanatory material into the newspaper columns was begun by the Associated Press in 1949 as the result of criticisms of its reports in a continuing study by a committee of the Associated Press Managing Editors Association. The managing editors and the AP make a distinction between explanation and interpretation. "How can the average reader understand what the story means if vital information and background are omitted?" asked one committee studying the domestic news report. Another committee criticizing the foreign news report declared: "What the reader wants is the essential facts PLUS sufficient explanatory matter to enable him to place the particular event in its true perspective."

Many editors commenting on the AP campaign expressed the opinion that interpretation really belongs on the editorial page or should be left to by-line writers and columnists; but explanation, they said, is just as essential in a spot news story as the reporting of facts about an event or the developments in a situation.

The copyreader is often in a better position than the reporter to see that a story contains the requisite explanatory matter. He is not so close to the event or the persons involved; he can view the story more objectively. Thus one of the duties of the copyreader should be to make sure that a story answers all the questions that a person unfamiliar with the event described might ask about it.

IDENTIFICATION OF PERSONS

Newspapers generally do a good job of identifying people in the news. The fundamental rule is that the full name and identification must be given the first time a person is mentioned. There are several ways of identifying people, and they may be used singly or in combination. The commonly used identifications are: address, age, occupation, title or position, reputation, connection with news in the past, relationship, and achievement.

Supposedly reporters know the methods of identification, but the copyreader should consider whether the identification is adequate and whether it is the appropriate one for the story.

It is a sound rule of newspapers that persons involved in accidents, arrests, and court cases must be identified by age and street address. Such stories may, and usually do, contain some defamatory elements. For its protection the newspaper must insist that the identification be sufficiently specific that two persons in the community with the same or a similar name will not be confused. The truly conscientious copyreader will seek to verify the reporter's identification by reference to the city directory or the telephone directory. If he is still in doubt about a name or identification, he should hold back the story and query the city editor or the reporter.

The copyreader should be on guard against letting identifications get by that might reflect against a race, nation, or religion. To identify a person accused of a crime as a Filipino, a Puerto Rican, a Jew, or a Catholic is undesirable because of the likelihood of contributing to prejudice against minority groups. After World War II, former servicemen were usually identified as veterans or ex-G.I.'s. The American Legion and other veterans' organizations campaigned against this practice in stories involving crime on the grounds that such identifications gave the public an exaggerated notion as to the number of veterans involved in criminal activities and law violations.

When more than one identification is available, the copyreader should see that the reporter has used the identification by which the person is best known, or the one that is most appropriate to the story. For example, a U.S. senator who is retired from public life by the vote of the people may for years thereafter engage in a private profession or business. His identification in news stories ordinarily will be "former U.S. senator." If, however, he were serving as chairman of the Community Fund drive in his city, he would properly be identified, in stories having to do with the fund, as chairman instead of former senator.

For a similar situation, the New York *Times* stylebook contains the following rule: "When a public official has several titles, he should first be referred to by his ranking title, then identified by the subsidiary title which is pertinent to the immediate story, and in subsequent references to him the ranking title is again employed." For example, the first mention in a news story might be: Senator John L. Smith, chairman of the foreign relations committee. Subsequent references in the story would be to Senator Smith.

When a reporter has used a long, multiple identification in the lead, the copyreader may shorten it and supply the additional explanatory matter in a later paragraph, preferably as the AP recommended in its report, "in one chunk rather than sprinkled throughout the story."

One of the worst practices of reporters is to use points of identification as substitutes for the individual's name or for personal pronouns. A story like the following may come to the desk:

PRAGUE, March 10.—Jan Masaryk, foreign minister of Czechoslovakia, plunged to his death today after staying two weeks in his country's new Communist-controlled cabinet.

An official government announcement said the son of the first president and liberator of the country, Thomas G. Masaryk, committed suicide.

The body of the veteran non-party leader and patriot was found in the stone courtyard underneath the bathroom window of his third-floor apartment.

The American-born Czech diplomat was reported by Communist officials as having received many letters and telegrams from friends abroad criticizing him for remaining in the Communist-dominated cabinet.

The references to Masaryk successively as "the son of the first president and liberator of the country, Thomas G. Masaryk," "veteran non-party leader and patriot," and "the American-born Czech diplomat" are considered an unobtrusive way of supplying background information and reminding the reader of details he may have forgotten. Hence this method is used by many reporters. They know that if they stopped the story at the second paragraph to tell the reader just who Masaryk was, some copyreader might chop out the explanatory material. So they slip it in piecemeal. And the result is grotesque, giving the person a Dr. Jekyll and Mr. Hyde character. The reader may be inclined to wonder where all the people came from.

The other practice of working in identification or biographical information is to interrupt a sentence in the body of the story with some additional facts. The reader may come across a sentence like the following:

After re-enacting the crime, the youth, who had served in the Forty-Fifth Division in Italy, was returned to his cell in the county jail.

Or:

Mr. Jones, who served two terms on the City Council, told police he was driving at 30 miles an hour when the accident occurred.

In both examples the information inserted by means of "who" clauses is irrelevant. It belongs earlier in the stories, but the reporter feared he couldn't get a paragraph of biographical background past the copy desk, so he put it in bit by bit.

IDENTIFICATION OF ORGANIZATIONS

Explanation of the general nature, purpose, function, membership, and reputation of organizations mentioned in the news is as essential to full understanding as identification of individuals. Many groups, institutions, foundations, committees, and commissions mentioned frequently are only vaguely known to readers.

The original failure of newspapers to give adequate identification of organizations has become more flagrant in recent years with the maddening practice of abbreviating the full name to the first letters of the words in the name. A collection of capital letters like AAA, USSR, MBS, CCNY, HOLC, and FTC has almost as little meaning to readers as the letters on an oculist's eye-testing chart. The name of the organization or agency should be written out in full the first time in the story; thereafter, the initial letters may be used. Readers may know that USSR means the Russian nation, but do they know that the initials stand for the Union of Soviet Socialist Republics? They may know that the CIO is a labor union, but do they know that the initials stand for Congress of Industrial Organizations?

In general, organizations may be identified by their purpose, general nature, membership, institutional affiliation, and reputation, as in the following examples:

By purpose: *The Women's League, an organization formed to support projects for child welfare.*

By general nature: *Phi Beta Kappa, honorary scholastic society.*

By membership: *The Baker Street Irregulars, a club made up of Sherlock Holmes fans.*

By institutional affiliation: *The Wesley Foundation, young people's society of the Methodist church.*

By reputation: *The National Council of American-Soviet Friendship, listed as a subversive organization by the attorney general.*

The mention of an organization in the news may raise some questions in the minds of readers. Who belongs to it? How big is it? Why does it exist? Did it ever do anything that anyone cares about? The copyreader should anticipate and answer these questions if the reporter who wrote the story failed to do so. Clubs, societies, foundations, endowments, professional societies, Greek-letter groups, fraternal organizations, publications, magazines—all may be made more meaningful if a word of explanation is added.

The American Farm Bureau Federation opposes a program of the U.S. Department of Agriculture; the significance of its attitude will become clear if the reader is informed that the bureau has 1,400,000 members and is perhaps the most powerful of the farm organizations. An American writer wins a Nobel Prize in literature; the importance of the award will be apparent if a brief statement about the Nobel Prize is made. A news story is based on an editorial in the *American Federationist*; it will have more significance for the reader if he is told that the publication is the official organ of the American Federation of Labor.

IDENTIFICATION OF PLACES

Rudolf Flesch, the Associated Press' advisory expert on readability, said in a report on explanatory writing that the most obvious need for explanation concerns facts of geography. "They must be explained to any reader who doesn't live right there." He cited the identification of Hong Kong as "this British colony" in a wire dispatch as a good example, saying that the explanation was absolutely necessary for American readers.

He gave as another good example an interpolation in a wire story about a proposed Columbia Valley Authority. The story was made more meaningful to readers by this explanatory paragraph:

> The Columbia river discharges into the Pacific and is the borderline between Oregon and Washington. Its basin reaches into Montana, Idaho, and Canada.

The explanation would not be needed for readers in Washington and Oregon; it was needed, in Mr. Flesch's opinion, for readers in other states.

Buildings and other structures not well known in a city should be identified by a street number. Little-known small towns and rural communities should be identified either by the county in which they are situated or in reference to large cities according to distance and direction. Since the general newspaper public is not well traveled, it seems a good idea for copyreaders to see that explanatory identification is given for such places as the Louvre, Fleet Street, the Parthenon, and even the Lincoln Memorial.

IDENTIFICATION OF EVENTS

The most common and simplest identification of events is the tieback to refresh the reader's memory about something that happened before the current development in a story. It usually appears in the lead, as in the following examples:

John Doe, who was arrested yesterday when he held up a First National Bank messenger in the midst of a noon-day crowd on Main Street, pleaded guilty at a hearing today in a justice of the peace court.

BOGOTA, Colombia, July 11—(AP)—Colombia sped relief Tuesday to the rich coffee-growing section 230 miles northeast of here where 270 persons were killed and 40,000 left homeless in devastating earthquakes Sunday.

Other identifications that may be necessary are a statement of the significance of the event, its relationship to other contemporary or previous events, and the auspices, if any, under which it occurred.

In a statement on explanatory writing, W. D. Barksdale of the Fort Smith (Arkansas) *Times-Record* said that the significance is often the real story and the actual event is "just window dressing." He cited a wire story from Berlin with the opening paragraph: "A Russian walked across an imaginary line in Berlin today and two nations were embroiled in a controversy as a result." This was followed by a parenthetical second paragraph explaining that the Allies and the Russians had agreed that the middle of a certain street would be the dividing line marking the authority of the two nations in the city.

The lead, Barksdale said, should have been: "A Russian crossed the agreed-upon boundary between the Red and the Allied zones today, and two nations were embroiled in a controversy." In the original story the explanatory matter was thrown in as an afterthought, according to Barksdale, and the fact that the Russian crossed a line was the main thought. "It seems to me the explanatory matter—that the Russian broke an international agreement—is the story and the crossing the line is merely the method," he said. In other words, the news was not the event but the significance of the event.

The tendency of copyreaders is to delete explanatory matter to save

EXPLANATION AND AUTHORITY IN THE NEWS

space or on the dubious grounds that it is not news. Not only should they beware of doing this, they should study the story to see if the reporter has overlooked needed explanations. Moreover, they should take care that the story's real significance has not been covered up by later but minor developments.

Lee Hills, managing editor of the Detroit *Free Press*, says that there is a tendency on the part of newspapers to overemphasize spot news developments:

> Spot news ceased to be the major selling point of newspapers when radio grew up. It may become even less important with the advent on a large scale of TV. I believe that newspapers must provide the "organized background" of past facts for today's events to give the reader the true meaning of the news. It cannot be done by cubs or hacks or hurried local reporters. Much of it has to be done by well-informed news writers with time to do a decent job.

Hurried reporters—even when good—can't always do the job. When they fail, it is the copyreader's responsibility to add what explanatory detail he can for quick comprehension of the story. If he can't supply the background, at least he shouldn't cut out any that the reporter has put in, in an excess of zeal for brevity and recency.

IDENTIFICATION OF WORDS

Just as the copyreader should not overestimate the information that people have about persons, places, organizations, and events, so he should not overestimate their familiarity with words.

A story about a labor-management controversy may be only half-understood by readers because they don't know the meaning of such terms as open shop, closed shop, yellow-dog contract, and vertical union. A story on atomic energy may be all but meaningless because readers don't know what plutonium, thorium, and Geiger counters are. An overly literary police reporter may write about a Fagin or a Raffles, but many readers will not recognize the two as types of criminals. The correspondent in Washington knows what protocol and *de jure* recognition are, but the reader probably does not. The copyreader must be on the alert to spot such terms and either substitute everyday words for them or supply an explanation or definition.

HOW THE EXPLANATION SHOULD BE PRESENTED

Some copy desks, in inserting explanations in a news story, especially if it is a press association dispatch, enclose the material in parentheses or brackets. This method is of course awkward and disturbing to the reader.

The Associated Press queried editors as to how they would like to have the explanatory writing presented. The almost universal reply was: Right in the body of the story, and well up in it. The editors opposed parenthetical interpolations or explanations appended to a story as dash-matter.

The AP instructed its staff members:

> There should be no attempt to disguise explanatory or background material. Don't try to sprinkle it throughout the story in an effort to make it look like fresh material. Put it boldly right where it belongs in the story, whether it is the second paragraph or dash-matter. A few words of background dropped here and there may be disconcerting and irritating. Editors and readers will thank you if you give it to them in a chunk they can easily understand.

Reporters and deskmen have been dominated so long by the inverted-pyramid news story structure and the doctrine of recency and so-called objectivity that the prejudice against putting explanatory material well up in the body of a story may be hard to exorcise. But journalistic practices must change to meet new demands of readers. Copyreaders are in a position to recognize these demands and to aid in bringing about necessary changes in news writing and presentation.

INDICATING SOURCES OF INFORMATION

Examination of stories coming to the copyreader reveals that most of them record information told to a reporter. The reporter does not see all the events that he covers, or even a large portion of them. He gets his information from people who saw them or from officials who talked to witnesses.

In consequence, newspaper practice requires that all news stories reveal the source of information or the authority upon which they are printed. It is a sound rule. It enables the reader to judge the authenticity and value of the information, and it relieves the newspaper of responsibility to some extent if the information is wrong. No paper should knowingly publish misinformation even if a source is given or accept the word of an unreliable source, but it is not always possible to verify everything that is written for publication.

In many routine reports a single mention of the source is sufficient. For example, if the reporter writes a story about a convention program and indicates early in his article that the material came from the president of the organization holding the meeting, the copyreader should not insist that the source be repeated throughout the body of the story.

Other types of stories, however, may require mention of the source not once but several times. Articles made up of statements and summaries given in speeches or interviews or in written form such as a proclamation or printed report must repeatedly indicate the source by a speech tag or credit tag. A source is required for almost every sentence, unless it is obvious that it was made by the speaker and not the reporter. The tag is needed for all direct and indirect quotations, paraphrases, and condensations.

The deskman must make especially sure that the reporter has pinned down every statement to the source when the copy deals with a controversial or potentially libelous topic. No ostensibly *ex-cathedra* statements, none that might be construed as being made by the reporter or the newspaper, should be permitted. All opinion in a straight news report must be credited to its source as quoted material or by a credit tag, or else be stricken out by the copyreader.

The copyreader must also be on guard against the reporter who thinks that such qualifications as "alleged burglar" free the newspaper of liability for libel, and who gives spurious authority for his statements by using such tags as "it is reported." The deskman should not pass stories with such vague attributions.

Points of law which the copyreader must know are taken up in Chapter 20. At this point, however, it is appropriate to remind him that the reporter's authority for news of arrests is that his information is a matter of record. If a person has not been booked or charged, the information is not privileged. Off-the-record statements of police or prosecuting attorneys are not privileged. It is preferable, however, to quote the sources directly than to rely on such expressions as "it was alleged" or "it is believed."

The copyreader must be able to distinguish between the legitimate use of anonymous sources and improper attributions by which the reporter attempts to disguise his own theorizings. When the political reporter writes that "an administration spokesman said" or "reliable information indicated," he is supposedly protecting a news source who wishes to remain anonymous. To give his name might close a pipe line of information. But when a reporter uses a general statement like "opinion here today was" or "it is regarded," the chances are that he has made no real survey of public opinion and that the belief expressed is chiefly his own. His whole story must be considered suspect.

EDITING SPEECH REPORTS

In editing speeches and interviews, the deskman must see that the reporter has properly attributed every statement to its source and that the article is correctly punctuated. The smooth and unobtrusive handling of speech tags and the correct placing of quotation marks demand a meticulousness beyond the ability of many reporters.

Some common examples of faulty leads in speech reports are the following:

1. A lead that doesn't emphasize what the speaker had to say.
2. A lead that lifts a sensational or striking statement from the body of the speech and thus gives a wrong impression of the speaker's attitude.
3. A lead with a long quotation that could be better expressed by a paraphrase or a partial quotation.
4. A lead that crowds in too many details about the occasion and the speaker.

If the reporter writes a lead that does not give the highlights of the speech or an adequate summary of it or a clear statement of the speaker's attitude toward his subject, the copyreader may have to write the lead himself. He will have to do this if the lead is no more informative than the following examples:

John R. Smith, noted archeologist and explorer, spoke in Town Hall last night as the fifth speaker in the Community Forum lecture series.

"The Mayan Temples in Mexico" was the subject of an address last night given by John R. Smith, noted archeologist and explorer, in Town Hall as one of the lectures in the Community Forum series.

These leads give no more information about the lecture than was revealed in the advance stories. Obviously the follow-up report should state what the speaker had to say about his subject.

On the other hand, the reporter may have striven too hard to get something interesting in his lead, sometimes to the extent of lifting a statement out of context and thereby distorting the speaker's meaning, or emphasizing something provocative that might have been uttered as an aside. This type of lead is often not entirely the reporter's fault, as Oswald Garrison Villard said in his book *The Disappearing Daily*:

On behalf of the reporters it should be said that they are as much sinned against as sinning. It is constantly dinned into their ears that when they go to public meetings or to interviews they must look for something "spicy," something to warrant a smart headline, something unexpectedly sensational or controversial. There must always be a bright, snappy "lead." So happenings of no real importance are constantly "played up" and really valuable statements or actions overlooked.

Distortions like those Villard justly condemned can usually be spotted by the copyreader, because the body of the story contains no amplifying details about the startling or spicy statement.

The objection to beginning a speech report with a direct quotation is that it is often difficult to find a pithy one that adequately summarizes the speaker's remarks. Moreover, the attribution for such a beginning must frequently take the form of the awkward shirttail dangler. Just as bad are the reports whose first paragraph is a complete quotation, the speaker being indicated in the second paragraph by such a clumsy device as "So said . . ." This type of lead before and after the copyreader has had a go at it is illustrated below:

"It is fatuous to maintain the pretense that anything is to be gained by continued recognition of the moribund and thoroughly discredited Kuomintang regime, which seems destined to lose its last strongholds in China proper and to be driven back to Formosa."

So declared Mortimer Rover, noted foreign correspondent, in a lecture in Town Hall last night.

With only his copy pencil, the deskman simplifies the foregoing to this:

It is silly to maintain the pretense that anything is to be gained by continued recognition of the dying and "thoroughly discredited" Nationalist regime in China, Mortimer Rover, noted correspondent, said here last night.

Mr. Rover, lecturing in Town Hall, said the Nationalist regime seems destined to lose its last strongholds in China and to be driven back to Formosa.

Reporters too well drilled in the theory that a lead must specifically answer the five W's and the H are likely to make their opening paragraphs too long by giving details that can be worked in unobtrusively in later paragraphs. When a speech has been given, there is no need, for example, to state the exact time and place in the lead. The copyreader can shorten the first paragraph by eliminating them. The details of the occasion may also be of minor importance, and the copyreader can move them to a subsequent paragraph in the story.

In editing the body of a speech report, the copyreader has no way of checking on the order in which the material was presented by the speaker, but he can see to it that the account is coherent. In attempting to follow the rule that information must be presented in order of diminishing importance, the reporter is likely to skip back and forth from topic to topic. The deskman can restore some semblance of order by switching paragraphs.

Another fault of reporters in writing speech reports, especially if they have a copy of the speech, is to rely too much on extensive quotation. It is easier to quote verbatim than to paraphrase and condense. Since public speakers are not noted for conciseness and simplicity, the copyreader may have to do the reporter's work of cutting the verbiage down to a simple statement of what the speaker meant. The style manual of the

International News Service gives the following example of a speaker's windy nonsense:

"It is scarcely possible to envisage the establishment of an international organization for maintenance of peace without having as a component part thereof a truly international judiciary body," the speaker said. "Steps must be taken to formulate such an instrument for consideration at the forthcoming conference."

This statement can be paraphrased thus:

The speaker said that he believes a workable peace organization must include a world court, and the court should be organized at the forthcoming conference.

USE OF SPEECH TAGS

Many reporters find it hard to achieve smoothness and variety in using speech tags. Monotony can be avoided by varying the location of the tags. They may come at the beginning of the sentence, at a natural pause within a sentence (at the end of a phrase or clause), or at the end of the sentence, as in the following examples:

Touching upon new demands by labor unions for wage increases, the senator said: "I don't see how we can raise wages and at the same time hold the line on prices."

"Is it a fair description," the senator asked, "to call this new bipartisan American foreign policy a 'get tough with Russia' policy?"

"Russia does not want war," the senator said. "America does not want war. We both are in the United Nations to prevent war. I hear much more war talk here than I did in Paris."

When there are several sentences of direct quotation, as in the last example, the tag is put at the end of the first sentence, not at the end of the last sentence of the quotation. In long quotations that extend for several sentences or several paragraphs the tag should come early in the quotation or should precede it, so that the reader will immediately know the author of the statements.

There is a tendency for reporters and copyreaders to strain themselves unnecessarily to find synonyms for *said*. The word itself is unremarkable and usually is the right one to describe the way most statements are made. *State* and *declare* should be reserved for formal utterances. *Claim* should be avoided; it is not a synonym for *assert* or *maintain*. *Pointed out* is weak, and it is not a synonym for *said*. *Add* should not be used except for a statement that is an actual addition to a previous remark. Such pretentious terms as *opine, asseverate, enunciate,* and others found in a thesaurus should not be used because they attract attention to themselves.

One of the worst newspaper practices is mixing direct and indirect quotations in the same sentence. The following is a horrible but commonplace example cited by J. Edward Meeman of the Memphis *Press-Scimitar* in the *Bulletin of the American Society of Newspaper Editors*: "Molotov said Byrnes' support of the Canadian proposal 'took me by surprise.'" The correct locution is: "Molotov said Byrnes' support of the Canadian proposal took him by surprise." The long-established grammatical rule is that any statement preceded by *said that, remarked that,* and similar expressions is an indirect quotation and does not require quotation marks.

The mixing of direct and indirect quotations is chiefly due to press association writers, but the baleful practice is spreading to other reporters. Such mixtures are desirable only when it is necessary to emphasize that a phrase or word in an indirect quotation or paraphrase is the speaker's actual expression. The necessity or desirability arises when the statement is striking, controversial, or otherwise unusual. Thus: The speaker condemned "appeasers" and "missionaries of confusion here at home." Or: He described his opponents as "blackguards and liars."

CHAPTER 6

Making Room for All the News

THE NEED FOR TRIMMING STORIES

Every newspaper receives many more stories than it can use. Much of this copy is not printed for the simple reason that there is not room for it. Stories are eliminated on the grounds that they will not interest enough people or are not sufficiently important to be worth publication.

But even after reports of inconsequential happenings and stories with narrow interest have been spiked, the news desk is still confronted with the problem of finding space for all the material that seems worth printing. The problem is greater on some days than on others, those days when the paper is "tight"—that is, when there is so much advertising that little space is left for news.

The copyreader must shorten stories to make the news conform to the space available. He does this routinely on all stories by striking out unnecessary words, phrases, and clauses. Sometimes he is handed a story with orders to "trim it to space." This means shortening it so that it will just fit the space assigned to it in the make-up editor's dummy. Occasionally the story needs to be "cut" or "boiled down." These terms call for drastic shortening so that only the most essential details are given. A 500-word story may be cut to 75 or 100 words.

If a straight news story has been written according to the inverted-pyramid structure of putting least important details last, the quickest and easiest way of shortening is to begin cutting at the end. Such butchery is justified only when the copyreader is hard pressed for time. A better way is to delete a superflucus word here and a redundant phrase or clause there. On an average, six words deleted means saving one line of type; six lines of type gained means one inch of extra space. At the same time,

MAKING ROOM FOR ALL THE NEWS

no essential or interesting details have been cut out of the story. Instead, it has been improved by careful editing.

In trimming a story to space, the copyreader must deduct from the available inches the space the headline will occupy. If the assigned space on the dummy is about six inches, for example, and the headline takes up one inch, the story must be shortened to fill about five inches when in type.

An experienced copyreader can gauge the number of column inches a story will require almost at a glance, but the beginner may need to resort to a mathematical estimate. His measurements are merely approximate. A half-inch or so either way does not matter.

For most newspaper body type of 7 or 8 point, the deskman can estimate that a single line of typewritten or teletype copy will require two lines of type. Thus, to fill one column inch he needs four lines of typewritten copy.

An approximate scale for different sizes of body type is:
    6 typewritten lines equal 1 column inch of   6-point type
    5 typewritten lines equal 1 column inch of   7-point type
    4 typewritten lines equal 1 column inch of   8-point type
    3 typewritten lines equal 1 column inch of 10-point type
    2 typewritten lines equal 1 column inch of 12-point type

This scale may have to be adjusted depending on whether type is set solid or leaded. Most newspaper body type is set on a slug one point larger than the type. Seven-point type is ordinarily set on an 8-point slug, 8-point type on a 9-point slug, and so forth.

The copyreader should train himself to look for superfluous words, phrases, and clauses in all the copy he reads. His purpose is not only to save space, but also to improve the story. Conciseness is an important element of informational writing. It makes the main ideas or information easier to comprehend, because the reader himself is not compelled to weed out extraneous matter. A lean, athletic prose style is wanted in newspaper writing.

The redundancies in most newspaper copy are so obvious that it would seem that reporters could write without them, but writing under pressure tends to produce diffuseness rather than terseness. The same verbiage appears again and again in copy, and cutting it out soon becomes almost reflex action for the copyreader.

UNNECESSARY WORDS

The italicized words in the following sentences are some of the pertinacious redundancies found in newspaper copy:

The meeting will be held *next* Thursday.
The *various* members have been assigned *different* duties.
The *total* amount received was $50.
The club will meet *on* Friday.
Merchants have been asked not to sweep dirt from sidewalks *out* into the streets.
He said 5,000 tickets *already* have been sold.
The suspect has not *as yet* been arrested.
The membership has reached *the* 200 *mark*.
The *new* initiates . . .
The *regular* weekly session . . .
A break in the case is expected within *the next* 24 hours.
The *present* incumbent . . .

WORDY PHRASES

Copy frequently can be improved and words saved by substituting action verbs for weak verbal phrases, as in the following:

Wordy: He tipped the scales at 200 pounds.
Concise: He weighed 200 pounds.

Wordy: He entered a plea of guilty.
Concise: He pleaded guilty.

Wordy: He was in receipt of the letter on Thursday.
Concise: He received the letter Thursday.

Wordy: He made his home in Chicago.
Concise: He lived in Chicago.

Wordy: They are of the opinion that the tax is necessary.
Concise: They think the tax is necessary.

Wordy: He tendered his resignation on Monday.
Concise: He resigned Monday.

Wordy: The play will be under the direction of John Smith.
Concise: John Smith will direct the play.

Wordy: Police will make an investigation.
Concise: Police will investigate.

Wordy: The prisoner made his escape.
Concise: The prisoner escaped.

Wordy: The police gave chase to the bandit.
Concise: The police chased the bandit.

Wordy: He was an eyewitness to the accident.
Concise: He saw the accident.

Wordy: They arrived at the conclusion that the change should be made.
Concise: They concluded that the change should be made.

Wordy: They held a discussion of the matter.
Concise: They discussed the matter.

MAKING ROOM FOR ALL THE NEWS

Wordy: He put in an appearance.
Concise: He appeared.
Wordy: The meeting was brought to a close.
Concise: The meeting ended.

Copyreaders can frequently shorten sentences by changing the passive voice to the active and rearranging sentences to eliminate *there is* and *it is* constructions.

Wordy: The Boy Scouts were presented with merit badges.
Concise: The Boy Scouts received merit badges.
Wordy: The suspect was identified by three witnesses.
Concise: Three witnesses identified the suspect.
Wordy: A proclamation was issued by the governor.
Concise: The governor issued a proclamation.
Wordy: There were 200 persons present.
Concise: Two hundred persons attended.
Wordy: It is expected that an announcement will be made soon.
Concise: An announcement is expected soon.

Unnecessary prepositional, infinitive, and other phrases are another source of weakness and wordiness in newspaper copy.

Wordy: The precipitation for October was 2.43 inches.
Concise: October precipitation was 2.43 inches.
Wordy: They collected a sum of $50.
Concise: They collected $50.
Wordy: Judge Smith will address a meeting to be held on Friday.
Concise: Judge Smith will address a meeting Friday.
Wordy: The program will open with a group of selections to be played by the high-school band.
Concise: The program will open with selections by the high-school band.
Wordy: A meeting of the Chamber of Commerce will be held on Friday.
Concise: The Chamber of Commerce will meet Friday.
Wordy: He was elected president of the club at a meeting held last night.
Concise: He was elected president of the club last night.
Wordy: He will serve as chairman of the meeting.
Concise: He will preside at the meeting.
Wordy: Members of the football team will leave on Friday.
Concise: The football team will leave Friday.
Wordy: The team scored a total of 21 points.
Concise: The team scored 21 points.
Wordy: John Smith acted as chairman.
Concise: John Smith was chairman.
Wordy: The meeting will be held for the purpose of electing officers.
Concise: The meeting will be held to elect officers.

Wordy: He was held in jail for a period of six hours.
Concise: He was held in jail six hours.
Wordy: A special meeting was called in order to elect a new president.
Concise: A special meeting was called to elect a president.

WORDY CLAUSES

The copyreader can save words by eliminating or shortening dependent clauses.

Wordy: Mr. Smith, who has been a member of the club for five years . . .
Concise: Mr. Smith, a member of the club five years . . .
Wordy: John Smith, who is majoring in English . . .
Concise: John Smith, an English major . . .
Wordy: Plans will be made at a meeting which will be held on Friday.
Concise: Plans will be made at a meeting Friday.
Wordy: Members of the club who were present were . . .
Concise: Club members present were . . .

The examples cited appear frequently in stories about meetings and other routine happenings. Since such stories account for a large quantity of local news, the elimination of redundancies alone will mean a great saving in space. Most of these reports are of interest only to the persons concerned. The space saved can be used for stories with wider appeal.

UNNECESSARY TRANSITIONS

In an earlier chapter it was pointed out that copyreaders in their zeal for brevity frequently eliminate transitions needed to make a news story cohesive. Keeping in mind that such bridges are often required, the copyreader should nevertheless be on the watch for those that merely take up space.

English composition teachers tell students to avoid abrupt shifts in ideas and subject matter—to lead into new material by means of transitional sentences, clauses, or phrases. Rhetoric books list devices designed to make the prose flow smoothly. Ponderous transitions, however, are not desirable in newspaper copy. They slow up the reading and delay the absorption of information. Jerkiness is not an aim in journalistic prose, nor is an even pace gained by means of wordy transitional expressions especially wanted. A brisk, even nervous prose is suitable to express the immediacy of much of the material in a newspaper.

The copyreader looking for ways to shorten stories can eliminate many of these space-stealing connectives. Some of the more common are *in accordance with, as a result of, as a consequence of, on the other hand,* and *inasmuch as.*

Two frequently encountered superfluous transitional phrases are *in the meantime* and *meanwhile,* sometimes improperly used by reporters to indicate simultaneousness in time. When two events happen at the same time, the phrase *at the same time* of course should be used. *In the meantime* and *meanwhile* indicate in an intervening time. They can often be deleted without loss to the story.

UNNECESSARY ATTRIBUTIONS

Told that each quotation and statement in a speech or interview story must be clearly attributed to the speaker by means of speech tags, reporters frequently become self-conscious about them and stick them in when they are not needed. The copyreader should check each attribution to see if it is necessary. Often it may be deleted, because the authority for the statement is obvious.

In a lead such as the following the source of information is clear and an attribution is superfluous:

Joseph P. Warrior, 31, an unemployed waiter, was arrested yesterday and charged with the burglary of the Elite Dinette, police announced.

Once the source is given, it is not necessary to repeat it throughout the entire story, as in the following:

More than 150 school administrators will meet here today for the annual conference of the Clay County School Directors Association, J. B. Martin, county superintendent, announced.
Mr. Martin said that Dr. Arthur L. Winters, assistant state superintendent of public instruction, will address the group. His subject, *the county superintendent added,* will be "The State's School Health Program."
The program will also include, *Mr. Martin said,* round-table discussions of budgeting problems, grade reporting systems, and extra-curricular activities.

Vague attributions that do not name an actual source of information are especially suspect. For example, the attribution in the following is needless:

Two intersectional football games, *it was announced today,* have been scheduled for next year by the University of Oklahoma.

Other attributions of this type are *it was learned today, according to an announcement made today, friends here were informed today,* and *it was reported today.* These often indicate doubt as to the authenticity of the information. The copyreader might be wise to question whether the entire story should be printed at all.

ELIMINATING TRIVIAL DETAILS

In addition to saving space by weeding out the verbiage, the copyreader must also prune some of the information. In eliminating factual information he must search for minor details that are not necessary for a full understanding of the story or are not interesting in themselves. Triviality is not easy to assess. A detail that is not significant and whose loss might not affect the meaning of the story may nevertheless be just the bit of information that gives the finishing stroke to the picture evoked by the words. In his zeal to preserve only the vital or the important, the copyreader must not eliminate the descriptive touches that enable the reader to visualize a scene or catch the tone or color of an event.

Typical of stories containing unnecessary detail is the following report; the information and words that could be left out are italicized:

Four persons named Smith, *from Middletown and Centerville,* met *each other* for the first time at 11:45 a. m. today when they became involved in an accident just south of the city on U. S. Highway 77, *and* a fifth Smith was called *in* to investigate.

The four Smiths in the accident received minor injuries. They are Mr. and Mrs. A. M. Smith, Middletown, and Mr. and Mrs. T. R. Smith, Centerville. They were taken to the Municipal Hospital *for treatment and observation, two of them by the Anderson Funeral Home ambulance and the other two by the Jones Funeral Home ambulance.*

Highway Patrolman T. K. Smith said a *1949 model* sedan driven by A. M. Smith *was going north and* was passing a tractor and hay baler driven by B. R. Potter, Route 1. The car was cutting back into traffic *ahead of the tractor* when it collided headon with the *1950 model* car driven by T. R. Smith.

The two cars hit about on the center line of the road, Patrolman Smith said.

Each driver was accompanied by his wife. At the hospital they were reported as having the following injuries:

A. M. Smith—*chest injury, a contusion of the left knee, and an abrasion on the right knee.*

Mrs. A. M. Smith—*A laceration on the forehead and multiple abrasions about the face.*

T. R. Smith—*facial lacerations and bruises on the body.*

Mrs. T. R. Smith—*multiple cuts about the face, a contusion of the left knee, and an injury to the right ankle.*

Potter swerved his tractor and baler into a ditch to avoid hitting the pileup of the Smiths' automobiles. He was not injured.

The story loses little from the removal of the italicized details, which total almost 150 words. Instead, it is strengthened by the deletion of extraneous information. While not perhaps essential to the story, the last paragraph has been retained because it answers a question that many readers may ask: What happened to the tractor and baler and the driver? The details of the injuries are not interesting, for the second paragraph describes them as minor and the persons involved in the accident are not local people.

UNNECESSARY REPETITION

The inverted-pyramid construction of news stories accounts for much of the repetition in newspapers. A story must be told at least three times—tersely in the headline, summarily in the lead, and fully in the body of the article.

This repetition is bad, but reporters make it worse by saying the same thing in different words in a story. A frequent fault is use of a quotation that repeats matter which precedes or follows it. The style manual of the International News Service warns against the following kind of repetition:

CENTERTOWN, May 30—Sheriff Oscar D. Blank disclosed tonight that he had warned operators that all race tracks not closed in Centertown by tomorrow will be padlocked.
"I have warned the operators that all race tracks not closed in Centertown by tomorrow will be padlocked," Sheriff Blank disclosed.

This repetition is obvious and few copyreaders would let it get by, but a deskman not really alert might miss the repetition in the following from a press association dispatch:

Meanwhile, Pennsylvania's veterans got some cheering news when federal internal revenue officials said the bonus payments won't fall under the federal income tax.
"No bonus has ever been taxed, and this one will not be taxable," said Stanley Granger in Pittsburgh.
The payments already are exempt from any state tax levies.
The bureau of internal revenue, Granger said, has consistently ruled bonuses given veterans for war service are tax-exempt. The ruling applied to federal and state bonuses distributed after World War I, and the same procedure will be followed for World War II.

OPINION AND INTERPRETATION

Notwithstanding the well-known theory that news stories should be factual and opinion should be confined to the editorial page, many stories that reach the copy desk are cluttered with the country-weekly variety of puffs and boosts for organizations and individuals, with unnecessary adjectives and descriptions, with interpretation of events that don't require interpretation, and with theorizing and conjecture instead of facts.

Among the more commonplace puffs and boosts that take up space are the following:

All members are urged to be present. (It is not the newspaper's function to exhort an organization's members to attend meetings.)

The public is invited. (This can best be expressed by describing the meeting as an open meeting.)

An interesting program has been planned. (It may not be interesting to many persons. Reporters who use this phrase almost never include the program so that the reader may determine for himself whether it is interesting.)

He has a broad experience in social work. (Not necessary if the background is given.)

He is one of the most outstanding students in school. (Not necessary if the achievements are listed. But they never are, for *most outstanding* is used to make an undistinguished person appear more important than he really is.)

One of the largest crowds ever to attend . . . (The number that attended is sufficient. The statement is meaningless unless comparative figures are given.)

A small but appreciative audience . . . (The newspaper need not apologize for the size of the audience.)

The list could be continued indefinitely, but enough examples have been given to indicate the type of thing the copyreader must be on the watch for, especially in stories by beginning reporters and country correspondents.

Properly chosen adjectives are not objectionable in news copy, but poorly chosen ones weaken rather than reinforce a description. Copy written by an adjective-prone reporter can be strengthened as well as shortened when the copyreader strikes out adjectives of an opinionative nature. A reporter who speaks of Ernest Hemingway as a well-known author is using an unnecessary adjective. If he describes the assistant professor of English at the state agricultural college as a well-known author because he once had a poem in *Winged Verse* magazine, he is falsifying the news. There is little need, in describing the slaying of a six-year-old girl by a sexual pervert, to use such emotive adjectives as fiendish, gruesome, and horrible. Normal persons will recognize the killing for what it is. Many adjectives should be eliminated because they mean different things to different people. How large is a large crowd? The woman on trial for murder is beautiful to whom? Is a person who is well liked in a small group really popular?

The reporter who tries to achieve an effect by overuse of adjectives is likely to overwrite in other ways, and he is especially addicted to clichés.

MAKING ROOM FOR ALL THE NEWS 79

He will start a lead with such a redundancy as: "All roads will lead to Centertown today as Clay County's 50th annual free fair gets under way." Or he will try to featurize a routine accident report by starting a lead: "In a freak accident caused by icy streets, one man was injured and two others escaped injury when two automobiles collided at an early hour this morning at Main Street and Hanford Avenue."

The copyreader should not be prejudiced against brightly written news stories. However, he frequently finds that the reporter who is suffering from featuritis shows little sense of judgment about when to be clever and when to turn out just a straight news report.

Typical of the tendency of some reporters to beat about the bush before telling their story is the following from a Pittsburgh paper:

> Georgia can brag of its cracker barrels and peaches, but when it comes to moonshinin'—
> Well, the revenooers up North here will give Georgia an argument any time.
> They broke up a right smart moonshine factory yesterday in the flats of Richland Township, outside Gibsonia.

Since Georgia is not especially famed in song or story for its moonshiners —we associate them more with the mountains of Kentucky and Tennessee—it's difficult to understand why the reporter chose Georgia for comparison. What he meant by cracker barrels is anybody's guess. The first two paragraphs of the story are superfluous from the informational standpoint. They would be all right if they were entertaining, but they are not. The copyreader who handled the story did much better in writing his headline than he did in editing the story. His caption told the news pertly and succinctly: "Gibsonia Joy Juice Factory Raided."

Another writer of diffuse stories is the reporter who tries to interpret everything he writes, who analyzes causes and motives on incomplete information or inadequate understanding, and who pads his stories with explanations of the obvious. The following, for example, appeared in a story about a community's plans for street decorations for Christmas and for events to drum up holiday trade:

> Details have not yet been completed, but plans call for a preliminary visit from Santa. On these visits St. Nick will determine what the children of Centertown and vicinity would like for Christmas.

The style manual of the International News Service cites the following example of explanatory phrases not needed for clarity:

> Under the contract now being formulated, the miners reportedly will receive a flat $75 vacation pay, instead of the $40 they get under the old contract.

The figure represents a compromise, inasmuch as Lewis originally asked for $100 vacation compensation for the UMW.

The style manual recommends cutting down these two paragraphs to two short sentences:

A flat $75 vacation pay reportedly is proposed, instead of the present $40. Lewis originally asked $100.

SPACE-STEALING REPORTERS

A few reporters are not content to state facts simply and directly. They are inclined to drag out inconsequential stories to wearisome length, either to flatter their egos by a good play in the paper or to please their news sources. The copyreader may be faced with many a story like the following:

A discussion of school bus laws and an address on the future trends in education will be the highlights of the 14th annual convention of the School Directors Association of Clay County to be held in the Courthouse in Middletown tomorrow.

Dr. Donald D. Pulver of the school of education at the University of Middletown will talk to the group on the following topic: "Where Are We Going in Education?" His address will begin at 2:30 p. m.

B. T. Morgan of the State Department of Public Instruction will present a summary of the school bus laws at 10:20 a. m. The new school bus laws were effective Sept. 1 of this year, and Mr. Morgan is expected to explain the duties of the school boards regarding these laws.

Rev. William R. Smith will present the invocation at this session at its opening at 10 a. m. T. B. Masters, president of the Clay County School Directors Association, will welcome the directors in a short address.

Following Mr. Masters' address, Dr. Kenneth T. Peters will discuss the dental program in the schools. He will be followed by Dr. Laurence C. Bosper, who will conduct a similar discussion on the health program.

A 30-minute business meeting will end the morning's activities. There will be reports from the nominating committee on officers for next year and the delegates to the state convention.

The annual report of the county office will be given at 1:30 p. m. with Arthur K. Ransome, superintendent of county schools, presenting the report.

The type of writing exemplified in the foregoing is infuriating to the copyreader, for it is almost impossible to edit. There is nothing terribly wrong with it. It is reasonably correct grammatically, and fairly sound news judgment has been exercised in the order in which details are presented. But it is a badly written story. The average copyreader will quickly pare it down to something like the following, knowing that it is probably the best that can be done without rewriting it:

MAKING ROOM FOR ALL THE NEWS

School bus laws and trends in education will be discussed at the 14th convention of the Clay County School Directors Association at the Courthouse tomorrow.

Dr. Donald D. Pulver of the school of education at the University of Middletown will talk at 2:30 p. m. on "Where Are We Going in Education?"

B. T. Morgan of the State Department of Public Instruction will speak at 10:20 a. m. on the new school bus laws which became effective Sept. 1.

The Rev. William R. Smith will give the invocation at 10 a. m. T. B. Masters, president of the association, will give a welcoming address.

Dr. Kenneth T. Peters will discuss the school dental program, and Dr. Laurence C. Bosper the school health program.

Reports from the nominating committee on officers for next year and delegates to the state convention will be given at the business session ending the morning's program.

The annual report of the county office will be given at 1:30 p. m. by Arthur K. Ransome, superintendent.

The story could have been cut more drastically, but that would not have been advisable. It is a fairly important local item, and it merits a good play. It has been made more readable by the excision of about 80 superfluous words.

Wasteful use of words is not the only problem that the space-stealing reporter poses for the copy desk. The reporter who writes slovenly, wordy prose is also likely to be inaccurate in getting his facts. He writes poorly because he does not think clearly. Hence in handling this reporter's copy the deskman must be on the alert for inaccurate details and false inferences.

The copyreader can trim almost any story because his mind is conditioned to detect verbiage, but he must be on guard against excessive pruning. He must realize that most of the newspaper's readers do not have his practice in reading for essential information. What seems an unnecessary explanation to a copyreader who has a memory for detail and background may be needed by the reader for complete understanding of the story. A story that gives only the quintessence is usually not sufficient for the general public.

When space is at a premium, the copyreader is entitled to cut stories ruthlessly. But he should not make it a practice all the time. He should remember that he is not the sole judge of the value of a story—that its newsworthiness, on the basis of both content and length, was previously evaluated by the reporter who wrote it, by the city editor who approved it, and by the chief copyreader or news editor who specified the heading it should receive. The right to trim copy does not give the deskman the right to butcher copy.

CHAPTER 7

On Guard Against Mistakes

THE OMNISCIENT COPYREADER

The copyreader is generally pictured as the guardian of the newspaper's accuracy. His mind filled with a multitude of facts like an encyclopedia, he is expected to draw upon this vast reservoir of information to detect and correct a reporter's error in giving the height of Pike's Peak, the number killed when the atomic bomb was dropped on Hiroshima, the date of the Duke of Wellington's death, the score of the first game in the World Series of 1946, the author of "When Irish Eyes Are Smiling."

With a clairvoyance greater than that of Nostradamus, the copyreader is expected to know that the reporter who wrote that 15 men were arrested for gambling at 115 East First Street really meant 1115 East First Street and that it was John W. Smith and not John M. Smith of Center Grove who was a guest at the Rotary Club luncheon.

His ears attuned to the infinite, he is expected to have heard the speaker say, as he did, that "these things do not happen in a vacuum," and not, as the reporter wrote, that "these things do not happen in a back room." With better eyesight than the reporter who saw the crowd, the copyreader is expected to correct the statement that the crowd was "angry" when it was merely noisy, and that 2500 persons instead of the actual 1500 were assembled.

Actually, of course, the newspaper copyreader can discover only relatively few of the factual errors in reporters' copy. He must handle too much copy too quickly to be able to verify every fact. The copy desk is set up to guard against errors, but the newspaper does not have the time or the resources to be 100 percent accurate. A weekly publication like *Time* can do better—each writer has the aid of research assistants whose job is to check every word and statement for accuracy and to pencil a dot over each to show that it has been verified. And even *Time* errs, not only

ON GUARD AGAINST MISTAKES

in meaning, interpretation, and implication but in *actual* facts like weights, dates, and measurements.

But through training and experience, copyreaders become astonishingly perspicacious in spotting errors, as if they had a sixth sense warning them that something is wrong. They are able, even in the hurly-burly when a fast-breaking story comes across the desk, to concentrate on the copy before them. Their minds are filled with a vast store of facts about events, persons, and places; they may have almost a photographic memory for these details. And, above all, they know what mistakes to look for.

KNOWING THE REPORTERS

In preparing himself to find errors, the copyreader must first learn to know the reporters on the paper. He knows that young Bill Jones on the police beat has a scoop complex, that he is likely to go off half-cocked when he hears of a story, that in his eagerness he often does not take time to get all the details or to check his information against all the sources. The copyreader watches Bill Jones' stories carefully.

The copyreader knows that Spike Malone, who has been a reporter for twenty years, is dissatisfied and bored with his job; that he can't be bothered with verifying a name in the city directory or making a telephone call to check on a bit of information. The copyreader watches Spike Malone's copy carefully.

The copyreader knows that Fannie Gibson is a hard-working girl, that she likes everybody and everybody likes her. But she just can't get things straight. She has to write three or four leads before she hits on one that is suitable. She is constantly x-ing out words and going back to insert phrases and whole sentences. The copyreader watches Fannie Gibson's stories carefully.

And there is Ernest W. Smith. A little slow and methodical, perhaps. His copy doesn't exactly sparkle. But he hardly ever gets anything wrong. The copyreader learns to rely on him. He can edit Ernest W. Smith's stories with only casual inspection.

THE NATURE OF NEWSPAPER ERROR

Knowing whose copy has to be checked carefully is one secret of the deskman's ability to spot errors. Another is knowing what errors are made most frequently.

Unfortunately, little research has been done in the field of newspaper accuracy. The most important studies are those by Mitchell V. Charnley of the University of Minnesota and by Carl E. Lindstrom of the Hartford

(Connecticut) *Times*. Charnley reported on his findings in an article, "Preliminary Notes on a Study of Newspaper Accuracy," in the *Journalism Quarterly* of December, 1936. Reports of the surveys made by the Hartford *Times* appeared in the *Quill* for June, 1949, and in *Editorially Speaking*, a publication of Gannett Newspapers, Inc., issued in 1948.

Charnley's method consisted of clipping stories chosen at random from three Minneapolis daily newspapers and submitting them to the news sources for verification. He found that 54 percent of the 591 stories returned to him were entirely accurate.

The frequency of types of error discovered by Charnley is of chief concern to the copyreader. His tabulation follows:

Errors in meaning	121	Errors in quotations	17
Errors in names	93	Errors in addresses	13
Errors in titles	83	Errors in dates	13
Mechanical errors	29	Errors in spelling	13
Errors in figures	21	Errors in grammar	9
Errors in times	20	Errors in ages	6
Errors in places	17		

Commenting on the large number of errors in meaning, Charnley said:

> This is, of course, a commentary on the skill and understanding—or lack of them—of the news writers who handled the stories. Perhaps this finding will not surprise any student of news writing. To me it seems that the figure should not be taken at face value, however. The individuals who checked the stories often knew more about the facts involved than any reporter would care to tell his readers, and such individuals might declare stories to be deficient in meaning merely because they did not present every fact, no matter how trivial.

Nevertheless, it is the frequency of this type of error that has most significance for the copyreader. He may have no way of checking the multitude of facts in the copy he handles, but if he is sufficiently attentive he can often see where the reporter has erred in understanding or interpretation.

The high frequency of errors in names and titles is also important, indicating a need for more attention in checking the names of local persons in city and telephone directories.

Although Charnley's survey seems to indicate an appalling percentage of errors in news stories, the figure should not be misinterpreted. It doesn't mean that 46 percent of the facts in a newspaper are wrong. It means that an average of 46 percent of the stories tested contained errors. Moreover, Charnley's study included typographical or mechanical errors and grammatical errors which, although bad, do not necessarily reflect upon the accuracy of the information in the newspaper.

The Hartford *Times*' method of checking on the accuracy of stories was similar to that used by Charnley. The newspaper mailed questionnaires to the persons mentioned as the source of information in 1000 stories. In the 1949 survey the newspaper received 536 returns from the questionnaires. Of these, 73 percent of the stories were marked correct and 27 percent incorrect.

A tabulation of the errors follows:

> Errors in names 77
> Errors in facts 54
> Stories incomplete 17
> Typographical errors 10
> Errors in headlines 9

The Hartford and Minneapolis surveys are isolated examples, and it is therefore impossible to draw definitive conclusions from them regarding newspaper accuracy. One is tempted, however, to say that accuracy apparently increased during the period from 1936, the year of the Minneapolis survey, to 1949, the year of the Hartford survey.

The opportunities for newspaper errors of course are legion. In his book *Freedom of Information* Herbert Brucker reports that a single edition of a newspaper contains almost 5500 statements of fact. These are gathered, written, and printed in just a few hours. Is it any wonder, he asks, that mistakes occur? Moreover, he says, many of the errors are the fault not of the newspaper but of unreliable sources and witnesses.

Another defender of newspaper accuracy, Lucy Maynard Salmon, declares in *The Newspaper and the Historian* that newspapers use "every known means to guarantee the reliability and the authoritativeness of the definite statements made by them . . . [and] they are to the best of their knowledge true and unimpeachable." She cites persistent fallacies in history, such as the belief that Hudson discovered New York Bay, that Bell invented the telephone, and that Cleopatra was beautiful, and says: "If history, with a thousand years' leisure at her disposal, cannot find out just who set up a new throne or pulled down an old one, let us forgive the reporter if he misspells the Christian name of the prominent citizen who was thrown from his automobile at 2:30 A.M."

The deskman is not concerned, however, with forgiving errors or offering excuses for them. His job is to find them and thus prevent their getting into type.

THE ABILITY TO FIND ERRORS

The copy desk itself is often a source of error. Carelessly edited copy and illegible corrections account for many mistakes. Another cause is laziness—the failure to verify verifiable facts.

The copyreader's ability to detect factual errors depends upon his ability to remember miscellaneous details as well as upon the close attention he gives his work. Within one hour he may handle stories on the city budget, a trial for murder, a lecture on art, a meeting of dermatologists, a report of the wheat harvest. The variety of material he handles makes it impossible for him to know everything that he should know in order to spot what is wrong and to make corrections.

The copyreader can, however, prepare himself to some extent for his impossible job. First of all, he should be a student of news and of newspapers. He cannot evaluate stories if he does not know what was printed the day before or the previous week or month. He should be familiar with details about persons and topics that reappear in the news, and with the background of developing situations. This information can be gained only by daily study of newspapers.

Second, he should become an authority on certain fields which furnish the bulk of the news. He should know local and state geography, street and place names, and the location of towns, streams, and landmarks. He should memorize the names of city, county, and state officials and learn something of their background. He should know the spelling of people's names that appear frequently in the news, not only those of public officials but those of prominent citizens—scientists, actors, writers, attorneys, physicians, athletes, and singers. Since the law and the courts provide a great deal of news, he must know legal terminology and legal procedures. He should know administrative government and political history, the election laws, tax and assessment procedures, and legislative procedures.

The copy the deskman edits will give him a few hints that something is wrong. A statement or fact inconsistent with something else in a story is an indication of an error. A person's age can be checked by subtracting the date of birth from the current year. Since reporters are usually poor mathematicians, the copyreader should add any figures to see if his totals match those in the story. If a reporter writes that five persons were killed, the copyreader should count the names to see whether the total is correct or whether any names were inadvertently omitted.

Beyond these few routine checks, there is little on the face of the story itself that will tell the copyreader that the information is wrong. He must draw upon his memory to spot the factual errors.

The copyreader should not ignore a hunch or a "feeling" that a story is wrong. The suspicion at the back of his mind or in his subconsciousness is generally sound. If he does question a fact or a statement but can give no reason for thinking it wrong, he should not pass the story without checking on it. If the questioned statement is not essential to the story, it can be deleted. If it can be verified in a reference book, he should look it up. When to his own knowledge the copyreader does not know whether the suspicious matter is right or wrong, he should hold back the story and query the city editor or the reporter who wrote it.

Since he has to verify a variety and quantity of information, the copyreader must be thoroughly familiar with standard reference works. He must know which books contain what information and how they are indexed so he can look up moot points quickly. When he is handling an important and complex story whose background is hazy in his mind, he should send to the newspaper's library or morgue for the clips on it to refresh his memory.

The misspelling of a name, a wrong street address, or an erroneous date may seem minor, but sometimes such errors have serious consequences. A wrong initial in a story about an arrest or the dropping of a digit in a street address may result in a libel suit. More often no one is harmed by these minute errors. But the newspaper's reputation for accuracy is damaged. The man whose name is misspelled is likely to consider the newspaper equally inaccurate in the other information it contains. Hence the frequency of the remark: "You can't believe what you read in the newspapers."

AMBIGUITIES AND HIDDEN MEANINGS

In addition to factual errors, another prevalent type of mistake occurs in ambiguities and hidden meanings that lurk innocently in the close-set columns of the newspaper. A stock source of humor for magazines is provided by these blunders, which inevitably result from the haste in which stories are written, edited, and set in type. The *Literary Digest, The New Yorker, Reader's Digest*, and others have immortalized many of these slips. Others with bawdy connotations are spread by word of mouth. One of the best assets a copyreader can have is a mind able to perceive the horrifying innuendoes in a seemingly harmless phrase or juxtaposition.

Typical examples of these humorous slips are:

In the parade will be several hundred school children carrying flags and city officials.

The upturned, serious faces below him were those of the rugged ancestors of the old pioneers. They had come to hear him speak.

The wedding is the termination of a romance extending over a period of years.

The accident occurred at Hillcrest Drive and Santa Barbara Avenue as the dead man was crossing the street.

A daughter was born Saturday to Mr. and Mrs. ———. She resides with her niece. She takes a keen interest in affairs of the day, reads the newspapers, does housework and enjoys an occasional automobile ride.

Her father will clasp the perfectly matched string of pearls about her neck which was once her mother's before he escorts her to the church.

The cutworm, that menace to tomato growers and to many other species of vegetables, is again making its appearance.

The President, starting out, was dressed in a battered hat, his customary fishing attire.

Friends here were sorry to learn recently that Mrs. George ———, a former resident of Oakville, is convalescing at Belleville, after suffering several broken ribs in a fall.

Electrically operated registers which accept only nickels, dimes, and tokens and drivers clad in new neat-fitting uniforms, are other outstanding features.

Her act [of taking poison] was discovered at once and a strong anecdote was immediately administered.

The well was ordered plugged because the water was found to be contaminated by the county health department.

Hearing a noise on his front porch, Joseph Gigliotti picked it up and threw it toward the street.

As we look down, we see a mass of faces on the floor, dancing arm in arm.

Cards were the order of the afternoon, and the results exceeded the sanguinary expectations of the committee.

Miss Alice Jones has been engaged as social hostess on the S.S. *Adonis*. Before leaving port she will have her bottom scraped.

She is getting along as well as could be expected under the care of Dr. ———.

After the execution, they said he made no new statements.

The many friends of Mrs. ——— will be sorry to learn that she is recovering from a severe fall.

Analysis of these editorial lapses shows that they fall into several classifications: misplaced phrases and clauses, ambiguous antecedents, overcrowding of facts in a sentence, words with double meanings, confusion of similar words, *non sequiturs*, and improper punctuation.

The copyreader who takes the trouble to study the errors analytically and to learn the forms they commonly take will be better able to spot them when he sees them in a story. The mistakes are funny, but they can be serious, too. A reader innocently made the butt of a joke is not likely to enjoy the humor in the situation.

FALSE EMPHASIS AND EXAGGERATION

In checking for accuracy, one of the greatest services the copyreader can do for journalism and his paper is to stand guard against the tendency to make every happening seem more important than it is.

The late Raymond Clapper was one of the critics, both within and outside the newspaper profession, who have found fault with this tendency. In an article in *Quill*, he wrote:

> Our curse in this business of turning out newspaper copy is overemphasis and straining for headline smashes.
> This comes about partly because of the kind of headlines we use, which attempt to freeze some sensational report into a fixed letter count. And it comes about partly from the pressure upon all newsroom workers, from managing editor on down, to whip up a lead that will knock the reader's eye out. This incessant pumping up of news leads and heads is, I think, and I believe a great many of my colleagues will agree, a curse which leads to overemphasis and distortion of news.

The practice of attracting attention in headlines and leads by using the strongest word was attacked by A. J. Liebling in his book *The Wayward Pressman*. He cited the use of the word "ultimatum" in newspapers to describe a note the United States sent to Yugoslavia stating that unless American airmen then held prisoners were released a complaint would be filed with the Security Council of the United Nations. Liebling also baited the press for referring to a scarcity of meat in the retail market in 1946 as a "famine." Actually, there was no shortage of meat; it was merely being held off the market in the expectation of higher profits if wartime price controls were removed. Liebling wrote:

> I have continued to note instances of that addiction to the strong word, even when it is not justified, which is destroying the values of the language in the newspapers. If, for example, you use the word "famine" in a headline to indicate that lamb chops are hard to find in markets that are gorged with poultry, fish, and eggs, what are you going to use when you mean the kind of famine they have perennially in India?

The copyreader should watch out for such exaggerations, not only in stories that come over the wire but in articles written by local reporters. The distortion of news usually does not arise from a deliberate desire to misrepresent. The reporter may merely want his story to sound bigger and better in his natural desire to have it make the front page. In large city papers the exaggeration is sometimes due to circulation pressure and the effort to get big street sales, for readers can be persuaded to buy a paper if they think something momentous has happened.

If the facts do not justify the strong language in the lead, the copyreader should tone down the story. Usually a reporter will put in some qualifications further down in his account, and his exaggeration is not difficult to detect.

Do three or four cases of polio in a community make an "epidemic"? Was the head of a state institution really "called on the carpet" when he was asked to give a report before an appropriations committee? Does a request from the city manager for people to be sparing in the use of water for lawns and flowers mean that the city is "facing a water crisis"? Did the city councilman "hurl charges" when he called for an inquiry into the handling of the new garbage contract?

The answer to these questions is frequently "no." The strong words were used merely for effect. Their use casts doubt upon the newspaper's reputation for accuracy. Their continued use will cause disbelief, just as no one is impressed when a new motion picture is hailed as "colossal."

CHAPTER 8

Readability and Understanding

NEWS AND LITERARY STYLE

In the past few years newspaper writing has undergone as careful an analysis, perhaps, as has ever been attempted of so large a body of prose. Despite criticisms that newspapermen write slovenly English, the fact is that few other groups of writing people have so carefully considered the problem of composition from the viewpoint of its ultimate end—the communication of ideas and information.

To find out if the writing in newspapers is adequate for its purpose, privately owned readability services, schools of journalism, and editors themselves have surveyed and analyzed millions of words. In addition, editors have carefully studied readership surveys in an attempt to discover why one story attracts a large number of persons and another only a few.

There have been times when newspapermen consciously sought to be "literary." And sometimes it seems that newspaper writing has been at its worst when reporters were more concerned with the way they said things than with what they had to say. James Russell Lowell ridiculed journalistic pretensions to fine writing in his introduction to *The Biglow Papers*. He printed a list of expressions that he felt were poisoning the language: "Commenced his rejoinder" for "began his answer"; "the conflagration extended its devastating career" for "the fire spread," and "was launched into eternity" for "was hanged."

But such high-sounding prose has not been the standard sought by newspapermen. The kind of writing editors have wanted was better described by William Cullen Bryant in a letter of advice to a young man seeking to be a journalist:

I observe that you have used several French expressions in your letter. I think if you will study the English language, that you will find it capable of expressing all the ideas you may have. I have always found it so, and in all that I have written I do not recall an instance where I was tempted to use a foreign word but that, on searching, I have found a better one in my own language.

Be simple, unaffected; be honest in your speaking and writing. Never use a long word where a short one will do as well.

Call a spade by its name, not a well-known oblong instrument of manual labor; let a home be a home, and not a residence; a place, not a locality, and so on of the rest. When a short word will do, you will always lose by a long one; you lose in clearness, you lose in honest expression of meaning, and, in the estimation of all men who are capable of judging, you lose in reputation for ability.

The differences between journalistic English and standard English are chiefly superficial—a matter of organization of material rather than a way of writing. Fundamentally, writing for a newspaper has about the same purpose as writing for any other medium, and the elements employed are the same—words, grammar, syntax, punctuation. Like any other writer, the reporter is expected to choose the proper word to express the meaning he wishes to convey, his grammar must be correct according to current usage, his sentences must be carefully constructed, and his punctuation should indicate pauses and stops and clarify expression.

Collections of "best" news stories contain stories of high literary merit. They show that there is no essential difference between journalism and literature. But the newspaperman who hurriedly typewrites a story or dictates one over the telephone to the editorial room is not consciously trying to compose literature. Most of the time he doesn't, but occasionally the piece he turns out has the emotional impact of a drama or a story. His articles are written in a style appropriate for the material and purpose, they are vigorous and forceful, they arouse an emotional or an intellectual response, they may even have beauty. Are these not precisely the values we discover in any literary work?

Nevertheless, the copyreader will find little coming to his desk that he will want to compare with the prose of Ernest Hemingway or Virginia Woolf. Newspaper writing has been called "literature in a hurry." All too often it is in too much of a hurry. Reporters trying to keep in mind a multitude of details, harried by the thought of facts they still must get and persons they still must see, and rushing to get their copy into the office to meet a deadline, are likely to make serious grammatical slips, to use the wrong word, to write clumsy sentences. If their piece turns out to be "literature," it is a lucky accident. Reporters write for today, not for the future.

MEASURING READABILITY

The recent studies of newspaper writing have been concerned with it not as literature but as a means of simple communication. Editors became interested in the surveys because they seemed to promise a method by which reports of the complex affairs of the world might be made quickly comprehensible to the average American—to the man or woman who snatches 30 minutes of the day's 1440 to become informed. As a result of these studies, a new word has entered editorial room vocabularies—readability.

Readability, or reading ease, is judged by three factors—short simple sentences, common everyday words, and human interest. There is nothing new in this concept. Writers of children's books have almost always written after this fashion. So have the authors who strive for huge sales. So have advertising copywriters. The something new that has been added to stir up interest in readability is the attempt at its scientific measurement by a formula.

Two yardsticks are in common use. One of these was devised by Robert Gunning, director of Readable News Reports. The United Press had Gunning analyze its news report in 1945. The other well-known formula is that of Rudolf Flesch. Flesch presented a formula in his *The Art of Plain Talk*, published in 1946, and revised it for another book, *The Art of Readable Writing*, published in 1949. Variations of these two basic formulas have been made by teachers in schools of journalism and applied to analyzing stories in a large number of newspapers.

Introducing a series of reports on readability studies made by the United Press, Earl J. Johnson, general news manager, said: "Writing is an art, but when its primary purpose is *to inform*, writing comes close to being a science as well. The scientific method has been used with success in almost every department of newspapering except the news-writing department." He commented that in letters written from his office he preached writing simply more than anything else. But when the UP report was measured for readability, most of the stories were scored "difficult."

The Gunning readability yardstick measures stories for the following factors:

1. Sentence pattern—the average number of words in a sentence. Mate-

rial with sentences averaging more than 20 words is considered hard to read.

2. Fog index—a measure of abstract or complex words: *prodigious expenditure* for *big expense, undoubtedly* for *no doubt, compelled* for *forced, rendezvous* for *meeting*.

3. Human interest—the number of times people are mentioned or named in a story.

The formula scores stories from 6 to 17, the figures corresponding roughly to the number of years of education a person would need to be able to read an article with the least difficulty. The census indicates that the average for people in the United States is nine years of formal schooling; hence an acceptable readability score is 9 or below.

The Flesch formula is similar. The readability scores are standard, fairly poor, poor, and very poor. The yardstick is as follows:

Standard: not more than 150 syllables per 100 words; not more than 19 words per average sentence; at least 6 "personal words" per 100 words; and at least 12 "personal sentences" per 100 sentences.

Fairly poor: 151-162 syllables per 100 words; 20-23 words per average sentence; 3-5 "personal words" per 100 words; 5-11 "personal sentences" per 100 sentences.

Poor: 163-186 syllables per 100 words; 24-27 words per average sentence; 1-2 "personal words" per 100 words; 1-4 "personal sentences" per 100 sentences.

Very poor: more than 186 syllables per 100 words; more than 27 words per average sentence; no "personal words"; no "personal sentences."

A danger in the readability formulas is that they may be followed slavishly. Executives of both the AP and the UP have warned against this. Thus Paul R. Mickelson, general news editor of the AP, said in a memorandum to staff members:

> A fundamental of AP operations is that no rule or idea is meant to be followed out the window. That applies to our use of Dr. Flesch's formula. For example, the fourth factor of his formula, dealing with the "personal sentence," should be used with care and discrimination. It applies best to feature writing or to columns.
>
> The point is, we do not want to break out in a rash of first and second person stories about things that call merely for simple, straightforward news writing.

And Johnson, in a memorandum to UP staff members, quoted the following from Gunning's report on readability as a warning:

> In this report the emphasis is placed on sentence pattern, rather than on average sentence length. Nothing is more boring than a dead level of sentences

READABILITY AND UNDERSTANDING

about 20 words long. There is no objection to a 30-word sentence. The point is that the 30-word sentence should be balanced with two or three of 10 words or less.

Johnson added:

> As the head specialist himself observes, *we don't want to strike a dead level of 20-word sentences.* We don't want the whole news report cast in one rigid mould. Different stories require different treatment and *variety is an important quality of the news report.*
>
> The important thing is that *stories that are written primarily to inform,* as distinguished from features written primarily to amuse or entertain, *must be done in simple, direct sentences made up of words that readers generally are familiar with.*

Judging newspaper readability with an arithmetical yardstick and syllable count has been popular with editors and publishers. Many of the men who *write* the newspaper, however, have taken a dim view of the practice. One of them was Robert Faherty of the Chicago *Daily News*. A readability expert's survey showed that the average sentence length in the *Daily News* was 21.6 words. Faherty said he was told to limit his sentences to 14 words. After several months of sticking to the 14-word formula, he wrote an angry article for the *Guild Reporter* making the following criticisms of the formula from the point of view of *writeability*:

1. The formula wastes writer-time, which costs money. It wastes writer-skill. It wastes writer-strength, thus cutting efficiency. It kills writer-creativeness, which some editors regard as desirable.

2. It is often difficult to achieve a 14-word lead that expresses the news element and properly identifies a principal. It is often necessary to discard two or three attempts. A formula 14-word story about anything more complex than a warehouse fire requires double or triple the time needed for a story written with a normal sentence flow.

3. The formula wastes space. A 14-word sentence very often becomes a 14-word paragraph because on fast-running and near-deadline stories the copy is snatched out of the machine a sentence at a time. Many sentences must be cut off at six or eight or ten words because an added phrase or clause would go beyond the limit—and in top-speed writing the writer has no time for studied rearrangement. So a six-word sentence may become a six-word paragraph. Meager paragraphs waste much space.

4. Frequently a satisfactory word count must be obtained by arbitrarily breaking a compound sentence into two sentences, even though this means starting the new one with a coördinate conjunction.

5. The structural faults of sentences that have been cut abruptly to the

formula give the stories structural faults. Abnormality and artificiality are instantly evident.

The establishment of a 14-word maximum for sentences is, of course, something that the originators of the readability yardsticks did not envision. The rule illustrates a fallacy of reasoning which says that if a sentence is readable, a shorter sentence will be more readable. The result of this application of the formula as a tool for gauging readability is choppy prose, numerous examples of which can be found in the copy of newspapers and press associations whose writers have taken the short-sentence rule too seriously.

An arithmetical formula for determining whether a piece of writing is good or bad, or even readable, is rather superficial. Conceivably, a piece of prose to which the yardstick gave a good score could have no meaning at all. As a matter of fact, passages from Gertrude Stein have come out well on the readability scale, nonsensical though they are to the logical mind.

The formula leaves out too many factors—rhythm, euphony, subject matter, individuality—which must be considered in determining the effectiveness of reading matter. Moreover, the readability experts have given no proof that the adult newspaper reader has the comprehension of only a seventh- or eighth-grader. The adult who didn't finish high school but has succeeded in making a living and rearing a family in our difficult and complex era is certainly capable of assimilating the day's news when written at a level above that of a school reader.

Moreover, the formula is perhaps a symptom of a retrogressive tendency in our age, a trend which Clifton Fadiman discussed in an article in the *Saturday Review of Literature*. He named this tendency "the decline of attention" (the name borrowed from Henry James, an *unreadable* writer).

"In general," Fadiman wrote of modern journalism, "a successful, technically admirable attempt is made to *attract* the attention without actually *engaging* it; to entertain rather than challenge; or, to use the editors' quite legitimate phrase, to be 'readable'—that is, to present material which can be read easily and forgotten quickly."

The logical conclusion is that if simplicity is good, more simplicity will be better. When all reading can be reduced to the primer level, journalism can go on from there—abandon words entirely and give us the news in the form of cartoon strips. Then we will have made the complete circle and have returned to where writing began—the pictograph.

The great danger in oversimplification is that, in demanding less attention from the reader, the newspaper will *get* less attention. Surveys indicate that the average adult spends only about 30 minutes a day reading the newspaper. Will the paper be better off if this time is reduced to 15 minutes or even five?

The readability faddists apparently tend to underestimate people's desire to know. It is possible, for instance, to get the gist of the news without reading at all—from a five- or fifteen-minute newscast. If this were sufficient to satisfy curiosity and the hunger for information, the total newspaper circulation would probably be falling instead of rising from year to year. What newspaper writing needs is not necessarily fewer syllables and shorter sentences but a prose that stimulates by its freshness of idiom, its avoidance of stereotypes, its vigorous pace, its logical neatness. The arithmetical formula is a help to better writing. It has directed attention to poorly chosen words, pointed out the prevalence of sprawling sentences, indicated the lack of dramatization of ideas in human terms. But its usefulness as a tool is destroyed when its application means chopping off a sentence at 14 words when 30 are needed to complete it, or when a reporter hesitates to write such an indispensable word as "radioactivity" because it contains seven syllables.

The conditions under which the reporter writes account for much of the unreadability of newspaper stories. It takes time to write well. Pruning unnecessary words, framing shapely sentences, maintaining pace and rhythm appropriate to the subject matter, choosing the exact word to convey an idea or evoke an image—such niceties of style come from studied effort. They are unlikely to appear in articles typed out quickly at deadline and sent to the composing room in takes. The deskman also works under pressure. His compulsion, however, is not to get the story written, but to get it in shape for publication. He can give it the finishing touches for which the reporter may not have had time.

Another explanation for unreadable newspaper stories is the rules established for news writing. By insisting that the whole story be told in the lead and that additional details be presented in the order of descending importance, editors sought to make it easier for their readers to keep up with the news. The theory was that the readers could find out from the opening paragraph what the story was about. If they were interested, they would read the rest of it. But the device has been too successful. Readers frequently do not get beyond the first few paragraphs.

One of the most beneficial results of the readability formulas has been the undermining of the inverted-pyramid pattern of newspaper writing by their insistence on short opening paragraphs. The structure still has its uses and hence will not be completely abandoned. But its rigid pattern no longer determines the shape of the news story. The lead should tell the important facts summarily, but it is no longer a requisite that it be written, to quote from a textbook on newswriting, "in such a form that the rest of the story may be cut off in the editing or the make-up without depriving the reader of any essential point."

The work of the copyreader of course is not to write the news. He is an editor. But if a story that lacks readability comes across the desk, he can often improve it with a few deft touches. Some suggestions for editing copy for readability are given in the remainder of this chapter.

MAKING SENTENCES READABLE

The value of the short sentence does not lie in the mere fact of shortness. The short sentence makes it impossible to use long qualifying phrases, dependent clauses, and other syntactical parts that delay comprehension.

Dependent clauses and long phrasal modifiers at the beginning of the sentence are awkward. The copyreader should recast the sentence to place these where they belong.

Example:
With returns in from 3,005 of the state's 3,107 precincts, James R. Smith had amassed a total of 253,000 votes at 2 a. m. to lead Robert B. Jones by 28,000 votes in the gubernatorial race.

Edited for Readability:
James R. Smith was leading Robert B. Jones by 28,000 votes in the race for governor at 2 a. m. He had 253,000 votes with 102 precincts yet to be heard from.

The unemphatic attributions of the shirttail variety in leads can often be moved to the second paragraph when there is no necessity for giving the source immediately.

Example:
Serial numbers of bills taken in the $25,000 robbery of the First National Bank gave police and FBI agents today their best hope of tracing the members of the holdup gang, according to Police Chief Joseph R. Chambers.
The bills listed varied in denomination from $1 to $100, Chief Chambers said.

Edited for Readability:
Serial numbers of bills taken in the $25,000 robbery of the First National Bank gave police and FBI agents today their best hope of tracing the holdup gang.
Police Chief Joseph R. Chambers said the bills listed varied in denomination from $1 to $100.

READABILITY AND UNDERSTANDING

Long modifying phrases or clauses separating the subject and verb are pitfalls for both writer and reader. They facilitate grammatical errors and they confuse the reader.

Example:
Under the contributory pension plan, members of the faculty, who may retire at the age of 60 with an annuity of approximately 50 per cent of their average salary during the five years preceding their retirement, pay into the fund 3 per cent of their wage each month.

Edited for Readability:
Under the contributory pension plan, faculty members may retire at the age of 60 with an annuity about one-half their average salary during the five years preceding their retirement. They pay into the fund 3 per cent of their wage each month.

Reporters frequently pick up long meaningless quotations from mimeographed speeches and reports simply because it's easy to do. The copyreader can turn these into sensible statements by paraphrasing.

Example:
"Whatever the merits of the new legislation—and I for one do not believe that it presents a workable solution to the situation—it is now the law of the state, and it behooves those officials whose duty it is to enforce it to do so with dispatch and efficiency," the senator said.

Edited for Readability:
The senator said he does not think the new law will solve the problem. But since it is the law, he declared, officials should enforce it vigorously.

THE SHORT PARAGRAPH

Of all the aids to readability, the short paragraph is the easiest to achieve. Remembering that each line of typewritten copy makes about two lines of type in the standard newspaper column, the copyreader can quickly gauge copy for paragraph length and mark in the symbol for a new paragraph where needed.

Because the newspaper column is narrow and the type is small, paragraphs should not have more than five or six lines. Two-line paragraphs are frequent.

Paragraphs should of course vary in length according to the content of the story. Too many single-sentence paragraphs—a result of excessive compliance with the rule of shortness—are monotonous. They may slow up the onward march of the story and hinder readability rather than advance it. When several sentences are closely related in thought, they should be presented as a paragraph unit, not separated by arbitrary paragraphing.

PERSONAL WORDS AND SENTENCES

The readability yardsticks measure human interest by the number of personal words and by the number of sentences addressed to the reader. Human interest or personal words are names, personal pronouns, group words like "folks" and "people," and nouns that have masculine or feminine gender like "father," "daughter," and "actress." Personal sentences include commands, questions, exclamations, and quoted conversation.

One of the AP stories given a high readability rating by Rudolf Flesch is the following. It ranked high in human interest as well as in word and sentence length.

INDIANAPOLIS, Jan. 2—(AP)—Are you shivering in this cold weather? Well, go gnaw a hunk of cabbage.
It all simmers down to a matter of vitamin C, says the state board of health.
"Cabbage," said Miss Lelia Ogle, nutritionist for the board, "is one of our most plentiful and inexpensive winter vegetables and is rich in Vitamin C."
Other foods recommended by Miss Ogle to ward off chattering of the teeth are citrus fruits, canned tomatoes, and raw vegetable salads.

By either journalistic or literary standards the foregoing is poor writing. The newspaper rule of objectivity in reporting events—which bars the first person and direct address—has too great validity for it to be abandoned except in feature stories. The intelligence level of the story, discounting the reporter's dubious interpretation of the nutritionist's statements about vitamin C, verges on the moronic. The wit of "Go gnaw a hunk of cabbage" is that of a boorish teen-ager's wisecrack.

Stories with human interest do not have to be written in a chatty vein. For purposes of study, Paul R. Mickelson, general news editor of the Associated Press, had science writer Howard W. Blakeslee rewrite a story that scored low on readability.

Example:
SEATTLE, Jan. 2—(AP)—University of Washington scientists reported today experiments have shown that microplankton organisms act as radioactivity "carriers" in Bikini waters, keeping the waters radioactive.
The report on the role of the organisms as aquatic "Typhoid Marys" came from Dr. Lauren R. Donaldson, director of the university's applied fisheries laboratory, and Arthur D. Welander, fisheries instructor. Both men participated in the Bikini atomic bomb test and a resurvey last summer.
Dr. Donaldson said the microplankton, the basic element of food changes

in the sea, carry the lethal radioactivity and transmit it to other forms of aquatic life that feed on them.

He said they apparently pick up the radiation from plant life deep in the lagoon and bring it to the surface. Barnacles and algae on the bottom of ships are believed to absorb the radiation as they feed on the minute organisms, thereby causing radioactive disturbances on the ships.

Rewritten for Readability:

SEATTLE, Jan. 2—(AP)—Discovery of the missing links that will spread dangerous atomic bomb atoms to human beings was reported today at the University of Washington.

The atom-spreaders were found in Bikini lagoon, and described by Dr. Lauren K. Donaldson and Arthur D. Welander. These carriers are tiny animals and plants that live in water. They are mostly too small to be seen. They number countless billions. They scour the bottoms and fish live on them.

The Bikini underwater explosion rained about a bushel of radioactive atoms from the bomb into the lagoon. This bushel spread over about 200 square miles of lagoon bottom, seemingly safely out of harm's way.

But the microscopic water creatures picked up the atoms, and fed them to the fish. Some fish took their own photographs with the radioactive rays from these atoms in their flesh and bones.

A man eating these Bikini fish for a few years might become equally radioactive, and that would kill him.

This danger will last a century, or more, because many of the bomb atoms will emit dangerous rays for that long.

What worries some scientists is that even when the atoms go up into the air, as they did in Japan, they will fall ultimately to earth, and be just as dangerous as the day when they went up.

Blakeslee's version of the microplankton story has human interest not because it addresses the reader familiarly but because it shows what the radioactive particles may mean to man—to the reader himself.

The deskman, however, should not rewrite stories to give them human interest appeal. But he can do a great deal to enliven impersonal newspaper prose by being alert to recast abstractions and generalizations into specific human terms.

The copyreader frequently finds stories in which the idea of people as individual human beings is replaced by the idea of them as a group or segment of society. These include such expressions as *population of the United States* for *people of the United States*; *the student body* for *the students*; *the medical profession* for *doctors*. Such terms can be changed quickly.

Example:

A venire of 200 names will be called for jury service for the fall term of court starting Sept. 15.

Edited for Readability:
Two hundred persons will be called for jury service for the fall term of court starting Sept. 15.

Often the copyreader finds sentences in which the reporter has made an idea the subject of a sentence, whereas the emphasis belongs on the persons involved.

Example:
Adjudication of differences between the workers and the management will be attempted at a conference to be held tomorrow.

Edited for Readability:
The workers and the management will attempt to iron out differences at a conference tomorrow.

Most examples of this faulty emphasis are found in sentences whose verb is in the passive voice. By changing to the active voice, the copyreader not only gives the sentence human interest appeal but strengthens it with a more vigorous verb.

WORDS THAT PEOPLE KNOW

Building a large vocabulary as a means of getting ahead in journalism is no longer necessary. Editors today do not want writers who raise the syllabic count of stories with long words. As a consequence, the thesaurus is one of the least-used books in the newsroom.

In recommending words drawn from the everyday speech of the people, editors and readability experts are not being antiliterary. They are merely advising newspaper writers to copy the great authors of the past and present. According to Greek scholars, Homer recited in a language easily understood by his hearers. Dante wrote his great epic in the Italian vulgate instead of literary Latin. Shakespeare wrote for the "groundlings"; his plays did not sound high-flown to Elizabethan audiences. "My purpose was to imitate, and, as far as possible, to adopt the very language of men," said Wordsworth of his poems.

Many reporters, confronted with a big story to tell, make the mistake of employing a high-flown style commensurate with the importance of the event they have to describe. What they intended to be deathless prose often turns out to be unreadable prose. Here, for example, is a story with a poor readability score in the United Press survey:

NEW YORK, Jan. 3—(UP)—Dr. John F. (Jafsie) Condon, whose rendezvous beside a graveyard with the Lindbergh baby's kidnaper catapulted him from classroom obscurity to national fame, will be buried tomorrow in Gate of Heaven Cemetery, Valhalla, N. Y.

READABILITY AND UNDERSTANDING

Edited for readability, the lead says:

NEW YORK, Jan. 3—(UP)—Dr. John F. (Jafsie) Condon, whose meeting beside a graveyard with the Lindbergh baby's kidnaper made him a national figure, will be buried tomorrow in Gate of Heaven Cemetery, Valhalla, N. Y.

The following example is taken from the Associated Press report cited by Rudolf Flesch:

DUBLIN, Feb. 4—(AP)—The Irish in great numbers voted today for a new parliament. The *dominant* issue was whether to *oust* Prime Minister Eamon de Valera from the power he has held for 16 years.

Many politicians saw in the unusually heavy vote a sign that the *Fianna Fail* leader might lose his majority. Mr. de Valera has *declared* that he would resign if his party failed to secure the 74 seats *necessary* for a majority. He has also *declared* that he *would refuse to* form a coalition government with other parties.

Conclusive results are not expected before Friday. The complicated count under the proportional representation system will start tomorrow.

The chief threat to Mr. de Valera is Sean MacBride's year-old *Clanm Na Poblachta* (Republican party). Government leaders *acknowledge* that the threat is *potent*. Mr. MacBride has drawn *considerable* old-time *Fianna Fail* support to his Republican *banner*.

The italicized words were singled out by Flesch as words that should be replaced by simpler ones. He regarded as essential to the story such complex terms as *majority, coalition government, proportional representation system*.

In editing stories, the copyreader should not automatically choose the shortest word. Instead, he should choose the *right* word. Most of us live in houses, but there is nothing wrong with a reference to the governor's mansion or residence. If a senator speaks for an hour and a half at a Fourth of July celebration and calls the roll of the founding fathers with appropriate remarks, let the reporter call it an oration instead of a speech.

Even unfamiliar big words are not necessarily hard to understand. They do not confuse because their meaning is clear from the context in which they appear. They are undesirable in newspaper writing not so much because they are hard as because they are artificial and affected—because the reporter was striving for effect and not for clarity.

More to be guarded against than the big word is professional jargon. All reporters become infected with the shop words they hear repeatedly on their runs (there is a newspaper jargon, too), and the words creep into their reports. Among the jargons most frequently met are those of the law, medicine, science, the stock market, education, and the federal government.

Of these jargons, perhaps the most mystifying is the federalese, or "gobbledygook," the word which former Representative Maury Maverick of Texas coined to designate government prose. Washington correspondence is likely to contain such terms as "deactivate," "reactivate," "units of currency," "vend program," "90 percent of parity," and many others that hurried reporters copy from a government report or press release.

Federalese, unfortunately, is not wholly a matter of diction. It is as much a way of thinking as a mode of expression. It is, moreover, insidious, for it creeps into news stories through the door of direct quotation. For example, this from a War Department report dealing with efforts to unify the armed services: "In the joint chiefs of staff and the joint staff, we have the benefit of coördinated thinking. Under [the joint chiefs of staff's] guidance, substantial strides have been taken in reconciling divergent professional opinions." The man on the street, if he understood the quotation at all, would translate it: The army, the air force, and the navy are still fighting one another, but not as bitterly as they used to.

The copyreader must also be on the lookout for the jargon of the law and the courts. The Latinisms sprinkled throughout the text of petitions, court orders, and lawyers' briefs mean little to the ordinary citizen. As a matter of fact, most people have only a vague understanding of some of the most common legal terms. They do not know the legal difference between robbery and burglary. They cannot distinguish precisely between an indictment and a presentment. They cannot describe what happens at an arraignment. They are likely to be completely baffled by sentences like the following:

> The district attorney nol prossed the indictment of James R. Jenkins, 32, of 220 E. First Street. . . .
> The state supreme court in a per curiam decision today . . .
> The United States Circuit Court of Appeals today issued a writ of certiorari. . . .

Stories dealing with the courts are hard to handle, from the standpoint of using terms the reader understands. Often, the reporter uses the proper legal terminology in minor items for the sake of brevity. He feels that the story is not worth the space needed for an explanation. At other times, the fault lies with the reporter's indifference to clear and readable writing. Instead of paraphrasing, he picks up sentences and passages verbatim from a petition or court ruling. Not uncommonly, the copyreader has to edit stories in which a negligent reporter always refers to the persons involved as "the defendant" and "the plaintiff" instead of by their names—which of course are easier for the reader to grasp. To make such stories under-

READABILITY AND UNDERSTANDING

standable, the copyreader must himself know the legal terms used and must have on tap ordinary expressions that have about the same meaning. Some examples follow:

The Legal Term	*A Familiar Equivalent*
nolo contendere plea	no-defense plea
capias	bench warrant
arraignment	hearing
per curiam	decision concurred in by the whole bench
ex parte	of one side
nol pros (nolle prosequi)	drop charges
move for a severance	ask a separate trial
venire	jury panel
veniremen	prospective jurors
writ of supersedeas	delay of judgment
mandate	order
writ of certiorari	order requesting a record of proceedings

The Latinisms in stories dealing with the courts often turn up in stories on the legislature and congress, many of them written by famous by-line reporters and correspondents. No matter how expert the political reporter or how well known the correspondent, the copyreader should not hesitate to translate the unfamiliar terms into everyday English.

Another department of the news that contributes its share of Latinisms and polysyllabic words is the medical profession. The reporter gets from the hospital information that the victim of an auto accident received lacerations about the head, abrasions on the face, and contusions on the body. What his story should say is cuts about the head, scratches on the face, and bruises on the body. Unless there is a special reason for giving the exact cause of death, it would seem just as well to say that a person died of heart disease or a heart attack as of coronary thrombosis or angina pectoris. If there is a popular name for a disease, it should be used instead of the scientific one. If there is no popular name, the scientific name should be explained.

SEMANTICS FOR THE COPYREADER

What word indicates a person who—

believes that change is the basic law of life;

recognizes that the sole aim of government is to insure the maximum freedom and well-being of all the governed individuals;

attempts to accomplish the greatest good with the means at his disposal;

believes that nothing less than the richest possible life is good enough for men;

is a radical with a wife and two children;

wants somebody else to support him;

believes in orderly progress;

believes that basic wants should be provided for people who are unable to provide for themselves;

believes in freedom of conscience, freedom of religion, freedom of speech and of the press, and the right of man to think and act for himself;

wants a better life for everybody;

thinks for himself;

has the welfare of all the people at heart?

A college class asked the foregoing gave such replies as a Democrat, a New Dealer, an evolutionist, an idealist, a Christian, a Communist, an American, a social worker, a philanthropist, an independent, a reformer. The correct answer is "a liberal"—correct at least in so far as the above descriptions were received by the New York *Herald Tribune* when it asked readers to send in their definition of "a liberal."

Commenting on the variety of answers received, the *Herald Tribune* said in an editorial:

Considering how universally the "liberal" tag is claimed by politicians and public men, we were unprepared for the number of our readers to whom the word is apparently one of opprobrium, connoting the impractical, the wishy-washy or mere "gimme" type of mind. The great majority, it is true, still define "liberal" as a word of honor; but even among these it is rather striking to note how generally vague are the definitions given.

One of the readers who sent in a definition hit the nail on the head when he wrote: "It is a useless word; it means something different to everybody."

This is the first lesson to be learned from the study of semantics—the branch of the science of language that deals with the meaning or signification of words.

Semanticists believe that many of our problems arise from the failure of communication, that is, from misunderstanding the words we use and confusing the words as symbols for objects with the objects themselves.

On a simple level, the trouble arises from something like this: The sound or the written symbol for a familiar four-legged animal is "dog." "Dog" is a label for the animal, but it is not the animal itself. When we use this general label "dog," the word does not create the same picture in the minds of everyone. Some may envision a dachshund, others a collie, a terrier, a spaniel, an Airedale. Or the mental picture may even be more remote from the four-legged animal: a beast, a pet, a nuisance, an expense.

The misunderstanding and the confusion of words increase, the further they are removed from an actual object. Thus in the final analysis, the word "liberal" as defined by the readers of the *Herald Tribune* had no meaning at all except in the mind of the user. This source of confusion was well expressed in a legal opinion by Elihu Root:

> Words are like those insects that take color from their surroundings. Half the misunderstanding in this world comes from the fact that the words that are spoken or written are conditioned in the mind that gives them forth by one set of thoughts and ideas, and they are conditioned in the mind of the hearer by another set of thoughts and ideas, and even the simplest forms of expression are frequently quite open to mistake, unless the hearer or reader can get some idea of what were the conditions in the brain from which the words come.

In making practical application of semantics the copyreader should consider the following questions:

1. Are there high-order abstractions—beauty, truth, idealism, democracy—about which people have vague and different ideas?

2. Are referents indicated for the labels, that is, naming the object or situation in the real world to which the word or label refers?

3. What is the date or time of the object or situation? This is important since facts and situations change.

4. What are the generalizations? For example, are pencils thought of as a class instead of as separate individual pencils, since no object is exactly like another?

In his book *The Tyranny of Words* Stuart Chase subjected one of his own pieces of writing to the semantic discipline. He had written:

> We need a new religion. The elder faiths have followed the economic secular trend downward. The system called capitalism, for all its sprinkling with holy water in the nineteenth century, is at heart irreligious, without internal unity of public spirit, often a mere congeries of possessors and pursuers. When it adopted as its basic principles the competition of tooth and claw and the supreme duty of selfishness, all the holy water in the cosmos could not disinfect it. Great religious movements have usually been grounded in collectivism, in the brotherhood of man, leaving laissez faire, in the last analysis, a cold and ferocious anti-Christ. Capitalism, though officially blessed by Christian priests, has all but killed Christianity. Western mankind is thirsty for something in which to believe again.

What was Chase trying to say when he wrote that? He confessed that he wasn't sure. Substituting "blab"—a wonderful device for exposing nonsense—for the meaningless abstractions, Chase produced the following:

We need a new religion. The blab faiths have followed the blab blab trend downward. The blab called capitalism, for all its sprinkling with holy water in the nineteenth century, is blab blab or blab, often a mere congeries of blabs and blabs. When it blabbed as its blab blabs . . .

Then he rewrote the original paragraph to get rid of the hazy abstractions and to tie his statements down to something concrete:

Established religious organizations are losing their members (1933). The economic arrangements of the nineteenth century in western countries—often called capitalism—were approved by many church officials. The arrangements, however, tended to produce slums, disease, and misery for many working people, and to put a premium on disagreement between $Adam_1$, a businessman, and $Adam_2$, his competitor. Religious organizations stress the principle of the brotherhood of man, and so contradict such economic practice. When priests blessed the economic system, their followers naturally became confused, and many of them are now looking around for a religion which better lives up to its principles.

The piece became clearer, with the exception of the confusing numbered Adams—an esoteric device used by semanticists to indicate that one object of a class is not the same as another object.

If the copyreader subjected all the articles that come to him for editing to a semantic test, he would have to discard many as nonsense. Fortunately, most news stories are simple reports of happenings and offer few semantic difficulties. The parts of them that are hard to understand are the quotations—from politicians, public officials, economists, teachers, and so forth. The newspaper's own editorials, many of the "interpretations" by columnists and by-line writers, and the commentary of the book, music, drama, and art critics would probably fail a semantic test.

One of the most valuable things that an editor could do to improve the readability of his newspaper would be to brief all reporters and deskmen in semantics. A big step toward turning out understandable reading matter would come from eliminating or from defining the following classes of expressions:

Political and ideological tags: *Communist, Fascist, Socialist, red, liberal, radical, conservative, reactionary.*

Philosophical abstractions: *idealism, virtue, beauty, truth, democracy, progress, equality, happiness.*

Group personifications: *labor favors, management opposes, the medical profession regards, capitalists believe, Democrats urge, the administration seeks, the opinion of the South.*

Broad generalities about groups: *the American mind, British reticence, German efficiency, New England thrift, Midwestern isolationism.*

Symbolization of abstractions: *Uncle Sam, the Russian bear, government red tape, the torch of freedom, bloated plutocrats, Wall Street.*

Catchwords and slogans: *the New Deal, economic royalists, freedom of the press, a war to end wars, behind the iron curtain, the welfare state.*

There is no denying that the phrases and words on this list—and it could be lengthened indefinitely—are emotionally effective. But, as Jeremy Bentham said more than a hundred years ago in *Fallacies of Confusion*, words have double meanings. He suggested for such words the label "impostor terms." Impostor terms, he said, are used "chiefly in the defense of things which under their proper names are manifestly indefensible." For example, persecutors have no such word as persecution; it is zeal. What Bentham called the substitution of "an object of approbation for the object of censure" is a reliable technique of present-day propagandists.

Deprive a politician, a rabble-rouser, a chamber of commerce orator, a labor leader, a music critic of semantically unsound words and he will be left almost speechless. Remove such words from the columns of newspapers and we'll all understand better what's going on in the world.

CHAPTER 9

Press Association News

WORLD-WIDE NEWS NETWORKS

The editorial room of almost every daily newspaper in America contains a pair of boxed typewriter-like machines that almost uninterruptedly tap out news stories at the rate of 60 words a minute—a total of more than 25,000 words during an eight-hour period. The machines—teletypewriters—are operated on alternate days so that one will always be available in case of a breakdown. They are the newspaper's link with the events of the world—the end point of a vast communications system for the dissemination of news.

Within a short time after an event happens—in Tokyo, Sydney, Buenos Aires, London, Rome, Jerusalem—a report of it reaches the copy desks of newspapers in the United States—not merely a report, but a completely written story that can be rushed into print after a little editing and the writing of a headline.

The bulk of the news throughout the world is gathered and written for American newspapers by three organizations—the Associated Press, the International News Service, and the United Press. Each employs hundreds of reporters and editors for getting and writing the news. Each maintains scores of bureaus in the principal cities of the United States and other countries as control points for the news. Each has developed a complicated communications network making use of leased telephone wires, ocean cables, commercial wireless, and short-wave radio. Each is the medium by which several hundred million people in the world learn about what is going on. Each is truly an international organization, gathering news from all over the world, not only for clients or members in the United States but also for publications in some 60 or 70 other countries—wherever foreign governments permit it to operate.

The three organizations have one other point in common: They are dedicated to recording truthfully, completely, and impartially what happens everywhere at any time.

Without such a policy they would be immensely dangerous, controlling as they do the means by which we are kept informed of world events. If they consciously slanted the news to accord with a political or economic bias, millions—not only anonymous newspaper readers but heads of governments, statesmen, and legislators—would receive a distorted version of events. But they serve publications of all shades of opinion and belief. They could not stay in business if their reports were not as objective as is humanly possible. Their size is therefore a partial guarantee of their factualness and impartiality.

The deskman does not need to know how the three systems operate except in a general way. The communications networks are so complicated that perhaps only people employed in the traffic divisions of the three agencies fully understand them.

The number of employees in a press association bureau ranges from one in a minor city to about 100 in a key point such as Washington or New York. In cities and towns where there is no full-fledged bureau the association stations a correspondent or employs a part-time stringer.

In the United States the bureaus in the major cities are linked by trunk wires, the New York office of each bureau serving as general news desk for the world. The news from Europe and South America is funneled into the New York office by cable, wireless, and short-wave radio. Domestic and foreign news goes out from this office via trunk wires north and east to newspapers and bureaus in Boston and New England; south to Philadelphia, Washington, Atlanta, and other points; west to Pittsburgh, Albany, Chicago, St. Louis, and Kansas City, and onward in an expanding network. On the west coast San Francisco is the gathering point of news coming in by radioteletype from the far reaches of the Pacific. A west-to-east trunk wire carries news of national or international import that originates on the Pacific coast and in other western states.

In each system there are relay points for breaking a news report down to serve regional interests. In the AP system the main east-west relay point is Kansas City. There news on the trunk wire from the west coast is sorted out for transmission to the East. A story of great interest in the central and western states may be of little interest in New England or the South Atlantic states. It is killed outright at the relay point or sent east in a condensed version. Similarly, news on the east-to-west trunk wire is edited for the central and western members of the organization. Twenty wire circuits pour into the Kansas City relay office every twenty-

Fig. 16. News of the world reaches the editorial room ready for use via teletype from a central bureau of one of the press associations. (*Washington Post* photo.)

four hours an average of one million words to be cut and edited to meet the needs of trunk, regional, and state wires serving all parts of the country.

In addition to the nation-wide trunk service, each network is divided into regional and state circuits. In sparsely populated areas several states may form a regional network. In more densely populated areas there may be a separate network for each state. For example, the Oklahoma City bureau of the UP is on a southwestern trunk circuit. This bureau's reports are edited as required for the client newspapers in Oklahoma and transmitted on a separate state leased wire. The Oklahoma wire carries a great deal of state news that is not considered of sufficient interest to be placed on the southwestern regional wire or the national wire.

The major bureaus in a circuit can both transmit and receive news on the national or regional wire. Thus newspapers on the Pennsylvania state AP wire may receive their stories from bureaus in Philadelphia, Pittsburgh, or Harrisburg. On a regional trunk wire, say one covering the Southwest, the sending and receiving points might be Kansas City, Oklahoma City, New Orleans, Houston, Dallas, and Denver.

In addition to the general news wire, the associations have special wires for sports and business news that serve primarily metropolitan publications which need a greater volume of these classes of information than the smaller-city publications. Both AP and UP also have a special wire for radio stations. Radio stations in the INS network get their news roundups and special features on the general news wire.

For their foreign clients the three services maintain wire networks when the number of member publications is large enough and there is no interference by government. News from the United States to foreign countries goes by cable, commercial wireless, and, in recent years, radioprinter.

Newspapers can obtain from the press associations almost any quantity of news they desire. For small-town publications abbreviated reports known as "pony" service are available. The pony reports are dictated by a reader in the bureau office to member newspapers over a telephone hookup. From six to a dozen newspapers may be on the wire at the same time. The pony calls last fifteen minutes, and a newspaper can have one or two of them a day, depending on the need. The paper must have a fast typist to take down the stories as they are read. In the past few years teletypewriters have been installed by many small newspaper offices to replace the typists.

Most daily newspapers need more stories than they can get in the fifteen- or thirty-minute pony report. They obtain full leased wire service for the state or region in which they are situated. This is usually an eight-hour report. Metropolitan publications with their voracious appetite for news may obtain a trunk-wire report as well as the state or regional report. Many supplement the reports of one association with those of one or both of the others. Some subscribe in addition to such special services as those provided by the Chicago *Daily News*, the Chicago *Tribune*-New York *Daily News*, the New York *Times*, the New York *Herald Tribune*, and the North American Newspaper Alliance.

The costs of press association news to individual publications vary according to the type of service received and the circulation of the newspapers. This sliding-scale arrangement makes it possible for even the smallest newspaper to obtain a fairly full report of the news of the world written by noted reporters and special writers.

AP, INS, UP

The oldest of the wire news services is the Associated Press, which dates its founding back to 1848, when a group of New York editors formed a coöperative news-gathering association to reduce the cost of the telegraphic transmission of the foreign news received from ships arriving at Boston Harbor.

Under successive mutations of the original organization the AP has held to the following policies:

1. It is a nonprofit organization devoted to the gathering and dissemination of news.

2. Costs are prorated among the members according to the circulation of each newspaper.

3. Members are obligated to make available to the AP news gathered by their staff members. The present bylaw covering this states that the AP is entitled exclusively to the use, for republication, of all the local news printed in a member newspaper, as well as all AP news dispatches.

As incorporated under Illinois law in 1893, the AP made its news available only to member publications which held exclusive franchises in most cities. In 1900 the Illinois Supreme Court ruled that the organization was a public utility and must sell news to all applicants. This ruling resulted in the dissolution of the Illinois corporation. The AP was then incorporated under a New York law governing social and nonprofit organizations. Again, as the result of an antitrust suit against it, the AP was ordered by the United States Supreme Court in 1945 to amend its bylaws to prevent one member's blackballing an applicant for membership. Today radio stations and newspapers as associate members may purchase news reports, but they have no voice in selecting the board of directors or determining policy.

In cities where there is an AP bureau, member newspapers usually turn carbon copies of stories over to it. In other cities the local newspaper is expected to get in touch with the AP if a story of state or national interest breaks. As an inducement to coöperation the association pays correspondents or stringers on member papers for their work.

Originally the AP engaged only in gathering and transmitting news. Demands of members, however, led to supplementary services. These

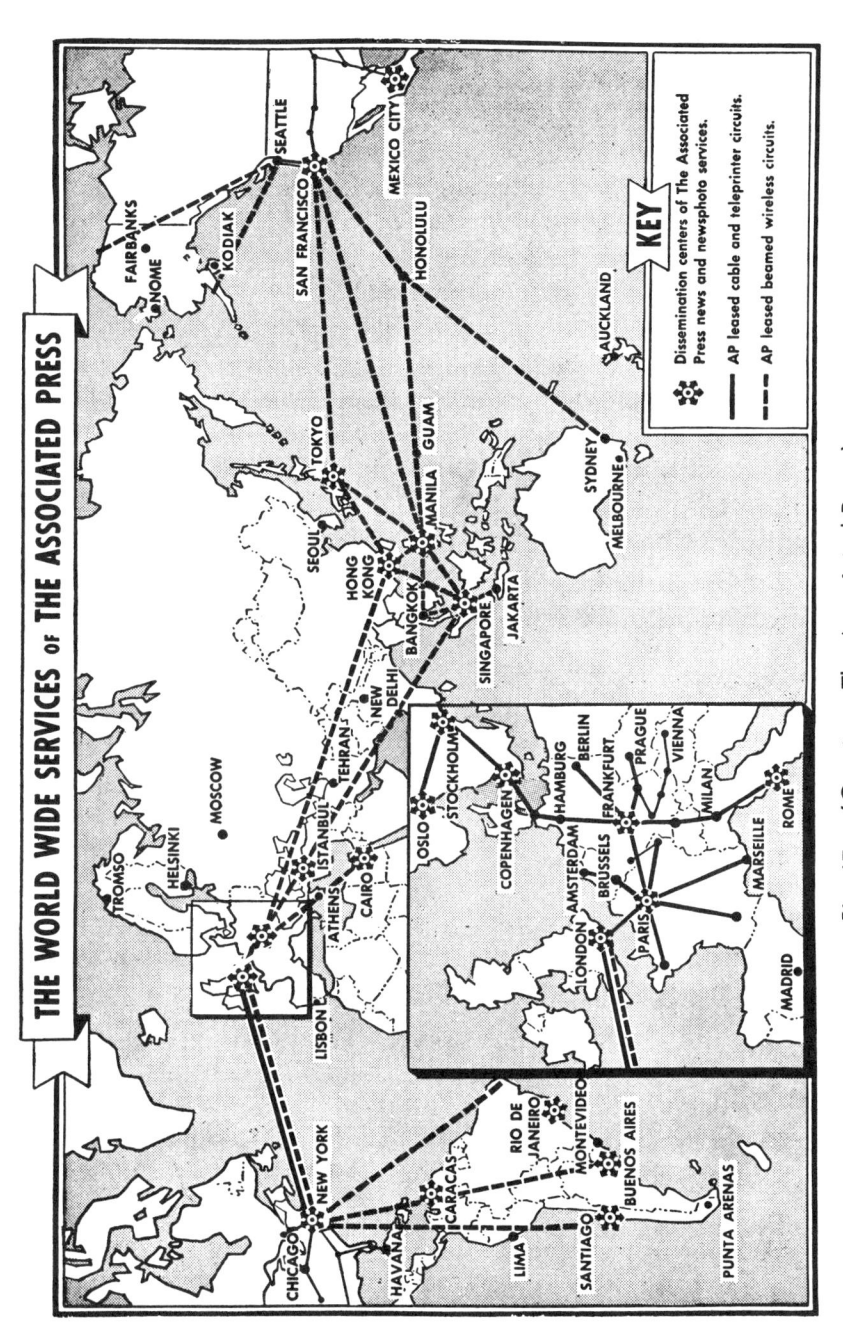

Fig. 17. (Courtesy, The Associated Press.)

include radio, sports, and business news wires; AP Newsfeatures, consisting of columns, special articles and features, cartoons, pictures and mats, crossword puzzles, and other material like that distributed by syndicates; AP Newsphotos, including pictures transmitted by Wirephoto and Telemat mailings of illustrations in matted form; and Wide World Photos, a feature picture service. A special assessment is made for all these services.

The International News Service and the United Press Associations (usually abbreviated to United Press) differ fundamentally from the AP in that they are commercial noncoöperative organizations engaged in the business of buying and selling news. Both owe their beginning to systems set up by large chain newspaper operators for exchanging news among the publications they owned.

William Randolph Hearst established the INS in 1909 for the sale of news to newspapers. It supplanted earlier services set up for the publications in his chain. Its reporting of the news has been flavored somewhat with the same journalistic sauce used in the Hearst newspapers. It has emphasized full coverage of big events rather than comprehensive coverage of all the news. It often draws upon a galaxy of big-name writers—novelists and magazine writers as well as newspapermen—to cover a sensational or important event. Many editors regard the INS as deficient as a general news service but valuable as a supplementary one because of its unparalleled big-name reports of events and its special articles by famous by-line writers.

The INS maintains International News Photos as a picture agency, with a mat mailing service and with wire circuits for transmission of photographs under the name of Soundphotos. The King Features Syndicate is a Hearst affiliate.

The UP was formed in 1907 by the merger of two organizations serving the E. W. Scripps chain of newspapers, and a third small association, the Publisher's Press, that served newspapers on the Atlantic seaboard. Under the direction of Roy W. Howard the UP produced lively, readable news reports in contrast to the purely objective and factual reports of the AP. Howard realized that the UP could not at first compete with the AP in comprehensiveness of coverage because of the latter's mutual interexchange of news among members. His policy of using a brighter, more dramatic style for news reports proved successful, and the UP grew rapidly. An important factor in its early growth was Howard's development of its foreign service, especially his signing up of South American clients. Today AP and UP serve about the same number of radio stations and newspapers and there is not much difference in the quality and comprehensiveness of their reports.

The UP service today includes its weekly Red Letter, a clipsheet of columns, features, and time stories, which supplements its wire reports. Members of the Scripps-Howard newspaper chain stand somewhat in the same relation to the UP as do AP member newspapers. The UP has close relations with the Newspaper Enterprise Association, a feature syndicate. On January 1, 1952, UP purchased Acme Newspictures, a division of NEA, and installed its own picture service, using the credit line, "United Press Telephoto."

THE WIRE REPORT

Compared with editing local copy, editing a wire report is comparatively simple. Once the deskman becomes familiar with the mechanics of the wire and the nomenclature used for numbering and identifying stories, the work is fairly easy.

The wire stories come to the desk in almost perfect form typographically. All of them have been preëdited in the press association bureaus, and few errors in fact, grammar, or construction slip by. Editing therefore may be confined mostly to indicating capitals, changing the style to conform to that of the newspaper, and trimming items to fit space requirements.

But there is more to the telegraph editor's work than these simple routines. To some extent the wire tells him which stories are big and which are mediocre, but his journalistic ability is tested by his judgment about what to do with an item. His decisions must be based on a thorough grasp of affairs and an instinct as to what will most interest his readers.

Moreover, the press wire is prepared for newspapers with different deadlines. This means that dispatches are more often revised to bring them up to date than many of the stories written in the newspaper's own office. The telegraph editor may have a complete story about a congressional hearing at 10 A.M. He must decide whether to send it to the composing room then or to hold it for a new lead containing later and perhaps more interesting developments.

The wire report each day usually begins with what is known as the budget—a forecast of the stories coming up. It consists of a short statement giving the point of origin of each story, its nature, and perhaps its approximate length. Occasionally there may be a word or two to help the editor anticipate the handling of a story. Some items may be marked "Developing," a hint to the desk that the first stories will probably not stand up. The tag "Much New" indicates that though the story is a follow-up of a previously covered topic there are enough additional developments to make it important. The budget is followed during the day with messages to the editor telling him when to expect a story, or that a good story not on the budget will be cleared soon, or that a budget story will be expedited.

Following is a UP budget, the first item sent when the wire opened:

KX1
   EDITORS:
      THE UNITED PRESS REPORT TONIGHT WILL INCLUDE:
   PITTSBURGH—STEELWORKERS JOIN MINERS IN STRIKE, SHUTTING DOWN TWO OF AMERICA'S MOST VITAL INDUSTRIES (A WRAPUP OF BOTH COAL AND STEEL).
   NEW YORK—(NEWSPAGE SPORTS)—RED SOX AND YANKEES MEET BEFORE 70,000 IN GAME THAT CAN DECIDE AMERICAN LEAGUE PENNANT WINNER.
   PHILADELPHIA—(NEWSPAGE SPORTS)—DODGERS MEET PHILLIES WHILE CARDINALS ATTEMPT KEEP NATIONAL LEAGUE PENNANT HOPES ALIVE AGAINST CUBS.
   BELGRADE—YUGOSLAVIA ACCUSES RUSSIA OF ENDANGERING WORLD PEACE BY PUTTING MILITARY, ECONOMIC PRESSURE ON TITO REGIME.
   SHANGHAI—CHOU EN-LAI NAMED PREMIER OF NEW COMMUNIST REGIME IN CHINA AT MAMMOTH CELEBRATION.
   COBH, IRELAND—IRISH AUTHORITIES TO PERMIT 400 BALTIC REFUGEES TO TRY ATLANTIC CROSSING IN BATTERED, OVERLOADED LANDING CRAFT.
   WASHINGTON—CONGRESSIONAL REPORT EXONERATING LILIENTHAL SAYS SOVIET SPEED IN GETTING A-BOMB IS "MONUMENTAL CHALLENGE" TO U.S.
   LAKE SUCCESS, N.Y.—ITALY'S SFORZA, IN "GUEST" SPEECH BEFORE UN, DENOUNCES RUSSIA, ASKS INDEPENDENCE FOR EX-COLONY OF TRIPOLITANIA.
                UNITED PRESS ASSNS., NEW YORK

The value of the budget is its usefulness to both make-up and telegraph editors in planning the day's work. They can make tentative decisions early in the day as to the length of stories, their headlines, and their location in the paper. But the budget is frequently an unreliable guide. Many important stories break without any warning, and a few in the budget peter out.

After the budget the wire transmits complete stories that are likely to stand up for the day, columns and interpretive articles which of course do not change, and early leads on budget stories.

The early stories on the day wire for afternoon newspapers are likely to be rewrites of material already carried in the morning papers. Yesterday afternoon's and last night's sports events clear early because after a game is over, little new can be written about it. Many overnight general news stories also are complete and may be used in the early editions or be scheduled for inside pages. Many stories give much of last night's material under an anticipatory lead covering expected spot developments during the day. These stories may be used in an early edition. They are revised for later editions as new developments are reported. The telegraph editor of a small newspaper with only one edition holds these stories for pickup material that may be needed after new leads have cleared the wire.

The night wire for morning newspapers is usually less complicated than the day wire. Afternoon newspapers must try to keep up with developing situations during the day, and the press service sends out many new leads and revisions of stories. Since most of the nation's business is transacted in the daytime, the night wire, except for dispatches from abroad, includes many stories that are completely wrapped up before transmission. The night wire carries financial news early, for example, because the security markets are closed. Sports, which clears early on the day report, is late on the night report except for events held in the afternoon.

The three press services employ similar methods of numbering, slugging, and timing articles to make it easy for the telegraph desk to keep track of them.

All dispatches are numbered consecutively. This number appears after a wire or bureau designation on a separate line flush to the left at the top of each item. A single letter usually indicates a wire or circuit of the service. Thus on a trunk-wire circuit stories might be numbered A1, A2, A3, and so forth. When a bureau on a split circuit takes the wire for a series of dispatches, it uses the bureau telegraph call letters, KX for Kansas City, NY for New York, and CX for Chicago. Each bureau's dispatches are numbered consecutively without reference to the number sequence of the main wire or of other bureaus.

Each dispatch or message closes with an end mark giving the initials of the operator who sent it and the time it was completed. The AP system uses an end mark like the following: PHS851AES. The first three letters are the initials of the operator, and the message was completed at 8:51 A.M. Eastern Standard Time. The UP end mark BR115P means that an operator whose initials are B. R. completed the dispatch at 1:15 P.M. The INS puts the sender's initials after the time—323PSC—the P standing for afternoon and S. C. being the initials of the teletype puncher. The word "more" at the end of course means that the story is not complete and that an add will follow.

Besides the message number at the beginning of a dispatch, an important story may have a slug. Frequently appearing slugs are "Congress," "United Nations," and "Weather." Many stories, however, are not given slugs until a new lead or an add is transmitted. The wire at 10 A.M. may carry a report of a plane crash without slugging it. Later, if new developments justify it, a second lead may be sent slugged not "new lead" or "second lead" but "first lead plane crash." When the deskman sees "first lead," he must remember that this is not the first story about the crash, but the second. The slug "second lead" means that there have been two previous stories, not just one; an item carrying such a slug is actually the third story on the event.

The press services as far as possible attempt to send complete stories in a single dispatch, but to expedite the transmission of news they often must interrupt a story. The add to a story has a slug giving the nature of the item, the place of origin, and a pickup line. A slug on the AP wire is in the following form: LOS ANGELES—FIRST ADD PLANE CRASH X X X BOULEVARDS. A subsequent add will be "second add," and so forth. The UP does not number adds; their slug will be: ADD PLANE CRASH LOS ANGELES X X X BOULEVARDS. The form used by the INS is: ADD NIGHT LEAD PLANE CRASH (SMITH) LOS ANGELES X X X BOULEVARDS. On by-line stories the name of the writer is usually given, as in the INS example. The three X's are used by press associations to indicate elisions. The word or words following them in a pickup line are the last words of the previous message. They tell the deskman exactly where the two parts of the story must be fitted together.

For the guidance of editors a new lead contains a pickup line at the end of it telling the desk where to fit the lead in the previous report and what portion of the earlier story should be killed. The pickup line gives the paragraph number and the first two or three words of the paragraph. An example of an AP pickup line is: THE PRESIDENT REPEATED X X X ETC., 3RD GRAPH PREVIOUS. The pickup line has the following form on the UP wire: PICKUP EARLY AT 6TH PGH STARTING: THE PRESIDENT REPEATED ETC. On the INS wire it is: PICKUP 3RD PGH READING IT X X X THE PRESIDENT REPEATED ETC.

Sometimes, however, the new lead ends with "No Pickup," indicating that the story is complete and that previous matter is not usable, or with

"Pickup Available," meaning that the editor can use parts of the earlier story if he wishes.

To expedite the transmission of important news, the three associations follow similar practices. For events of transcendent importance—a declaration of war, a major calamity, or the death of a great public figure—they use a flash. The flash is short—just a few words telling of the event and giving the point of origin—and it has priority on all circuits. It is repeated once. The flash is very useful because it enables the newspaper to make immediate preparations for revising make-up, getting out an extra, and assembling art or background information.

A bulletin of 50 words or less immediately follows the flash. As quickly as information can be obtained and a story written, adds giving details follow the bulletin. Since the bulletin and the adds are written rapidly under extreme pressure, they are usually followed after a short period by a first lead containing a better account of the event. Bulletins are also used for other news of first importance; they do not necessarily always follow a flash. As a matter of fact, flashes are extremely rare.

Both the AP and the UP have another label for stories of more than average importance but not worth flash or bulletin treatment. The AP slugs such stories "95" and they are usually sent in one piece not exceeding 200 words. The UP slug for such stories is "Urgent"; the story moves in takes of three to five paragraphs, with no more than 200 words in the first take. The INS has no comparative symbol; it makes greater use of bulletins (often abbreviated to "Bun"). It frequently slugs first and second leads "bulletin" if the wire filer considers the story worth calling to the attention of editors. The 95 slug used by the AP to indicate a better-than-average story is used by UP and INS for important messages from one bureau to another. The INS uses "Box" for short, lively items and "Interesque" for human interest and feature stories.

In addition to new leads and adds to revise news dispatches and bring them up to date, the press associations employ a variety of devices to correct errors. When the information in a story is entirely erroneous, unprivileged, or potentially libelous, the story is killed. A kill ordinarily is sent as a bulletin. The AP, for example, sends a message like the following:

BULLETIN KILL
CHICAGO—KILL STORY JOHN SMITH ARRESTED. SMITH NOT ARRESTED.
THE AP

The kill is followed immediately by a warning to editors:

EDITORS
CHICAGO—THE STORY ABOUT THE ARREST OF JOHN SMITH
HAS BEEN KILLED. A KILL IS MANDATORY. MAKE CERTAIN
THE STORY IS NOT PUBLISHED.

The receipt of a kill message means, therefore, that the desk must hunt the story and make sure that it is not printed. This may even mean stopping the presses to remove an offending article.

For stories not libelous or dangerous but objectionable on the ground of triviality or fundamental error the AP uses a bulletin elimination. The AP stylebook gives the following example:

BULLETIN ELIMINATION
KANSAS CITY—ELIMINATE MAN BITES DOG. TRIVIAL.
THE AP

Minor errors in stories are brought to the attention of editors by means of corrections. These ordinarily show exactly what is to be corrected and give sufficient information so that the desk can locate the place easily. An example is the following from a UP wire:

C O R R E C T I O N
IN 5TH PGH LSU-RICE FOOTBALL BATON ROUGE READ IT
X X X BOBBY LANTRIP THROUGHOUT (RATHER THAN
LANTROP AS SENT).
UP

Revisions in stories may also be indicated by substitutions (abbreviated to "Sub" in wire report slugs), inserts, and notes to editors. An example of a sub follows:

SUB FOR 2ND PGH STORM NEW ORLEANS STARTING:
THE WEATHER, ETC.
AT 10 P. M., CST, ADVISORY LOCATED THE STORM AT
LATITUDE 20.7, LONGITUDE 92.8, OR ABOUT 200 MILES WEST
OF MERIDA, MEXICO. STRONGEST WINDS NEAR THE CENTER
WERE ESTIMATED AT 40 TO 50 MILES AN HOUR. THE
STORM WAS MOVING NORTH, NORTHWESTWARD ABOUT
EIGHT MILES AN HOUR.

To expedite the transmission of certain types of stories—speeches, government reports, and important announcements—the press associations frequently send articles slugged "Advance" or "Hold for Release." In some cases the release is automatic at a stipulated time; in others the time of release is given in a special message. To avoid timing mix-ups and discriminatory practices, the three press associations have signed an agreement covering the following points:

1. They will accept advance material on condition that the stipulated release does not discriminate between newspapers and radio.

2. When the source stipulates release to morning newspapers, the material will carry a slug showing that it is for release at 7 P.M. New York time. When the source stipulates release to afternoon papers, the material will carry a slug showing that it is for release at 7 A.M.

The desk need not wait until the release time to send an advance story to the composing room. If the story is set in type, however, it should be slugged with the time of release if known or with "hold for release" if the time is not known.

The teletype machine used for wire reports is of strong construction and ordinarily operates during an eight-hour period without trouble. It has a simpler keyboard than the standard typewriter, and there are three type bars instead of four. The characters include only capital letters, figures, and punctuation marks. The machine used by the AP is as follows:

```
           1  2  3  4  5  6  7  8  9  0
           Q  W  E  R  T  Y  U  I  O  P
           -  '  $  !  &  £  '  (  )
           A  S  D  F  G  H  J  K  L
           "  /  :  ;  ?  ,  .
           Z  X  C  V  B  N  M
```

The UP and INS machines differ from the AP's in that the apostrophe is omitted from the "J" key.

Occasionally the machine may fail to shift from letters to figures or back to letters after setting figures. The result is one or more lines of garbled copy. When this happens, the desk can correct the errors by reference to a code chart. Arranged in alphabetical order, the matching characters on the type bars are:

A	-	G	&	L	)	Q	1	V	;
B	?	H	£	M	.	R	4	W	2
C	:	I	8	N	,	S	'	X	/
D	$	J	'	O	9	T	5	Y	6
E	3	K	(	P	0	U	7	Z	"
F	!								

If the machine begins sending a jumble of characters and incomplete lines, the stand-by machine should be turned on immediately. If it also acts up in this fashion, the fault is in the telephone circuit and the press association bureau should be notified immediately. Since it may take time to find the source of the trouble, the newspaper may miss part of the wire report. If the part missed is short, the bureau will transmit a rerun for the newspaper. If a considerable portion of the report is lost, the bureau may send a schedule of the missing items and ask the telegraph editor to indicate which ones he wants rerun. To avoid taking up the wire time of other newspapers with reruns, the material is sometimes sent to the newspaper by commercial telegraph.

ASSEMBLING THE STORIES

The large quantity of material sent on the wire and the practice of transmitting stories in takes and bringing them up to date with new leads mean that the telegraph editor must systematize his work. One of his major problems is to maintain an even flow of copy to the composing room while keeping track of scores of stories and parts of stories.

His problem of assembling stories sent in takes with new leads and adds is illustrated by the following from the UP day wire:

KO31
    BULLETIN
    DENVER, OCT. 1—(UP)—A WRECKED AIR FORCE B-17 WAS SIGHTED ON THE GROUND 10 MILES SOUTH OF TRINIDAD, COLO., AT 7:45 A. M., MST, (9:45 P. M. EST) TODAY AND AIR FORCE OFFICERS AT LOWRY BASE SAID THEY BELIEVED IT WAS A PLANE MISSING SINCE YESTERDAY AFTERNOON ON A FLIGHT TO DENVER FROM EL PASO.
                          MORE FY936A

KO33
    ADD B-17 DENVER X X X EL PASO.
    THE PUBLIC INFORMATION OFFICER AT LOWRY BASE SAID THE PLANE WHICH SPOTTED THE DOWNED B-17 REPORTED THAT ONLY THE TAIL SECTION OF THE WRECKED CRAFT WAS INTACT.
    THERE WAS NO WORD AS TO WHETHER ANY OF THE 10 CREW MEMBERS ABOARD HAD BEEN SIGHTED FROM THE AIR.
    LOWRY BASE OFFICIALS SAID THAT SEARCH PLANES WHICH HAVE BEEN SCANNING THE SOUTHERN COLORADO AND NORTHERN NEW MEXICO AREA SINCE LAST NIGHT FOR THE B-17 WERE CONVERGING ON THE TRINIDAD AREA AND A PARA-RESCUE TEAM WAS PREARING TO PARACHUTE TO THE WRECKED PLANE.
                          MORE FY941A

PRESS ASSOCIATION NEWS 125

KO41
   ADD B-17 DENVER X X X PLANE.
   THE B-17 WAS FROM THE FIFTY AIR RESCUE SQUADRON AT BIGGS AIR BASE, EL PASO, TEX. NINE PLANES HAD BEEN SEARCHING FOR IT SINCE EARLY FRIDAY EVENING.
                        FY1004A

KO45
   CORRECTION
   IN B-17 DENVER LAST PGH 1ST LINE READ IT X X X FROM THE FIFTH AIR ETC (STED FIFTY).
                      UP
                        FY1024A

It took exactly 28 minutes for that item to clear the wire, not counting the 20 minutes necessary for the correction to be discovered and sent. In its present version so early in the morning the story is not usable except in an early edition of a metropolitan newspaper where it might be worth a page-1 spot. The details are so vague that the editor knows immediately that the story will not stand up for long. He pastes the takes together, makes the correction, and lays the story aside, knowing that it is potentially a good item. In his first hasty reading he may or may not have noticed two errors not indicated by correction messages—the 9:45 P.M. statement in the bulletin lead (it should be 9:45 A.M.) and the misspelling of "preparing" in the add. The UP did not bother to send corrections, for it knew that any reasonably alert deskman would observe and remove the errors. The correction message changing "fifty" to "fifth" was essential, because an editor would have no way of knowing the correct number.

The next follow-up on the story comes as a bulletin from another sending point; it has a new number sequence and a different date line:

X43
   BULLETIN
       LEAD DENVER
   RATON, N. M., OCT. 1.–(UP)–AN AIR FORCE B-17 CRASHED IN RUGGED MESA COUNTRY SIX MILES NORTH OF HERE SOMETIME LAST NIGHT AND CIVILIAN AUTHORITIES SAID TODAY THEY FEARED NONE OF THE 10 CREW MEMBERS ABOARD HAS SURVIVED.
                   MORE VR1110A

X44
   ADD B-17 RATON X X X SURVIVED.
   TWO RANCH EMPLOYES DISCOVERED THE WRECKAGE OF

THE FOUR-ENGINE BOMBER SCATTERED OVER A QUARTER-MILE AREA IN THE ALMOST INACCESSIBLE WILDERNESS COUNTRY OF THE BARTOLINO RANCH NORTH OF HERE SHORTLY AFTER DAWN.

[The item continues with seven more paragraphs giving additional details and background.]

(ELIMINATE DENVER DATE)

VR1113A

Although the story from Raton is obviously more complete than the first reports from Denver, the deskman realizes that it still is not ready for headlining and sending to the composing room. Unless it is near deadline for an edition, he will hold the story until the deaths of the crew members are verified. The dispatch contains two bits of information to guide the desk: (1) the "Lead Denver" at the beginning notifies the desk that a previous dispatch date-lined Denver has been sent; (2) the "Eliminate Denver Date" at the close tells the desk that the earlier dispatch can be killed.

The next installment comes from a different sending point but has a Raton date line:

DA3
BULLETIN
       1ST LEAD RATON CRASH

RATON, N. M., OCT. 1.—(UP)—AN AIR FORCE B-17 CRASHED IN RUGGED MESA COUNTRY SIX MILES NORTH OF HERE SOMETIME LAST NIGHT AND AUTHORITIES AT ITS HOME BASE, BIGGS FIELD, TEX., SAID ALL 10 CREWMEN WERE KILLED.

(IN EL PASO, BIGGS FIELD SPOKESMEN SAID IT HAD CONFIRMED THAT THE CREWMEN, FROM FLIGHT B OF THE FIFTH AIR RESCUE UNIT, HAD NOT SURVIVED THE CRASH.)
—0—
PICK UP EARLY AT 2ND PGH: TWO RANCH EMPLOYES, ETC.

EF1130A

The story is now in a stage where it is rather definite—at least the deaths of the crew members have been verified by responsible authority. The only information lacking is their names, and these can be expected though perhaps not immediately. As a matter of fact, they were available about an hour and a half later and the UP sent a new lead:

X72
  2ND LEAD B-17

RATON, N. M., OCT. 1.—(UP)—TEN CREW MEMBERS AND PASSENGERS WERE KILLED WHEN AN AIR FORCE B-17 ON A

PRESS ASSOCIATION NEWS 127

ROUTINE FLIGHT FROM EL PASO, TEX., TO DENVER CRASHED IN RUGGED MESA COUNTRY NEAR HERE, AIR FORCE OFFICIALS ANNOUNCED TODAY.

THE PLANE CAME TO EARTH SOME TIME LAST NIGHT, SIX MILES NORTH OF HERE.

SEVEN OF THE DEAD WERE OFFICERS AND NON-COMMISSIONED OFFICERS OF LOWRY AIR BASE, DENVER. THE THREE OTHERS, PRESUMABLY THE PLANE CREW MEMBERS, WERE STATIONED AT BIGGS FIELD AT EL PASO, THE PLANE'S HOME BASE.

THE SEVEN LOWRY BASE PERSONNEL KILLED IN THE CRASH WERE IDENTIFIED BY THE BASE PUBLIC INFORMATION OFFICER AS:

[There follows a paragraph of names and an additional paragraph explaining that the names of Biggs Field men were withheld pending notification of next of kin.]

—0—

PICK UP 1ST LEAD AT 3RD PGH: TWO RANCH EMPLOYES, ETC.
VR122P

The foregoing example illustrates an important factor in editing wire reports: No story can be considered complete until all reasonable questions about it are answered; the press association is expected to keep on the story until the loose ends are tied up. The telegraph editor's deadline and his own intuition, derived from experience, tell him when he must send the story to the composing room.

The bomber crash story has been isolated from the complete UP report, and the problem of assembling the adds and the new leads has been oversimplified. The telegraph editor may have a dozen or a score of such stories to keep track of. Unless he follows an orderly routine he may find himself losing stories or parts of stories and unable to decide what to do with items.

His first endeavor should be to keep up with the wire. If he gets an hour or so behind, he may find himself swamped. Most deskmen find a ruler—a brass column rule from the shop if one is available—better than scissors for cutting stories apart. Many items on the wire report obviously do not fit the needs of his newspaper. He gets these out of the way immediately by putting them, in the order received, on the kill hook or spindle. They should not be thrown away, for the editor may reconsider and use some of them or he may find it necessary to refer to them. Specialized copy such as sports and financial reports is sent to the appropriate departmental editor as soon as received.

Stories for potential use may be sorted into groups. For example, features may be placed in one stack, filler items in another, Washington dispatches in another, and the international situation in another. There may be a separate pile for possible front-page stories. The grouping may vary from day to day. A wave of strikes may bring a half dozen or so related items from different news points; these might form one group of material. All the takes and new leads on each story should be folded together, with the latest dispatch on the outside. Some deskmen paste the separate parts together as they are received and also make corrections immediately; others wait until they are ready to send the story to the composing room. In assembling stories it is better not to cover or cut off slug lines and pickup lines. If the deskman should make a mistake in pasting an add to a dispatch, it would be hard for him to paste it correctly if the pickup line has been concealed or torn off. The guide and pickup lines should be marked out in copyreading.

Since he must maintain a steady flow of copy to the composing room, the telegraph editor keeps the operators busy with a variety of inside-page stories, columns, features, and shorter items while making up his mind about dubious stories. Only front-page stories are held back until late in the day, although some of these which are obviously complete can go to the shop early.

NEWS BY PERFORATED TAPE

Newsroom desk procedures of newspapers in several states were revolutionized in the latter half of 1951, when the three press associations successfully put into operation state teletypesetter networks.

The teletypesetter is a device attached over a line-casting machine keyboard for mechanical operation by means of a perforated tape fed through it. The chief advantage of the teletypesetter is that one man can supervise the setting of type by several machines, thus reducing labor costs. Casting of type lines is also somewhat faster than by manual operation.

The punching of tapes in a number of newspaper offices simultaneously from a central point has long been possible. Rising costs of newspaper publishing finally made it desirable in 1951, and editors throughout the country, especially those of small-city publications, welcomed the new service.

News coming from a central press association bureau automatically perforates the tape in the newspaper office. Stories appearing on the tape can be checked against a monitoring machine which reproduces the copy line for line in typewritten form. The new system of transmission is slower than that of the old—53 words a minute by tape as compared with the 60 words a minute by teletypewriter.

The editing of copy received by tape is not fully standardized. In some newspaper plants the reperforating machine is set up adjacent to a typecasting machine, into which the tape feeds automatically. Stories are eliminated, shortened, and otherwise edited on galley proofs. In other newspaper plants the editing is done on the tape by referring to copy received on the monitoring machine.

Three immediate difficulties stand out in the handling of tape copy:

1. The newspaper's style as regards punctuation, capitalization, spelling, and abbreviations must be made to conform to that of the press association.

2. The tape copy is uniform for all the newspapers on the circuit. The individual editor must have material reset if he wants it wide measure, indented, boxed, or in boldface; or he must eliminate such material from the tape and have it set from monitor copy according to his desires.

3. Though the editor can make insertions in a tape story and can kill part of a story, he cannot change a word or a phrase except, of course, by correcting a proof and having the material reset.

The filing of stories by the press services on the teletypesetter circuit to some extent reverses the order on the conventional wire. The order, as a matter of fact, is better adapted to the small newspaper. First stories coming on the tape are shorts and features. These are followed by longer stories for the inside pages—stories that will stand up during the day or night. A story that will require a new lead or revision for later developments is laid aside by the wire filer—just as an editor holds back a story which he knows will be changed by new developments. Then, at a time to conform with most of the network newspapers' deadlines, come the page-1 stories. Editors, in the meantime, have been kept informed of these by "advisories" which give the nature of the stories and their lengths. They thus can plan their dummies in advance. The last portion of the wire time is devoted to late breaks, bulletin precedes, substitute leads, markets, and advance stories for the next day.

Editors using tape copy point out as an advantage the elimination of the desk chore of marking capitals and making minor changes to conform to style. Time thus saved, they say, can be devoted to improving the headlines and giving closer attention to local stories. On many small newspapers wire copy is only casually edited, anyway, and many desks leave the question of style up to the composing machine operators.

Critics of the latest method of news transmission say that in adopting it editors are relinquishing their responsibility. The result, they say, is a more standardized product in both typography and content. The newspaper, in their opinion, becomes just another mass-produced product with no more individuality than canned string beans or processed cheese.

COPYREADING WIRE STORIES

In using press association stories the newspapers have great freedom to edit, shorten, and rearrange. They cannot, however tamper with the facts or make alterations that will substantially change a meaning or impression from that intended in the wire service version. Except for routine trimming—cutting out verbiage and eliminating minor details—the desk must be careful of changes that may affect the accuracy of the report. The press association initials (AP, UP, and INS) in the date line, or in the credit line in stories not carrying a date line, are their voucher for the accuracy and reliability of the news.

When a story is rewritten in the newspaper office, it is often better to drop the logotype or credit line and indicate the source in the body of the story. One occasion for rewriting arises when a story can be given a local angle. For example, suppose a local person is elected president of an organization at its national convention. The list of officers may be buried far down in the AP story, but the deskman will write a new lead putting the local person's name to the front. The attribution in the lead may be "according to the Associated Press" or "the Associated Press reported today."

Another occasion for rewriting a wire story occurs when the deskman wishes to combine information in the dispatches of more than one of the associations. The sources of individual items of information may be given by attributions in the body of the story, or the basis for the article may be indicated by the following credit line: "Compiled from Press Dispatches."

When one service's dispatch conflicts with that of another or has information that the other does not contain, the desk can avoid rewriting by interpolating a note in parentheses pointing out the conflict or supplying the additional information.

Faults in wire copy not found so often in copy written by the local staff include the following:

1. Overqualification and attribution and excessive use of partial quotations. Because their news is more widely disseminated than that in newspapers, press associations tend to be overly meticulous in fixing responsibility for statements in their stories. Thus statements are hedged

around with qualifications, and unnecessary quotation marks are placed around individual words or phrases in an indirect quotation. Such practices sometimes make for an awkward, hard-to-read news account.

2. Burying of the real lead under new developments. Press associations boast of scoops in terms of minutes; there is an incessant endeavor to get on the wire first with the latest happenings. Sometimes the real meat of the story is found not in the last lead sent but in an earlier one. This is especially true of the night leads for stories that broke on the day wire and of second-day accounts of events that occurred on the night wire. For example, one wire report carried the story of the senate's passing a new bill affecting labor. Later in the day it sent a new lead stating that one of the labor unions would fight the law in the courts. The real story was still the passage of the bill; the union's fight against it should have been an insert in the body of the story, not a new lead.

3. Discrepancies between an early story and one filed later. When a press association sends a new lead or a revision of a story with a pickup from an earlier dispatch, it sometimes indicates the correction of a name or number in the new material by inserting the word "correct" or the abbreviation "CQ" immediately following. Unless the desk is careful, this change may be overlooked. Careless assembly of stories may also result in the inclusion of incorrect material. For example, a newspaper story said in the lead paragraph that a man was fatally beaten in a robbery attempt. The fifth paragraph, however, said that the victim died shortly afterward of a bullet wound between the eyes. The statement about the fatal beating was contained in a first lead which picked up at the third paragraph of an early story. The statement about the victim's dying of a bullet wound was in the early story.

4. Confusion regarding the day of the week in night wire stories. The press associations use the terms "today" and "tomorrow" with reference to the day of the month in the date line. This causes no trouble on afternoon publications, but it is likely to prove confusing to readers of morning newspapers. The date line says October 1, but it is October 2 when the subscriber reads the newspaper. To add to the confusion, the headline may say "today" when the dated story says "tomorrow." To get around this, many newspapers change "today" or "tomorrow" in the wire story to the day of the week. Others eliminate the date from the date line and substitute "yesterday" or "last night" for the "today" or "tonight" of the story.

CHAPTER 10

Headline Fundamentals

HOW HEADLINES EVOLVED

Headlines are the most prominent and characteristic feature of American newspapers—and the most influential. When we say that the American people are well informed, we really mean that they have merely a smattering of knowledge about current affairs gained from reading headlines. As has often been said, we are a nation of headline scanners. What that means in terms of events only half understood or misconstrued because of the limitations of headlines is a matter especially for newspapermen to ponder. In recent years, editors who have subjected themselves to soul searching about their profession have concluded that their duty is to inform the public by interpretive and explanatory reporting. Perhaps they should also consider changes in the headline, which as much as anything else stands in the way of understanding the complex problems that the newspaper seeks to report and make comprehensible.

As it has developed over the years, the headline has evolved into a rigid form. The rules that govern its composition are almost as unalterable as the law of the Medes and Persians. In literature the only forms comparable in tightness of structure and inflexibility of composition are a few French verse patterns and the Japanese hokku. To many copyreaders a headline is an exercise in literary composition; and if they are susceptible to aesthetic appreciations, a good one is a thing of beauty, as worthy of an ode as a Grecian urn.

The word "headline" is often defined as a title or caption. It is neither, though it has some of the functions of both. A title or caption indicates what a book, article, or document is about. So does a headline. But it does more. It summarizes the content. As they say in newspaper offices, it *tells* the story. It is a synthesis, a crystallization, a distillation put into a capsule for easy swallowing.

HEADLINE FUNDAMENTALS

The first newspapers in this country printed the news with almost no typographical differentiation between the separate items. The early headings were what today are called date lines; they merely gave the place of origin of the news and the date. They consisted of nothing more than the heading for a letter; as a matter of fact, this was all that many of the early news stories were—letters written by correspondents to the editor of the newspaper.

Later, as the papers began printing more news, items were segregated under such headings as "Washington Correspondence," "Political Affairs," and "Police Court." Today we would say that the news was departmentalized. In the first part of the nineteenth century the label heading was used on many news stories. Sometimes the labels were placed on a separate line above the article, but more often they appeared in all-capitals on the same line with the first words in the story. The labels occasionally were provocative, as though designed to lure the reader into perusing the article. Typical label heads were: THANKFUL FOR SMALL FAVORS, TRIAL FOR LIBEL, FINANCIERS IN TROUBLE, LOCAL POLITICS, RETRIBUTION, MORALS IN BOSTON.

The first notable tendency toward modern headlines came during a period of big news stories—the Mexican War. To herald stories from the battle fronts, newspapers began printing stories under headings consisting of a half dozen or so single-column parts. During the Civil War, a long series of headlines sometimes taking up half a column was used. This pattern prevailed until the Spanish-American War. During this period of headline development, column rules were seldom broken for a heading more than one column wide. The reason was chiefly mechanical. The early rotary presses printed from type locked in forms around a cylinder and held fast by wedge-shaped column rules. If these rules did not extend the length of the form, it was difficult to make it tight and secure.

With the invention of modern rotary presses and the development of stereotyping processes in the 1890's, the way was cleared for the use of heads running across several columns or clear across the top of the page during the Spanish-American War. In this period of yellow journalism big black headlines, sometimes several inches in depth, were used. The more sensational newspapers printed their headlines in red ink.

By the beginning of World War I headlines had become standardized. Several conventional patterns for type size and style had evolved, and the rules governing what a headline should say and how it should be said had become fixed. There was a new outbreak of big headlines during the war, of course, but no drastic changes in form took place.

The prevailing pattern was unchallenged until the 1930's, when John E. Allen, editor of *Linotype News*, and others campaigned for simplification of headlines and more readable typography. They criticized all-capital headlines as being hard to read, and urged a reduction in the number of parts. They recommended the abandonment of symmetrically balanced headlines for headlines set flush to the left with uneven margins on the right. These new heads were easier to write and easier to set up in the composing room. Despite the adverseness of newspaper editors and publishers to change, modernism or streamlining took hold because of lowered costs—an important item during the depression years of the 1930's. The shortage of experienced copyreaders and headline writers during World War II led other newspapers to go modern. Today, because we are accustomed to them, streamlined heads seem just as attractive in appearance as the older balanced patterns.

The next development in headlines? The trend toward simplification continues, with many newspapers now using only single headings. Perhaps the pendulum may swing back to label heads. Some critics recommend this form because it tends to eliminate any distortion of meaning resulting from attempting to force too much content into the few words in which a headline writer is expected to tell the whole story.

FUNCTIONS OF HEADLINES

The foregoing account of the evolution of headlines indicates something about their function. Their primary purpose, it would appear, originally was to advertise what a newspaper contained. The display headings over important stories attracted attention, aroused interest, and led to the newspaper being bought. This function was especially important in cities, where a dozen or more papers might compete for circulation. The advertising function is still important there, because metropolitan dailies rely to a great extent on street sales.

Some doubt about this function was raised in a study by Walter A. Steigleman. Questioning buyers of newspapers at street stands, Steigleman found little to indicate that readers chose their papers because of headlines. People asked for their favorite newspaper without noticing the headlines or comparing those on the different papers. In an article in the January, 1949, issue of *Journalism Quarterly* Steigleman drew the following conclusion:

HEADLINE FUNDAMENTALS

With this study indicating the headline has little direct sales appeal, with newsboys at times nullifying the editorial judgment, and with readership surveys showing the streamer story does not always obtain maximum readership, journalists may well re-examine some present theories about the worth and function of today's headlines. Front-page typography then could be designed in the light of the function that headlines serve today, rather than the function they may have served in the past. Perhaps newspapers have been indulging in a wasteful and expensive ornament.

Whatever the merits of Steigleman's study, it is clear that newspapers in smaller cities do not have to rely upon headlines to sell their product. There is less competition—in fact, today only about 115 cities have competing newspapers—and most readers have their paper delivered instead of buying it on the street or at a newsstand. But since the metropolitan dailies set the standards for excellence in journalism, the smaller papers tend to imitate them in news display and typography.

Big headlines advertising a scoop or a momentous happening are less important today than they were formerly, because, by the time a newspaper can be brought out with the news, people have already heard it on the radio or television. Newspaper extras are almost a thing of the past, and metropolitan publishers have found that numerous editions during a day are likewise uneconomic.

With the growth of newspapers from small, four-page publications to large, multiple-page ones, headlines took on another function—that of promoting rapid reading. This was accomplished by abandoning the label head, which gave only the subject matter of the story, in favor of the headline, which was a condensation of the news report. Publishers did not expect everyone to read the entire paper—few persons had the time. But people could inform themselves quickly about the happenings of the day by reading the headlines. The headlines today also facilitate selecting the stories to be read. The newspaper contains items that are of interest to only a small segment of the reading public. The headline tells the reader what the story contains and thus prevents him from wasting time on a story that does not interest him.

Although a headline is expected to tell the full story in a few words, feature articles and suspended interest stories excepted, it is nevertheless supposed to be sufficiently provocative to make a person want to read the story. Thus its function sometimes is contradictory: A headline makes it unnecessary for a person to read a story, and yet it is expected to inveigle him into doing so. That this feat of legerdemain can be done is evident from examining the headlines of some newspapers, especially the tabloids.

For example, the following tells the story succinctly and clearly, yet few readers would be likely to skip reading the story on that account:

> 3 JUDGES WEIGH
> HER FAN DANCE;
> FIND IT WANTON

HEADLINE PATTERNS AND TERMINOLOGY

Newspaper headlines have only six fundamental patterns, but these can be arranged in different combinations to give variety in form and appearance. The basic patterns are: the crossline or keyline, the dropline, the full line, the flush left, the inverted pyramid, and the hanging indention.

1. The Crossline. The crossline or keyline is a single line of type either centered in the column or set full column width. Most newspapers use it as a single-line heading over short one- and two-paragraph items or as a division line in a headline consisting of several sections.

Example of a crossline:

> Three Hurt in Crash

2. The Dropline. In the dropline pattern the separate lines that form the headline are approximately equal in length and are arranged in a stair-step pattern. Most often the head contains two or three lines. Other names for this pattern are "step" or "staggered" heads. It usually is a main display head.

Example of a dropline:

> MAYOR APPOINTS
> THREE TO SERVE
> ON HEALTH BOARD

3. The Full Line. In the full-line head all the lines are set so that they are flush with both left and right margins. The head usually runs to two or three lines and is generally a main display head.

Example of a full line:

> 4 Are Injured
> In Harlem Fire
> In 3 Buildings

4. The Flush Left. Headlines set flush left are aligned on the left and have an irregular margin on the right, depending on the length of each line. The most common pattern consists of two or three lines. It is used for both main and secondary headings.

Example of a flush left:

> New Tax Bill
> To Eliminate
> Wartime Excises

5. The Inverted Pyramid. The first line of the inverted-pyramid head is set full column measure; succeeding lines, each shorter than the one above it, are centered. It most often consists of three lines, but is used in two- and four-line patterns. It is primarily used as a secondary head under a main display head.

Example of an inverted pyramid:

> City Council Votes to Annex
> Sunbury Addition Despite
> Residents' Protests

6. The Hanging Indention. The first line of a hanging idention head is set full column measure; the other lines are indented equally at the left and, with the exception of the last line, must be flush to the right-hand margin. It is used in three-, four-, and five-line patterns, and is most often used as a secondary head under a main display head.

Example of a hanging indention:

> Blaze Causes Damages
>   Of $25,000; Smoke
>   Overcomes Fireman

Headline terms and special-type headings with which the copyreader must be familiar include the following:

1. Bank or Deck. The divisions of a headline that consists of more than one part. The first deck of big display type is usually called the *top deck*.

2. Top Head. A head, usually single column, at the top of the page.

3. Banner, Streamer, or Line. A headline extending across the entire page. Most banners consist of a single line of type, but there may be two- or even three-line banners.

4. Spread Heads. Large display headlines extending over two or more columns but not across the entire page. A variety of the spread head is the *blanket head*—a multicolumn headline extending over two or more related stories.

5. Hanger or Read-Out. A bank descending from a banner or spread head.

6. Eyebrow. A single line of small type above the main or top deck of the head. The eyebrow is a recent innovation in headlines. Its function is to give a clever twist to the headline. Other names for the eyebrow are *snapper, kicker, tickler, overline, read-in,* or *topline.*

7. Box Head. Any heading enclosed by borders on all four sides. Those with borders at the top and two sides are known as *heads in a hood.*

8. Jump Head. The heading over the part of a story carried over ("jumped") from the front page to an inside page.

9. Standing Heads or Stock Heads. Headings used unchanged from day to day for regular features.

10. Feature Head. A heading set in italic type, or one which, instead of merely condensing the story, is designed to attract attention by clever phraseology or a play on words.

11. Captions. Identification or explanatory matter for photographs. A heading above a photograph is often called an *overline,* and the information beneath it an *underline.*

COUNTING OUT HEADS

A deskman can be a good headline writer without knowing much about typography. Some deskmen never learn to distinguish type by its family or name, nor can they give reasons why one type is preferable to another for specific uses. Hence the subject of typography will be discussed in a later chapter.

However, before he can begin to write headlines, the deskman must know two typographical fundamentals: the newspaper's headline schedule and the method of counting out letters and spaces so that the completed headline will meet space requirements.

The length of line in a heading is strictly limited by the column width used in the newspaper. A line even the tiniest fraction too long cannot be used, for the space cannot be stretched. In certain headline patterns balance and symmetry are destroyed if the lines are too long or too short. Getting exactly the right number of letters and spaces in a headline is a matter of arithmetical count.

In determining the length of a line the deskman counts the letters and the spaces between words; they are the units that make up each line of the heading. The number of units in a headline is determined by its column width and by the width of the letters in the words.

The letters in a family of type are not all the same width. Casual examination shows that M and W are wider than the other letters in the alphabet. These are often spoken of as "fat." Capital I is narrower than other capitals. Of the small letters, $f, i, j, l,$ and t usually are thinner than the other characters.

HEADLINE FUNDAMENTALS

Counting-out systems take into consideration these differences in width. There is, however, no universally used system. The difference in the width of the characters used for headlines makes it impossible to apply a single formula to all kinds of type. The flush-left headline does not require so precise a count as do the symmetrical patterns, and in many offices composing machine operators are instructed to adjust irregular lines to make them balance. Thus some desks employ a loose system of counting out, and others employ a carefully exact count. The counting-out systems below apply in most newspaper offices.

The system for all-caps headlines is fairly simple. The following may be used:

Capital I	½ unit
Capitals M and W	1½ units
All other capitals	1 unit
Punctuation marks	½ unit
Figure 1	½ unit
All other figures	1 unit
Space between words	1 unit

This scale may have one difference from that used in many offices, for some editors prefer to count the space between words as ½ unit. Counting it as 1 unit, however, seems preferable. A wider space between words makes them easier to read; furthermore, the count is quicker and easier because there are fewer fractions.

In counting out headlines in which both capitals and small letters are used, the small letter is considered as the basic unit. The scale that is used follows:

Lower-case i, f, l, j, and t	½ unit
Lower-case m and w	1½ units
All other lower-case letters	1 unit
Capital I	½ unit
Capitals M and W	2 units
All other capitals	1½ units
Punctuation marks	½ unit
Figure 1	½ unit
All other figures	1 unit
Space between words	1 unit

Variations of this scale sometimes include counting *f*, *j*, and *t* as 1 unit, since in most type faces they are slightly wider than *i* and *l*. Some newspapers also count the space between words as ½ rather than 1 unit.

The exactitude necessary in counting out depends to some extent upon the headline pattern. But the deskman should never go above the maximum count for any headline. Sometimes the line can be squeezed in by using less space between words, but it is safer not to take any chances. A headline that won't fit is expensive. The writer wastes time writing it, the composing machine operator wastes time setting it, and other time is wasted in returning it to the copy desk for revision.

The dropline head is attractive only if the lines balance; hence it must be counted more precisely than the flush-left head. So also must the full-line head, because it is unsightly if there is either not enough or too much space between words. The count for inverted-pyramid and hanging indention decks set in small type is not ordinarily so precise as for top decks. In some plants the composing machine operators make a badly counted line balance by letterspacing the words, but they should not be depended upon to do the headline writer's job. Letterspacing takes extra time; and if the operator is rushed, he may not bother to make the small adjustments necessary to stretch out a short line.

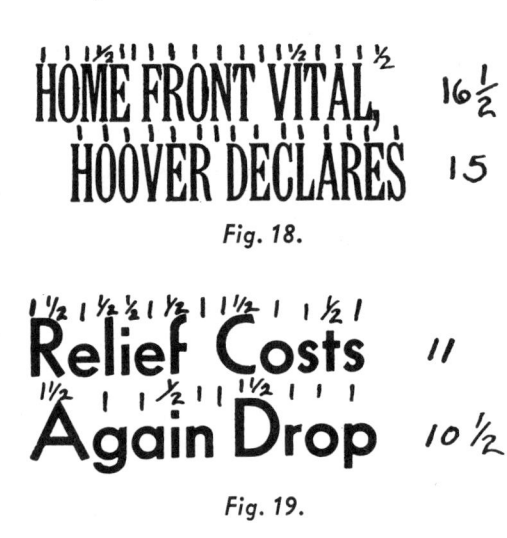

HOME FRONT VITAL, $16\frac{1}{2}$
HOOVER DECLARES 15

Fig. 18.

Relief Costs 11
Again Drop $10\frac{1}{2}$

Fig. 19.

The method of counting out an all-caps headline is shown in Fig. 18. Fig. 19 shows how a headline with both caps and lower case is counted.

In the latter headlines counting out is complicated by the presence of numerous fractions. Keeping track of them slows up computing the total units in the line, and it is easy for the writer to become confused and miscount. He can facilitate the counting-out process by an arithmetical short cut. Instead of tortuously counting out "Chungking" as 1½, 2½, 3½, 4½, 5½, 6½, 7, 8, 9, he can quickly get the total by counting each letter as a full unit and adding or subtracting mentally to justify the half units. Thus "Chungking" has 9 letters. He adds ½ unit for capital C—making 9½—and subtracts ½ unit for the small *i*. The result of course is still 9 units. The veteran copyreader simplifies the process even further. He notes at first glance that the fat *C* and the thin *i* balance each other and that a flat count can be taken.

The student should learn these short cuts for counting out lines. In his

HEADLINE FUNDAMENTALS

first few heads he may write the count above each letter, as in the figures, but he should abandon this kindergarten method as quickly as possible.

HEADLINE SCHEDULES

Most newspapers have a headline schedule for the information and convenience of desk workers, compositors, and printers. A schedule is a chart showing type faces, sizes, and unit count for the paper's headlines.

The most frequently used headline patterns or combinations are designated by a number or letter. A one-column headline used for stories at the top of a page may be designated as a No. 1 or an "A" head. Other heads may be No. 2, No. 3, or "B," "C," and so forth. Thus the deskman does not have to indicate the type face, the type size, or the column width. In a more elaborate system, single-column heads are designated by the figures 1, 2, 3, and so forth; double-column heads by 21, 22, 23; and three-column heads by 31, 32, 33.

Since headings more than two columns wide are relatively rare, numbered or lettered symbols are seldom used for longer heads. Instead, the deskman indicates the width in columns, the size of type, and the kind of type, in that order, at the left of his headline or above it. Thus "3-36 gothic" directs the composing room to set the headline three columns wide in 36-point gothic type. It is not necessary to indicate the number of lines because each line in the head appears as a separate line in copy. Additional information that may be necessary concerns the use of caps and lower case. The proper designations are: "3-36 gothic caps" and "3-36 gothic c & l." Boxed heads are indicated by drawing a box around the headline or by including the word "box" with the other instructions for the compositor.

CHAPTER **11**

Rules for Writing Headlines

HEADLINE APPEARANCE

The composition of headlines requires a craftsmanship not demanded in any other kind of newspaper writing. The headline writer may not be a creative artist, as is the poet who must conform to the rules of prosody, but his problems are somewhat similar. Just as meter, rhyme, and verse patterns impose limitations upon what the poet can say and how he says it, so rules govern the composition of headlines.

The first requirement is that a headline must conform to the unit count for its size and pattern. If it is longer than the maximum count, it may not fit within the column rules at all. If it is shorter than the minimum count, it will present an unattractive appearance.

The rigidity of the unit count depends upon the headline pattern. The flush-left pattern gives the writer the most freedom. When this pattern was first used in the early 1930's, the tendency was to take full advantage of the freedom. The only rule was the line must be within the maximum count. As a result, many of the heads were unsightly because of great irregularities in the length of lines. In a three-line head a first line of 16 units, a second line of 8 units, and a third line of 12 units was so ragged on the right-hand side that it offended the eye, especially of persons accustomed to symmetrical headings. Today more attention is paid to the appearance of the flush-left head. Ordinarily a difference of more than 3 units in length of line is avoided. Also, the maximum count is set a little less, usually 1 unit, than that required for copy to set flush to the column rule on the right.

The dropline head, formerly the most popular pattern for top headline decks, is attractive only when it "steps" properly. Consequently a difference of only 1 to 1½ units is desirable in the lines of these heads. A greater difference is allowed only if the typesetters are instructed to letterspace words in order to obtain proper symmetry. Note the unattractive appearance of a badly fitting dropline head:

>AUTO SMASHES
>TELEPHONE POLE;
>DRIVER KILLED

The full-line head likewise does not allow much variation in unit count. If lines are too short they must be letter spaced, and unattractive white gaps may appear between letters. Another danger in counting out these heads is getting the lines too long so that no space is left between words.

The inverted-pyramid and hanging-indention patterns are used mostly in secondary banks. Since a small type size is used for them, they do not have to be counted out as carefully as the larger top decks. In using the inverted pyramid, the deskman must be careful to avoid unsightly differences in the length of lines, and he must not write lines of approximately the same length. A hanging-indention head is unattractive when the last line is too short. The following examples illustrate faulty heads:

>Mayor Tells City Council
>That Parking Meter
>Revenue Shows Loss

>Mayor Tells City Council
>Parking Meter Revenue
>Drops

>Mayor Tells City Council
>Parking Meter Revenue
>Drops

ACTION IN HEADLINES

The label headline was abandoned by American newspapers not only because it was uninformative but also because it was static. It did not give a sense of the immediacy of news. Reporters got news by rushing to the scene of an event. Copyreaders worked under pressure to edit the story. Compositors set it in type at high speed. But no feeling of this drama and of the pressure of time was aroused by such inert labels as "Drowning at Sandy Point" or "Storm in Florida." Hence newspapers that wanted their readers to share the excitement of an event put verbs in headlines and insisted that they say something. Today the rule is that every headline and every bank of a headline must have a verb or else imply one so clearly that the reader automatically supplies it.

The sense of immediacy in headlines is further conveyed by the historical present—the use of the present tense to tell about a past happening.

The historical present is seldom employed in standard English writing, but it is found often in speech. A person telling about some exciting experience he has recently had may unconsciously lapse into the present tense. The experience is so vivid to him that in describing it he relives it. Something of this feeling of being on the scene is conveyed in the newspaper headline through the present tense. "Heavy Rain Lashed City" is not so effective as "Heavy Rain Lashes City."

There are two pitfalls in using the present tense in headlines. Used with a day of the week, the present tense indicates futurity. Thus "Smith Dies Thursday" means the death will occur Thursday. The only time this verb would be appropriate for this type of head would be over a story about an execution. The present tense also should not be employed with a word denoting the past. "Smith Dies Yesterday" strikes us immediately as incongruous. The correct locution is "Smith Died Yesterday." The past tense is properly used in such constructions as "Smith Shot Boy, Witness Testifies" and "Accident Toll Last Year Was 500 Persons."

The future tense in headlines is indicated as in ordinary speech by the auxiliary verb "will" or the infinitive construction. Since "to meet" takes up less space than "will meet," the infinitive is often found in headlines. The passive construction in which "slated" or "planned" is used for an event in the future should be avoided. Thus, "Dinner Slated by Lions Club" should be changed to "Lions to Hold Dinner Meeting" or "Lions Announce Dinner Meeting."

Forceful, vigorous heads that will attract attention and tell the story tersely require the active voice rather than the passive. Of the following heads, the one at the right gives more information and has more power than the one at the left:

**Robbery Suspect   New Clues Clear
Cleared by Police   Robbery Suspect**

The headline writer, however, should not shun the passive voice if it tells the story more naturally and clearly than the active voice or if, to get the most important information in the first line, the passive voice is required. The head at the left below has a strong, active verb but it does not tell the story so well as the head with the passive verb at the right:

**Boiling Water   Infant Scalded
Scalds Infant   In Fall into Tub**

In the following example it is desirable, even though an active verb is sacrificed, to get into the first line the fact that the police chief was shot:

RULES FOR WRITING HEADLINES

Youthful Robber   Police Chief Shot
Shoots Police Chief   By Young Robber

If possible, the verb should come in the first line of the head. To delay it until the second or third line makes the statement wooden. Note in the following example how the head is improved by getting the verb in the second line:

Heat from Crowd   Heat from Crowd
At Berlin Exhibit   Warps 3 Paintings
Warps 3 Paintings   At Berlin Exhibit

Since headlines should be written to be read at a glance, it is undesirable to shift from active to passive voice or to change the tense within a single deck. The reader may have to take a second look to get the meaning in such headlines as the following:

Governor Asks   Mayor to Seek
Tax Rise; Given   New Tax Source;
House Support   Asks Suggestions

As verbs are the action words, it is preferable not to omit them even though the meaning may be clear. The head to the right in the following example is an improvement over the one to the left, because it states an action:

Smith New President   Kiwanis Club Elects
Of Kiwanis Club   Smith New President

The objection to omitting verbs, however, does not apply to "be" as an auxiliary. In fact, the omission of auxiliaries makes the heads stronger; about the only time they are used is when they are needed to fill out the line:

Policeman Shot   Youth Is Shot
By Two Bandits   By Two Bandits

Headline writers should avoid forms of "to be" as the principal verb because this verb is weak:

New Tax Bill Is   Smith Is Chairman
Ready for House   For Fund Campaign

These heads can be made livelier by stronger verbs stating an action:

New Bill Boosts   Smith Heads Drive
Excise Tax Levies   To Raise $10,000

Or forms of "to be" may be and often are omitted:

Films Indecent,
Minister Says

Living Costs Up,
Bureau Reports

In the head, "Films Indecent, Minister Says," the verb will be required if the speech tag precedes the statement. "Minister Says Films Indecent" sounds wrong and is wrong, because we ordinarily expect "films" following a verb to be in the objective case, whereas the object of the verb is the implied clause "that films are indecent." For instant comprehension the head would have to read: "Minister Says Films Are Indecent." Then there is no confusion and no awkwardness. A general rule here is that if the speech tag precedes the statement, the verb is probably needed; if it follows, the verb may be omitted.

Another type of weak headline is the one stated negatively because it contains "not." If a story says that the president of the university refuses to grant an extension of a vacation asked by students, the headline should not read: "Students Do Not Get Vacation Extension." It should tell the story positively: "President Refuses to Extend Vacation."

OMISSION OF WORDS

As indicated previously, it is permissible to omit an auxiliary verb in the passive voice and "to be" used as the principal verb. Other words commonly dropped from headlines are the articles "a" "an," and "the," and conjunctions. The articles should not be omitted when needed for smoothness or for avoidance of ambiguity. The headline, "Wedding Plans Secret, Star Says," would read better if the article "a" were included: "Wedding Plans a Secret, Star Says." The conjunction "and" is often left out, its omission being indicated by a comma.

One of the most characteristic newspaper practices is the use of a noun as an adjectival modifier when normally a prepositional phrase would be used—what grammarians call the attributive noun. This use of nouns is legitimate in English (horse race, cinder track, college classes), but headline writers (writers of headlines) are likely to overdo it for the sake of brevity. These two headlines illustrate an awkward use of the attributive noun:

Council Opposes
Mayor Proposal

Court Frees Four
In Yacht Brawl

What the headline writer meant was "Mayor's Proposal" and "Brawl on Yacht."

Many newspapers bar "verb" heads, that is, headlines in which the subject is omitted. Such a head is particularly bad when it reads like a command:

> Arrest 14 Men
> In Strike Riot

> Make Plans to Aid
> Needy in County

If the verb ends in *s* the verb head is not offensive. In fact, if the subject is not important and it is difficult to include both subject and predicate, it is often desirable to omit the subject. The New York *Daily News*, whose headlines are among the brightest and best of any headlines in the country, frequently uses "verb" headings, as do other well-edited publications. Following are heads in which the omission of the subject is not objectionable:

> Shoots Wife, Baby
> After Drunken Party

> Steals Penny Bank,
> Overlooks $1,500

SPLIT HEADLINES

One of the theories of writing headlines maintains that each line should be a unit in itself. The basis for this theory is that the eyes take in only one line of type at a time and must be refocused when starting a new line. Consequently, there is a pause after each line is read when the eyes are shifting to the new line. It is believed that reading and comprehension are facilitated if a thought unit or a syntactical unit is not carried over from one line to the next. Thus no word, at least in top display heads, is divided or split. An adjective and the noun it modifies should not be separated; a preposition should not be separated from its object; the verb and the sign of the infinitive should not be put on different lines; an auxiliary verb and a principal verb should not be divided. In brief: the lines of a head should not end with an adjective, adverb, auxiliary verb, or preposition.

The following headings violate the rule that each line should be a unit:

> Oldest Banks In
> City to Combine

> Mayor Opposes Rent
> Control Measure

> 4-H Clubs Will
> Hold Conference

> Two Hurt in Car
> Crash at Rollins

> Three Are Badly
> Injured in Wreck

> State Editors To
> Meet at Harrisburg

BLIND FIRST LINES

As was said above, it is desirable to have a verb in the first line of a head. One reason is that a verb tells the story in the headline better than any other part of speech. Since the headline is designed to give information quickly, it should convey as much as possible at once—in the first line. Hence blind first lines—those that say little or nothing in themselves—should be avoided. The reader should not have to read the second or third line to get the main idea of the story.

One of the commonest types of blind first lines occurs with a single word or proper name that takes up the full line. Long words are the nemesis of headline writers because they leave little room for other information. If they are in the first line, they delay getting the idea across to the reader. Note the increased liveliness and intelligibility of the heads on the left as rewritten on the right:

    John C. Roberts   Roberts Named
    Named by Mayor   Chief of Police
    As Police Chief   By Mayor Jones

    Disagreements   Workers Strike
    Over Wages   When Refused
    Cause Strike   Wage Increase

IDENTIFICATIONS IN HEADS

The brevity of headlines does not permit extensive identification of persons and places. The name of a well-known person can of course be used in a headline without explanation. But if a name standing by itself means nothing to the general reader, it should be sacrificed, the head writer concentrating on telling the story. The fact that a person's name may be unknown to the public is the principal excuse for the verb headline previously described. The story under the following headline will create little interest if the person mentioned is not well known locally:

    James B. Roberts
    Killed in Crash

Other elements in the story may be chosen to make the headline arouse more interest in the reader:

    Speeding Driver
    Killed in Crash

Or:

    Death Stops Car
    When Police Fail

Or:

    Wild Ride Ends
    In Fatal Crackup

RULES FOR WRITING HEADLINES

In other words, the writer of the first headline missed the real news in the story by concentrating on the name rather than on the event.

Before using a name in the head, then, the deskman must be sure that it is sufficiently familiar to the public to convey some idea of the person involved. A previously unknown name that has appeared in the news several days may be used in a headline over follow-up stories.

Often a generic term like "man" or "woman" or "child" or "suspect" will mean as much to the reader as a name. Following are some examples:

**Girl Is Drowned
At School Picnic**

**Clerk Taps Till
For Racing Bets**

**Woman Is Fined
For Sassing Cop**

**Chinese Leader
Periled by Bomb**

An important identification that the headline must often make is place—letting the reader know whether the event happened locally or somewhere else. For example, the following head over a story about a school principal in another town would be inappropriate, because readers might believe that the person mentioned was a local individual:

**Board Removes
School Principal**

It would be better to include the name of the town:

**Canton Principal
Fired by Board**

The problem of place identification arises chiefly in handling wire copy. A headline reading "State Revenues Decline" naturally will be taken by the reader to mean his own state. If it is another state, the headline should say so: "Texas Revenues Drop." Similarly, the headline, "City to Change Zoning Laws," is inappropriate over a story about another city.

Indication of the place of origin is not always necessary, however. The place is obvious in many instances. Thus, readers will know that a small headline reading "Mayor Killed in Wreck" does not concern their mayor. If their mayor were involved, the story would be worth a much bigger headline in the local newspaper. Similarly, most national and foreign stories, because of their content, are not mistaken for local stories.

Though it is important that local stories be recognized immediately as such in the headlines, copyreaders should avoid as much as possible such geographical adjectives as "local," "city," "area," and "county"; the adverb "here"; and the name of the city and the word used to indicate residents of it, such as "Atlantan" and "Kansas Cityan." If deskmen are not careful, they may fall into the habit of using these terms indiscriminately and too often. Four or five stories on a page, each containing the word "local" in the head, would be excessive. Similarly, the word "state" or the name of the state is not needed on all stories concerning a state's affairs or events in it.

ABBREVIATIONS

The need for extreme compression due to the rigid limitations of headline units makes abbreviations enormously attractive. Yet, in general, no abbreviations should be used that would not be used in the body of the story. The newspaper stylebook indicates what abbreviations are permissible in headlines.

Abbreviating has become endemic in newspapers in the last decade or so. The proliferation of "alphabetical agencies" during Franklin D. Roosevelt's administrations was perhaps the prime cause for the telescoping of words, not only in the headlines but in the body of the stories as well. Beginning first with the use of initials to designate government agencies, headline writers let down the bars against abbreviations for other organizations and institutions. Thus the program to help Europe rehabilitate itself after World War II became the ERP (European Recovery Program); the requirement that young men should serve in the armed services for a period became UMT (Universal Military Training); and many other cabalistic letters came into frequent headline use.

The principal objection to these abbreviations is that they are not understood by newspaper readers. For example, test yourself on the following, which appeared in headlines: "Army PIO Chief Dies in Blast"; "Tentative Actions Cuts AF Funds"; "Mayor Urges VD Clinic"; "Chairman Named for ARC Drive." If you had to pause at all to figure any of them out, you can be sure they should not have been used in headlines.

Another objection to initial-letter abbreviations is their unattractive appearance typographically. In headlines set in caps and lower case they stand out too much and make the headline look unbalanced. If used without periods in all-caps headlines they look like typographical errors.

Another unsatisfactory shortening device adopted by headline writers is the use of first names and nicknames for persons in the news. Occasionally, abbreviated forms are unavoidable. The last name of Franklin D. Roosevelt was almost impossible to use in most headlines. Its 8½- or 9-unit count, for caps and lower case or all-caps respectively, was too short for a single line but too long to use with another word. Because the name appeared so frequently, newspapers were justified in shortening it to

RULES FOR WRITING HEADLINES

F.D.R. But when headline writers began referring to Mrs. Roosevelt as "Eleanor" they showed lack of proper respect. Similar bad taste is shown in calling well-known people by a nickname. Such terms should be used only when unavoidable—which usually means never. So firm a hold has the vicious habit of abbreviations on deskmen that they often use them when unnecessary. Harry S. Truman's last name is not a difficult headline word, yet some deskmen persist in such abominations as this: "Expect HST to Drop Tax Drive."

Omitting the title "Mr." in headlines is of course standard practice for newspapers, even those which are meticulous in using it in the body of the story. Women's names in headlines usually require "Miss" or "Mrs." unless the full name is used.

Certain long place names may appropriately be abbreviated when frequently used. Thus Philadelphia newspapers refer to their city as "Phila."; Los Angeles papers use "L.A."; San Francisco papers, "S.F."; and Pennsylvania papers, "Penna." Only distantly removed newspapers, however, would be safe in using "Philly" and "Frisco" since local residents resent them.

Many clipped forms and colloquial expressions are permissible in headlines, though they should be avoided. Thus we find "gas" for "gasoline," "photo" for "photograph," "quake" for "earthquake," "A-bomb" for "atomic bomb." Nouns are likely to replace longer adjectives; "Swedish" becomes "Swede," "Finnish" becomes "Finn," and "Arabian" becomes "Arab." "Russia" or "Russian" is cut down to "Russ" or "Red"; a Japanese becomes a "Jap," and an Australian an "Aussie."

HEADLINE STYLE

The punctuation, capitalization of words, and use of figures in headlines are governed by the newspaper's stylebook. However, certain typical practices will be discussed in this section.

Many newspapers omit the period in all headlines. Others drop it in top display decks but use it at the end of secondary decks set in small type.

The comma is used to indicate the omission of the conjunction "and":

**Mother, Daughter
To Receive Degrees**

Independent clauses not joined by a conjunction require a semicolon:

**Car Strikes Pole;
Driver Is Killed**

Single quotation marks are customarily used instead of the double to save space. Quotation marks are used to enclose the exact word or phrase employed by a speaker, to show that a word is used in an ironical sense, and to indicate slang:

'Truce' Declared
In Transit Strike

A question mark at the end of a headline conventionally indicates doubt as to the authenticity of a statement. This use should be avoided; many newspapers do not permit it.

T. B. Smith to Run
For City Council?

The dash is occasionally employed as a substitute for such verbs as "says" or "states" in a quotation. This short cut should be avoided.

'Comics Are Menace
To Youth'—Roberts

Only one comma is used to set off an identification or apposition when the second comma would come at the end of the last line of the heading, as in the following instance:

Death Takes Smith,
Former School Head

The capitalization of words in headlines and banks set in caps and lower case is a matter of newspaper style. Most papers use small letters for conjunctions and prepositions unless these words begin or end a line. Some typography experts say that capitalizing the first word on every line gives a more attractive appearance than using small letters on prepositions or conjunctions. Compare the two styles in the following:

Britain, U. S.
Reach Accord
on Trade Pact

Britain, U. S.
Reach Accord
On Trade Pact

Whether words or Arabic figures are used for numbers is another matter that is determined by newspaper style. Some publications insist on the same style for headlines as for the body of a story; that is, numbers under 10 are spelled out. Others permit the use of figures for single-digit numbers. There is no reason why one style is better than the other. The rule that is adopted should be followed consistently; a number should not be spelled out in one headline and written as a figure in another. Some newspapers advise against beginning a top deck with a figure. This is probably based on the rule that a sentence should not begin with a figure. Applied to headlines, however, the rule seems nonsensical.

THE DICTION OF HEADLINES

Critics of the language and grammar of newspapers have most frequently found fault with headlines, and journalism has been accused of being a corrupter of speech. The exigencies of space require the headline writer to use short words; the necessity of saying much in little causes him to load these short words with symbolical meanings. The result is a new language—headlinese.

Pedants criticize headlinese; and newspaper editors, self-conscious about their journalistic sins, warn their staffs to avoid the jargon. But nothing avails. Headlinese persists, primarily for the convenience of copyreaders. So long as legislatures conduct investigations, we apparently will continue to read about probes and quizzes. So long as politicians lambaste one another, we will continue to read that a candidate raps, flays, hits, or blasts his opponent. So long as there are differences of opinion, we will continue to have rows, clashes, and splits. When two cars collide, there will be a crash; when an agreement is signed, there will be a pact; when public expenditures are reduced, there will be a budget cut or a budget slash; when a robber escapes, he will flee. Those who condemn these fine monosyllabic words probably never tried to write a headline.

H. L. Mencken in *The American Language* says that English is naturally rich in very short nouns. Copyreaders, however, are not content with them as they stand. Mencken cites the following samples of headline words that have extended their meaning:

Ace. In the sense of expert or champion it came in during the World War. It has since been extended to mean any person who shows any ponderable proficiency in whatever he undertakes to do. I have encountered ace lawyers, ace radio-crooners and ace gynecologists in headlines.

Aid. Its military sense has been extended to include the whole field of human relations. Any subordinate is now an aid.

Balm. It now means any sort of indemnity or compensation. A derivative, love-balm, means damages paid to a deceived and deserted maiden.

Ban. All prohibitions are now bans.

Boat. It now means any sort of craft, from the Queen Mary to a mud scow.

Cache. This loan-word, one of the earliest borrowings from French, now signifies any sort of hidden store.

Car. It is rapidly displacing all the older synonyms for automobile, including even auto.

Chief. Any headman, whether political, pedagogical, industrial, military or ecclesiastical. I once encountered the headline "Church Chiefs Hold Parley" over a news item dealing with a meeting of the Sacred College.

Drive. Any concerted and public effort to achieve anything.

Edict. An almost universal synonym for command, order, injunction or mandate.

Envoy. It now signifies any sort of superior agent. Ambassador and minister are both too fat for the headlines.

Fete. Any celebration.

Gem. Any jewel.

Head. It means whatever chief means.

Hop. Any voyage by air.

Mecca. Any center of interest. Mecca has an M in it, and is thus troublesome to copyreaders, but it still is shorter than any other word signifying the same thing.

Plea. It means request, petition, application, prayer, suit, demand or appeal.

Row. Any sort of dispute.

Slate. Any programme, agenda, or list.

Snag. Any difficulty or impediment.

Solon. Any member of a law-making body.

Talk. Any discussion or conference.[1]

Is this jargon bad? The answer depends upon one's point of view. Perhaps such words should be avoided as much as possible, not because purists don't like them (no one can stop the language from changing) but because the terms have become colorless and ineffectual with overuse. The American people like novelty in language—witness their predilection for slang—and the headline words that once were forceful and pungent have become inane with repetition. The newspaper reader is not excited when he sees a headline, "Solon Raps Edict of Chief." He translates it into something like this: a member of congress opposes (probably for partisan reasons) an order issued by the president.

Whatever the attitude of the copyreader and his newspaper toward headlinese, he must nevertheless develop a vocabulary of headline words. This means that he must have on tap a ready flow of short synonyms. If a word with a seven-unit count is one unit too long, he must immediately know a six-unit word to substitute, or else revise his whole deck. If he uses a key word in one deck, he must have a synonym for it in the next deck, for one of the first rules of headline writing is that important words are not repeated. The reasoning behind this injunction is that a word repeated conveys nothing new. The avoidance of repetition, however, can be overdone. For example, a headline writer used the word "snow" in his first deck; in the second he called it "white precipitation." If there is no

[1] H. L. Mencken, *The American Language*, Alfred A. Knopf, 1936, p. 181.

convenient synonym for a word and it is needed again in a secondary deck, the copyreader should not be afraid to repeat it.

THE ETHICS OF HEADLINES

Most criticisms of newspapers for sensationalism stem from the headlines. It has been a problem since "scare" headlines were first used in the circulation war between Joseph Pulitzer's New York *World* and William Randolph Hearst's New York *American*. Copyreaders, like reporters, seem to suffer an itch to make every story a smash, to use the strongest word to describe every incident, even when it may not be the policy of the newspaper to insure mass sales.

The copyreader's first rule should be to write a headline that accurately says what the news story reports. An example of one that did not, given by the late Raymond Clapper in an article in *Quill*, appeared over a dispatch saying that President Roosevelt and Secretary of State Cordell Hull were reported to have "disagreed on the language of a neutrality message to congress." But the headline over the dispatch in the first newspaper to reach the president's desk said: "Neutrality Note Splits FD and Hull." "That colored the whole dispatch," Clapper wrote, "and pumped it up into an inside crisis and gave an exaggerated emphasis to the differences over technique in dealing with congress." The result was that the president issued a denial accusing the press service which sent out the story of falsifying the news.

Such things happen every day. The first reports of a disaster almost always have about twice as many persons dead or injured as the final tabulation of the casualties. Some newspapers have a rule that when a story says 100 to 200 lives were lost, the lower figure is the total for headline purposes. Exaggeration of casualty totals often has unfortunate results. Scare headlines cause unnecessary worry to persons with relatives or friends in the area of the disaster; people flocking to the scene hinder rescue efforts; and anxious people trying to get in touch with their families swamp telephone facilities.

Headline writers should be hesitant about labeling an outbreak of disease an "epidemic," in calling every difference between the United States and a foreign power a "crisis," in describing every diplomatic protest by a government as a "threat" or "ultimatum."

Jenkin Lloyd Jones, editor of the Tulsa (Oklahoma) *Tribune*, urged editors to check their papers to see whether they were putting scare heads on stories that were not likely to have as dire consequences as the headlines indicated. He declared that "it is further the duty of the press to give a reasoned, not an hysterical, picture of the world. It is its duty, so far as it can, to separate that which is accidental or frivolous from that which is meaningful and indicates a trend. Sensationalism is a poor yardstick for genuine news value, for it rarely distinguishes between one and the other." Jones accused the press, partly because of its big headlines and the blowing up of differences between the United States and Russia soon after World War II, of creating a near-panic in the nation.

Newspaper headlines which make unwarranted use of smear words also do untold damage. Name calling is one of the most common propaganda devices, and newspapers should be careful not to let themselves be duped by propagandists or to harm individuals or groups with smear words. For example, the American Medical Association tagged compulsory health insurance "socialized medicine." Newspapers used this inaccurate term. On their own, the papers contributed to the prejudice against labor organizations by calling their leaders "reds," and they gave the public a false impression of liberal college professors by speaking of "Communist teachers."

The headline writer must be on guard against unconscious editorializing. Because of space limitations it is difficult to work in an attribution or to cite authority for statements, yet the headline should not assert as truth what someone merely says is truth. The following headline is an illustration:

Labor's Demands
Peril Economy

In a two-line head it is probably impossible for a copyreader to work in the authority—that the above statement was made by the president of the National Association of Manufacturers. But somehow he must avoid pronouncing judgment on labor's demands, as in the following:

Labor's Demands
Called Menace

Labor's Demands
Seen as Menace

In the same category are the headlines indicating that a person is guilty of a crime when he has only been arrested and charged with it. A newspaper cannot correctly say that a person is an arsonist or a burglar until he has pleaded guilty to such a charge or been found guilty by a jury. The two headlines below are faulty, because they do not say what the story says—and they are potentially libelous:

Police Arrest
Girl's Assaulter

Attorney Arrested
For Drunk Driving

RULES FOR WRITING HEADLINES

They should be rewritten as follows:

**Suspect Is Held
As Girl's Attacker**

**Attorney Accused
Of Drunk Driving**

In writing headlines the deskman is subject to the conventional standards of good taste. A British critic of American sensationalism said that our press "dabbles much of the time in scatological jargon calculated to appeal to mob curiosities." He had in mind such headlines as "Wife Slays 'Torture' Mate" and those favorites of tabloidia that feature "love nest" tribulations. But even more conventional publications sometimes fall from grace in this respect. Moreover, in his efforts to write a sparkling headline the copyreader should avoid levity when telling about tragic events. Conscienceless tabloids are guilty of this every day, but such cynical treatment of human errors and weaknesses should not be imitated.

CHAPTER 12

Composing the Headline

GETTING STARTED

A veteran deskman can write a headline that fits and tells the story on his first try. Often he does not even count the letter and space units. His practiced eye tells him whether the count is correct. The novice also may occasionally write a suitable heading immediately, but more often his first one doesn't fit. One line is too long or too short. He strives to adjust it by substituting another word. The count is still wrong. He starts all over again and perhaps a third time. The more he ponders the more impossible his task seems. Minutes go by and he begins to worry. He thinks of the approaching deadline, of the insatiable typesetting machines and their idle operators, of the yawning space in the newspaper forms on the composing stones. His nervousness makes his mind go blank. Headline writing, he decides in despair, is too hard for him to master.

This experience is one that every deskman has undergone. The art of writing headlines has to be learned through practice. But once you learn how, it is easy.

You cannot learn to write headlines by reading how they should be composed or by memorizing a set of rules. You have to take a story and restate it in headline terms. One of the best methods of practicing is to write several headings for the same story. Choose a definite headline pattern with a definite count. Then write three or four heads to fit. Next, choose another kind of pattern and write several heads in it. This practice will give you needed training in saying the same thing in different ways. You will learn that when a certain phraseology doesn't work out, there are always other expressions you can use.

The veteran deskman who writes a perfectly counted head apparently without stopping to think about what he wants to say very likely has the exact phraseology in mind before he puts pencil to paper. The headline writes itself for him, in his subconscious mind, while he is editing the story. One of the first rules in writing headlines is to edit the copy and then compose the head. The deskman should not skim through the story to get the main facts and then write his headline. Instead, he should mark the copy for the composing room. By the time he has edited the story, his mind will have absorbed the information and the words for the headline will have come to him without his having to concentrate on them.

Another reason for writing the headline after editing the story is to avoid putting into it any facts altered or eliminated in the editing. The head, of course, should not contain any information that is not stated in the story. If the deskman writes the headline first, he runs the risk of mentioning in it something he later may trim out of the story. The result is lost time and effort in recasting the headline.

In most newspaper offices deskmen write their headlines in pencil instead of typing them. The reason is that the copyreader's work is done mostly with pencil. Moreover, several copyreaders are crowded around the rim of the copy desk, and there is no room for typewriters.

Many editors on smaller newspapers, however, compose their headlines on a typewriter. There are several advantages in using a typewriter. It is quicker to type a line than to write it in longhand or print it; the copy is neater and more legible; and counting out can be done automatically with the marginal scale on the machine.

Since headlines are not set on the same composing machines as straight matter, most newspapers require that they be written on separate sheets of paper from the stories. The only exceptions are subheads in the body of the story and the small headings over one- or two-paragraph items that are set in the same type size as the stories.

Unless the newspaper uses long multiple-deck patterns, headlines may be written on half sheets of copy paper. The deskman puts the headline number or designation and the slug or guideline for the story at the top of the sheet. Underneath, he writes the head, line by line as it is to be set. Block letters or print is preferable to script, because such copy is easier to count and more legible.

Flanking lines may be used (though they are not necessary) to indicate to the operator how the head is to be set—flush left, dropline, centered, and so forth.

EXERCISE IN CONDENSATION

As was said earlier, the chief function of the headline is to give the essence of the story. The lead ordinarily summarizes the news; the head-

#2 Legislature

| House Group
| Defeats Six
| Tax Proposals

] Measures to Hike
] Levies Are Postponed

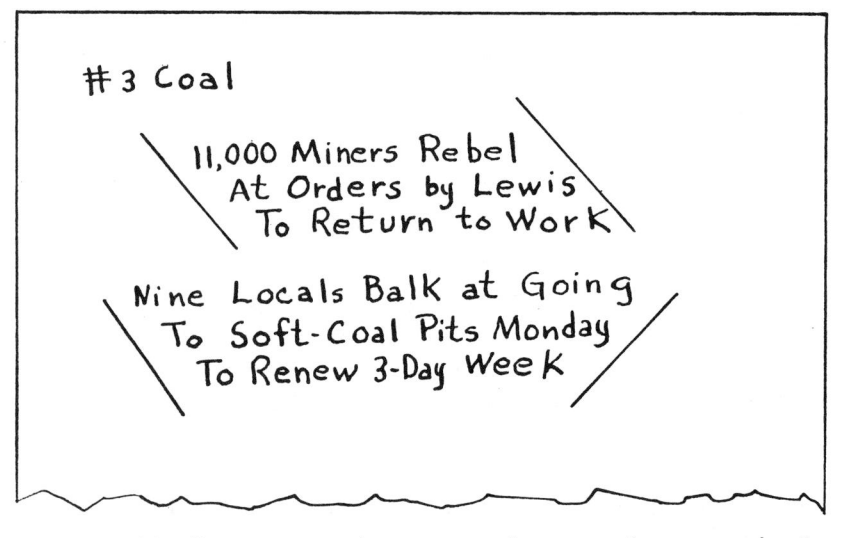

#3 Coal

\ 11,000 Miners Rebel \
\ At Orders by Lewis \
\ To Return to Work \

\ Nine Locals Balk at Going /
\ To Soft-Coal Pits Monday /
\ To Renew 3-Day Week /

Fig. 20. Headline copy ready to go to the composing room, showing headline designation, the story slug, and flanking lines.

COMPOSING THE HEADLINE

line says the same thing even more briefly. Every word not absolutely necessary to convey meaning is discarded; only the kernel of information is left in the completed head. According to newspaper convention, the lead answers the questions Who, What, Why, Where, When, and How. Of the five W's and the H, the only one almost always essential to the headline is the what. The others may or may not be included in it, depending on how important or how interesting they are. But a headline is no headline if it does not say what happened, if it does not tell about the action in the story.

A good way for a beginner to start writing a headline is to reduce a story to a single short sentence, and use that as the basis for his headline. This method is used by most copyreaders, especially for complex stories, although they may not be conscious of it. Its application may be illustrated by writing a single-line heading with a maximum count of 30 units for the following item:

John T. Winters, 33, of 418 E. Tenth Street, received a three-inch cut on his left arm this morning when his automobile skidded on the icy pavement and crashed into the curb at E. Tenth Street and N. Walnut Avenue. He was treated at the Good Samaritan Hospital.

Reducing this paragraph to a short sentence, we have: "John T. Winters cut his arm when his car skidded on the icy pavement and crashed against the curb." The identification, the time, and the place have been eliminated as of secondary importance. But the sentence must still be drastically shortened.

At this point the beginner, recalling numerous headlines he has read, will see the light and dash off the following with a flourish: "Man Hurt in Car Crash." There's the headline; it tells the story and it fits. There is nothing wrong with this headline, *except* that it could be used over any story about a man injured in an automobile accident. It is not sufficiently specific.

The really critical deskman will try again. He still decides to omit the name because the victim is not well known and his name will mean little to the reader. He shortens the sentence further to: "Man Cuts Arm When Car Skids on Icy Pavement." This is too long, but it is closer to what he wants. As a last try, he saves several space units with the following: "Man Hurt as Car Skids on Ice." This is within his 30-unit count, and he decides that it is satisfactory.

Of course, the process does not always reach such a favorable conclusion. There are times when the deskman knows what he wants to say, but try though he may he cannot make the count come right. In such situations he must try another approach; or, if copy is piling up, he may have to send the composing room a headline that does not please him. A better way is to lay aside the story with the balky headline and return to it later. Often a headline comes naturally and easily after a lapse of a few minutes. On the above story three deskmen out of four would have used "Man Hurt in Car Crash," because the item is unimportant. It is filler material, and its presence or absence in the paper will make little difference to anyone.

The single-line heading over filler material may seem the easiest of all heads to write, but the ease of writing it is deceptive. True, there is a rather large unit count and the line does not have to balance with other lines as in the two- and three-line patterns, but the fundamental rules for this heading are the same as for any top-deck heading up to a 120-point banner.

CHOOSING THE "MUST" ELEMENTS

The headline we have been considering, "Man Hurt as Car Skids on Ice," emphasizes the what and how of the story. The who is also given but in such general terms as to be almost meaningless. In all the stories he edits the deskman must decide which of the five W's and H must be included in his headline. The what, as we have seen, is essential for nearly all headlines. The who should be emphasized if the name is known to the public; if not, the person can be indicated by a generic term such as man, woman, boy, girl, policeman. The rule that the verb in a headline must have a subject makes the who nearly always necessary in some form. The when is seldom used except for stories dealing with future events. Present-tense verbs indicate past action, presumably sometime in the twenty-four hours since the last edition of the paper, and the future tense tells the reader that something will occur, although the exact time may not be stated. The where may be essential if the location is newsworthy in itself or if for any reason the deskman decides that it is required to avoid confusion. Whether the why and the how are used depends upon the nature of the story. If they are especially important or especially interesting, they should be in the headline.

In addition to stating the most important or most interesting of the five W's and the H, the headline should emphasize the feature of the story— the element that is likely to affect or interest the greatest number of people and that distinguishes it from reports of similar events.

After the deskman has stripped the story down to a thesis sentence and

COMPOSING THE HEADLINE

has selected the most important questions that the headline should answer and the feature that should be emphasized, he most often finds himself with two or three words that are essential in the headline. These are the key words around which he must build it.

With these requirements in mind, let us consider writing two-line flush-left top decks for several varieties of stories; the maximum count for each line is 16 units.

1. The *who* as a key word:

John T. Springer, speaker of the House of Representatives, announced today that instead of asking re-election to the legislature from Clay County he will seek the Democratic nomination for the U. S. Senate in the July primary election.

A headline based on this lead can hardly be written without the man's name. The use of the word "legislator" as a substitute will not tell the story; there may be a hundred or so legislators in the state. "Clay County legislator" cannot be used because it is too long; moreover, there may be more than one legislator from Clay County. "Speaker" is short enough, but would be almost meaningless alone in the headline. "House Speaker" is a possibility, but the man's name is preferable. The headline that best tells the story begins with the man's name:

Springer to Run
For U. S. Senate

2. The *what* as a key word:

A 2-cent increase in the gasoline tax—from 3 cents to 5 cents a gallon—to finance the state's highway improvement program was agreed upon today by Senate and House conferees.

Quite clearly any headline for this lead must contain the words "gasoline tax" or, in the abbreviated form, "gas tax." Any head that omits one of these two words will not tell the story. A deskman might write, "2-Cent Hike in Tax Voted" or "Conferees Agree on Tax Hike," but neither tells the real story. A heading that might be used is:

Gas Tax Boost
Of 2 Cents Voted

If the deskman wishes to emphasize the amount of the increase because there has been a controversy over it, he might write:

2-Cent Increase
In Gas Tax Voted

3. The *when* as a key word:

Enrollment in the city's grade schools and the junior and senior high schools will be held Sept. 10, T. R. Smethers, superintendent, announced today.

The when is seldom an imperative element of headlines, but in stories like this one it is needed. A headline which merely said "School Enrollment Date Announced" would not satisfy the reader's desire for information. One giving the specific date, such as the following, is preferable:

**School Enrollment
Set for Sept. 10**

Or:

**City's Students
Enroll Sept. 10**

4. The *where* as a key word:

T. C. Walters, 41, an unemployed bookkeeper, shot and killed himself in front of the Keystone Building on Main Street this morning when his application for a job at the Economy Shoe Store was turned down.

The where in this lead certainly is one of the major elements of interest in the story—men seldom commit suicide on a busy main street. Thus the deskman might write the following head:

**Man Kills Self
On Main Street**

Some deskmen might prefer: "Refused a Job, Man Kills Self," in which the motive is emphasized; but the location, because of its unusualness, has a strong point in its favor.

5. The *why* as a key word:

Unseasonably warm weather caused a 5 per cent decline in department store sales in the state during January, according to the monthly report of the Bureau of Business Research of the state Chamber of Commerce.

Although in this lead the important news element is the 5 percent drop in retail sales, the reason for it is also of special interest. The headline, "January Sales Drop 5 Per Cent," tells the story; but the fact that the decline was due to the weather and not to bad business conditions in general, unemployment, or some other cause is important enough to make the following preferable:

**Weather Causes
Decline in Sales**

6. The *how* as a key word:

John P. Martin, captain of the North High School football team, broke his left arm after the game with Emerson High School yesterday when he slipped on a bar of soap and fell down in the shower room.

Football players are frequently hurt in games and in practice; but when one is injured in a comparatively safe place like a shower room the how is unusually newsworthy. Thus this lead might give the deskman the following headline:

**Fall in Shower
Injures Grid Star**

Or:

**Grid Star Felled
By Bar of Soap**

While not often the main element in a news story, the how is frequently the most interesting or most unusual. When it is, it is a must for the headline.

HEADS WITH MORE THAN ONE DECK

The principal change in newspaper headlines in recent years has been the elimination of long, multiple-deck heads. Until the 1930's most newspapers used for top-of-the-column headings a pattern consisting of a top deck, a second deck of the hanging indention or inverted-pyramid type, a crossline, and a final deck which repeated the pattern of the second deck. Headlines over secondary stories usually had two decks. The streamlined newspapers of today have eliminated these long headlines. Many have reduced the maximum number of decks to two, and many others use only single-bank headings.

Writing banks is easier than writing top decks. The banks are set in smaller type, and the deskman has more freedom in his choice of words. The unit count in top decks may be from 12 to 16 units; in the secondary decks it may be as high as 25 to 30 units. Moreover, many newspapers have no rule against splitting phrases and dividing words in the subordinate parts of headings.

The function of the bank or banks in a heading is to elaborate upon the top deck and give additional details needed for better understanding the story. For example, if the top deck says, "Man Injured in Auto Crash," the second bank may give his name, the nature of his injuries, or details of the accident. The lower parts of multiple-deck headings may also be used to introduce another topic covered in the story.

In writing secondary decks, the deskman should be on guard against merely repeating the idea in the first deck in different words. The bank should have something new to offer; it should be more than a paraphrase of the top deck. Hence one of the rules of headline writing is that a secondary deck should not repeat an important word in the top deck. The following headline illustrates faulty composition in the lower deck:

**4 CARS DERAILED
NEAR WESTMORE**
**Three Passenger Cars,
Mail Car Leave Track**

The second deck does not give enough new information to make it worth the space it takes. Other questions it might have answered include the number of persons injured, if any, the name of the railroad, the cause of the derailment, and the extent of the damage.

If the top deck does not contain a subject, the first word in the next bank should indicate it, as in the following:

**ASSERTS KILLER
IS A 'GOOD KID'**
**Mother of Slain Girl
Says Youth Deserves
Chance at Freedom**

A subject in the top deck may be used in the next division of the headline, provided the subdeck begins with a verb:

**BOY DISCOVERS
BURIED MONEY**
**Finds $900 Believed
Hidden by Robbers**

The multiple-deck headline differs from the two-bank patterns illustrated only in that it permits the addition of more details and the introduction of new topics perhaps not covered in the first deck. The crossline in the four-deck pattern may be used for a striking subordinate fact or a new topic, and the last deck may elaborate upon the crossline.

The method of constructing a multiple-deck headline and variations in choosing elements to feature can best be illustrated by an example. For illustrative purposes the headline has the following pattern: a top stepline deck of three lines, maximum count 15 units; a second deck, inverted pyramid, maximum count for first line 26 units; a crossline, maximum count 22 units; and a bottom deck the same as the second deck.

COMPOSING THE HEADLINE

The story to be headed starts as follows:

Six hundred indignant school people last night mapped a program of political pressure to force Gov. Robert T. Allen to increase the common-school fund by $12,200,000 a year.

The strongest undercurrent at the meeting was talk that public-school teachers may stay away from their classrooms until their demand for money is met.

To finance their proposal to increase the common-school fund from $22,300,000 to $34,500,000 a year, the school people endorsed a tax program designed to raise $14,301,000 a year in additional revenue.

They recommended that the legislature increase the tax on beer from $1.50 to $3 a barrel; raise the present 2-cent-a-pack tax on cigarets to 5 cents; boost the 3 per cent tax on pari-mutuel betting to 10 per cent; and increase the production tax on whisky from 5 cents to 10 cents a gallon.

Only 237 school superintendents were invited to the meeting, but enough principals and teachers showed up to swell the crowd to around 600. T. Alfred Bond, president of the state association, presided.

Analysis of the story shows the following principal elements:

1. Teachers to use political pressure to force increase in common-school fund.
2. A strike may be used as a weapon in the campaign.
3. The increase sought is $12,200,000.
4. New taxes are proposed to obtain the additional money.

The factor common to all these four points is the increase in school funds. Hence this factor must appear in any top heading the deskman writes. Some possibilities for the first bank of the headline are:

(1)
TEACHERS WEIGH STRIKE TO FORCE BOOST IN FUNDS

(2)
TEACHERS SEEK INCREASED FUNDS OF $12 MILLION

(3)
TEACHERS TO ASK INCREASED TAXES TO HELP SCHOOLS

(4)
SCHOOLMEN PLAN PRESSURE DRIVE TO BOOST FUNDS

Although these headings do not exhaust the possibilities, they illustrate several ways in which the key element—the increase in school funds—is used in conjunction with different aspects of the story.

The content of the subordinate decks is of course determined by the top bank the deskman selects. Complete headings that might be written from the first two banks above are:

(1)
TEACHERS WEIGH STRIKE TO FORCE BOOST IN FUNDS

Indignant Educators Are Set To Bring Pressure On Governor Allen

600 PRESENT AT MEETING

They Propose Higher Taxes To Increase State Aid By $12,200,000

(2)
TEACHERS SEEK INCREASED FUNDS OF $12 MILLION

Threaten Strike as Weapon In Pressure Campaign Against Allen

NEW TAXES PROPOSED

Money Would Come From Levies on Cigarets, Racing, Whisky

Two faults are frequently found in multiple-deck headlines. If, after writing his top deck, the deskman introduces a new topic in either the second deck or the crossline, he should not revert to the subject of the top deck in his concluding deck. The second deck is the place for the theme in the first deck to be amplified. While it is permissible to use the same subject for the verbs in the first and second decks (as in No. 2 above), the deskman should not continue to use it for the verbs in succeeding parts of the headline.

HANGERS FOR SPREAD HEADS

Writing hangers or read-outs for banners and spread heads involves no new rules. The deskman should regard the multiple-column heading as the top deck and the read-out as a bank.

The spread head that covers the content of two or more separate but related stories, however, creates some special problems. The spread head may or may not cover all the stories under it. This depends on whether the deskman has all the stories at hand when he writes it. Very often he does not. He may write a three-column head with a read-out. Later a related story comes to the desk, and the slotman then decides that he wants the two stories printed under the same spread. Since it is time-consuming and costly to rewrite and reset the original spread, it is used for both stories.

For example, a newspaper carried a roundup story on a big increase in the governor's budget for the biennium. Under a five-column spread the paper printed not only the roundup story but two other stories dealing with separate items in the budget.

UN Sidetracks U. S. Charges To Study Peiping's Truce Offer; Yanks Win Big Jet Air Battle

33 U. S. F-84s	Austin Brands
Shoot Down 4	It Transparent
Russian-Made	Effort To Split
MIGs; Damage 4	The Free World

Fig. 21. A three-column spread head for two related stories originating from opposite sides of the globe—one in New York, the other in Tokyo.

Even though stories are date-lined from widely distant points, they can be carried under the same spread head. In Fig. 21, two lines of a three-line, three-column spread concern United Nations action in New York regarding the Korean war; that story drops to the right. The third line and the hanger at the left deal with the battle front and summarize a story date-lined Tokyo.

JUMP HEADS

Stories worth multiple-deck heads or spread heads are likely to be too long to be completed on the front page. The copyreader must therefore write "jump" captions for articles that are continued to another page.

Practice differs in newspaper offices, but in most the jump head is sent to the composing room with the original headline. This means that the copyreader who handles the story also writes the heading for the continued portion of the article. Some newspapers require that jump heads be written for all long stories slugged for the front page. A copyreader's failure to send back a jump head may delay making up the paper at deadline. In the hectic minutes before the pages are justified and the forms are locked, the make-up editor has too much on his mind to have to spend time writing jump heads.

One variety of jump head duplicates the headline on the front page. If the carry-over is short, only the top deck may be repeated. If the con-

● **Food–**
(Continued from Page 1.)

HOUSE
Continued From Page 1

King George
Continued from First Page

Traffic Snarl Here Called Worst Ever
Continued from First Page

Wage Freeze Is Relaxed
(Continued from Page 1)

KICK—*From Page 1*

Bevan Is Given Kick in Pants

Solon Makes Bribe Charge Against RFC
Continued from Page 1

Fig. 22. Examples of newspaper jump heads.

tinued portion is long and is to be given top-of-page display on the inside, the entire head of several decks may be repeated. In such a case, the deskman has only to write on the headline copy either of the following instructions to the compositor: "Set Double" or "Set Jump Head."

One practice is to repeat the first line of the heading or the key word or words, in either the same size or a smaller size of type. Another practice is to use an entirely rewritten head, perhaps in smaller type. If the original heading is not duplicated, the copyreader should write the jump head on a separate sheet of paper and slug it "jump head."

SUBHEADS WITHIN STORIES

Stories that run a half column or more present an expanse of type that looks uninteresting and gives the page a gray appearance. Most newspapers therefore require that long stories be broken up by subheadings or other typographical devices—initial letters, dashes, or extra spacing between paragraphs.

Subheads usually are set in blackface type of the same size as the body type. They may consist of one line centered or set flush left. Some papers set them in all-caps, print them as two lines, use a larger type than body type, or set them in italic type.

If the newspaper has a standard form for all subheads, as is likely, the copyreader needs only to indicate them by the word "subhead" or the abbreviation "sh" written and circled in the left margin of the copy. Specific instructions to the compositor may be used, as "bf c & l" for boldface caps and lower case or a wavy underscoring to indicate boldface.

Since one of the principal functions of subheads is to improve the appearance of the page, some newspapers require that they be placed regularly every four or five inches for balance and specify that there must be two or more to a story—never just one. Other papers, while desiring symmetrical placement, specify that the subheads are to come at natural "breaks" in the story. No subhead should follow a paragraph ending with a colon and introducing a quotation in the next paragraph, or between paragraphs in a direct quotation.

Subheads must conform to the standard rules for headlines. Label subheads are barred. Subheads should be based on information in a following paragraph, preferably the second one.

The theory of the subhead is that it will lure a reader into reading more of the story, but readership studies at the University of Illinois indicate there may be a fallacy in this conception. Surveys showed that many persons stopped reading at the subhead; they thought it meant that a new topic or phase of the story was being taken up and decided that it was a good point at which to shift to another story.

HEADS FOR FOLLOW-UP STORIES

The headline for second-day or follow-up stories must be written so that the reader will not be misled into thinking that the story concerns an entirely new event. The copyreader follows the reporter's technique in emphasizing the new development in the headline and then hastily indicating the previous action by means of a tieback.

Newspapers have developed a handy device for refreshing a reader's memory about an event. They give the story a name or label. Any newsworthy murder, for example, receives an identifying name before it has been long in the news. Sometimes the identification emphasizes the method of the killing, as "hammer killing" or "ax murder"; sometimes it is a peculiar circumstance, as "black dahlia slaying" or "picnic killing"; sometimes it is the motive, as "mercy killing" or "insurance death." A series of unexplained killings in Cleveland, Ohio, in which the victims were decapitated and dismembered has had a long career in the press as the Cleveland "torso murders."

Other events also soon become known by brief descriptive epithets. The state legislature's investigation of alleged Communists on a university faculty becomes "Red probe." A series of firings and demotions in the police department to improve efficiency may be known as "police shake-up" for several days during the life of the story.

To illustrate the use of a descriptive label for a continuing story, let us assume that the first news report tells of the finding of a woman's body with the head crushed by a claw hammer lying nearby. This might have the heading: *Woman Killed by Hammer.* A later story might report that police are questioning the woman's husband. This headline might say: *Husband Held in Hammer Death.* The phrase "hammer death" would probably be used in most of the other headlines about the man's being charged with murder, his trial, his conviction, and his execution. Later on, of course, the man's name may become so well known that it alone will be an adequate reminder for the readers, and the label will not have to be used.

The descriptive-label tieback is not needed for all follow-up stories. In some continuing stories all the copyreader needs to do is to emphasize the new development. Suppose a state senator is killed in an automobile crash. The news story is headed: *Senator Smith Killed in Crash.* The follow-up story might have the head: *Smith Services to Be Private.* Another follow-up might read: *Manslaughter Charge Filed in Smith Death.*

FEATURE HEAD TECHNIQUES

If a headline tells a story clearly, accurately, and concisely, it will achieve its principal function—informing the reader. This is the goal sought by most copy desks for the bulk of the stories.

Yet many stories require a different headline—one that is bright or clever. Sparkling heads are especially desirable for feature stories. Such headlines are needed to give readers relief from the long menu of the stories of crime, disaster, politics, and social significance served daily by newspapers, just as Shakespeare found it desirable to interlard his tragedies with comic scenes. Most editors like at least one "brightener" for the first page—an amusing story under an amusing headline.

Asked by the slotman to write a clever head for a story, the copyreader is likely to fail. Wit and humor are not on tap like the chlorinated water that flows through city mains. The sparkling headline usually comes from a sudden inspiration.

Nevertheless, there are a few tricks which every deskman has up his sleeve. His wit may not be up to that of Oscar Wilde or George Bernard Shaw, but it probably is no worse than the humor of some highly paid radio comedians. Anyway, a fine and subtle wit is likely to be lost on the majority of headline scanners.

Let us consider that much-maligned variety of wit known as the pun. The pun has suffered from being misunderstood. It is called the lowest form of wit—the place given it by neoclassic critics of the eighteenth century. These critics did not mean by wit what we mean today. To them wit meant rhetorical devices for the adornment of poetry—similes, metaphors, conceits, personification. For serious poetry the pun was inappropriate, and hence given an inferior position. It could be used by a barbarian like Shakespeare, but not by the cultivated people of Queen Anne's reign.

Because it is recognized by all and enjoyed by most, the pun is suitable headline wit. Even bad puns are funny—the worse they are the funnier they are. Here is one a paper used for a story about a woman who asked for help in getting a refund on a girdle: *Mayor Will Look into Squeeze on Dissatisfied Girdle Buyer.* Or this about the high cost of supplies causing legislators to refuse to appropriate money for repairs on the chamber in which they met: *The Overhead Is Even Higher Than Congress' Weak Roof.* And now for a pun so bad that it's good: *It's Too Hot and Wet for the Wetter Man,* used over the daily weather story.

Alliteration can be legitimately used to enliven a headline. Copyreaders, however, do not employ it subtly for its melody as do poets; instead, they hit the reader in the face with the Peter-Piper-picked type of tongue twister. A story about two locksmiths locking themselves in a vault had the following heading: *Lock-Unlockers Locked in; Lack of Luck Licks Them.* And this for a feature about official stenographers of the U.S. senate asking for extra help to spell them from recording senatorial oratory: *Senate Stenos Seek Surcease from Speeches.* Most alliterative headlines are probably suggested by phrases in the story. In the first example, it was probably "locksmiths locked in a vault," and in the second, "senate stenographers," that made the copyreaders think of the tongue-twister headline.

Another device that any deskman can employ in turning out feature heads that will get by, though they may not be much as wit, is twisting a well-known proverb, saying, song refrain, or line of poetry to tell the story. *Where There's Cinders* was used as the eyebrow for a story about three trainmen being fined for violation of a city smoke ordinance. A story on the decline of communism in South America was headed: *Latins Decide Communism Isn't the South American Way*. A feature about the effort of "Lucky" Luciano, the former gang leader, to lead a law-abiding life in Italy was headed: *Luciano Toes the Straight and Narrow*. And a story of Margaret Truman's earning $60,000 for her concert appearances had: *Margaret Truman Hits High G—60 Grand*.

Occasionally a copyreader may break the monotony of counting out heads and finding shorter synonyms for "must" words in headlines by turning out a rhymed head. Stories for which verse is appropriate are seldom encountered; but when the story concerns a poet or poetry, the deskman is warranted in concocting a bit of doggerel for variety's sake. Thus a prisoner's poetic request to the pardon and parole board was headed: *Board Gets Prisoner's Rhyme, But He's Still Serving Time*. It's terrible, of course, but again headline readers are not harsh critics.

Apt figures of speech make a headline stand out from the routine summaries of the day's news. The imaginative deskman has available such devices as metaphors, similes, and symbols. A story about a town that overlooked a celebration for the anniversary of its founding was headed: *Cudahy Is Rubbing Its Eyes; Overslept Date of Jubilee*. Instead of saying routinely that the president had no comment, a deskman stated it neatly and differently: *Truman Buttons Lip on Super Bomb Plan*. And *Wings Clipped on Air Force* was a natural for a story about the enforced curtailment of air force activities in an economy program. Well-chosen imagery, provided it is not overdone, furnishes the copyreader with endless opportunities for varying and brightening his headlines.

Questions, exclamations, colloquialisms, quotations, direct address, and typographical novelties are other possibilities in the bag of tricks the veteran copyreader can reach into for feature headings. The question head: *Where's the New City Market? Well, It's Still Under Study*. The exclamation: *Big Steam Engine Went with Scrap; But Stolen? Oh, No!* A colloquialism: *'Hill Billy' Ain't No Name Fer a Sad Cowboy Singer*.

A quotation: *'I'm a Success, but I Dunno Why,' Says Gary Cooper*. Direct address: *Yes, Sir, Boys, You Really Saw What You Saw*. Typographical oddity: *Diners Find 'Devil's Coffee' Hotter Than—* and *This Landlord Pays Bonus FOR Babies*.

Occasionally a feature story will tickle the public fancy and newspapers across the land will break out in a rash of whimsical headlines. Such a one was the story about Grady the Cow that jumped through the door of a silo near Yukon, Oklahoma, and couldn't get out. The exhibits collected by the Associated Press included:

New York *World-Telegram:*
Cow in His Silo Places Farmer in Dell of a Fix
Kingsport (Tennessee) *Times:*
Swing Your Honey, Dosey Doe; Cow's in Silo—Door's Too Low
Dallas *Times-Herald:*
Cow Freed Slick 'as All Get Out' With Grease, Strong Push-Pull
Akron *Beacon Journal:*
Grease, Winch, Heave, Whoopee, Cow's Free!
Hartford *Times:*
Big Beef Gets Relief

In looking for angles from which to write a feature head, the copyreader should find his suggestions and hints in the nature and quality of the story itself. The headline should have the same flavor as the story. Especially should he avoid writing a flip head for a story about a tragic or pathetic circumstance. Often a straightforward summary is better than rhetorical pyrotechnics. For example, *Legless Boy Passes Scout Hike, Swim Test* is so moving in its simplicity that whatever the headline writer's skill, it could not heighten interest in the story.

HEADLINES FOR NONNEWS FEATURES

Formerly newspapers printed columns and regular features and departments under standing heads. Although these are still used today, probably such columns are more often given live headings—even the ponderous interpretive and analytical columns on the editorial page. The reason for this change is fairly obvious: persons not addicted to the column or department may be attracted to it by a brightly written, timely headline.

Today and Tomorrow
Problem of Chiang, Formosa Tied to Any Truce in Korea
By Walter Lippmann

Hollywood
★ ★ ★
Old Publicity Fibs Plague Stars
★ ★ ★
By HEDDA HOPPER

Showdown In Guatemala

BY CHARLES FERNANDEZ
Daily News Foreign Service

GUATEMALA CITY, Guatemala—A new government program for economic development of this Central American country within the framework of free enterprise appears headed for an early showdown.

It may well come in negotiations set for June on a new collective labor contract for the banana-producing United Fruit Co., backbone of the country's economy.

FERNANDEZ

Hard Water Not Harmful
BY WILLIAM BRADY, M.D.

for
WOMEN
of Today
Matrimony Hazards
Warning to Brides
And to Bridegrooms
Home Safety Rules
Booby-Trap Gadgets
—By Inez Robb

Fig. 23. Examples of headings for regular columns and features.

COMPOSING THE HEADLINE

On some newspapers the live headings for nonnews features are subject to some of the same rules as the headings for news stories—they have a subject, the verb is in the present tense, the content gives a summary or states the highlight of the article. On others the headline may be like the title of a magazine article or book.

Some of the ways of handling such columns typographically include the following:

1. Often a headline is written for the feature, and there is no indication that it is syndicated matter or that it appears regularly. The author's name appears as a conventional by-line.

2. The name of the column may be printed as an eyebrow above the heading for the article, with the author's name appearing as a by-line.

3. The name of the columnist, especially if well known, may appear alone as the column heading, or it may be given typographical emphasis in the eyebrow above the headline for the column.

4. The headline may be set off by rules and borders.

5. A thumbnail half-tone or line drawing may be printed regularly with the column, either as part of a standing caption or live heading or in the first or second paragraph.

6. A standing head may be used with a live heading.

In writing headlines for feature and syndicate material the copyreader should take the same precautions as he does for straight news. His headline must accurately state the columnist's or writer's point of view or conclusions. In trimming, special care must be taken not to change the writer's meaning. A headline that misses the point or distorts the meaning is not fair to writer or reader.

CHAPTER 13

Typography for the Deskman

COMPOSING ROOM MACHINERY

It is possible for a copyreader on a metropolitan newspaper to get along for a time with no knowledge of typography and printing, but his usefulness to his paper and his advancement to more responsible positions depend upon his learning something about type and what goes on in the back shop. In contrast, the deskman on a small newspaper comes into immediate contact with the mechanical department and cannot avoid learning something of the intricacies of setting type, placing it in the forms, and printing the paper.

The desk's duties include not only getting copy ready for the printers, writing headlines, and indicating where stories are to go in the paper, but also checking page proofs and the first printed copies for typographical details. The make-up editor is chiefly responsible for these mechanical matters, but everyone on the desk must be able to help out. Good typography and presswork depend upon a multitude of minor niceties; and one person, with only a few moments for checking, cannot observe them all.

The deskman should have almost a printer's knowledge of typography, although he doesn't need to be able to set type by hand or operate a typecasting machine or make up page forms at the stone. As a matter of fact, union rules are so strict as to forbid his picking up a piece of type or a slug and handing it to a printer. But the make-up editor must be able to tell whether the printer has done his job properly and direct attention to slipshod work when necessary. A good printing job requires painstaking effort, and a lazy or hurried printer may take advantage of an editorial department that doesn't know good craftsmanship from bad.

Until the latter part of the nineteenth century each letter of the alphabet and other characters such as punctuation marks were cast as separate pieces of type. Foundry type, as it is called, is set by hand. The type is kept in a shallow drawer known as a type case. When setting copy in type, printers set the words in a shallow metal holder called a composing stick. A stick holds about 2½ inches of type, and thus a "stickful," a term still used in print shops, means about 2½ inches. After foundry type has been

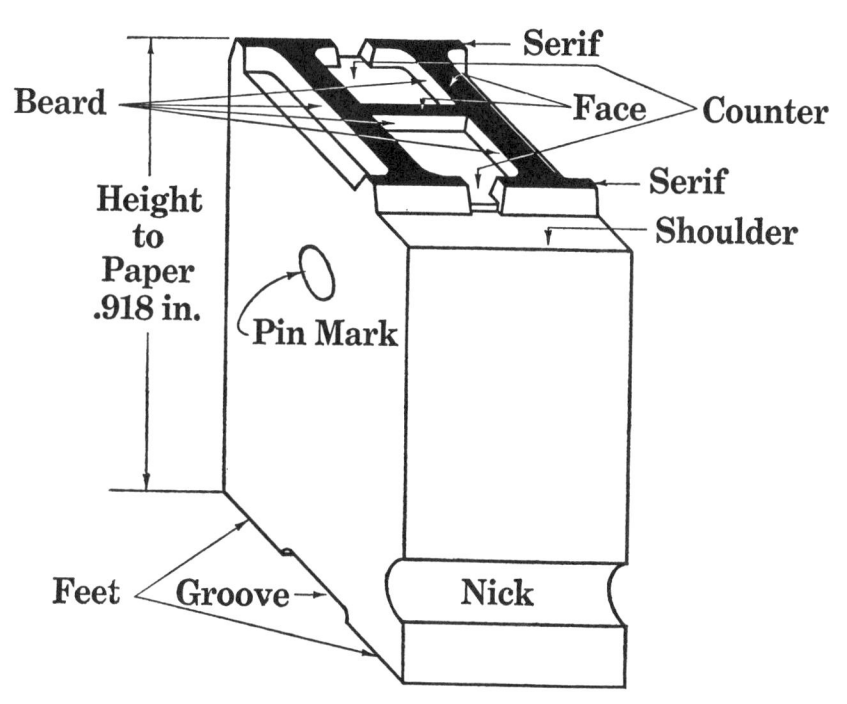

Fig. 24. The parts of a piece of type. (Courtesy, American Type Founders Sales Corporation.)

used, it is redistributed in the cases. Molded from a steel alloy, it can be used over and over again.

The printing surface of a letter is cast in relief on the surface of a metal block called the *body* or *shank* of the piece of type. The body of the type stands on two *feet* that are separated by an open space called the *groove*. The rounded depression at the end extending from the bottom of the letter is called the *nick*. The location of the nick or nicks varies according to the size and kind of type. The nicks of all the characters in a given size and kind of type line up. By feeling the nick, the printer can tell if the letter is right side up. The hole on the side of some pieces of type is the *pinmark*. It is left by the pin used to hold the mold together when the type is cast.

The printing surface of the letter is the *face*. The thin strokes of the face are *light elements* and the broad strokes are *heavy elements*. The endings of strokes marked by spurs or crosslines are *serifs*. The hollow areas between the elements or strokes are *counters*. The top part of the

Fig. 25. Printing procedures, No. I: The first stop after a news story leaves the copy desk is the composing room, where it is set in type on a typesetting machine. Here the operator is at the keyboard, setting from copy clamped to a metal holder. (Photo by Richard O. Byers.)

body on which the face rests is the *shoulder*, and the metal from the body to the face is the *neck* or *beard*.

After the development of the first mechanical type-casting machine in 1886 by Ottmar Mergenthaler, handset type for the main content of newspapers rapidly became outmoded. Today foundry type is used in newspaper offices for headlines and advertising display matter, but machines have been perfected for setting type of almost any size that a newspaper wants.

TYPOGRAPHY FOR THE DESKMAN

Type-casting machines impose the letter surfaces in one line on a single piece of metal called a slug. Machine typesetting is much faster than the hand composition of type, and the assembly of type in the forms is greatly facilitated. Modern newspapers would not have been possible without the invention of the type-casting machine, one of the most important developments in the history of printing. The slug produced by a type-casting machine is a lead alloy. It can be melted and the metal used over and over again.

Two types of slug-casting machines are in general use on American newspapers—the Linotype and the Intertype. They differ only in certain mechanical details. Although the deskman does not need a mechanical engineer's understanding of the operations of a composing machine, he should know what kinds and sizes of type are available on the machines in his newspaper's shop. This information will enable him to utilize the facilities economically and efficiently and will prevent his making unreasonable demands on the composing room.

In operation the slug-casting machines are extremely complex. The type face is cast from a mold called a matrix, a flat brass piece with the character or letter stamped on the side. The matrices are stored in a container called a magazine. When a letter on the keyboard is depressed, a matrix is released from the magazine and slides down to the line being assembled. The letters that make up a line of type are made to come out even on the right-hand side, or justified, by means of sliding metal spacebands. The full line of matrices and spacebands is brought against a mold into which hot metal is forced. The end result is a slug with the faces of type raised on its surface, ready for printing. While the matrices are being returned to the magazine to be used again, a new line of type is being cast.

Fig. 26. A Linotype matrix. Arrow at top points to the teeth which guide the matrix into the proper magazine channel when matrices are distributed after a line is cast. Lower arrows point to letter molds. (Mergenthaler Linotype Co. photo.)

By using interchangeable magazines, a single machine can set type of various sizes and styles. Most newspaper plants practice division of labor in using type-casting machines. Thus some machines are used exclusively for setting straight matter and others for setting headlines and advertisements.

The straight-matter machines usually have only one magazine; it contains one size of type in two faces—light and bold. This explains why

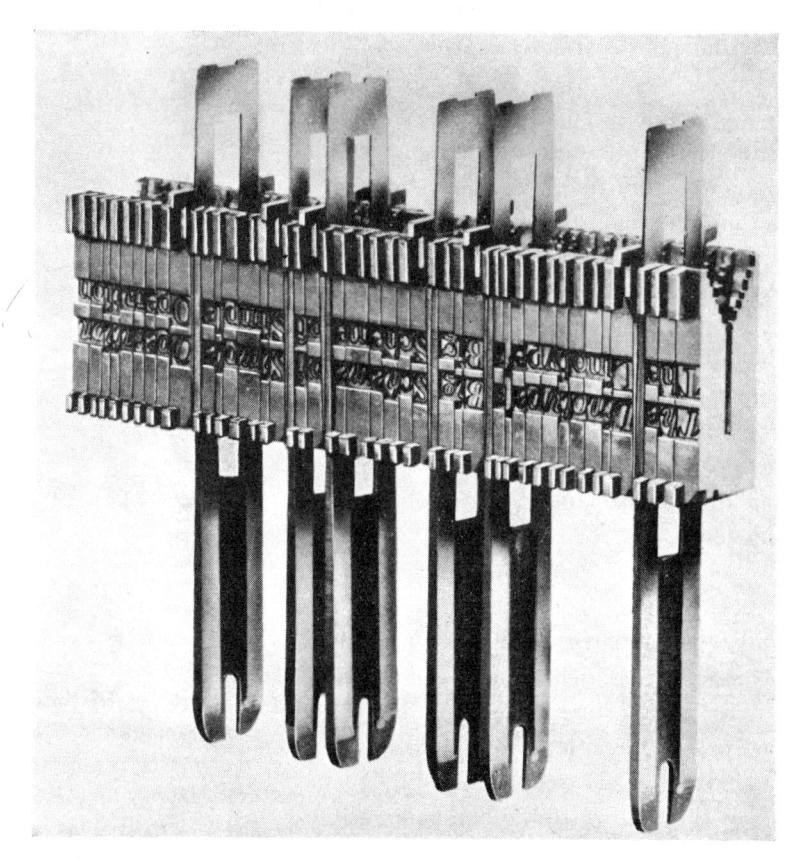

Fig. 27. A line of matrices with spacebands. The sliding spacebands push up automatically to justify or fill out the line. (Mergenthaler Linotype Co. photo.)

newspaper stylesheets call for quoting titles of books instead of setting them in italics. It is possible, of course, to obtain a magazine with an italic face, but newspapers find more use for the light and dark faces than for the italic.

TYPOGRAPHY FOR THE DESKMAN 183

The machines for setting headlines and advertisements are built to handle several interchangeable magazines. The magazines can be changed by turning a crank, and a great variety of sizes and styles of type is available.

If he works for a small newspaper, it is especially desirable for the news editor to know the shop's facilities for setting type. In a plant with only

Fig. 28. Lines of type cast on the Linotype. The letters which form the printing surface are raised above a metal slug. (Mergenthaler Linotype Co. photo.)

four machines, for example, three may be used for setting display matter. When the ad composition is about complete, one or more of the machines may be switched to straight matter, enabling the shop to catch up on news material quickly. But on days when the volume of advertising is heavy, the machines may be tied up with ad composition longer than on other days. Hence the desk may have difficulty in getting all the type needed for the news. The deskman takes care of this situation by trimming stories and by having as much material set the preceding day as is feasible. Often

Fig. 29. Placing display Ludlow type matrices by hand in the stick preparatory to casting a line of type. (Photo by Richard O. Byers.)

it is necessary to fill up the inside pages with time copy and picture mats.

Another kind of line-casting machine found in newspaper plants is used primarily for setting bigger type than is possible on regular Linotype and Intertype machines. The best known of these machines are the Ludlow Typograph and the All-Purpose-Linotype, or A-P-L. These machines require hand composition in assembling the matrices in the stick and inserting them in the machine which casts the slug or line of type.

Fig. 30. A close-up of the Ludlow composing stick with matrices being inserted. (Washington *Post* photo.)

Less often found in newspaper plants is the Monotype, a type-casting machine that casts individual letters and justifies them instead of casting a slug with the letters in relief. The Monotype operator sits at the keyboard and punches out on a narrow tape a pattern of holes that direct the selection of letters when run through the casting unit. The Monotype is used mostly in book and magazine publishing, but metropolitan newspapers use it in setting tables such as stock market quotations.

Fig. 31. Printing procedures, No. 2: After the story is set in type, a galley proof is pulled. The galley proof is checked for errors, and lines containing mistakes are reset. (Photo by Richard O. Byers.)

Fig. 32. Printing procedures, No. 3: Stories and advertisements in type are placed in a page-size steel framework called a chase. The printer works at a steel-topped table called a composing stone. The completed page when made up is called a form. (Photo by Richard O. Byers.)

Fig. 33. Printing procedures, No. 4: The completed form is placed in a matrix rolling machine. The matrix, or mat, is a cardboard-like sheet which takes the impression of the form when subjected to pressure. (Photo by Richard O. Byers.)

TYPOGRAPHY FOR THE DESKMAN

In many newspaper plants the Linotypes and Intertypes have teletypesetting devices attached to the keyboard. The keyboard is punched electrically by means of a perforated tape punched on another machine. The teletypesetter was developed as a means of lowering the cost of composition. Punching the tape requires no more skill than using a typewriter. Typists can be employed at lower salaries to operate the perforating unit than newspapers have to pay for expert typesetting machine operators.

Fig. 34. Printing procedures, No. 5: A curved stereotype plate is made from the mat when hot lead is poured around it in a casting box. Here the plate is being trimmed after casting. In the last step in the process, the stereotype is attached to the press for printing. (Photo by Richard O. Byers.)

One man can oversee as many as four typesetting machines equipped with teletypesetters.

In addition to machines for casting type, there is additional equipment for casting rules, borders, leads, and ornaments. These include the Elrod caster and the Monotype-Thompson type caster.

MEASUREMENT OF TYPE

Since 1887 in this country type foundries have employed a standard system of measuring type. Thus a type of a given size made by one foundry or appearing on one kind of casting machine will be exactly the same size as type of a different foundry or casting machine.

One measurement that need not concern the deskman is the height of the slug or piece of type from the face or printing surface to the bottom or feet. This is universally .918 of an inch. All presses are constructed to print from type of this height.

The measurement most important to know is what we generally think of when we refer to the size of type—the length from the edge of the shoulder at the top of the letter to the bottom edge of the shoulder. This length is expressed in *points*, a point equaling approximately $1/72$ of an inch. Type about an inch in length is 72-point type. Thirty-six-point type is approximately half an inch, 6-point type about one-twelfth inch, and so forth.

One mistake frequently made in measuring the size of type is using the depth of a printed letter. A printed letter by itself cannot be used to determine size. The reason is that all the letters do not take up the same space on the body. Tall letters like *l* and *t* extend above such letters as *a* and *e*. Letters like *g* and *y* extend below. The portion above is called the *ascender*; that below, the *descender*. Thus to determine the size of type from printed letters, the measurement must be made from the top of the highest ascender to the bottom of the lowest descender. A capital letter is likewise an inaccurate measure, because it does not occupy the entire shoulder. A space is left at the bottom for the descender in the letter *Q*. The printed characters in a newspaper are slightly smaller than their true size because of the shrinkage of the mat from which stereotype printing plates are cast. Printers and experienced deskmen, however, can usually guess the size of type from the printed characters.

Type used by newspapers ranges in size from 5½ point, the smallest, to 144 point. Larger type—cut from wood—is available but it is seldom used. Up to the 10-point size, type comes in whole and half-point measures—5½, 6, 6½, 7, 7½, 8, 8½, 9, 9½, and 10 point. Thereafter there are jumps of 1, 2, 4, 6, 12, and 24 points as follows: 11, 12, 14, 18, 24, 30, 36, 42, 48, 60, 72, 84, 96, 120, and 144 points. In-between sizes—16, 20, 28, and 34 points—are available. The 28- and 34-point sizes have come into rather popular use in recent years for headlines. The deskman should keep this range in mind as a guide in estimating type size. He brands himself as a novice if he asks the shop to set material in 33- or 61-point type.

The frequently used sizes of type are shown below:

This is 5-point type.
This is 5½-point type.
This is 6-point type.
This is 7-point type.
This is 9-point type.

This is 10-point type.
This is 12-point type.
This is 14-point type.
This is 18-point type.

This is 30-point type.

This is 36-point type.

This is 48 point

This is 60 poi

This is 72 p

Before the point system was adopted, types of different sizes were given names. Most of these names are now obsolete, but several have specific uses today. The old term *agate*, which approximates 5½-point type, is employed in measuring the depth of advertising. Fourteen agate lines equal approximately one inch. Most large newspapers quote their advertising rates by the agate line; smaller papers use the column inch. *Nonpareil*, or 6 point, is often used to express the thickness of leads and rules. *Pica*, or 12 point, is the standard measurement of width. We speak of a newspaper column, for example, as being 12 or 13 picas wide. The printer's ruler, or *line gauge*, is marked off in picas, nonpareils, and agates as well as in inches. The term *em* is often used instead of pica. The letter M is on a square body, and thus, in pica-sized type, the M is a pica in width as well as in length. A column is often loosely referred to as 12 ems wide instead of 12 picas or 12 pica ems wide.

In addition to its lengthwise measurement, type is also described by width. A type of a given design may come in five common widths—extra condensed, condensed, regular or medium, expanded, and extended. The regular or medium width is the width in which the body of the *M* is square.

Examples of five widths of type in the same face and same point size follow:

Cheltenham bold extra condensed.
Cheltenham bold condensed.
Cheltenham medium.
Cheltenham expanded
Cheltenham extended.

Variations in the width of the strokes in a letter give another characteristic of type—its weight. A lightface type is one in which the elements of the letter are thin; a boldface type, one in which the elements are thick. Some types come in four weights or faces—light, medium, bold, and extra bold or heavy. They are illustrated below:

18-point Airport light.
18-point Airport medium.
18-point Airport bold.
18-point Airport heavy.

CLASSIFICATION OF TYPE BY DESIGN

Typographers generally recognize six broad classifications of type: text, script, italic, roman, gothic, and square serif.

Text. The oldest of the type designs is of German origin. Text type, or black letter, is copied from the letters used by monks in writing ecclesiastical manuscripts. Text type is infrequently used today. It is found on calling cards, wedding announcements, and printed material where a religious flavor is desired. Its use in newspapers is confined to advertisements and to special occasions such as Christmas and Easter. Many newspaper nameplates are set in text type.

𝕮𝖍𝖎𝖘 𝖎𝖘 𝖙𝖊𝖝𝖙 𝖙𝖞𝖕𝖊.

Script. Script type is an imitation of handwriting. Most scripts slant to the right, but in some designs the type is vertical and in a few the slope goes to the left, as in backhand writing. Script is sometimes used in newspapers for feature headings and for standing headings for columns and departments. A variation of script type is known as *cursive*. In script type the letters are linked together as in handwriting; in cursive they are not joined.

This is script type.

This is cursive type.

Italic. Type letters that slope to the right are known as italic. They come in hundreds of faces. In fact, most perpendicular styles of type have a matching italic face. A variety of italic is *oblique*. Most newspaper people do not distinguish between the two, and the term oblique is seldom used. Italic letters may be slightly modified in form from the perpendicular letters. In the oblique faces the perpendicular letters are slanted to the right; there are no changes in the basic design. Italic and oblique faces are seldom used for long passages because they are hard to read. Newspapers use them chiefly for feature and contrasting heads.

This is Caslon italic.

This is Futura medium oblique.

Roman. The most widely used type design is roman. It is a vertical type characterized by serifs and different weights for the strokes of the letters. There are two main divisions of roman type—*old style* and *modern*.

In old-style roman there is less difference between the light and heavy elements of letters than in modern. The serifs of the old-style letters are slanting or curved, often appearing wedge-shaped, and the ball finials are oval. The modern faces have straight serifs right-angled to the main stroke of the letter, and the ball finials, as in the descender of the letter *y*, are round. Modern roman type is sharp and clean-cut in contrast with the blended-in serifs and strokes in old-style type. Some type faces have characteristics of both old-style and modern and are often referred to as transitional or mixed romans.

Roman faces are considered the most legible of all types and they are used in most printing today. Because of their great popularity, they are made in a great many different designs. Deskmen do not need to know all the roman faces by name, but they should be able to distinguish at least between old style and modern and should be familiar with the faces commonly used in headlines.

Caslon old-style roman.

Bodoni modern roman.

Gothic. Type designs with no serifs and with strokes of the same or approximately the same weight throughout are known in America as gothic. This term is not accurate, for the type has no characteristics in common with the literary and architectural uses of the word. Typographers prefer the term block letter or sans-serif.

Gothic faces, because of their boldness, have for a long time been popular headline types in this country, especially for all-cap top decks. Gothic was often used in extra condensed faces to give headline writers a large unit count. Gothic lost in popularity for a time when newspapers began changing to cap-and-lower-case roman faces for more legible headlines, but in recent years it has come back into favor because of the development of new designs with varying weight in the strokes. The latest designs have a "modern," streamlined appearance which, combined with their strength and blackness, has made them preferred for flush-left heads in cap and lower case.

This is Franklin gothic.

This is Erbar type.

Square Serif. A variation of the block-letter design is a group of faces with square or flat serifs. In this design the strokes of the serifs have the same weight as the main strokes in the letters. Though not widely popular, flat serif designs have been adopted recently by a number of newspapers for headlines.

Memphis bold square serif.

The designer of a type face or the foundry manufacturing it usually gives it a name to distinguish it from other designs. Type generally is made in a variety of sizes, widths, and weights. The term *family* is employed to designate all the type faces of a given design, and the term *series* to indicate the range in size. The complete identification of type includes its body size in points, the name of the family, the degree of blackness, the slope if italic, and the width, as in the following from the Linotype catalogue:

18-point Erbar bold condensed.
18-point Cheltenham bold italic.
18-point Franklin gothic.

Type is purchased in group lots known as *fonts*, which consist of complete sets of characters of one size and style. Thus a font of 14-point Bodoni bold includes all the letters of the alphabet in capitals and lower case, punctuation marks, figures, and miscellaneous characters known as sorts. Except in the larger sizes of type, the magazines of type-casting machines contain two-letter fonts—lightface or regular combined with boldface or with italic. A matrix or piece of type mixed in with a font of type of another size or design is called a *wrong font*. In proofreading it is designated by the abbreviation "wf."

LEADING, RULES, AND DASHES

The average person who looks at a newspaper page is conscious only of such prominent features as the size and design of the headline type and the pictures. He does not notice the important small details that help determine the overall attractiveness and readability of the newspaper. These include such elements as leading or the space between lines, rules of several kinds, and dashes.

Editors who don't know their way around the print shop have a tendency to leave these matters up to the printers. This is a mistake. The make-up editor especially must be cognizant in these matters if he wishes to get out a superior newspaper.

Leading. The space between lines of type is an important factor in legibility and appearance. Body type set solid—that is, without any space separating the lines of type—is hard to read because the outlines of the letters on a line tend to blend with those above and below. Moreover, in shifting his eyes from the end of a line back to the right to start a new line, the reader often makes a mistake and finds himself reading the same line again. The leading of body type, however, is not a regular concern of the desk, because newspapers set body type on a slug a half point or a point larger than the letters. Nor is the leading between the lines and elements of headlines often a problem, because proper spacing is provided for in standard practices for setting the heads.

Where the make-up editor must be alert is in seeing that the printers lead properly in justifying a page of type before locking the forms. In their hurry to get the forms ready, the printers may use excessive leading. Extra leads customarily are inserted between stories, above and below subheads and dashes, and between the lines of type at the beginning of stories.

If leading is done properly, the extra space is unnoticed. For justifying, printers should be asked to use 1-point leads, not 2 point or larger. Leading between paragraphs should be avoided, especially if the last line of a paragraph does not make a full line of type. John E. Allen recommended interlinear leading in the first paragraph of news stories. "Extra 1-point leading at the beginning of a story," he said, "usually helps the reader to 'get into it better' without seriously marring the appearance of the story or page."[1]

Column Rules and Cutoff Rules. The thin printed lines separating areas of type in newspapers are called rules. There are two types. Those running vertically are column rules; those running horizontally are cutoff rules. The rules used by newspapers are predominantly plain lines, as in the specimens below:

Hairline: ————————————————
2 point: ————————————————
6 point: ████████████████████████
Oxford: ════════════════════════
Parallel: ════════════════════════

Newspaper practice in the use of column rules is fairly well standardized. Such rules uniformly are thin, a 1-point line or hairline usually centered on a 6-point body. During World War II, however, many newspapers cast the rules on 3- and 4-point bodies to save space and conserve newsprint. Typographers recommend the 6-point body or even a wider one. Generous white space between columns of type makes the page more attractive and easier to read.

The copy desk must take the width of the column rule into consideration in establishing the count for headlines extending across more than one column and in ordering engravings more than one column wide. For example, if the columns are 12 picas wide and are separated by a nonpareil rule, the width of a two-column headline is not 24 picas but 24½ picas.

A few newspapers have dropped column rules in favor of white space between the columns of type. White space instead of column rules is especially popular for editorial and feature pages and magazine sections.

[1] John E. Allen, *Newspaper Designing*, Harper & Brothers, 1947, p. 98.

When rules are not used, the spacing between columns must be greater than 6 points; typographers recommend 10 points.

Publishers who have abandoned column rules argue that the page is more attractive. They point to the fact that in many newspapers the rules are broken and bent and that often they are not properly aligned.

One disadvantage of not using column rules is that horizontal or cutoff rules are often needed to indicate to the reader where the story descends from a multiple-column heading. Abandoning column rules usually means that the newspaper's make-up necessarily departs from conventional standards.

The cutoff rule most often used is a hairline, but some newspapers use a 2-point line in certain situations and a few an Oxford or a parallel rule. Cutoff rules have a variety of uses. They are employed to separate advertisements from news matter. They are placed under spread heads to separate them from stories not related to them and to direct the reader to the column in which the related story drops. Multiple-column headings "sunk" on the page (those that are not placed at the top) require a cutoff rule above them. Cutoff rules are put under the cutlines for engravings that are not placed within a story and above engravings that are not at the top of the page.

Stories squared off at the bottom and running across two or more columns require cutoff rules unless they come at the bottom of the page. Cutoff rules also are used under the shoulders of stories in which the lead is set two columns and the story drops in one column. Their use is conventional under continuation lines of stories jumped to another page and to separate "wrap-around" stories (those breaking from one column to an adjoining column) from other stories they touch.

Formerly most newspapers used small simple ornaments, such as a diamond-shaped figure, at the place where cutoff rules and column rules met. Although it gives a finished appearance, this practice has been abandoned in recent years because of the extra trouble and expense. Since cutoff rules are easily misplaced or omitted, they must be carefully checked by the make-up editor.

Dashes. The most commonly used dashes in newspapers are the 30-dash or end dash at the end of stories and the "jim" or "dinky" dash used to separate the elements in a headline or story.

Thirty-dashes customarily are plain 2-point lines either 6 or 8 ems in width. They should be heavier than the hairlines used in column and cutoff rules, but not bold enough to attract undue attention. A great many ornamental 30-dashes are available, but they are shunned by most newspapers. The theory is that 30-dashes should be black enough to notify the reader of the end of the story, but at the same time they should be unobtrusive so as not to distract him or destroy the typographical harmony of the page.

Jim dashes formerly were used to separate the decks in headlines, but most newspapers have abandoned them for this function; white space is left instead. Jim dashes are shorter than 30-dashes. The conventional lengths are 3 and 5 ems.

Newspapers still use a jim dash to separate elements in a story. For example, a story that is followed by a closely related article either with or without a headline takes a jim dash rather than a 30-dash. The story under the jim dash is called "dash matter." Jim dashes or small ornamental dashes such as star dashes are frequently used to separate elements in columns, to break up long editorial and feature articles, and to separate items in columns of personals and society notes.

CHAPTER 14

Newspaper Use of Type

TREND TOWARD LARGER BODY TYPE

Newspaper publishing practices are so rigidly fixed that an editor can do little toward changing his mass-manufactured product to make it easier to read. Most persons agree that the conventional eight-column publication is unwieldy and that the body type is too small for legibility. Yet little can be done about it.

The only major change in format in this century has been the tabloid or half-size newspaper, and it is found chiefly in cities. The tabloid has not been popular in small towns. There are probably two reasons for this. Readers are accustomed to a big newspaper, and the tabloid is associated in their minds with sensationalism.

An editor of almost any newspaper must get out a newspaper under these limitations:

1. A narrow column of 12 or 12½ picas (13 on some weeklies). He cannot increase the width, because all advertising mats and plates for newspaper use are designed for a 12-pica column.

2. A small body-type face. The size of the type cannot be materially increased for legibility, because a bigger face would be unattractive and awkward in the narrow column.

3. A poor grade of paper. Newsprint costs are so high that no newspaper could afford better stock even if it could be obtained in sufficient quantities.

4. A relatively poor quality of printing. To get out a daily newspaper, quality must be sacrificed for speed. This means high-speed rotary presses, with consequent loss of sharpness of impression when stereotype plates are made.

In recent years the tendency has been for newspapers to shift to larger body types. For instance, the photographic process by which newspapers were published during the 22-month printers' strike in Chicago involved the use of larger type. Since readers had become accustomed to this size, two of the papers shifted to bigger type when the strike was settled in 1949 and regular production processes could be used again. The *Daily News*, which before the strike used 7½ point on an 8-point body, and the *Sun-Times*, which used 7½ point on an 8½-point body, both changed to 8 point on a 9-point body. The *Herald-American*, which had switched to 9 point just before the strike, continued using it on a 9½-point body. Dozens of other newspapers throughout the country have recently changed their type from 7 or 7½ point to 8 point or larger.

One result of the use of larger type sizes is the need for more careful editing on the copy desk. To cover the news as completely and comprehensively as they did before they adopted the larger type, newspapers must devote more attention to eliminating verbiage and unnecessary minor details in stories.

Suppose, for example, a newspaper had been using 7-point Excelsior on a 7½-point body. It can get approximately 1260 words in a 12-pica, standard-length column. If the type is changed to 8 point on a 9-point body, the number of words is lowered to about 1000. This is a loss of 260 words a column, or 2080 a page.

When the copy desk has material set to a wider measure than the standard one-column width, the size of the type must be increased in proportion if it is to be easily read. Two-column leads and editorials are customarily set in 10 point. Column-and-a-half matter, the measure used by many newspapers for editorials, can be set in 9, 9½, or 10 point.

To conserve space, newspapers occasionally set certain material in 5½ or 6 point. Such material includes long lists of names, stock market reports, vital statistics, and box scores of sports events.

Italic type, which tests show is less legible than roman type and hence a cause of eyestrain, is seldom used for body type. Some newspapers use it as a contrasting type for cutlines and editor's notes. But since most straight-matter type-casting machines are not equipped with italic fonts, the regular roman boldface type is more often used for this purpose.

HEADLINE TYPE FACES

Though there are hundreds of type faces, comparatively few are used for headlines. It is fairly important for the deskman to be familiar with them. The headline, more than any other single factor, gives the newspaper its character. A newspaper that wants to be known as a dignified, careful purveyor of the news cannot achieve that reputation if it chooses a gaudy display type; nor can a publication that seeks to be known as a lively, impertinent sheet win its way with conservative typography.

Fashions in typography change—slowly, to be sure, but to the extent that the typographical historian can note them. Up to twenty-five years ago, the most popular face for top-deck heads in this country was the all-cap gothic. There were several reasons for this: Lacking serifs, it did not take up as much space as roman type; since foundry type was used for headlines, gothic was more durable than roman because there were no serifs to break off; it attracted attention by its blackness. Following the example of the New York *Herald Tribune* in the late 1920's, many newspapers changed to the more attractive and more legible roman cap and lower case. In recent years, with the introduction of new sans-serif designs, the swing has been toward gothic in cap and lower case.

A survey of daily newspaper headline faces made by the author in 1950 showed that approximately 40 percent used gothic cap and lower case for their main news headings and approximately 33 percent used roman cap and lower case. All-cap gothic faces were used by 7 percent; all-cap roman, by 2 percent; and cap-and-lower-case flat serifs by 5 percent.

Thirteen percent of the papers surveyed used mixed faces. These included all-cap gothic and cap and lower case for contrasting heads; gothic with roman for contrasting heads, and vice versa; and mixtures of the two with no apparent design.

Flush-left headline patterns, which became popular during the 1930's, are the overwhelming favorite of newspapers, according to the survey, with 78 percent using this style and 22 percent using dropline and other patterns. The percentages are the same for cap-and-lower-case headings and against all-cap top decks—78 and 22 percent.

Similar findings were reported by N. W. Ayer & Son, Inc., in a study of entries in the firm's annual newspaper typography competition in 1948. Of the 913 entries, 644, or about 70 percent, used cap-and-lower-case letters. Sans-serif faces were found in 389 entries, and a "predominant" use of roman faces in 485 entries. Forty-two of the entries employed flat-serif types. The conclusion of the judges for the Ayer awards was that the change-over to new faces and the flush-left patterns had resulted in "cleaner, more legible, better-balanced newspapers."

Roman Faces. Even though the use of roman headline faces has declined in the last few years, roman still has certain advantages over gothic. The chief one is its greater legibility. The serifs and the variations in the weight of the elements of the letters give each character of the alphabet a distinctive, easy-to-read pattern, especially in the capitals. The old-fashioned all-cap gothic headlines were extremely hard to read, especially in their extra condensed versions. Once newspaper editors gave more attention to readability of type than to blackness and prominence they preferred the roman faces.

Among the old-style roman faces, the most commonly used are Caslon and Cheltenham, although Cloister, Garamond, and Goudy have also been popular. They are illustrated below.

This is 18-point Caslon bold condensed.
This is 18-point Cheltenham bold condensed.
This is 18-point Cloister bold.
This is 18-point Garamond.
This is 18-point Goudy.

Probably the most popular of all modern roman faces is Bodoni. Century is also often used; Caledonia is employed less frequently.

This is 12-point Bodoni bold.
This is 12-point Century bold.
This is 12-point Caledonia.

Gothic Faces. The old-time black, squared-off gothic faces told the news with considerable authority, but their unattractive appearance caused them to be abandoned except for banner headlines. Railroad gothic condensed, which comes only in capitals, is still used for banners by newspapers which otherwise have streamlined their typography. A larger-size Railroad gothic is sometimes called "studhorse" gothic because of its use in farm sales bills. Another old-time gothic is Franklin gothic, still used frequently for banners but less often for smaller headings. The newer sans-serif faces have become immensely popular. In an era of "modernism" in architecture and furnishings and of streamlining in automobiles and airplanes, the sans-serifs because of their simplicity of design seem more appropriate than the roman-style faces.

This is 18-point Franklin gothic condensed.
This is 18-point Franklin gothic.

This is 18-point Erbar bold condensed.

This is 18-point Lydian.

This is 18-point Futura bold.

This is 18-point Vogue bold.

Flat-Serif Faces. The flat-serif faces are new designs that have not yet won wide popularity; they are probably used by no more than 50 or 60 daily newspapers in the country. The three best-known designs are Memphis, Karnak, and Stymie.

This is 18-point Memphis bold.

This is 18-point Stymie light.

This is 18-point Karnak.

HEADLINE PATTERNS

The selection of headline patterns, type designs, and type sizes has been simplified in recent years by the acceptance of a few rules suggested by typographers. These can be summed up as follows:

1. Use cap-and-lower-case type for all headings. This style is easier to read than all-cap heads, and the unit count is greater, allowing more freedom in writing them.

2. Reduce the number of decks to one or two. Multiple-deck heads take up too much space, and they require valuable time on the copy desk for writing and in the composing room for setting. Readership studies indicate a tendency to skip the bottom decks and jump immediately into the story. In his surveys of small-town dailies and weeklies, George H. Miller of Butler University, Indianapolis, found that many readers bypassed the headlines entirely, the stories having a higher readership than the headlines.

3. Keep the number of lines in a deck down to two or three, depending on the pattern and the position on the page. Decks with more than three lines are unattractive and hard to read.

4. Set all headings flush to the left. They require less time from the deskman than do other patterns and permit him to concentrate on content rather than on the count. They also save time in the composing room,

since compositors do not have to spend time spacing to make the lines balance.

5. Keep all headings within one family or two closely related families, and limit the variations in size to a few. A mixture of gothic and roman types, for example, should be avoided.

To illustrate the variety that can be obtained from a few faces and sizes, John E. Allen in his *Newspaper Designing* showed 25 different single- and double-column heads that can be set up with six fonts of type—more than enough for the most frequently used headlines for a newspaper.

Allen used single-letter fonts of 34-point Erbar medium condensed, 24-point Erbar medium condensed, and 30-point Metromedium No. 2. His two-letter fonts in the vertical and italic faces were 24-point Metromedium No. 2, 18-point Metromedium No. 2, and 14-point Metromedium No. 2.

Albert A. Sutton prepared a similar example for his *Design and Makeup of the Newspaper*. He used one-letter display matrices of 30-point Bodoni bold condensed, 24-point Bodoni bold condensed, and 30-point Bodoni bold, and two-letter matrices of 18-point Bodoni bold and Bodoni bold italic and 14-point Bodoni bold and Bodoni bold italic.

The majority of winners in the country's two biggest typography competitions—one conducted by the Inland Daily Press Association and the other by N. W. Ayer & Son, Inc.—follow the foregoing rules in the main. The chief exceptions are the New York *Times* and the New York *Herald Tribune*, both frequent winners of the Ayer trophy. The *Times* uses multiple-deck heads, all-cap top decks, and stepline and inverted-pyramid patterns. The *Herald Tribune* uses full-line top decks and hanging-indention secondary decks.

HEADLINE TYPE SIZES

For purposes of discussion on the basis of typography and size, headlines needed for a newspaper may be divided into the following classifications: (1) headings for shorts and fillers; (2) subordinate headings for two-, three-, and four-paragraph stories; (3) secondary headings for stories not important enough for top-of-the-column position but big enough to stand out from other stories on the page; (4) top single-column headings for major news stories; (5) spread heads; (6) banners; (7) contrast heads; (8) special feature and departmental heads.

Shorts and Fillers. Usually one paragraph in length, shorts and fillers are important for filling up holes in a page. The headline schedules of many newspapers specify for them a single-line heading, centered or flush left, set in boldface body type—in other words, in 7-, 7½-, or 8-point boldface. If the item runs over five lines, a 10-, 12-, or 14-point type may be used, preferably in a single-line head.

Political Signs OK On State Vehicles

SPRINGFIELD, Ill. — (*AP*) — A bill to bar display of political campaign stickers on state-owned vehicles was killed by the Illinois House.

The house also defeated a measure calling for one automobile license plate instead of the usual two, if a shortage of steel or aluminum should develop.

4 Sentenced as Spies

Belgrade, Yugoslavia, June 1— (AP)—A Yugoslav army captain, his wife and two Czech nationals were sentenced to prison at hard labor today on charges of spying for Czechoslovakia on orders from their "Moscow masters."

Fog Grounds Planes in N. Y.

NEW YORK, May 28 (*AP*).—Fog halted air operations at Idlewild Airport this morning and kept all but a few planes from taking off at LaGuardia Field.

Port Playground Fund Boosted

Contributions totaling $45 were received last week for the Port Matilda community playground fund, Parent Teacher Association officials announced today.

Additional contributions were from the Tyrone Elks Lodge, $25; Port Matilda Garden Club, $5; and Port Matilda Rebekah Lodge, $5.

Fire Auxiliary To Meet

The Auxiliary to the Boalsburg Fire Company will meet at the fire hall today at 8 p.m. with marching unit practice scheduled immediately after. All members are urged to attend.

BIG HOLE, NO GEMS

MONTEVIDEO, Uruguay, May 27—(UP)—Week-long digging for a fortune in jewels and gold which a former California woman believes is buried in a cemetery here today had produced only a big hole in the ground.

Fig. 35. Boldface type ranging from body to 14 point is used for heads on one- and two-paragraph filler stories.

Subordinate Heads. Headings for minor stories of two to four paragraphs (five if the paragraphs are short) range usually from 12 to 24 point. The pattern may be a two-line head for shorter items, and a three-line head for longer items. A two-paragraph story could use a two-line 12- or 14-point heading; longer stories, a two-line 18- or 24-point heading or a three-line 14- or 18-point heading. The tendency in recent years has been to use larger headings to give the bottom of the page a lively appearance. The use of too many such stories in make-up may give a spotty,

Air Raid Test Alert Planned Here Feb. 10

Economy League Reports on County

U. S. Bans Imports Of Soviet CrabMeat

Vinita Man Listed As State's Eleventh Korean War Loss

Charges It Is Produced by Slave Labor

Landon Asks U.N. Blockade of China

Six Air Force Men Die In Fiery Crash of B-29

BAN PLEASES MAE WEST

Five Parachute to Safety Before Plane Falls in Texas.

Actress Cheered by Publicity Value of Atlanta Censorship

Fig. 36. Typical subordinate headings from 12- to 24-point type used for short items.

unattractive appearance. Newspapers that use dropline or full-line headings use for these minor stories a crossline of 12, 14, or 18 point, with an inverted-pyramid, two-line deck of 8- or 10-point boldface.

Secondary Heads. Two or three headlines are needed for properly displaying and grading longer items on the front and inside pages. Such stories seldom are shorter than five paragraphs; they may run as long as ten paragraphs.

A fundamental principle of conventional newspaper make-up is that the largest headlines appear at the top of the page, and come down in size to smaller heads below the fold and at the bottom of the page. Thus, in planning a headline schedule, the headings for shorts and fillers will be smaller than those for subordinate stories; those for subordinate stories smaller than those for secondary stories, and those for secondary stories smaller than those for top-of-the-column stories. The proper gradations can be obtained by the size of type used or the number of decks and lines in the heads.

The display decks of secondary headings may be in 24, 28, 30, 34, or even 36 point if a condensed type face is used. For stories above the fold,

500-Lap Midget Race Due in City

Marathon Slated At Fairgrounds

HUGE GARAGE PLAN BACKED BY MAYOR

Moses Seen as 'Czar' in Vast Traffic Control Program Tied to City Defense

Physician 'Pays' Patients, Then Takes His Life

Attlee Warns Britain to Arm Against Russia

In His Stiffest Attack on Stalin, He Says Soviets Exceed Old Imperialism

Businessmen Pledge Support Of Controls

Call for Consumer Cooperation; Predict Some Shortages

Hold Five Men In Theft Ring

Waupaca, Outagamie County Officials Continue Investigation

THAWING OF COAL PRICES IN SIGHT

Boost Expected as Miners' Pay Hike Is Cleared

Ship Fire Rages In Hurricane

Crippled Vessel Airs Desperate Aid Plea

Fig. 37. In these examples of secondary headlines the type ranges from 24 to 36 point.

the larger sizes are used. The size of the second decks for these depends upon the size used for the top decks, the range usually extending from 12 to 18 point.

If the top-of-the-column heading consists of three lines with a deck of three or four lines, the above-the-fold secondary heading may be of the same type as the top-of-column head, with the number of lines in the top deck reduced to two. The below-the-fold heading may drop the deck entirely, but this is not recommended. A single-column heading toward the bottom of the page in the same type size as the top-of-the-column heading will be too prominent, even without a second deck.

A more attractive arrangement results from using a smaller size of type than the top-of-the-column heading for the above-the-fold secondary heading, and reducing the size for the longer stories below the fold.

Top-Column Headings. Stories at the top of the page require emphatic headlines. Top headings formerly consisted of multiple decks, but today the majority of newspapers have reduced them to two. A number of the more conservative papers that still use more than two decks follow the plan of the New York *Times*, whose top-page heads consist of a three-line step deck, an inverted pyramid second deck, a crossline, and an inverted-pyramid bottom deck. A few newspapers, among them the St. Louis *Post-Dispatch*, use a four-line heading, with either an inverted-pyramid or a hanging-indention deck.

But by far the greater number of papers, and practically all that use the flush-left pattern, have a top deck of three lines and a second deck of three or four lines. The first deck should be 30-, 34-, or 36-point type. The size of type for the second deck depends upon the size used in the top deck. It should not be too big and black, or it will detract from the effectiveness of the top deck; but if it is too small, it will be lost under the bigger and bolder type. In the flush-left pattern, the second deck should be indented.

Spread Heads. A great variety of practices are found in the use of spread and blanket heads. These heads range from two to five or six columns. Many newspapers use them instead of banners to give stories an emphatic display; the banners are reserved for stories of transcendent importance.

One of the great advantages of the two- or three-column spread head over the banner is that if slated for the right-hand side of the page, it can be moved to the left side in case a more important story breaks and it is necessary to change the front-page display of stories.

Spread headings for outside-column display on the front page range

Food Price Rise Bares OPS Fetters

TRUMAN WILL ASK TAX HIKES TO COVER COSTS

To Present Pay-as-You-Go Policy Friday; Sales Levy Possible

Dewey Asks Defense Unit Above Laws

Would Give It Right To Seize Property

Also to Ration Foods, Conscript Man Power; Bill Ready Tomorrow

Greatest Allied Tank Attacks Smash Reds

Bayonet Assaults Mop Up Enemy

Senate Passes Bill Expanding Social Security

Truman Expected To Sign Measure Upping Pay Roll Tax

Allied Forces Attack Reds With Bayonets

Fail To Smash The Unyielding Resistance Of Dug-In Chinese

Fig. 38. Type in the first deck of top-of-the-column headlines ranges from 30 to 36 point.

in size from 36 to 72 point, depending on the number of lines they have and their width in columns. A two-line, two-column 36-point head is likely to be too weak for an important outside position, but in three lines it would be sufficiently bold for the story. On the other hand, 48 point in three lines might be too large for a two-column heading but just right if only two lines were used. Three lines of 48 point, however, could be used for a three-column spread heading. For spread headings four or more columns wide in 60 or 72 point, the best effects are obtained if the headings are kept to two lines. One-line spread headings are used infrequently for outside columns.

Read-outs or second decks for spread headings have a great variety of forms. If the spread head extends over several columns and the type is big enough, the single-column hanger may be the regular top-of-the-column heading. Some newspapers use only the top deck for the hanger, and others use only the second deck. Many employ a different size of type than that used in top-of-the-column heads. The read-outs are not restricted to one column. Many are two-column, and some are three or even four columns for the wider spreads in important stories. Two or more related stories may be played under a spread head; this headline offers almost innumerable opportunities for typographical treatment. After experimenting with hangers for spread heads, most make-up editors generally settle upon a few that can be utilized for almost any make-up.

Two- and three-column and sometimes longer headlines employed to give variety to make-up are not properly spread heads. They are not major display headings; hence they can be placed below the fold and at the bottom of the page as well as at the top. They usually are set in smaller type than the spread headings.

Two-column headings, with or without decks, can run from 24- to 36-point type; three- and four-column headings, from 30 to 42 point. Smaller type is preferable for stories at the bottom of the page, in order not to contrast too sharply with the subordinate and secondary headlines below the fold. If a story is worth big display type, a place should be found for it in the positions of emphasis at the top of the page.

Banners. Many newspapers use banners every day regardless of the importance of the stories. This practice, however, is followed chiefly by metropolitan newspapers on the theory that banners help street and newsstand sales. Of late years, especially in smaller cities, spread headings have become more popular for display purposes, banners being reserved for stories of extraordinary importance.

In using banners, there should be no timidity in selecting the size of type. The banner should be big, bold, and blatant, or it should not be used at all. Consequently, although it is not an especially attractive type, Railroad gothic in 72, 96, or 120 point is the most popular face for eight-column streamers. Most banners have a single line of type, but for truly big stories two lines may be used. Even newspapers which use cap-and-lower-case headings often set banners in all-caps.

LABOR CHIEFS BATTLE WAGE FREEZE
Rail Men Obeying 'Work Or Be Fired' Order

TAFT URGES 1-9 U.S. TROOP RATIO IN EUROPE
Easing Of Freeze To Raise Some Prices

QUIT STALLING, U. S. TELLS U. N.
Girl Typist Slashed by 'Copter Blades

Truman Requests $71 Billion Budget, Increase of $16.5 Billion in Taxes

New A-Bomb Is Exploded
Hold-the-Line Freeze of Prices and Wages Is On

Fig. 39. Railroad gothic is the most popular type for banners. Two banner lines require the use of contrasting type.

Two or three banners in contrasting types may be run simultaneously. Newspaper practices vary. The major banner may be in all-caps, with the secondary in caps and lower case or in italic. When three banners are used, one line usually is in all-caps, one line in caps and lower case, and the third line in italics. The smaller or contrasting line for a two-banner head may be put above or below the bolder line.

Since the play position on page 1 is the right-hand side, the story under a banner should drop from or read out into the last column or columns. The hanger deck for a banner may be one or more columns. When two banners are used, the story for the smaller line should drop into the first column.

Inside banners or "lines" are printed in smaller type than those for the front page. The sizes range from 36 to 60 point. Since advertising is customarily pyramided from the right, the stories dropping from inside banners are placed in the first column. If the advertising is arranged so as to form a "well" for the news matter, it is better to avoid a banner for the page.

Contrast Heads. In addition to the type faces used in regular news heads, a headline schedule should include several heads in contrasting type. They add to the newspaper's attractiveness typographically by the eye appeal of variety and they give the publication a livelier appearance.

Make-up editors avoid "tombstoning" heads (two headlines of the same kind and size of type that align with each other in adjoining columns) and "bumping" heads (two headlines of the same kind and size of type that touch each other in adjoining columns). These unattractive juxtapositions can be prevented by using contrast heads.

Many newspapers use an italic type of the same family as the news heads for their contrast heads. Satisfactory contrasts, however, can be obtained with vertical types that are heavier or lighter and wider or narrower than the news heads. Some papers that use all-caps in their regular news display decks use the same type in caps and lower case for contrast heads.

There should be contrast heads for all the divisions of regular news headings except the filler captions. Contrast heads are needed for subordinate and secondary headings, top-of-the-column headings, spread headings, and banners.

Additional methods of securing variety in typography include the use of boxed stories, boxed headlines, and the small overline or "eyebrow" above the regular headline.

Feature and Departmental Heads. Regular features such as signed columns, advice to the lovelorn, homemaking hints, and etiquette are often set off from other material in a newspaper by standing heads that employ a variety of typographical devices. These include script type, boxed captions, the author's photograph worked into the caption design, cartoons, and hand-drawn letters.

In recent years, however, newspapers have tended to avoid standing heads, because they lose their attention-attracting ability if used monotonously day after day. They are being replaced by "live" headings that are changed daily and are based on the content of the current article or column. So that regular readers can easily find their favorite columnist, commentator, or critic, the live headings are usually combined in some way with a standing head. For example, the name of the column or author may appear as an overline above the live heading.

Special typographical devices sometimes are used for departmental pages and sections, such as society, drama, music, sports, editorial, and financial. For society and women's pages many newspapers adopt a type face entirely different from that used in the rest of the paper. A lighter and more "feminine" face is used—Garamond, Goudy, Caslon, or the lightface versions of the sans-serif types.

TYPOGRAPHICAL BRIGHTENERS

Early newspapers in this country, with their long columns of small print unbroken by headlines or photographs, appear dull to modern readers. Many present-day editors feel, however, that even headlines and pictures do not give enough variety, and they employ various devices to avoid unbroken stretches of gray print in long articles.

One of the most common and most effective methods of making long stories look less formidable is the use of subheads. Since eye appeal is the chief justification for subheads, they should not be placed too close together, nor should they come at irregular intervals. A subhead every three or four inches is desirable. A single subhead should be avoided. Hence, a story should be at least six paragraphs long to warrant subheads—one at the end of the second paragraph and another at the end of the fourth.

To save time and trouble in the shop, subheads are commonly set in boldface or all-caps of the body type. They would be very expensive if the operator had to change magazines to set them or if they had to be set on another machine like display headings. The most popular form of the subhead is set in boldface upper and lower case centered. The line should not be full, for the chief value of the subhead is the white space at the beginning and end of the line. Next in popularity perhaps is the boldface cap-and-lower-case subhead set flush left. Since this form allows no white space at the beginning of the line, extra leading above and below makes this subhead more effective. All-cap subheads either centered or flush left, and two-line subheads in either all-caps or caps and lower case, are other varieties.

Instead of using subheads, a few newspapers set the first line of some of the paragraphs in the body of the story in boldface; sometimes the first

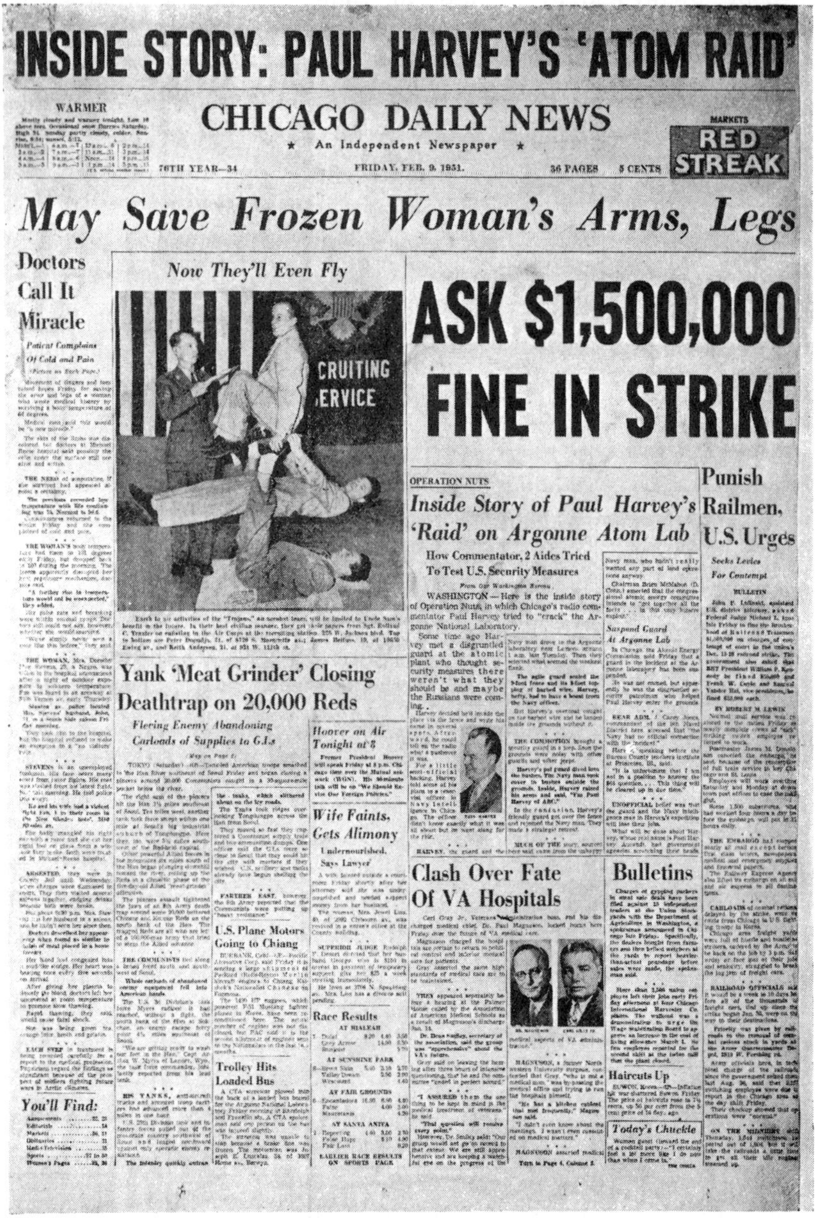

INSIDE STORY: PAUL HARVEY'S 'ATOM RAID'

WARMER

CHICAGO DAILY NEWS

★ An Independent Newspaper ★

76TH YEAR—34 FRIDAY, FEB. 9, 1951. 36 PAGES 5 CENTS

MARKETS RED STREAK

May Save Frozen Woman's Arms, Legs

Doctors Call It Miracle

Patient Complains Of Cold and Pain

Now They'll Even Fly

CRUITING ERVICE

ASK $1,500,000 FINE IN STRIKE

OPERATION NUTS

Inside Story of Paul Harvey's 'Raid' on Argonne Atom Lab

How Commentator, 2 Aides Tried To Test U.S. Security Measures

WASHINGTON—Here is the inside story of Operation Nuts, in which Chicago's radio commentator Paul Harvey tried to "crack" the Argonne National Laboratory.

Punish Railmen, U.S. Urges

Seeks Levies For Contempt

Yank 'Meat Grinder' Closing Deathtrap on 20,000 Reds

Fleeing Enemy Abandoning Carloads of Supplies to G.I.s

Hoover on Air Tonight at 8

Wife Faints, Gets Alimony

U.S. Plane Motors Going to Chiang

Trolley Hits Loaded Bus

Race Results

Clash Over Fate Of VA Hospitals

Bulletins

Haircuts Up

Today's Chuckle

You'll Find:

Fig. 40. The Chicago *Daily News* achieves a lively front page by typographical brighteners that break up stretches of body type. (Reproduced by permission of the Chicago *Daily News*.)

two or three words are in capitals. If this device is used, the boldface line should be separated from the preceding paragraph by extra leading, a three-star dash, or some other ornament. This device is especially appropriate for feature stories, editorials, and columns. News stories can seldom be broken up this way in natural divisions.

Large initial letters are used to break up masses of type in longer articles and editorials, but seldom in news stories. In using initials, two or three lines of type must be indented and the slug sawed out for the

Axford Asks Pledges

Herbert Axford, campus chest chairman, yesterday asked all students not yet contacted by solicitors, to sign a pledge card in the PSCA office, 304 Old Main.

Members of Alpha Phi Omega, national service honorary, canvassed town twice but were unable to contact everyone. Students who do not have a pledge card, but want to donate, should sign their names and matriculation numbers on paper and present them at the PSCA office before Friday. Students are warned not to give a donation unless they are given a receipt.

The drive ends Friday, and $8,000 has been given. The goal of the drive is $14,000.

Kind to Animal Gesture Costly

CARLISLE, Pa., Jan. 29 (P) —Cloyd W. George, of Carlisle, will think twice before he does another good deed for a rabbit. The last one cost him $25.

Game Warden Homer Thrush ordered George to pay a $25 fine on a charge of disturbing a trap set by an officer of the State Game Commission. Thrush said George admitted releasing a hare from a rabbit trap set under Game Commission supervision. George paid the fine.

Fig. 41. Boxes are more attractive when there is ample white space. Compare the crowded appearance of the box on the left with the more inviting appearance of the one on the right.

insertion of the oversize initial. Since this is costly, newspapers use initials sparingly.

Other devices for breaking up type masses involve the indention of single paragraphs and the use of boldface type for whole paragraphs. Lead paragraphs may be emphasized by being set in type larger than body type. In wire stories or articles sent in by a newspaper's own correspondents, the place name in the date line usually is set in capitals.

Setting by-lines in boldface, all caps, or caps and small caps—whatever style seems most pleasing to the editor—is another method of giving desirable typographical variety to the page.

One of the best ways of brightening the page and giving special emphasis to stories is to use boxes and boxed effects. Complete stories can be set in boxes, and boxes can also be used effectively for news summaries, bulletins, indexes, weather reports, inserts in long stories, and notices or announcements to the public. A box effect is obtained by indenting a story but omitting the borders, or having them only at the top and bottom.

A single-column box or box effect is suitable only for shorter stories. One of the principal faults with boxes is crowding them with material and headings. Another is using an inappropriate border. The single-column box should be oblong rather than square. The reading matter should be indented on both sides to give white space—6 to 9 points on each side—and there should be ample leading in the head. Borders should not be obtrusive; hence heavy borders and ornamental ones should be avoided. A 2-point rule is perhaps the most popular rule for newspapers. An Oxford rule with the outer line 2 points and the inner line 1 point, and a parallel rule of two 1-point lines, are also attractive.

PRINCIPLES OF GOOD TYPOGRAPHY

We look upon printing as a craft; yet it is also an art, especially in its typographical elements. Because of the speed with which it is carried on, newspaper publishing does not call for the finest in printing. Yet the newspaper should be both pleasing to the eye and easy to read.

A survey of recent books and other writings on newspaper design and make-up shows that students of the subject agree fairly well upon the following principles set forth under legibility, simplicity, and attractiveness.

Legibility. Lines set entirely in capital letters are more difficult to read than lines set in capitals and lower case.

Sans-serif or gothic faces are more difficult to read than faces with serifs.

Vertical type faces are easier to read than italic.

Faces of medium or normal width are easier to read than expanded or condensed faces.

Type lines are easier to read when leaded, but too much leading makes for difficult reading.

Words without adequate space between them on the line are hard to read.

A small-size type set two or three columns wide is hard to read.

Simplicity. Multiple-deck heads are too long and complicated.

Step heads with rigid unit counts are not desirable; flush-left heads are preferable.

Decks of more than three lines are too long and complicated.

Jim dashes between decks of heads are superfluous.

Typographical devices that intrude on the consciousness of readers should be avoided. These include heavy cutoff rules, fancy borders for boxes, and ornate 30-dashes.

Attractiveness. The use of more than two families of type in headlines should be avoided.

Proper proportion between type sizes is necessary. A 36-point top deck with a 10-point lower deck is out of proportion.

A blackface top deck with a lightface second deck lacks proper emphasis.

Great variations in the length of lines in flush-left heads give a ragged and unattractive appearance.

Flush-left headlines that are too short are unattractive because there is too much white space on the right-hand side.

Prepositions and conjunctions beginning or ending a line in a head give a better balance if the first letter is capitalized instead of lower case.

Too much large black type is unattractive.

Too small type for headlines makes for a gray appearance and an uninteresting page.

A page can be given a more sparkling appearance by the restrained use of such typographical devices as large initial letters, indention of stories, boxes and box effects, subheads, wide-measure columns, setting lead paragraphs in type larger than body type, and using boldface for emphasis.

CHAPTER **15**

Principles of Make-Up

POSITION AND RANK OF PAGES

News stories come to the copy desk continuously for several hours before they are assembled in the composing room, placed in the chase, and put on press for printing. The editor cannot wait until just before press time to decide which stories to discard, which to print, and where to place them in the paper. He has to make most of his decisions when the stories first come to the desk. He never knows at nine o'clock what the situation will be at ten o'clock or at noon. To get out a newspaper under these conditions, any plan he adopts for the arrangement of material must be flexible—one that can be changed in major as well as in minor details.

The erratic flow of information to the paper explains why there is little order in the way news is presented, why there is so little segregation of news in departments, why the reader never knows whether he will find a certain type of story on page 1 or on page 15.

Another complicating factor in making up a newspaper is that the amount of space the editor has available varies from day to day. He knows of course that the publication's dimensions do not change—each page will have eight columns 20 to 22 inches long—but until he starts to work on each issue he does not know how many pages there will be and how much of the space will be devoted to news. The number of pages and the space available for news are determined by the amount of advertising.

The flexible systems of make-up employed by the majority of American newspapers have evolved partly because of these two factors—the changing news picture and the varying amount of space available for news.

Other principles have developed during the growth of the newspaper. These include the basic ideas that the most important news should go on the first page and the biggest story of the day should be played in the upper right-hand corner.

The first newspapers in this country were small folio sheets of four pages. Colonial editors began the news in the first column of the first page. That was the practice followed later by magazines.

The next stage in the development of newspaper make-up was the printing of advertising; it appeared on the front and back pages—a wrapper for the news and editorial material on pages 2 and 3. Advertising went on the outside sheets because the early publishers were primarily printers and businessmen rather than editors.

With the growth of competition in the 1840's and the development of news enterprise, editors began attracting the attention of readers by playing important stories on the first page, usually in the right-hand columns. Gradually advertising was pushed from the front page to the inside pages, but on some newspapers the right-hand column remained the most important position for news. A reading habit had been formed—one that persists today.

Later, in the 1890's, this reading habit was fixed more firmly with the use of banner lines. It is natural for the reader, after scanning a streamer eight columns left to right, to look for the story to drop from it in the last column on the page.

As a result of using news to sell papers, editors today look upon the front page as a show window where the most important and most interesting stories are displayed. Conventionally, as we have seen, the biggest story goes in the right-hand spot at the top of the page. Other conventions of front-page make-up are that the second best story goes in the upper left-hand column, and the third best in the middle columns. The midsection and bottom of the page are devoted to news of secondary interest or importance.

After the front page, page 3 is usually considered the second in importance. This is primarily due to the fact that page 2 is difficult to read. It has no sheets backing it, hence the light may shine through; and it is hard to hold it up to eye level because the weight of the pages in the right hand tends to drag it down.

For many years editors held to the theory that the odd-numbered pages were read more than the even-numbered pages. Many advertisers requested a position on an odd-numbered page. This belief seems to have been blasted by *The Continuing Study of Newspaper Reading*. This survey, conducted by the Advertising Research Foundation, shows that there is little difference in the readership of odd and even pages. Editors today have concluded that the readership of a page is determined by its content and its typographical attractiveness.

A newspaper printed in two sections has a second front page, which may have high readership. Many newspapers place no advertising on this page; instead it is used for a feature or local news page.

On the inside pages the columns rank in importance in numerical order, column 1 being the place for the biggest stories. This is due to the fact that advertisements commonly are pyramided from the right. A story under an inside line or banner, therefore, should drop in the first column.

Whatever standard system of make-up is used, the foregoing general principles guide the placement of stories in the newspaper and on the page. The only exceptions are found in a few newspapers which departmentalize their news more than conventional publications. By departmentalization is meant the grouping of related news on the same page or in the same section of a paper. These departments customarily are sports, society and items of special interest to women, financial and business reports, and news and commentary about the theater, motion pictures, and music. A story of extraordinary interest in any of these fields, however, may be taken from its department and played on the front page.

TYPES OF FRONT-PAGE MAKE-UP

The system of make-up in a newspaper depends to a great extent upon the kind of readers the editor wishes to attract. The editor selects the headline style and size and arranges the stories and pictures on the page—he chooses the dress for the newspaper—much as an individual selects his clothing. The make-up is the outward sign of the paper's character and personality.

Just as clothes do not always make the man, type and make-up do not always make the newspaper; but a great deal can be gathered from a paper's appearance. The restrained typography and make-up of the New York *Times* tell us that the paper is solid, serious, and careful; perusal of its content reinforces the impression made by its outer dress. An entirely different character is revealed in the New York *Journal-American*, with its big headlines, liberal use of pictures, and shorter stories broken up by boldface type, subheads, and other devices. The *Times* is designed for the well-educated and thoughtful reader. The *Journal-American* is planned for the masses.

These two newspapers represent two extremes in newspaper personality. The majority of our daily papers strike a compromise between conservatism and radicalism in typography and make-up. They seek to appeal to all the members of the community in which they are published. Most papers have little or no newspaper competition—only about 115 cities in the United States have opposition dailies. Hence their appeal is aimed not to any one segment of the community but to the entire population.

Make-up patterns for the front page fall into five classes, two of which are comparatively rare: (1) exact balance; (2) contrast and balance; (3) brace or focus; (4) broken page; (5) unconventional or experimental.

Exact Balance. Formerly one of the most common make-up patterns, exact balance is found only occasionally today. In this pattern the center of the page serves as a fulcrum, with headlines and type masses exactly repeated on either side. Thus a one-column headline in the first column is balanced by the same heading in the eighth column; a two-column headline over columns 3 and 4 is balanced by the same heading over columns 6 and 7. This equipoise is maintained for all the headings on the page. The most notable example of a newspaper that frequently uses this extremely formal pattern is the New York *Times*.

The symmetrical front page is in disfavor today largely because it violates the principle that the make-up pattern should be chosen to fit the news, not the news to fit the pattern. There are days, of course, when there is little choice between the stories to be played on the front page, and none deserves special emphasis. When this happens, an exactly balanced page may be appropriate.

A disadvantage of balanced make-up is that this pattern is feasible only if all the front-page stories are long enough to be continued on an inside page or the editors are willing to slash stories to fit. An article not long enough to fit the space assigned to it cannot be used. Often, to avoid jumps, editors using exact balance ruthlessly chop a story down to size.

Many typographers and editors object to balanced make-up on aesthetic grounds. For example, John E. Allen wrote:

> Why should studied symmetry—unnatural balance—be a desirable quality for a news page? What high merit attaches to it? Experienced painters purposely avoid it. Artistic photographers instinctively shy away from it. So why should such a cramping, inhibiting and unnatural thing as studied symmetry be striven for on a news page when a page can be such a dynamic, fluently alive thing when it seems natural and spontaneous?[1]

Contrast and Balance. As the name indicates, a make-up pattern employing contrast and balance uses balance as the basis of its appearance, but avoids absolute or geometric symmetry. The center of the page may still form a fulcrum, but the typography and masses on one side are

---

[1] John E. Allen, *Newspaper Designing*, Harper & Brothers, 1947, p. 173.

Fig. 42. A front page of the New York *Times* showing exact balance make-up. (Reproduced by permission of the New York *Times*.)

Fig. 43. Contrast and balance are exemplified in this front page of the Washington *Evening Star.* (Reproduced by permission of the Washington *Evening Star.*)

not duplicated on the other. For example, suppose a single-column headline has been chosen for columns 1 and 8. In columns 2 and 3 there may be a story squared off under a double-column heading. This is "balanced" in columns 6 and 7 by a double-column cut. Or suppose a two-column heading is used in columns 7 and 8. This can be "balanced" on the left by a single-column heading in column 1 and a single-column cut in column 2. Both examples show balance of the masses.

In a departure from using the middle column as a fulcrum, type masses at the top of the page can be matched with type masses at the bottom of it. A cut at the top of the page in columns 2, 3, and 4 can be balanced by a three-column spread story in columns 5, 6, and 7 at the bottom of the page.

The contrast and balance system pleases because of the harmony of its design, but it has a more subtle appeal than absolute symmetry does. It is not so artificial, and it permits the make-up editor to play stories according to their importance and length. Since contrast and balance can be used in innumerable ways, the front page can always be varied.

Brace or Focus. Because the upper right-hand corner of the page is conventionally the place for the most important story of the day, an extremely popular make-up pattern has been developed to focus attention on this spot. Attention is directed to it by using there the largest display type on the page, the headline usually spreading over several columns. Since this has the appearance of a wall bracket, the name "brace" make-up has been applied to this pattern.

With many newspapers dropping the banner in favor of a spread heading over the day's principal story, a large number of page-1 make-ups either intentionally or unintentionally follow the brace pattern.

Despite the fact that in brace make-up the type is massed in the upper right-hand corner, editors strive for relative symmetry for the rest of the page. Often the principle of contrast and balance is applied in other parts of the page.

Advantages of brace make-up are its extreme flexibility, its possibilities for infinite variation, and its adaptability for emphasis in terms of the type size used and the number of columns over which a headline extends. A disadvantage is that a story played in the first column may be completely overshadowed.

Broken Page. The make-up patterns thus far considered have emphasized panel or perpendicular effects gained by having most of the stories and headlines run up and down single columns and using relatively few multiple-column headings. A make-up in which many multiple-

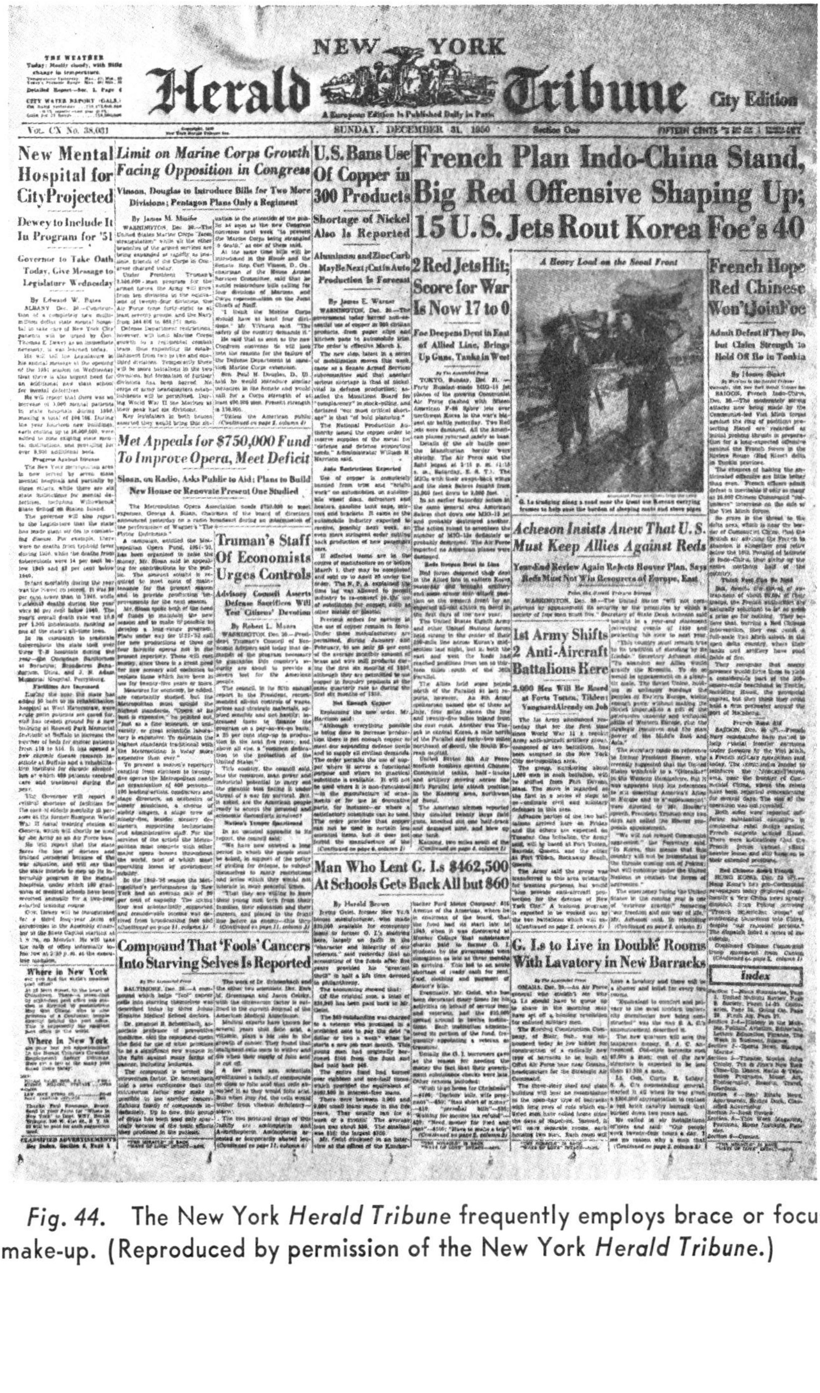

NEW YORK
Herald Tribune
City Edition
SUNDAY, DECEMBER 31, 1950

New Mental Hospital for City Projected

Dewey to Include It In Program for '51

Governor to Take Oath Today, Give Message to Legislature Wednesday

Limit on Marine Corps Growth Facing Opposition in Congress

Vinson, Douglas to Introduce Bills for Two More Divisions; Pentagon Plans Only a Regiment

U.S. Bans Use Of Copper in 300 Products

Shortage of Nickel Also Is Reported

Aluminum and Zinc Curb May Be Next; Cut in Auto Production Is Forecast

French Plan Indo-China Stand, Big Red Offensive Shaping Up; 15 U.S. Jets Rout Korea Foe's 40

2 Red Jets Hit; Score for War Is Now 17 to 0

A Heavy Load on the Seoul Front

French Hope Red Chinese Won't Join Foe

Met Appeals for $750,000 Fund To Improve Opera, Meet Deficit

Truman's Staff Of Economists Urges Controls

Acheson Insists Anew That U.S. Must Keep Allies Against Reds

1st Army Shifts 2 Anti-Aircraft Battalions Here

Man Who Lent G. I.s $462,500 At Schools Gets Back All but $60

Compound That 'Fools' Cancers Into Starving Selves Is Reported

G. I.s to Live in Double Rooms With Lavatory in New Barracks

Index

Fig. 44. The New York *Herald Tribune* frequently employs brace or focus make-up. (Reproduced by permission of the New York *Herald Tribune*.)

column headings are spotted on the page with little attention to symmetry or balance is called broken-page make-up. The result is lack of emphasis, with every story competing for attention with every other story on the page. In this style of make-up even the name plate may not have a fixed spot at the top of the page. If cut to three or four columns in width, it can be "floated," sometimes appearing at the left, sometimes in the center, and sometimes at the right. Headlines and stories are often placed above the name plate. When broken-page patterns are used without restraint, the result is called "circus" or "helter-skelter" make-up.

Formerly broken-page make-up was employed only by sensation-mongering newspapers. Many of these papers still employ circus make-up, but more conservative papers in recent years have used restrained versions of broken-page patterns. They use more subdued and smaller type than the big black headlines on the publications that delight in circus make-up, and, while wanting an eye-catching appearance, they place headlines so that the page as a whole gives an impression of harmony. The names "modern" and "streamlined" are often applied to the latter type of broken-page make-up. It appeared with simplified headline schedules in which headings were set flush left and multiple-deck forms were abandoned.

Unconventional or Experimental. Just before World War II several newspapers experimented with make-up primarily to achieve better organization of news material. Many editors felt that readers were being given a disordered picture of world happenings by the scrambled way in which stories were placed on the page. One result of this experimentation was the departmentalization of news after a system suggested by the weekly magazines *Time, Newsweek,* and *United States News.* These experiments led to a deëmphasis of headlines, with label captions often being used, and of course to radical changes in the appearance of the paper.

One interesting innovation in make-up was made by the *Christian Science Monitor.* To avoid jumping stories to inside pages, the *Monitor* adopted a horizontal make-up pattern. Stories are carried over from column to column under a multiple-column heading. Rules are not used within a story, but column and cutoff rules are employed to demarcate individual stories. This system reduces the number of stories that can be played on page 1, but it is sufficiently flexible to take care of the half-dozen more important stories of the day. It can also be varied sufficiently so that the front pages do not look the same every day.

The make-up classifications discussed above are not rigid. The names are more useful in the classooom than in daily work on a newspaper. Few

Fig. 45. An example of helter-skelter make-up. (Reproduced by permission of the Boston *Post.*)

Fig. 46. The Pittsburgh *Sun-Telegraph* uses an interesting version of broken-page make-up. (Reproduced by permission of the Pittsburgh *Sun-Telegraph*.)

Fig. 47. Flush-left headlines and a broken-page pattern characterize the streamlined make-up of the Los Angeles *Times*. (Reproduced by permission of the Los Angeles *Times*.)

Fig. 48. The *Herald-Journal* of Spartanburg, South Carolina, drops column rules, and employs a panel effect in the first two left-hand columns. (Reproduced by permission of the Spartanburg *Herald-Journal*.)

editors, in planning the layout of stories for the front page, say to themselves, "I think I'll use a brace make-up today" or "The news picture today is such that a broken-page make-up is in order." Nor are the classifications mutually exclusive. Elements of contrast and balance, for example, can be employed in almost any of the systems.

Actually editors are perhaps overly concerned with make-up. The reader does not approach his newspaper with the attitude of a typographer judging a competition. He does not hold the paper at arm's length to see if it presents an attractive arrangement of heavy and dark type. As a matter of fact, he may not see the page as a whole, because the newspaper is hard to handle and hence he tends to fold it for easier reading. Changes in typography are not noticed by the majority of readers. The New York *Herald Tribune* in 1947 dropped one of the decks in its top-of-the-column headings on page 1. The change went unnoticed even by newspapermen. A midwestern editor completely streamlined his paper's typography and make-up, adopting flush-left headings in a new sans-serif face instead of the usual roman type and eliminating column rules. After several days he made an informal survey to find out how the townspeople liked the paper's new dress. He found few persons who had noticed any change.

The pride an editor takes in his newspaper's appearance is chiefly professional, for the readers don't know good typography from bad. But no good editor is content unless he is getting out the best-looking paper possible with the equipment he has and the journalistic talent he can afford to hire.

RULES FOR MAKE-UP

Because of the differences in make-up patterns used by newspapers, few rules can be laid down for obtaining an attractive page. Moreover, harmonious arrangements of type and the use of headlines to grade the news and give the page a lively appearance depend so much upon such variables as the make-up editor's sense of design, the personality of the newspaper, and the changing news situation that rigid rules cannot be found to cover all exigencies. However, several conventions are followed more or less regularly.

In all make-up patterns except the broken page, a rule ordinarily followed is that the biggest headlines are at the top of the page, type sizes becoming progressively smaller as stories are placed lower on the page. The theory is that the important stories above the fold require emphatic headlines and that the reader's attention should not be diverted from them by a more conspicuous headline at the bottom of the page.

Thus most newspapers, in planning a headline schedule, use big type for top-of-the-column headings, smaller type or fewer decks or fewer lines in the headings of secondary stories, and still smaller type for the subordinate short stories on the page.

The rule of "biggest heads highest" of course has exceptions. A short story is often required for the top of a column to separate masses of type and provide eye relief and contrast. To keep this short story from being entirely lost in the midst of the larger type, it can be made to stand out by such devices as being boxed or having a boxed headline. Headlines two or more columns wide at the bottom of the page need larger type than the short items used to fill holes higher up on the page. Despite these exceptions, the conventional newspaper gives an overall appearance of heads descending in size as they go down the page.

Headlines lose their effectiveness if type of the same or a similar family, size, and blackness is massed together. There must be contrast. Hairline column rules and cutoff rules are not sufficient to make headings stand out as definite units.

One unattractive and hard-to-read juxtaposition that is banned in most newspapers is tombstoning, in which more than two headlines of the same kind are aligned side by side in adjoining columns. Two such headlines may be run together under a cut or under a story squared off at the bottom. Three or more should never be used. The make-up editor can avoid tombstone effects by using italic or boxed headings, a boxed story, or an engraving.

Bumping of heads—when headlines of the same type touch in adjoining columns—should also be avoided. Such careless juxtaposition ruins the balance or design of the make-up. The solution to this problem involves shifting a longer or shorter story above one of the bumped headlines to prevent the two from coming together.

Another awkward massing of type occurs when a large headline is placed under the shoulder of a double-column headline whose story drops in a single column. This can be avoided if the lead of the story is set double-column. To avoid this contingency, many newspapers set all leads under two-column headings wide measure. The double-column lead can be used as readily with stories that are wrapped around under the shoulder.

Since newspapers are folded once at the middle, it has become established practice not to have headlines at the fold. If only half the headline

SHOCK OF ALLIED FIREPOWER HITS CHINESE MORALE

Chinese Prisoners Said They Did Not Expect Such Force Of A Modern Army

TOKYO, Nov. 20. (*P*)—The shock of allied firepower has demoralized Chinese Communist morale in Korea, General MacArthur's headquarters said today.

The word comes from Chinese Communist prisoners, who also deny they came to Korea as volunteers, headquarters reported. Red China insists only Chinese "volunteers" are fighting in Korea.

An intelligence spokesman said

The U. S. charged this was an attempt to barter peace.

The 60-nation assembly beat down each section of the Soviet resolution in a paragraph-by-paragraph vote. Its vote for the nine-power plan was 51 in favor, five (Soviet bloc) against, and one (Continued On Page Four)

CENTRAL PARK TO GET OLD CAROUSEL

Old Merry-Go-Round From Park Near Reading Attracts New York

NEW YORK, Nov. 20. (*P*)—The kids—and nostalgic grownups—who mourned over the charred remains of the Central Park merry-go-round were given new hope today.

Fig. 49. An unattractive juxtaposition is the bumping of headlines of the same size in adjoining columns.

can be read when the paper is folded, as when stacked on a newsstand, the sales value of the heading is lowered. Moreover, the break at the fold may inconvenience the reader in unfolding the paper to find out what the headline says.

Newspaper rules regarding jumping stories from the front page to inside pages vary. In recent years a definite prejudice has developed against it. A few newspapers forbid jumping; others limit the number of continuations; and still others have no limit at all, permitting as many jumps as the exigencies of make-up require.

Newspapers which do not limit jumps hold to the theory that it is desirable to get as many stories as possible on the front page—the paper's show window—and that if readers are interested in a story they do not object to hunting up its continuation. A survey made by the University of Oklahoma School of Journalism seems to support this theory. Only a few of the readers polled objected to jumps. Others seemed to appreciate the difficulty of getting all of a long story on the first page.

Cardinal Dougherty Dies On 61st Ordination Anniversary

Four New Play Areas Planned By City Board

The addition of four new areas to the growing num-

PHILADELPHIA — (AP) — Dennis Cardinal Dougherty, fifth citizen of the United States to attain the highest rank of the Roman Catholic church, died Thursday a short time after celebrating mass on his 61st anniversary in the priesthood.

The 85-year-old archbishop of Philadelphia was the senior prelate of the church in this

Rachel Hill, Hooversville Pull Upsets in Windber

Rachel Hill and Hooversville Fire Company pulled slight upsets in the Windber Community League last night in Recreation Hall.

Rachel Hill dumped Sedlak Four-Leaf Clover, 48-43, while Hooversville defeated Ferndale Fire Company, 38-32.

Hiner with 13 and Bill Matey with 12 points helped the Rachel Hill team win its second straight game. Another strong fourth-quarter pulled the game out of the fire. Earl Fisher was high for the losers with 19 points.

DeWayne Berkebile dumped in 22 points as Hooversville moved

STANDING OF THE CLUBS
                    W. L. Pct.
Windber VFW 16   2 .889
Whalley Motor Co.....15 2 .882

Cresson High Matters Win

Cresson High's wrestlers scored a 38-15 victory over visiting Yeager-

Fig. 50. Setting the lead to wide measure prevents unattractive massing of type when a story is placed under the shoulder of a two-column heading.

Studies at the University of Illinois shed new light on jump stories. In an article in the December, 1947, issue of *Journalism Quarterly*, Professor Wilbur Schramm drew the following conclusion in a survey of the "depth" of newspaper readership: "Skipping a story to another page is not so bad for readership as has commonly been supposed. Most of the readers who are going to leave the story have already left by the time they come to the skip. A skip seems to lose about one-third of the readers *who are still reading* when they come to the skip."

On the other hand, the Laramie (Wyoming) *Bulletin* decided to avoid all jump stories on page 1 after a survey by journalism students at the University of Wyoming indicated that the continuation of stories lost about 50 percent of the readers. According to an article in *Editor &*

US Accepts New UN Cease-Fire Plan For Korea

Proposal OK'd by Austin Calls for 4-Nation Talks on All Far East Problems After Fighting Stops.

Hit by Malik

Five Points Include Truce Immediately, Withdrawal of Foreign Troops; Wait on Assembly Approval.

Dulles Going To Tokyo To Push Treaty

Republican Adviser Given Rank of Ambassador for Mission by President.

Ends Doubt on US Policy

Fig. 51. An unattractive massing of type sometimes results when multiple-deck headline patterns are used.

Publisher on February 14, 1948, the *Bulletin* before the survey carried twelve to fifteen pictures, stories, and features on page 1 on the theory that most of the important stories of the day should appear on the front page. About half the stories were jumped. In accordance with the new policy following the survey, the editor used horizontal make-up in order to get long stories completely on the front page, reduced the number of stories put in the "show window," and drastically trimmed other stories to avoid continuations.

The Continuing Study of Newspaper Reading also reveals low readership for the continued portions of stories. Most of them seemed to attract under 10 percent of the readers. This low readership, however, may be explained by the University of Illinois "depth" studies which indicated that the stories had already lost their readers before they came to the jump.

One factor that has led to a reduction in continued stories is that more and more newspapers are adopting a policy of using shorter news articles. One reason for this was the wartime and postwar newsprint shortage necessitating more careful use of space, but the most important reason is the revelation by readership studies that only a small part of any story is read unless it is of extraordinary interest.

To cite only one bit of evidence—again from the University of Illinois "depth" studies—indications are that the average news story loses readers rapidly after the first few paragraphs. The rate computed by Schramm was a 5 percent loss at the end of the first paragraph and another 5 percent at the end of the second. Two out of ten readers who began a story stopped reading it at the end of the fifth paragraph.

Two other conclusions were reached by Schramm in the survey:

1. The smaller a paper and the lower its frequency down to once a week, the more likely it is to hold its readers for a complete story. A weekly holds its readers better than a daily and a small daily better than a large daily.

2. The longer a story, the smaller the proportion of it that is likely to be read and the faster it loses readers. A story nine paragraphs long, for example, loses three out of ten readers by the fifth paragraph, whereas a shorter story loses only two.

The policy a newspaper adopts regarding length of stories and jump stories, of course, depends upon the aims of its owners. All the readership surveys in the world might not convince the New York *Times,* the *Christian Science Monitor,* the St. Louis *Post-Dispatch,* and other newspapers of their standing of the desirability of printing only the highlights of the day's events in short, flashily written stories. The purpose of these newspapers is to present a complete and comprehensive historical record, no matter if all the stories are not read by all the readers.

The radio, with its five-, ten-, and fifteen-minute programs of news highlights, is the natural medium for those who want news in small doses. The function of the newspaper is to give the details to those who want

Fig. 52. The *Christian Science Monitor* avoids jumping stories from page 1 by its horizontal make-up. (Reproduced by permission of the *Christian Science Monitor*.)

them. Only a few readers may want a full and complete account of a political campaign, the sessions of congress, a baseball game, or a convention of doctors, lawyers, or wholesale merchants. But in the aggregate these limited segments are more important than the averages that seem to be the principal preoccupation of many who make readership studies.

In setting up a policy for handling jump stories, the editor should consider the following:

1. The jump should be long enough to make it worth while for the reader to hunt it up. Nothing is more irritating than to search through the inside pages for the continued portion of a story and find only a paragraph or two.

2. The front-page jump should be continued in the same section of the newspaper. It is irritating for the reader who has only the first section in his hands to have to lay it aside and hunt for the jumped story on page 44 of the second section.

3. If feasible, all the jumped portions of stories should be printed on one page. An alternative is to print jumped stories on a page where related news is carried. For example, a story about the legislature should be continued on the page on which other legislative news is printed; a story about the stock market should be jumped to the financial page.

INSIDE-PAGE MAKE-UP

The placing of the advertisements determines the make-up for news on the inside pages. If the business office insists upon cramming too many advertisements on a page or in spotting them at random so there is no clear area for news display, the make-up editor cannot match the front page in the attractiveness and readability of his layout for the inside pages.

Fortunately, most advertising departments realize that readership traffic increases when a page has an interesting display of news with headlines large enough to attract notice and pictures that have attention-getting power. The business office is not desirous of killing interest in a page by crowding out the news. The advertiser's appreciation of the importance of news is indicated by the rule that advertising must be placed next to "reading matter."

And for their part, make-up editors in recent years have learned that advertisements increase readership. The high readership of advertising is shown repeatedly in the reports of *The Continuing Study of Newspaper Reading*. It equals and sometimes surpasses readership of the main news and feature stories on the same page. Short news items and filler material

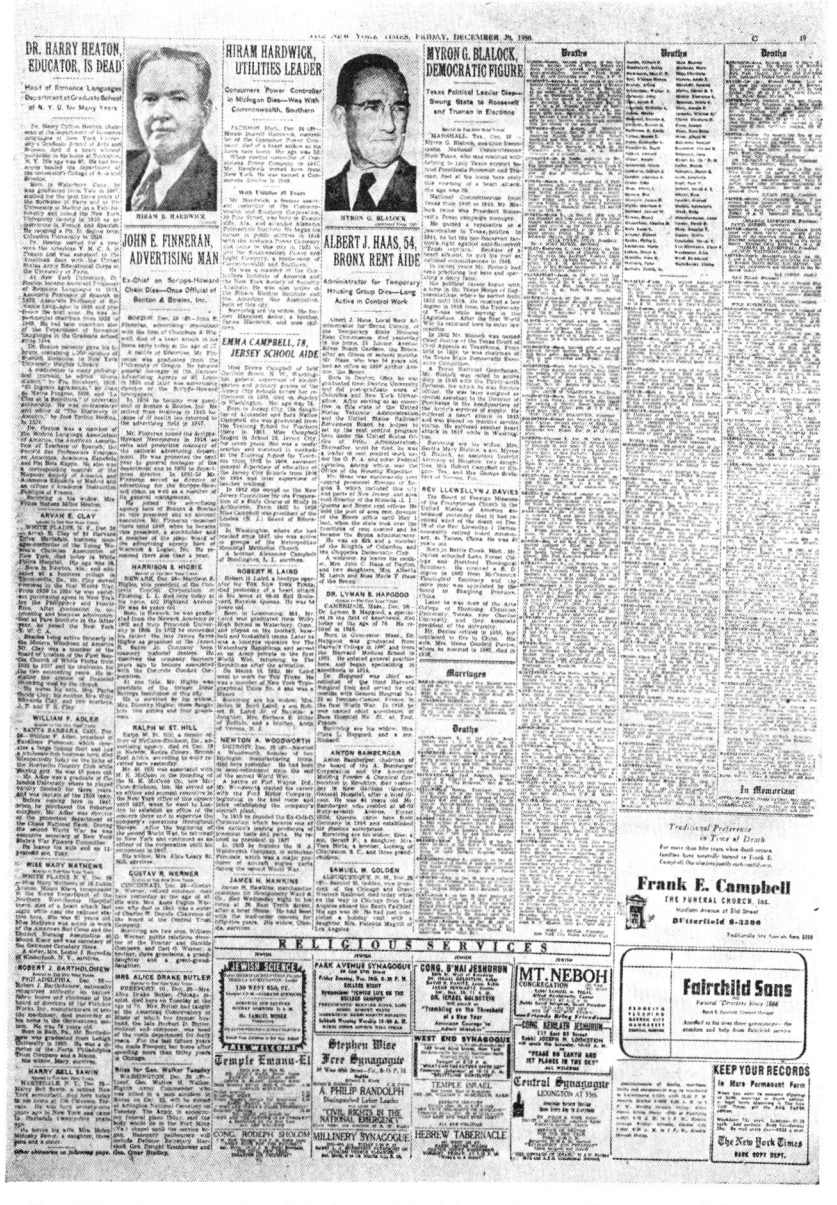

Fig. 53. An example of balanced inside make-up that is used frequently when the page does not carry much advertising. (Reproduced by permission of the New York *Times*.)

often attract a smaller percentage of readers than does advertising. Recognition of this fact, supported by about 150 studies of newspaper readership in the past decade, should do much to change the make-up editor's conventional attitude that advertising is a necessary nuisance.

Except for comparatively few newspapers which use or permit a hit-or-miss arrangement of advertising, the make-up editor will find advertisements placed roughly in only two ways—the half-pyramid arrangement and the double-pyramid or "well" arrangement.

The half-pyramid calls for the largest advertisement to be placed in the lower right-hand corner at the bottom of the page, with smaller advertisements stepped off diagonally up the right of the page. The appearance is that of one half of a pyramid with the apex in the upper right-hand corner and the base at the bottom of the page. Placing the advertisements in this manner permits all of them to be next to news material.

When a large amount of advertising is scheduled, it is sometimes impossible to pyramid them to the right and at the same time get all of them next to news material. A compromise is effected by pyramiding some of them to the right and others to the left. This leaves a "well" in the central part of the page for the news.

The make-up editor's utilization of the space available for news depends upon how the advertising is arranged on the page. He tries to follow these general principles on the inside pages:

1. The stories with the biggest headlines go at the top of the page. This principle also applies in front-page make-up.

2. The main display position on the page is the left-hand side; hence the most important story should go there. This is the reverse of the rule for the front page, where the biggest story conventionally goes in the upper right-hand corner.

Because the general inside news pages usually have advertising at the bottom, the make-up editor's theories of design and arrangement can be applied only to the top of the page. The possibilities are limited, and his pattern will probably fall into one of the following three categories:

1. Balanced Make-Up. The make-up editor secures balance by his placing of the same size of headlines in the upper portion of the page.

2. Descending Order Make-Up. In this style, the strongest headline is placed in the upper left-hand corner, and the other top-column headlines grow successively smaller across the page as the columns are shortened by the advertisements.

3. Single-Story Display. When advertising occupies most of the page, the space for news may be dominated by a single story under a

Fig. 54. Advertising pyramided both left and right leaves a "well" for news. Here the well is almost filled with a single story. (Reproduced by permission of the Johnstown *Democrat*.)

Fig. 55. When advertising pyramids high on the page, descending order make-up may be used, with headlines becoming progressively smaller across the page. (Reproduced by permission of the Appleton *Post-Crescent*.)

spread heading, possibly with illustrations. Any holes are used for short items whose small headlines are not conspicuous enough to require orderly arrangement.

Many make-up editors make the mistake of thinking that the inside pages offer little opportunity for emphatic news display. The tendency is to concentrate on the front page and make up the inside in a hit-or-miss fashion. By a little planning, a make-up editor can vary his pages and direct attention to good stories by such devices as streamers and spread headings. When there is sufficient room, each inside page should have a good "starter" story in the upper left-hand corner.

In adopting a headline schedule for the inside pages, it is a good plan to use for the one-column top heading the same head that is employed for secondary stories on the front page. If any of the page-1 stories must be shifted inside, there will be no need to rewrite the heads.

When advertising runs high on the page, as it often does, the long story under a one-column heading creates a problem in make-up. When a story fills the available space in one column and must break over or wrap around into another column, there are two possibilities for handling it:

1. The story may be continued in the column to the right beginning at the top of the page. Many newspapers ban this on the theory that it leaves a dead area at the top of the page.

2. The story may be continued in the column to the right but put under another story and separated from it by a cutoff rule. The danger here is that the long story may fill all the space in the second column and wrap around under a story in a third column. Unless the make-up editor is careful, the printer may let such a story stagger across several columns.

When a story wraps into a second column, the make-up editor must see that the breakover comes in the middle of a sentence. If the column ends with a sentence or paragraph, the reader may think that is the end of the story.

MAKE-UP OF TABLOIDS

The modern tabloid newspaper in America owes its existence to the huge success of the New York *Daily News*, established by Joseph Medill Patterson in 1919 in imitation of Lord Northcliffe's London *Daily Mirror*. The *Daily News* has the biggest circulation of any newspaper in the country. Though originally tabloid referred only to size—that of a conventional newspaper page folded in half—the term now also carries a connotation of sensationalism because of the rowdy journalism that

Fig. 56. Headlines for stories on the inside pages and pictures with captions appear on the front and back pages of many metropolitan tabloids. The New York *Daily News* devotes the front page to general news and the back page to sports. (Reproduced by permission of the New York *Daily News*.)

Fig. 57. The Gazette and Daily of York, Pennsylvania, is a frequent winner of typography awards for tabloids. Its make-up is similar to that of full-size newspapers. (Reproduced by permission of The Gazette and Daily.)

marked the competition of publications of this genre in New York in the 1920's.

The tabloid newspaper with general circulation is found chiefly in cities, where it proved popular because it was easy to read in crowded subways and buses. Although it has not made its way in smaller cities, its format is popular for school newspapers and for weekly and monthly trade journals. Ordinarily it has five standard-width columns and a page depth of 15 to 17 inches.

In the typical metropolitan tabloid the front and back pages are filled with attention-getting headlines and pictures. All the news stories to which the front- and back-page heads refer are on the inside pages; pages 2 and 3 carry the important items. In recent years it has become usual to devote the front page to general news and the back page to sports. Except for bigger and blacker headline types, the inside pages follow the make-up patterns of conventional-size papers.

The metropolitan tabloid, however, differs from the conventional daily in more than appearance and size. Since its appeal is a mass appeal, the emphasis is on sensational and human interest news. More space, also, is devoted to pictures. In fact, Patterson conceived of his newspaper as a picture-newspaper and first named it the *Illustrated Daily News;* a short-lived competitor established by Bernarr Macfadden was called the *Daily Graphic.* The writing, moreover, is of stronger voltage than that in conventional newspapers, and there is a premium on brevity, for tabloid editors expect the interest of their readers to flag quickly.

Outside the big cities, tabloid-size newspapers follow about the same make-up conventions as full-size newspapers. Headlines with one or at most two decks prevail, because the multiple-section patterns take up too much space. One advantage of the tabloid format for small newspapers is that it facilitates departmentalization. A regular-size daily of six or eight pages finds it difficult to get in all its advertising and have a page for editorials, sports, society and women's news, finance, and comics. This difficulty disappears when the six pages are increased to twelve tabloid pages and the eight pages to sixteen.

CHAPTER 16

Make-Up Procedures and Problems

COMPLEXITIES OF MAKE-UP

The process of making up a newspaper is extremely complex. It does not involve simply choosing an attractive design for stories and headlines and getting the type to fit the forms according to this design. An important part of the process consists of copy control—determining how much material is needed, how long the stories should be, and when copy must be sent to the composing room. The process also includes coördinating the work of the news departments—the city desk, the wire news desk, the sports department, the society department—and collaborating with the advertising department on the size of the paper and the allocation of space. Finally, the process involves working with the printers so that the type will be properly placed in the forms.

Putting a newspaper together is a continuous process. While reporters are writing stories, while the teletype is ticking off articles from all parts of the world, while copyreaders are correcting stories and writing headlines, while compositors are converting words into type, the make-up editor is busy getting the forms ready for press. He operates on a clockwork schedule, for page forms are locked up and stereotypes are cast at stated intervals.

The complexity of the process increases with the size of the newspaper and the frequency of editions; but, small or large, one edition or many, make-up is complex. A small newspaper with a single news executive who directs two or three reporters while acting as a one-man copy desk does not have as elaborate a system as does a larger daily whose great volume of news requires a man to devote full time to make-up. But on neither newspaper is the job an easy one.

As with most newspaper jobs, the work of the make-up editor must be learned by experience. Systems vary on newspapers; therefore any description of procedures and of the handling of problems must be generalized. On a small newspaper, make-up is but one of several tasks of the person employed as city editor or news editor. On larger papers, the slotman or one of the copyreaders may have the extra job of supervising the making up of the publication. On metropolitan dailies, make-up is specialized work and a full-time job for one or more men.

DETERMINING SPACE

The volume of advertising determines the number of pages and the percentage of the total space that are available for news and editorial matter. The ratio of news to advertising matter varies from day to day and from newspaper to newspaper. Increasing the number of pages does not necessarily mean more space for news. A Saturday issue of 10 pages light in advertising may provide nearly as much room for news as a 20-page Friday issue packed with grocery and other advertising.

The decision as to number of pages and the ratio of news to advertising is not made by the make-up editor. Other executives—the managing editor, the advertising manager, and perhaps the mechanical superintendent—determine how big the newspaper is to be. Nor does the make-up editor have anything to say about placing the advertisements. This is determined by the advertising department, which turns over to the make-up editor layout sheets with page designations indicating the position of advertisements.

When the make-up editor receives the dummies from the advertising department, he is ready to begin his task of planning the newspaper. He first estimates how many columns of news space is available. Suppose the plans call for a 20-page newspaper, with 90 columns of advertising. This leaves 70 columns which are the make-up editor's problem. But from these 70 columns he must subtract the space occupied by regular features— comics, the editorial page, crossword puzzle, bridge lesson, short story or serialized novel, and so forth. These cannot be omitted, no matter how tight the paper. No one is likely to telephone the editor because a news story has been left out, but to hold out a standard feature brings "kicks" ranging from a few for something like a crossword puzzle to hundreds for a popular comic.

With the news allotment decided, the make-up editor confers with the news executives as to their requirements. Some departments—sports, society, financial—have a regular amount of space according to the day of the week. Except in unusual circumstances the normal schedule is followed for these sections. If space is limited, however, the make-up editor may inform these editors of a reduction in the number of columns. Sometimes—often, as a matter of fact—departmental editors request additional space. A less accurate estimate of space requirements is obtained from the city editor, the state editor, and the wire editor. They ordinarily prepare a schedule of stories that are coming up, but it may be knocked out of kilter at any moment by a big spot news break.

After checking with department heads, the make-up editor almost invariably finds himself confronted with the same problem: The estimates and requests for space run higher than the columns he has available. When the paper is extremely tight, he may pass along an order to boil down stories. Occasionally there is a happy day when the paper is wide open and the desks can splurge on features, long stories, and art.

On most newspapers the make-up editor does not have charge of the layout and assembling of departmental pages. He merely has to turn over to the departmental editor the page dummy with the advertisements marked in. He is then free to concentrate on the general news pages.

The time schedule for making up pages in the composing room depends upon the type of information they contain. The first pages completed are those whose content is mainly nonnews. The editorial page may be the first assembled; often most of the copy for that page is sent to the composing room the day before publication. The society and women's pages also are made up early, because there are few late-breaking stories that have to make the day's edition. On afternoon papers the sports page can be completed early, for most of the material is a rehash of events of the day or night before; late-breaking sports stories—afternoon baseball games, for example—go on the first page of the street edition for the people going home from work. On a morning paper, however, the sports page is one of the last to be made up. The last pages to be completed are the front page and the inside pages carrying jump stories.

Since the size of the paper varies from day to day, it is not practicable to attempt to give departmental pages the same number every day; nevertheless, some uniformity is sought to make it easier for the reader to find the departments he wants. For example, if the newspaper usually appears in two sections, the second page of the second section may be established as the editorial page, and the opposite page may be the feature page or the society page. The business and financial page customarily precedes the classified advertising. A favorite location for comics and features like crossword puzzles and fiction is the next to the last page.

KEEPING THE RECORD

Unless a system of bookkeeping is employed to record the number of stories sent to the composing room, their length, and the headlines that go over them, the make-up editor will quickly find himself in difficulties. He will not know what stories are available for the inside, and thus he cannot dummy up his pages properly. If he does not keep a check on the flow of copy, he may discover that the city editor and the telegraph editor are exceeding their space allotments. The result may be too much copy set in type. Overset is undesirable from two points of view. It means that some good stories may be crowded out that could have been included by more careful trimming on the copy desk. It also means that time and money are wasted. An efficient editorial department has set in type only as much material as is needed to fill the paper.

On a small publication, the city editor or the slotman may find it unnecessary to keep a written record of major news stories and pictures, except perhaps to jot down the tentative location on the dummy sheets. From day-to-day experience he has learned to gauge the quantity of material that has gone to the composing room and the space it will take in type without having to add the totals of individual stories.

On a large publication, where copy passes through several hands on its way to the composing room, the make-up editor keeps a written record. At the start of his day's work, he has tentative estimates of upcoming stories from the city editor, the wire editor, the state editor, and the cable editor if the newspaper has its own correspondents abroad. But customarily the copy is channeled to the make-up editor after it leaves the copyreader but before it goes to the composing room, or he is given the record of stories kept by the slotman. The make-up editor may also receive galley proofs, but ordinarily he cannot wait for them before deciding how to place the stories in the paper.

The make-up editor's written record is called a slugsheet or schedule. It may be a simple affair of his own devising, or it may be a printed form. It usually includes the story's guideline, the head designation, and the length of the item. Additional information that may be helpful is the source of the story, the name of the copyreader who handled it, the time it cleared the copy desk, and the page of the newspaper for which it is scheduled.

In keeping his record the make-up editor often groups the stories

MAKE-UP PROCEDURES AND PROBLEMS 251

according to the news departments—city and local, wire, state correspondence, cable, and art or engravings.

The estimates of length may be in inches or columns. Some publications

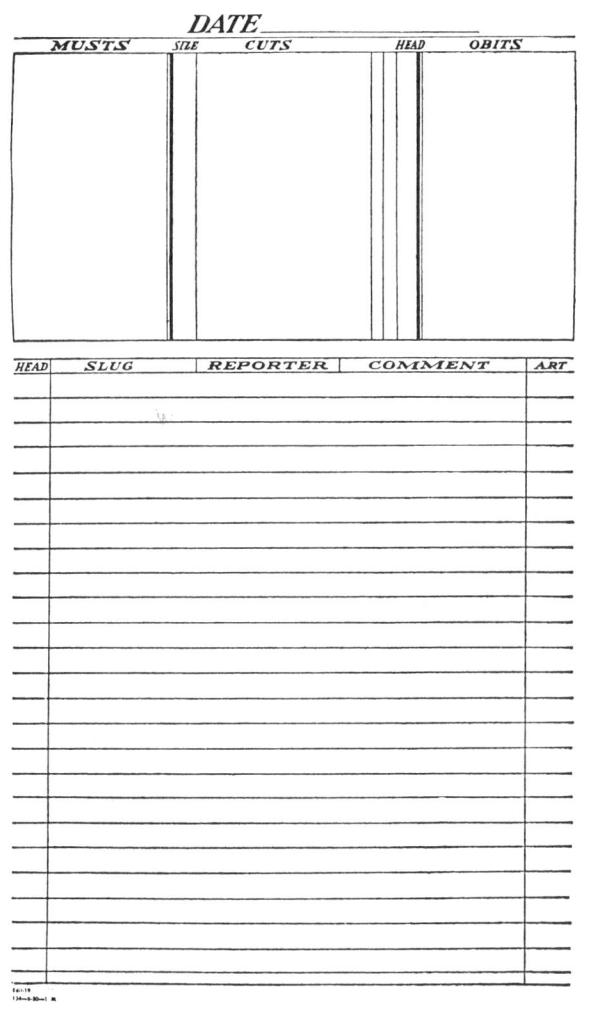

Fig. 58. Printed copy schedule or slugsheet used by the Philadelphia Inquirer.

use numbers as symbols for length; 100 represents a full column, 75 three-fourths of a column, 50 half a column, and so forth. It is important that the make-up editor watch the space of the various departments so that none will exceed its original allotment unless another has agreed to sacrifice some of its space. The city editor, for example, may have anticipated a dull day; instead, there are several unexpected stories of such interest and importance that they must be played to the hilt. This means that the state editor or the wire editor may have to reduce his space allowance.

THE PAGE DUMMY

While he is recording the stories that go to the composing room, the make-up editor keeps in mind the arrangement of stories on the page. He plans the make-up on a small-scale representation of the newspaper page called a dummy. From the advertising department, as has been said, he receives dummy sheets of the inside pages with the advertising blocked in. Duplicates have also been sent to the composing room so that the printers can put the advertisements in place as they are set.

Dummy sheets commonly are the size of an ordinary sheet of typewriting paper—8½ by 11 inches. They are ruled for the eight columns of the newspaper page. At the top is a blank for the date, the page number, and, on large papers, the edition. Along the sides the depth of the newspaper is indicated by numbers, either in inches or in agate lines. If the measurement is in inches, the numbers run from 1 to the figure that represents the length of the page—usually about 22. If the measurement is in agate lines, the numbers run from 10 to about 300.

On the dummy the make-up editor indicates the column or columns where stories and pictures will go in order to guide the printer or floorman in putting the type into the chase. Only the most important stories are designated on the dummy. The holes remaining after the major articles are placed in the forms are filled with any short items or fillers that fit.

The dummy should contain the following information:

1. The headline number or type designation.
2. The story's guideline.
3. The column into which stories under spread headings will drop.
4. The approximate length of the story or how far down the page it is to be run in case it is jumped.
5. The number of the jump page, if known.
6. The space to be taken by pictures and cutlines.

Some make-up editors indicate the length of a story by a straight or wavy line ending in an arrowhead. Others use an end mark—the figure 30 or a double cross or a dash. If the story is a jump story, the point of breakover may be shown by a cutoff rule, with the page number of the continuation written immediately above. Multiple-column headings may be

MAKE-UP PROCEDURES AND PROBLEMS

indicated by a horizontal line across the columns over which the headline will spread. Stories that "wrap around" into another column are shown by a line with arrows.

On many small newspapers that have only one news executive, the inside pages may be made up by the printer without a layout sheet. If there are special instructions for the printer, the editor gives them orally; very likely he does not stand by to supervise the placing of type in the chase except for the front page.

On a larger newspaper the slotman or other staff member who acts as make-up editor may not have time to stand by in the composing room while the floorman puts the type in the forms for the inside pages, but he does give the printer a dummy. This dummy must be complete and detailed. If any questions arise, the printer may send for the make-up editor. The printer follows the layout sheet for the major stories and pictures and fills in the holes with whatever short stuff is available.

On metropolitan newspapers and on the more carefully edited smaller papers the make-up editor usually goes to the composing room to watch while the type is placed in the chase and the forms are locked up. If stories do not fit, he may have to shorten them by lopping off the last one or two paragraphs, and he indicates the shorter items he wants used to fill up the vacant spots on the dummy. The printer works from the top of the page down, and the make-up editor stands on the opposite side of the stone. Although he is responsible for the appearance of the page, there is one liberty he cannot take. He is not permitted to change the position of an advertisement even if it will simplify the problem of make-up and result in a more attractive page. The reason for this rule is that the advertiser may have been promised a definite location. Before an advertisement can be moved, permission must be obtained from the advertising department make-up man.

Since the front page is the show window of the newspaper, the make-up of this page requires more attention than do the inside pages. Whatever the size of the paper, the news editor or make-up editor goes to the composing room to make sure that the printer follows instructions on the dummy and to make any last-minute changes that will perfect his page design and the arrangement of stories.

He may have many other details to attend to. Much of the front-page copy has been held up to as near deadline as practicable; operators are still busy setting page-1 stories. The make-up editor, especially on a small newspaper, can save precious minutes by reading galley proof of these stories. If the paper carries an index of inside features and departments, he prepares the index. He checks to see if the volume and issue number and the date line have been changed. If a headline doesn't fit, he may

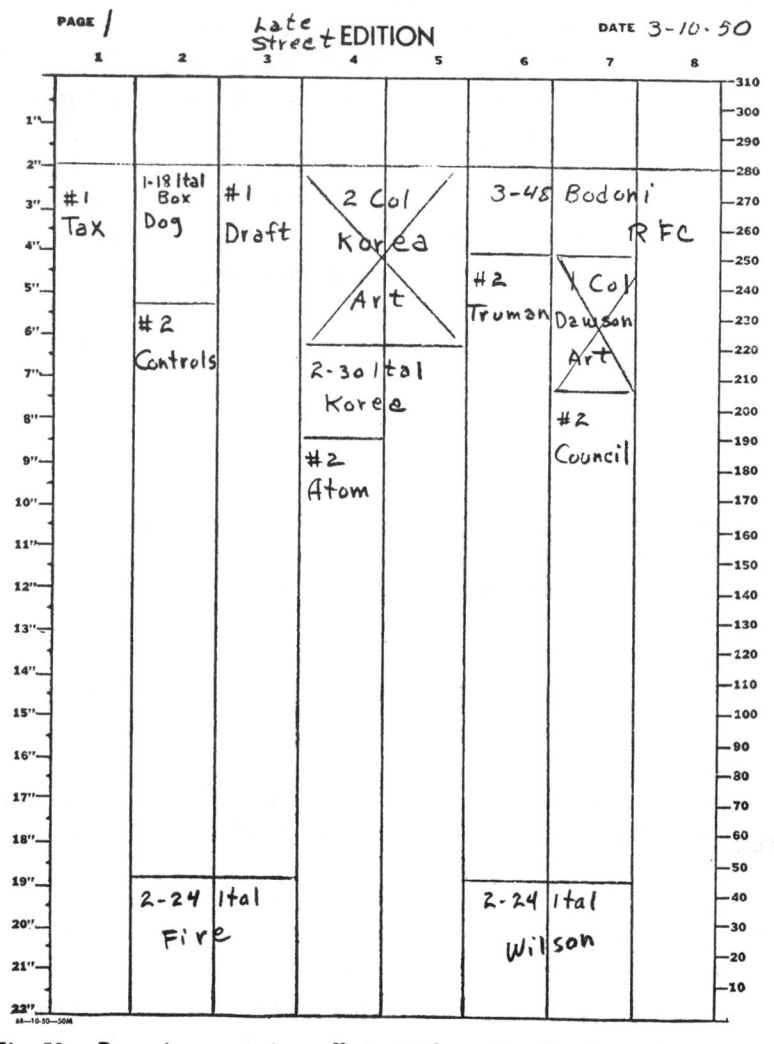

Fig. 59. Dummies must give sufficient information for the make-up man to place the major stories and cuts. Here is a page-1 dummy.

rewrite it. If a blank has been left in the weather report for the latest hourly temperature or for the high reading up to press time, he supplies the information. He reads the headlines in type to make sure that there

MAKE-UP PROCEDURES AND PROBLEMS

are no typographical errors or egregious blunders. He checks the correction lines in stories; they are easy to spot because they have not been inked for proofs and hence stand out from the other type.

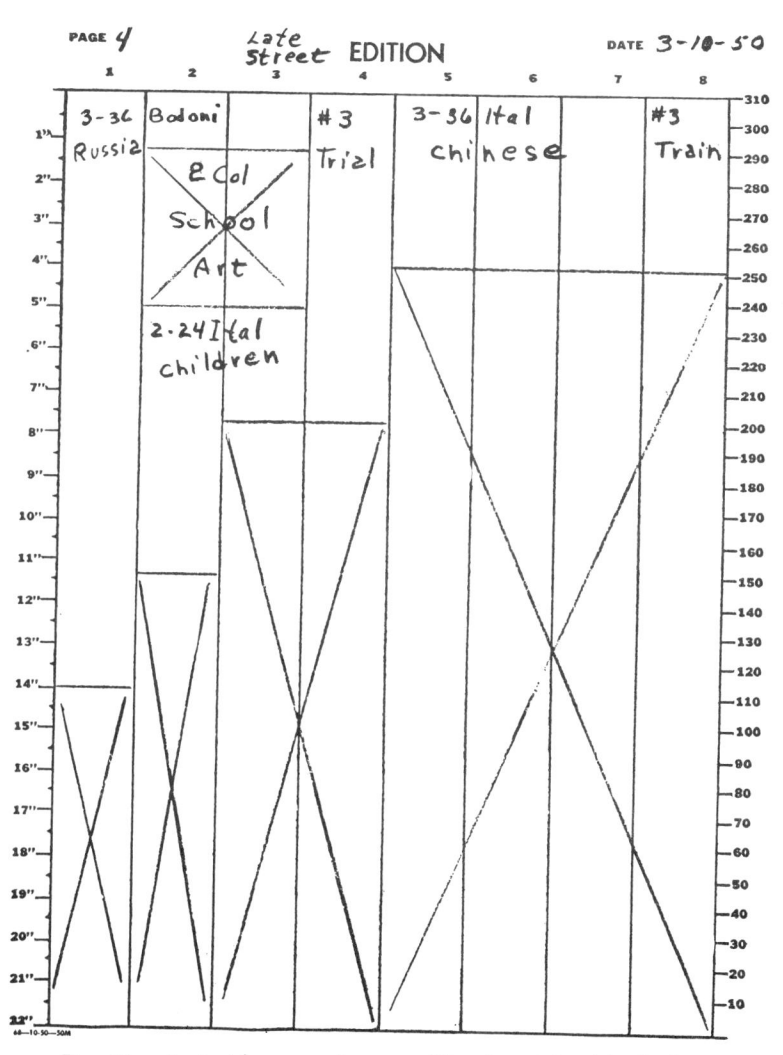

Fig. 60. An inside-page dummy with advertising blocked in.

When the page has been justified and the form locked, there may be time for a stone proof—made by placing a sheet of tissue paper or a moistened sheet of newsprint over the form and tamping it down with a felt-covered wooden block called a proof planer—before the form goes to the press or to the matrix rolling machine. Catching and correcting serious errors then may make it unnecessary to stop the presses or replate.

CHECKING FOR MAKE-UP ERRORS

In a short time the make-up editor without previous experience should by careful observation know as much about the details of getting the forms ready for press as the printer. While he does not handle the type himself, he checks the printer at his work, suggests changes to improve the appearance of the paper, and guards against such matters as omission of cutoff rules, incorrect leading to make stories fit, misplacement of legends under cuts, and dozens of other minutiae that have to be attended to in putting the paper to bed. It is better to watch for these details during the process of making up rather than after proofs are pulled, for after the forms are locked any changes or corrections can be made only with considerable difficulty.

An invaluable aid to a good make-up editor is the ability to read type the way the printer reads it—upside down from left to right. As he stands on the opposite side of the stone from the printer when forms are made up, he may also learn to read headline type from right to left.

On smaller newspapers where the make-up editor has other duties (he may edit copy and write headlines besides acting as city editor) he usually goes into the shop to supervise the making up of only the first page. The printers make up the other pages from his dummies, or very often without a dummy. Extra care must of course be taken in checking these pages for errors.

Make-up editors and deskmen should systematize their search for errors. The first check should be the volume and number of the issue and the date in the date line under the front-page name plate. On inside pages the date and page number must be watched. The continuation lines of jump stories and the index, if there is one, are then verified. Other routine checks of major importance involve making sure that the proper headlines are on all stories and the right cutlines are on pictures.

Other chances for error include cutoff rules and dashes improperly placed; subheads too near the bottom when a story is jumped or has been cut; subheads wrongly spaced because one was thrown away by the printer to make the type fit; stories flipped or breaking over to another column at the end of sentence or paragraph; improper and excessive leading; guidelines at the beginning of stories not discarded; wrong correction lines put in or lines with errors not thrown away; column rules

MAKE-UP PROCEDURES AND PROBLEMS

bent or broken or not properly aligned; boxes not fitting neatly at the corners; slugs and leads projecting; and headlines sawed too closely on the right. On the first press run the make-up editor should check to see that stereotype plates are not trimmed too closely at the edges or are not sufficiently gouged out in the white spaces, or, if the paper is printed direct from type on a flatbed press, that the cuts are backed up to print clearly.

SOME FRONT-PAGE PROBLEMS

As was pointed out in the preceding chapter, the front pages of newspapers are made up according to several possible arrangements or patterns. The same newspaper of course does not ordinarily employ all of them. If it did, it would have no prevailing personality, no recognition values for the reader.

But whatever the pattern, it must be planned carefully. The inside pages can be made up according to a hastily improvised pattern decided upon by the make-up editor from material available. But for the front page, headlines must be written and stories chosen to fit a pattern. This does not mean that the make-up editor blueprints the front page at the beginning of the day's work and then selects news articles and headings to fit the design already decided upon. Instead, the design evolves during the day as the make-up editor and other desk executives decide what stories are worth the front page and which are to have top-of-the-page display. This may mean planning several dummies and frequently reconsidering the value of news stories.

The make-up pattern for the front page may be determined largely by a single decision: the size of headline chosen for the lead story—the one in the upper right-hand corner. If this decision can be made early in the day, a blueprint for the rest of the page can be made into which other stories can easily be fitted. If not, the make-up editor may not know exactly how his page will shape up until a short time before deadline. A late-breaking story may upset any make-up pattern. Hence one of the requirements for make-up is sufficient flexibility so that the plan can be altered without any need to rewrite headlines and reset stories previously sent to the composing room.

Variety in front-page make-up is sometimes hampered by newspaper policy. Some papers, especially those in cities where there is competition, require a banner every day. A few—the Chicago *Tribune*, the Milwaukee *Journal*, and the Pittsburgh *Post-Gazette* are examples—carry a three-column cartoon every day, and this must be fitted into the overall design.

Some have a personal column that always goes in the first column. But most newspapers permit the make-up editor or news editor to play the news stories according to their essential importance and do not have regular front-page features that complicate the make-up problem.

A check of newspaper front pages shows that most carry three top-of-the-column news stories, not counting features and short articles printed under contrast heads. Unless there is a great deal of art taking up several columns or unless all the stories are multiple-column ones, it is hard to make up the page with less than three top stories. Four or more top stories can be worked in attractively only if there are no three- or four-column spread heads. A picture is almost a requisite for an attractive layout; hence a front page with no art at the top is a rarity.

The front-page make-up depends on the stories and art available for the day, but the news editor should not hold these back from the composing room while he decides how to play them. He should decide on a headline as soon as the stories are written and edited. This is not hard, because the city editor's assignment sheet and the wire report budget tell him what stories are upcoming. Some of them may not develop as expected. They may either collapse entirely or build up into bigger yarns. Moreover, the whole news picture may shift with the sudden breaking of a good story. The make-up editor should be able to revamp his plans as the necessity arises.

In his early planning, the make-up editor or the head of the desk should keep the following points in mind:

1. Do not evade deciding about a headline by sending to the composing room stories marked "HTC." This device may be used occasionally, but it solves no problems if it is used for several stories.

2. Do not mark too many stories for single-column top headings. Most make-up patterns permit only three or four of them. If these stories are ousted from the top of the column, the headings have to be rewritten for use lower on the page.

3. But don't forget that almost any front-page story with a secondary heading can be moved inside and replaced by a top story with a rewritten headline. If the top story is too long for the space, it can be shortened or jumped.

4. Put two-column italic or contrast headings on one or two of the stories worth top position. If better stories come in later, the earlier ones can be pushed down the page.

5. Schedule for the front page a good local feature whose interest does not depend upon its timeliness. If a good news story breaks near deadline

and the feature can't be moved inside, it can be taken out and saved for the next day.

6. Make sure that plenty of one-, two-, and three-paragraph items, preferably local stories, are slugged for page 1. If you don't, the best shorts and fillers may be used in the inside pages, leaving small pickings for the front-page holes.

These suggestions are made with the idea that rewriting and resetting headlines should be avoided as much as possible. Frequent changes add to mechanical costs, and near deadline it often is not possible to take time to write and cast new heads.

The same considerations are important in selecting the headline for the most important story on the right-hand side of the page. In assigning heads for this story, the make-up editor should keep in mind the possibility that a late-breaking story may suddenly force him to shift his original play item to the left of the page.

Such a switch is easy if the right-hand story is given a single-column headline. But a one-column heading in this spot is used infrequently. Most editors don't like it because the page has no point of highest interest. The page looks as if nothing was happening. And in truth this is usually the case. When any of three or four stories of routine interest might be chosen for the spot, the single-column heading is appropriate. Metropolitan newspapers, however, seldom follow this practice; they prefer a spread heading or a banner even when the news value does not warrant the play. On the other hand, small-city "home" papers do not object to the conservative one-column heading in the last column.

A two-column head for the main story is often an excellent choice, chiefly because it can easily be moved to the left-hand outside column or to the center in case a later story deserves the main play position. The two-column heading, especially in a three-line version, is sufficiently emphatic to draw attention to the upper right-hand corner and yet it is never sensational. It can be used in several ways—with a one-column readout, with a two-column deck with the story dropping in a single column, or with a two-column lead with or without a second deck. If a one-column piece of art is to go with the story, it can be placed under the shoulder of the two-column head.

On newspapers that use brace make-up, the three-column spread heading is a favorite. Like the two-column heading, the triple-column spread can be switched to the left of the page without tearing up the whole layout in case a bigger story breaks. If the story is big, the head can be made extremely emphatic by being set in three lines. For a less important story sensationalism can be avoided by using it as a two-line head. It can be used several times a week without becoming monotonous, because of the great variety of possible read-outs and the many ways it can be employed with pictures. Some of these are:

1. A single-column read-out.
2. A double-column deck with the story dropping in one column.
3. A double-column deck with the first part of the story set two columns.
4. Related news stories dropping in the sixth and eighth columns.
5. A one- or two-column cut placed under the shoulder.
6. The story descending in the sixth or seventh column instead of the eighth.

An attractive feature of the three-column spread is that, although forceful, it does not weight the right-hand side of the page so strongly that it seems topheavy. A regular one-column top heading and especially a two-column heading look well in the first or the first and second columns when a three-column spread is used on the right.

When spread headings are increased to four or more columns, their versatility of course declines. If a late-breaking story demands the right-hand position, the wider headlines must be rewritten for another spot on the page. Nevertheless, they are extremely useful, for they permit the playing of stories according to their news importance and they give variety to the front page from day to day. One difficulty with their use is that unless care is taken the left side of the page will be blacked out. Devices to avoid an uninteresting left-hand side and to restore balance include the use of pictures, stories set double column, a two-column three-line heading set in vigorous type, and a story squared off under a two- or three-column headline.

MAJOR NEWS DISPLAY

Many newspapers restrict banners for use only when a truly big story breaks; they present on the front page a cross section of the important news of the day. Although there may be several important stories about national affairs in Washington, for example, editors hesitate to play all of them on the front page. They are more likely to put the best of them on page 1 and to carry the others inside, using the front page for other items that appeal to their diverse readers.

Yet when there is a momentous story, such newspapers may thunder in type with one or two banners; and when a single event overshadows everything else, the whole front page may be devoted to the story about it.

MAKE-UP PROCEDURES AND PROBLEMS

The eight-column headline may be a single line of type or, if it tells of a world-shaking happening, two or three lines. The standard banner ranges from 72 to 120 point, frequently in all-capitals; Railroad gothic is a favorite. If the story is of extraordinary interest or importance, the read-out may be a spread of 48 or 60 point, with the story itself set two or three columns wide in 10- or 14-point type. The story under a banner should drop in the right-hand columns, because readers have been taught to look for the most important news in that spot.

When two or more stories are played under individual streamers, the banners should be in contrasting type. Thus if a 72-point all-cap banner goes over the biggest story of the day, the streamer for the second story should be set in italics or in caps and lower case. If three banners are used—this is to be avoided because they are confusing—one can be in all-caps, one in caps and lower case, and one in italics. Because of the rule of big-type-highest, the banner in the largest type or in all-caps should go above the banner in contrasting type. This rule, however, is not followed on all newspapers.

The story under the biggest type should drop on the right-hand side of the page, and the second story on the left-hand side. If there is a third banner, one of the stories must of course descend into a center column. If the make-up editor uses multiple banners frequently, he should follow a regular system on which the reader can depend.

Variations in handling banners include placing one above the name plate. Some newspapers cut the name plate down to three or four columns and run big spread headings or banners above, with the name plate shoved to one side or centered. There are numerous typographical possibilities for using banners and near-banners, and the alert make-up editor will have enough of them in mind to handle any news situation that arises.

There are times when a single story dominates the day's news, and the make-up editor must be prepared for it. One story of this type that comes along regularly is an election—local, state, or national. The make-up for an election issue calls for careful planning to give adequate display to the most important contests, to tabulations of the results, and to pictures of the winners and of scenes at the polls.

The biggest election takes place every four years when the voters choose the president. This is actually the easiest election for the make-up editor, because most states schedule local elections so as not to conflict with the national election and interest is thus focused on the outcome of one race. For a presidential election the make-up editor must plan

Fig. 61. The editor with a sense of design can depart from conventional patterns. Here is an attractive front-page experiment by the *Daily Oklahoman* of Oklahoma City. (Reproduced by permission of the *Daily Oklahoman*.)

MAKE-UP PROCEDURES AND PROBLEMS 263

banners and spreads for the following stories: the results of the election nationally—always the main story of the day; the voting in the city, the county, and the state; statements of victorious and losing candidates; results in the state senatorial race; and several side-light and feature stories. The whole front page thus is likely to be devoted to the election, with additional stories on the inside. The election blacks out most of the other news of the day.

For a state and local election, the make-up editor may have to plan his layout for the following stories: the governor's race; the senatorial race; the congressional district races; the races for both houses of the state legislature; the races for minor state offices; the country races. Which of these stories are most newsworthy depends upon the circumstances. An upset in a contest for a relatively unimportant office may make a story as good as or better than the gubernatorial or senate race in which the outcome is a foregone conclusion. Hence the make-up editor may not decide about the play of stories until the last minute.

Another fairly regular occasion when much of the front page is given over to a single event is the adjournment of congress or a state legislature. The final session may last for hours as the lawmakers work against the clock to secure final passage of bills that they debated and fought over for months. Very often measures of far-reaching importance are passed at this time, and the make-up editor must be prepared to give adequate play to stories about them.

But many stories that dominate the news come with stunning suddenness. Disasters like a tornado, fire, explosion, train wreck, or airplane crash; the death or slaying of a notable such as the president or the head of a foreign state; an incident that might provoke war—these occur without warning. And the make-up editor, with most of his stories in type and in the forms, may have to tear up his front page to make a place for the new story.

If he has been content to work with a few tried-and-true typographical arrangements, he will be caught short when the unexpected happens and he has to decide in a minute or two on the type and size of the headlines for the big story and on the pictures to use. No rules can be set down in advance for such a situation, for no two ever develop alike. The make-up man who has not been afraid to experiment from day to day and who has developed the faculty of visualizing the printed page from his dummy can meet the unexpected situation with confidence that his quickly made decision will be right—that his display of the news will be effective.

MAKE-UP WITH PICTURES

Despite the fact that wire transmission of pictures and fast engraving processes enable newspapers to have art available almost as quickly as they can get a story into type, they have not fully utilized the potentialities of illustrations to tell news stories. One reason for this is that pictorial journalism requires more space than they can usually afford for a single story unless it is of extraordinary importance or interest. Although this topic is discussed in Chapter 21, any discussion of make-up requires consideration of the problem of illustrations.

Conventionally, newspaper pictures are of two types: (1) pictures used to illustrate a story, (2) pictures used for their intrinsic interest and given only brief explanatory captions.

The second type offers no particular make-up problem. Sometimes they are used together to make up a picture page, and sometimes they are printed alone primarily to "dress" a page. They are separated from other material by cutoff rules. Many newspapers strive to have at least one picture on every page.

Formerly rules of make-up specified that cuts should not go in an outside column or be "sunk" on the page or be placed at the bottom. These rules had no particular validity, and only a few newspapers today restrict art to the top inside columns. If, however, there is only one illustration on a page, it should go at the top, not at the bottom. No matter how strong the headlines at the top, they lose their attention-pulling power when made to compete against a picture below the fold. Illustrations therefore should be placed at the bottom only when there are illustrations at the top.

Photographs that accompany stories should form an integral unit with the stories. The reader should know at once that the picture he sees belongs to a certain story and not to another in an adjoining column. Newspapers frequently err in not making it immediately apparent what story the art belongs with.

It is not enough that the picture be placed beside the story. It should be made an entity with the story by means of the headline, cutoff rules, and the elimination of column rules between it and the story it illustrates. The major difficulty is that a headline that encompasses both story and picture must be several columns wide. Sometimes the story is not worth such a spread head, and often it is hard to work such an arrangement into the page make-up. One solution to this problem adopted by some newspapers is to put the picture and story in adjoining columns, with an

Fig. 62. The picture and the story it illustrates should constitute a typographical unit, as in these examples of one- and two-column art.

arrow pointing to the illustration mortised in the story. This device does what is wanted but it is awkward and unattractive.

When the story and the picture drop under a spread heading or banner, the three elements can be isolated by omitting both the cutoff rule between the picture and the headline and the column rule between the picture and the story.

But since not all illustrations go with major display stories, other methods must be employed for other stories with pictures. Among them are the following:

1. A headline, then the illustration, then identifying underlines if needed, then the story. If the cut is more than one column, the story may drop in a single column or start in two-column measure and then break down to one column.

2. An overline, then the cut, then identifying underlines if needed, then the headline, then the story. The head may be one, two, or more columns according to the size of the picture.

3. The cut, then identifying underlines if needed, then the headline, then the story.

4. The headline, then the illustration, then identifying underlines if needed, a second deck for the headline, then the story.

5. A single-column cut, especially if a head-and-bust picture of an individual, placed or "sunk" in the text of the story.

These five methods of handling the make-up problem when illustrations are used can be adapted to almost any situation—even those in which there may be two or three cuts for one story. Of course not all the methods should be used by one newspaper; for if no consistent plan is followed, the reader is likely to become confused.

Pictures that illustrate a news story require only the briefest of explanatory captions, since it is expected that the reader will get from the story any background he needs to understand the illustration. Often the only underline required is the identification of the persons in the photograph. If the headline or overline says "Legion Names New Officers," the reader will assume that the men shown are the new officers. The underline need give only the names and offices. When the headline or overline says that twenty are killed in a hotel fire, the reader will know that the burning building in the picture is the hotel. No underline is necessary.

When a person's picture shows a profile or three-quarter view, the make-up editor should try to place it so that the individual is looking toward the center of the page or toward the story the photograph illustrates. This means that the picture of a person looking to the left must

MAKE-UP PROCEDURES AND PROBLEMS

go on the right-hand side of the page and to the right of the story it illustrates. If this rule is not followed, the reader's eyes will be directed away from the point of interest—the newspaper page itself or the story the picture illustrates.

INSIDE-PAGE PROBLEMS

The problem of fitting headlines to stories and stories to space on the inside pages is not difficult. The inside-page pattern is a simple one, and almost any arrangement of stories that avoids bumping or tombstoning heads gives sufficiently attractive composition.

Ordinarily the copy desk sends the composing room a sufficient variety of headlines and stories so that the make-up editor can plan the inside pages without much effort. If, however, the slotman chooses too many headlines of one size, the make-up editor may remind him that others are needed—more two-column heads, more italic heads in one, two, and three columns, one or two spread heads or a streamer for outside column display, several boxed heads or stories, and more short items to fill the lower parts of the pages.

One common fault of make-up editors, especially on smaller papers, is failing to use enough big headlines. Commenting on the lack of care given the inside pages, Dean Kenneth E. Olson of the Medill School of Journalism said in his criticism of entries in the 1949 typography competition for members of the Inland Daily Press Association:

> Many of our smaller dailies are now turning out well made up front pages, but when you turn inside it's like walking into a graveyard. Their inside pages are dead. And that's not playing fair with your advertisers. You don't allow them to advertise on the front page and yet you don't display your news on inside pages interestingly enough to create reader traffic through these inside pages where you do carry your advertising.
>
> There are just two little simple typographic tricks to this. First, instead of heading your inside columns with little insignificant 12- and 14-point heads that make your news columns look insignificant and dull and gray, get some good display—30-, 24-, and 18-point heads at the top of your inside columns. Second, if possible, pyramid your advertising on inside pages to the right, to leave the top left free for interesting news display.
>
> If you have a lot of small ads on a page and have to use the well-type of advertising make-up, don't build your left-hand pyramid clear to the top of columns one and two. That upper left-hand corner is where the eyes of your readers enter the page.

Because of newsprint shortages and high production costs, newspapers since World War II have been inclined to carry too much advertising to

Fig. 63. The size and style of headlines should give the reader a clue to the importance of news items. He gets no such help from this newspaper, which uses the same heading for almost every story. (Reproduced by permission of the Hazleton *Standard-Sentinel*.)

Fig. 64. Stories can be given good typographical display even when advertisements almost fill the page. The top example is dull. Note the use of multiple-column headlines in the other examples to attract the reader's attention.

the page. Since advertisers want their ads "next to reading matter," the well arrangement mentioned by Dean Olson frequently poses a problem for the make-up editor. When advertisements run high on the left side of the page, he often can achieve the effect he desires with an emphatic two- or even a one-line heading extending over several columns. This is better than starting the page with a one-column heading. But if only an inch or two of space is left, his only recourse is to lead off the page with a small heading.

Pages crowded with advertising also create a problem in handling pictures, for a basic rule of make-up is that a cut should not touch advertising. This juxtaposition is not attractive, and the effectiveness of the picture is lost if it is squared up against an advertisement, especially if the advertisement itself contains illustrations.

CHAPTER 17

Deciding the Paper's Content

THE PROBLEM OF THE NEWS

The typical American newspaper today is shaped by a number of conflicting forces. The owner or publisher sometimes has little control over them. He gets out the kind of paper that circumstances compel, not the kind that he perhaps would like. These circumstances influence the evaluation and treatment of news articles and the selection of other editorial matter. They must be thoroughly understood by the deskman.

The principal circumstances that shape the newspaper are:
1. Conventions of what constitutes news.
2. The need for getting readers and making money.
3. Concepts as to the functions of the newspaper.
4. The conditions of publication—size of city, competition, type of readers.

The circumstances are not inseparable, and their influence is not the same either for all newspapers, or for a single newspaper at all times. The publication of a successful newspaper—not only in a financial sense but also in service to the reader—depends to a great degree on understanding and adapting to these circumstances.

To a person traveling across the country, American newspapers are much alike in appearance and content. They are of the same size, have the same column width, and follow closely similar headline and make-up patterns. They publish articles and pictures from the same press news service bureaus, the same syndicated columns and features, and the same comic strips. Their judgments of what stories are worth front-page play are likely to coincide. There are differences, to be sure, just as an electric refrigerator made by one manufacturer differs in detail or size from that made by another; but standardization is the prevailing characteristic. This standardization is due to conventions regarding the nature of news.

The traditional conception of news is that it is a perceptible change in any *status quo*—an individual, an organization or institution, a state or nation. The more drastic the change, the more obviously it is news.

An individual may live for years without coming to the attention of a newspaper. Then something happens—he is involved in an automobile accident, he commits a crime, he heads a civic organization, he dies. There is a change in his *status quo*; he becomes news. A business building may be noticed by thousands of persons only casually for years. Then something happens—it is sold, it is damaged by fire or explosion, a decision is made to remodel it or tear it down. The building becomes news.

Almost anything is potential news; it becomes news when something happens. Explaining this fundamental of the nature of news, Walter Lippmann said:

Something definite must occur that has unmistakable form. It may be the act of going into bankruptcy, it may be a fire, a collision, an assault, a riot, an arrest, a denunciation, the introduction of a bill, a speech, a vote, a meeting, the expressed opinion of a well known citizen, an editorial in a newspaper, a sale, a wage-schedule, a price change, the proposal to build a bridge. . . . There must be a manifestation. The course of events must assume a certain definable shape, and until it is in a phase where some aspect is an accomplished fact, news does not separate itself from the ocean of possible truth.[1]

News, traditionally, is the report of a change or, in Lippmann's words, "of an aspect that has obtruded itself." If the change is a violent one, it arouses immediate interest. Hence the newspaper concern with catastrophe and crime. If it affects a large number of persons, it immediately becomes important. Hence the newspaper space devoted to government and public affairs.

Most of these observable manifestations about people make themselves known when their affairs touch public authority. Much of what is printed in newspapers, therefore, originates in governmental offices—the police station, the city hall, the courthouse, the state legislature, the governor's office, congress, the office of the president of the United States.

The places where change is recorded are comparatively few. They constitute the beats or runs to which reporters are assigned. Thus the problem of discovering news is immensely simplified. By maintaining contact with a few points, the newspaper can obtain information about a newsworthy event as soon as it happens, or perhaps even anticipate it.

[1] Walter Lippmann, *Public Opinion,* The Macmillan Company, 1947, p. 340.

DECIDING THE PAPER'S CONTENT 273

Until recent years newspapers were content with objective reports about these overt manifestations. Events were recorded in daily papers almost as isolated phenomena. What went on before an event obtruded itself—the currents and movements underneath that swept something to the surface so that it was observed—was not considered the business of the paper. For practical purposes it might be said that to a newspaper an event had no past. Nor, if we confine ourselves to the knowledge presented in the paper, did an event seem to have much of a present or future. The event was noted when it first appeared. It might reappear, but often it was forgotten as other events erupted to the surface. Newspapers confined themselves to recording "news breaks"—events that had obtruded themselves.

But recently newspapermen and the public have realized the deficiencies in merely reporting the surface manifestations. An early expression of this recognition came from an editor, J. Charles Poe of the Chattanooga *News*. In a talk before the American Society of Newspaper Editors in 1934 he said:

> Is not the time ripe for a shift away from the diet of dull routine, inconsequential crime and cheap flippant entertainment in our news columns to a more intelligent and withal more nourishing news menu? . . . [The people] want a chance to know about those social questions which heretofore have been chiefly the concern of scholars. They would like, perhaps, to try to relate themselves constructively to the pattern of their times.

This broadened concept of news was subsequently expressed in a resolution adopted by the society "that it be the consensus of the society that editors should devote a larger amount of attention and space to explanatory and interpretative news and a background of information which will enable the average reader more adequately to understand the movement and significance of events." In other words, events need to be interpreted as well as reported. As the Commission on Freedom of the Press said, newspapers should give "a truthful, comprehensive, and intelligent account of the day's events in a context which gives them meaning." The reporting of isolated phenomena, no matter how accurately, is meaningless; they must be related to other phenomena to be understood.

This concept of news coverage is summed up in the expression "interpretative reporting." Lester Markel, Sunday editor of the New York *Times*, defines it as "the deeper sense of the news. It places a particular event in the larger flow of events. It is the color, the atmosphere, the human elements that give meaning to a fact. In short, it is setting and sequence and, above all, significance."

Not all events need interpretation. A fire, an explosion, an automobile accident, a storm, a club meeting—most happenings recorded by the newspaper can be handled as isolated phenomena. Other events—the decision of congress to increase taxes, to establish new international trade agreements, to adopt a new program of social service for the people—may require explanation. Newspaper reports, then, are of two types—those that describe merely what happened and those that say why it happened and what it means.

JUDGING THE NEWS

In handling news, the reporter and the deskman have sharply divergent responsibilities. They both deal in the same commodity—news—and they judge it, broadly speaking, by the same values—interest and importance; but there the points of mutuality end.

In his work the reporter is faced with a fact, an event, a situation. If he considers it interesting or important or both, he gets the information he needs for his story. During his day's work he may encounter many facts, events, and situations. He has to make an immediate decision about each one of them. If he considers them news, his course is laid out for him. He decides whom he must see to get details, what questions to ask, how much information is needed. Then he writes his story, carefully evaluating the information he has gathered on the basis of the interest and significance it has, in his opinion, for readers.

The deskman (except insofar as he directs news coverage) is faced with the *report* of a fact, an event, a situation. He has the reporter's story before him, and he judges it. He weighs the reporter's coverage. Did he see the right people for details? Did he get answers to the right questions? Did he get enough information? The deskman also evaluates the reporter's account of the event. Is it well written? Does it emphasize or feature the most important and interesting details? Is it easy to read and understand?

But the reporter's story cannot be judged for what it is in itself. The deskman must compare it for interest and importance with the stories of other facts, events, or situations turned in by other reporters, with those received from the paper's correspondents, and with those ticked off over the press association teletype at the rate of 60 words a minute.

The deskman or editor pronounces the final verdict on a story's news value when he decides what "play" to give it. The play has several elements—the space the story is worth, the size of the headline it merits, the page it goes on, and its position on the page.

DECIDING THE PAPER'S CONTENT

In the pressure of the day's work there is little time to ponder over these questions of play. Various analyses have been made to account for a newspaperman's ability to make these quick decisions. Some explanations attribute it to instinct, to a "nose for news"; others consider it the result of training and experience; and still others say such decisions are possible only through the use of generally recognized stereotypes. Among the latter is Walter Lippmann, who has the following explanation of an editor's ability to handle incoming news bulletins with dispatch:

> The editor deals with these bulletins. He sits in his office, reads them, rarely does he see any large portion of the events themselves. He must . . . woo at least a section of his readers every day, because they will leave him without mercy if a rival paper happens to hit their fancy. He works under enormous pressure, for the competition of newspapers is often a matter of minutes. Every bulletin requires a swift but complicated judgment. It must be understood, put in relation to other bulletins also understood, and played up or played down according to its probable interest for the public, as the editor conceives it. Without standardization, without stereotypes, without routine judgments, without a fairly ruthless disregard for subtlety, the editor would soon die of excitement. The final page is of a definite size, must be ready at a precise moment; there can be only a certain number of captions on the items, and in each caption there must be a definite number of letters. Always there is the precarious urgency of the buying public, the law of libel, and the possibility of endless trouble. The thing could not be managed at all without systematization, for in a standardized product there is economy of time and effort, as well as a partial guarantee against failure.[2]

As Lippmann indicates, most of an editor's judgments must be almost automatic. They are determined by a somewhat crude but efficient scale of values whose application requires little thought. These determinants of newsworthiness are well known to all newspapermen: recency, timeliness or topicality, proximity, prominence of persons and places, significance, and human interest. These are, in a way, intrinsic elements of news interest by which all stories can be judged.

As a supplement to this scale, the deskman in choosing what stories to print and how to play them relies upon his own knowledge of what interests people. He doesn't have to be a psychologist or a public opinion pollster to know. People are interested, first of all, in themselves and, second, in other people. They are concerned about food, sex, money, clothing, shelter. They may be appealed to through their emotions—pity, fear, anxiety. They are attracted by the novel, the horrible, the spectacular, the beautiful. All newspapermen understand these primary preoccupations

[2] *Ibid.*, p. 352.

of people. Without such native understanding, they would be entirely unfitted for journalistic work.

NEWS AND NEWSPAPER ECONOMICS

In choosing the content of a newspaper—in determining the play of a story, for example—the editor may have several objectives in mind. These include informing the people so they can perform their duties as citizens, creating public opinion, exposing corruption in public officials, and protecting traditional liberties. These are often cited as the functions of the press. Actually, the editor's immediate task does not concern any of these functions. His first job is to get out a salable product. Gathering and printing news of whatever sort is merely a means to an end—the end being circulation.

According to the most generally accepted definition of news, the chief basis for selecting the material that goes into a newspaper is its appeal—the greatest appeal to the greatest number of persons. Often quoted is a definition given by Willard G. Bleyer in a journalism text popular thirty years ago. Bleyer said that news is "anything timely that interests a number of persons, and the best news is that which has the greatest interest for the greatest number." The profit motive is implied; it is not stated. Curtis D. MacDougall, in a later popular text, was more frank about the economic basis of news judgment. He defined news as "an account of an event which a newspaper prints in the belief that by so doing it will profit."

The reason for this emphasis on a pragmatic evaluation of news is the economics of newspaper publishing. As a product the newspaper is sold below cost. The money paid by the buyer generally amounts to about one-third the paper's total revenue. The other two-thirds comes from money received for advertising. But advertising rates are determined by the number of readers. Hence the editor's concern is to get as many readers as possible.

When an editor fails to maintain a circulation that produces adequate advertising revenues, his paper is doomed. Subscription premiums and prize contests may give the paper a transfusion that will keep it alive for a while, but in the long run its existence depends on a news and feature content for which the public is willing in large numbers to pay good money.

Great newspaper editors have been those with the ability to win large followings. Their formulas have varied according to the time and locality. James Gordon Bennett, preëminently a news gatherer, satisfied the public's desire for information about current affairs. Although his contemporary, Horace Greeley did not ignore news, he was the great political controversialist in an excessively political era. Charles A. Dana appealed to his public's interest in novelty of subject matter and treatment, especially the type of article called a human interest story. Later masters of mass circulation like William Randolph Hearst and Joseph Medill Patterson sensationalized the sensational in the crudest terms for the masses of metropolitan populations.

In attempting to attain as broad and numerous a readership as possible, editors today seem to have one of two paths.

One is that taken by the tabloids and sensation sheets—an appeal to the millions who enjoy violence, scandalous goings on, melodramatized events, and entertaining stories and articles. Big headlines blazon the news: COUNTS OUT HUBBY AT THE BELL; BOY'S SLAYER HEARS DOOM ON BIRTHDAY; AIRMAN'S WIFE DRAWS $5 FINE FOR CUTTING BLONDE'S TRESSES. Other space is devoted to the newspaper's features: comic strips, pages of photographs, gossip columns, advice to the lovelorn.

The other path is that taken by the majority of newspapers. These papers print as comprehensive and varied reports of the day's affairs as space permits. The theory, roughly, is that nobody will read everything in a paper but everybody will read something. This accounts for the miscellaneous content of most newspapers—the dozens of items that concern only a few score persons. All editors know that stock market quotations, for example, have low readership. They are printed for the few who are interested in them.

This theory of newspaper publishing is not new. The salutatory of the London *Daily Universal Register* of January 1, 1785, expressed the role of the newspaper in words that most editors would accept today:

A newspaper, conducted on the true and natural principles of such a publication, ought to be the register of the times, and faithful recorder of every species of intelligence. It ought not to be engrossed by any particular object, but like a well covered table, it should contain something suited to every palate.

Today's newspapers fit this description better than those of the past. When it was possible for almost any printer with "a shirttail full of type" to start a newspaper, the paper could succeed by appealing to a small, specialized group. The enormous cost of publishing today means that the paper must have a large circulation—that it must have universal rather than specialized appeal. Cities today are served by one newspaper that half a century ago could support six to a dozen papers. The few survivors have had to broaden their appeal to provide something of interest for every possible reader.

POPULARITY POLLS AND SURVEYS

In selecting material, the editor attempts to give most space to items he thinks will appeal to the greatest number of readers. That of course is the general aim. In actual practice it is seldom feasible. The reason is brought out in a study by the Louisville *Courier-Journal*.

A survey of preferences of men and women showed that out of every 100 persons, 94 looked at the picture page; 69 read "Blondie," the paper's most popular comic; 71 read the weather forecast; 60 looked at the editorial-page cartoon; 44 read the radio schedules; 72 liked a cartoon called "Private Lives"; and 36 read the sports column. Except for several front-page stories, the news articles individually did not rank high in the list of preferences.

Commenting on the results of the survey, James S. Pope, managing editor, said:

> If you were designing a newspaper from that survey, and knew nothing else about your job, you would carry a front page of news and fill the remainder of your paper with comic strips, cartoons, and sporting features.
>
> Such a product ought to be perfect. But it would not be. It would be like a huge market which displayed meat and bread in the windows, but offered for sale over the counters inside nothing but chocolate candy. Your customers would soon get the stomach-ache. They would look elsewhere for meat and bread.

Nevertheless, no editor can afford to ignore the likes and dislikes of his readers, or their reading habits. Knowing what the public wants and will accept is the secret of success in publishing a newspaper.

In the past few years editors, like sales managers and advertising directors, have turned to survey statistics to discover reader preferences. The most extensive of these survey projects is the Advertising Research Foundation's *The Continuing Study of Newspaper Reading*, already mentioned. Others are sponsored by schools of journalism and by private research organizations. Editors, at first hesitant regarding these studies, now accept them as tentative guides in selecting and playing editorial matter.

The interview-polling method by which the surveys are conducted has not produced a magic formula to solve the editor's problems. But it has resulted in a few general conclusions, such as the following:

DECIDING THE PAPER'S CONTENT

1. It's the story, not where it's run, that counts. Often a story played up with big headlines has much lower readership than one buried on the inside pages.

2. The big wire stories about congress, the United Nations, diplomatic maneuvers, and so forth may get banner headlines, but they don't attract the greatest number of readers.

3. A good human interest story, no matter if it's only two paragraphs long and printed under an inconspicuous headline, is almost always sought out and read by a large percentage of the people.

4. Women read a newspaper more thoroughly than men, but neither men nor women read all of it.

5. The tastes of men and women readers differ. Women show a preference for local news, whereas men lean slightly toward national and international news.

6. The stories most read by men are generally on the front page; those most read by women are often on the inside pages.

7. Pictures have a high interest value, but it is not so high as some persons contend. The median readership score of pictures for men and women is 56 percent. Median scores for other types of material are: best-read news story, 68 percent; page-1 banner story, 49 percent; weather, 49 percent; best-read wire story, 58 percent; best-read local news story, 59 percent.

8. Readership of the entire newspaper is high. The first page has the highest score, but the inside pages are also well read.

As Pope implied in his comment on the Louisville *Courier-Journal* preference survey, an editor cannot succeed if his newspaper is made up only of best-read features. The readership studies should be used for clues for getting out a better all-round newspaper. All the clues, however, cannot be considered universally valid because too many factors intervene. Small-town papers, for example, are read more thoroughly than city papers, and weeklies more so than dailies. People who work usually cannot spend as much time on a morning paper as they can on an afternoon paper. The newsworthiness of an individual item or feature is relative to other items or features in the issue in which it appears. Its score one day may be lower or higher in a survey conducted another day.

Editors have found readership studies extremely valuable as a guide in deciding whether to drop a column or feature, to buy a syndicated feature or strip, or to do away with a department like book reviews or music and art news. Space is at a premium in a newspaper, and such material is not worth while if it is not read.

Fig. 65. The Continuing Study of Newspaper Reading gives the readership score of each item. In the Athens (Ohio) *Messenger* the best-read story was not the play story but one farther down on the page.

DECIDING THE PAPER'S CONTENT

Among the newspapers that have made extensive changes as the result of readership studies are the Utica (New York) *Observer-Dispatch* and *Daily Press*. In a booklet entitled *By Guess and by Guide*, Vincent S. Jones, executive editor, described how his staff spruced up these two papers. The general goal was "to make things easy for the reader—easy to find, easy to read, easy to understand."

Built-in cap lines replaced old-fashioned subheads; the straight-up-and-down appearance of the page was changed by using more multicolumn headlines; gray masses of 8-point type were brightened by indented full-face paragraphs, and broken up by asterisks and king-size periods; more 10-point type was used and more material was set double column; long involved stories like reports of city council meetings were broken up into headlined sections; local statistics and records—deaths, births, marriage licenses, real estate transfers—were put into one column where readers could quickly find them; standing heads for columns were dropped in favor of live heads; the editorial page was enlivened with more display type and illustrations—maps, charts, pictures; the page-1 index was moved up on the page and set double column to comprise not only a guide to the inside contents but also a lively and readable summary of the day's news.

Jones summed up his views on the editor's problem in trying to give his readers what he thinks they want:

Many editors have pointed out the danger of paying too much attention to what readers want. I would be the last to suggest that there is anything but disaster in groping for a "synthetic" newspaper, geared to play upon reader tastes and weaknesses.

But I am keenly concerned with the problem of improving readership.

If a story or an editorial which I believe to be important is ignored, is it the subject or the treatment?

Does it need better writing, or more attractive presentation?

Some of the better newspapers and magazines have shown how to make even the most ponderous subjects readable.

So it's not a case of pandering to the reader. It's a problem of finding out how to interest him in things like atomic energy control and the United Nations, or good city government.

HOW MUCH ENTERTAINMENT?

The newspaper, whether or not it wants to be, is one of the media of mass communication, along with radio, television, movies, and magazines. To survive, it must appeal to the masses, preferably by not pandering to the lowest common denominator of interests and tastes. The temptation is for editors to give a disproportionate amount of space to entertaining their readers in order to get and hold circulation. But traditionally the newspaper's role as a medium of entertainment has been minor. Its valid role, historically, has been as a carrier of information.

Before the motion picture, radio, and television, the newspaper had almost exclusive access to the attention of the public. Its struggle for existence in recent years has been not with other newspapers so much as with the newer media—not only for the advertising dollar but for the attention of the public.

In fighting its competitors the newspaper has resorted to tactics that many persons condemn, among them the majority of newspapermen. Typical of the criticisms is the following from an article by Ferdinand Lundberg:

> In order to attract readers, an American newspaper must do the following things: it must devote a disproportionate amount of space to the reportage of commercialized "sports" events; it must devote a disproportionate amount of space to the reportage of isolated crimes of violence and sexual scandals; it must give heavy emphasis to the entertainment world—Hollywood and Broadway; it must discuss important political affairs in the same juvenile terms it devotes to sports, crimes and sex; and it must devote a disproportionate amount of space to "comics" and to various entertainment. "Serious" news it must almost invariably present in terms of the most primitive sort of conflict: "Vandenberg Flays Byrnes," "Economists Scorch President," "Pope Slashes Communists," and "Republicans Nail Democrats."

Newspapermen recognize that these practices exist in spite of their honest desire to present a well-balanced report of the significant happenings of the day. Few persons advocate the elimination of all features, human interest stories, crime reports, and sports news. But how to keep them "disproportionate"?

It is the desk's problem, and it is not an easy one to solve. The desk has what is called a "news hole" to fill—the space left in the paper after advertising is allocated and regular features such as comics, the bridge lesson, and sports pages are provided for. In an average metropolitan newspaper—say one of 30 pages containing 240 columns—the space left for live stories and pictures—the news hole—may run only from 30 to 50 columns.

What can be done to provide space for all the news that should be printed? Leave out the advertising? No; the paper needs the money. Leave out the comic strips? The switchboard will be swamped with protesting readers. Leave out some of the popular features? The editor will hear from the circulation manager. Cut down on the space for sports and society? The sports and society editors will argue loudly that they need more space, not less.

The editor usually must submit to these pressures. There is the unmistakable evidence of readership surveys that articles reporting what congress did, what the State Department said in a note to Russia, what the excise board decided about raising the tax rate, and what the school superintendent said about the difficulty of hiring primary teachers do not interest a large number of readers. There just doesn't seem to be the demand for solid informational articles that there is for sports stories, crime reports, and human interest oddities.

Nevertheless, editors have not given up their attempt to educate their readers' taste for serious and important news. They still put the big headlines on the stories they think people should read; they still find a place for Walter Lippmann as well as for Walter Winchell; they still send an expert to cover the state capitol as well as a baseball game.

Moreover, there is the possibility that, in overloading with entertainment material, newspapers may be slowly committing suicide. The fact is that a newspaper is ill equipped to compete with radio, television, and movies in entertainment. To these three news is merely incidental; to the newspaper entertainment should be merely incidental. The situation is pretty much that described by John R. Herbert of the Quincy (Massachusetts) *Patriot Ledger*:

Today we have radio, television, and motion pictures locked in mortal combat, and the fight is strictly to capture the great American entertainment audience rather than trying to take over the field of public information. Thus we have the public information field all to ourselves by default.

This should be our great opportunity to serve America and serve it well. I am disturbed when I find some newspapers thinking their primary job is to provide entertainment. I am not against crossword puzzles and other such items in a daily newspaper, but they should be a minor rather than a major part of our activity. Our job and the task to which we have been dedicated is to provide public information. It is our responsibility to see that we do this above all else. If we turn away from this job and go into the entertainment business we will be sunk in the fight for the entertainment audience.

Similar sentiments were expressed by Robert U. Brown, editor of *Editor & Publisher*, in an address before the National Editorial Association:

Too many editors, in my estimation, have lost sight of the importance of news and have misdirected their efforts in the presentation of entertainment. They are heading for trouble.

These editors are laboring under the delusion they must publish a heavy budget of entertainment items in their columns in order to compete with the movies, with the radio, and other media in competition for the reader's time. . . . Newspapers are not and never have been designed to compete in the entertainment field. Their one purpose and function—the one thing to which they owe their existence—is the presentation of local news and opinion.

Is there any positive evidence that newspapers should not compete in the entertainment field? Yes; for the new media, despite their spectacular growth, have not reduced the total circulation of newspapers. Except for one or two years during the depression in the 1930's, newspaper circulation in this country has shown a rise every year. Even in competing for the advertising dollar, daily newspapers have held their own with appropriations greater than those for any other single medium.

No other medium matches the newspaper in the volume and quality of current information. Whenever another medium does offer competition in the field of news, the newspapers should begin to worry. The newspaper's answer to the question of popular appeal is not to sacrifice news, but to make it easier to read. The techniques for this are becoming better understood—readable writing, humanization of issues and events, and attractive typographical presentation.

PUBLICATION CONDITIONS

In addition to the broad considerations of the nature of news, the economic problem raised by the necessity of attracting readers, and the function of the newspaper, the editor's task in determining content is complicated by the conditions under which his newspaper is published.

One of the most important conditions is the size of the town in which the paper is published and the nature of the geographical region whose news it reports.

A small-town daily and a metropolitan daily differ by much more than merely the number of pages. The small-town newspaper emphasizes local news; as someone has said, it is the printed diary of the community. It carries news not only of public affairs, which touch the lives of all the population, but also of individual affairs. The metropolitan newspaper lacks this intimate contact with its readers; it tends toward impersonality. Its news must interest a much more numerous segment of the population. This factor often tips the scales in favor of a wire story against a local story. On a small-town paper local news is front-page news. On a metropolitan paper, unless an item is extraordinary, it goes inside, perhaps on a page set aside for local stories.

This difference in outlook, as well as space limitations, accounts for the fact that in a small newspaper national and international news is boiled down to the minimum of information required to make a story understandable. A story worth a column in a big-city newspaper may be worth only a paragraph in a small-city paper.

The small-town newspaper is also more likely than the metropolitan newspaper to play up constructive news. Crime, for example, is seldom reported fully in the small-town press. A Chicago or Philadelphia newspaper can print gory accounts of murder and salacious details of a scandal that a Prairie Grove or Millvale newspaper could not print without offending its readers. The small-town editor who searched out his community's peccadilloes and played them up under big headlines would soon find himself losing friends—and subscribers. His readers may not be enthusiastically interested in news about the chamber of commerce, churches, or civic clubs, but that's the sort of information they think it proper for the newspaper to print.

The newspaper must mirror the interests of the geographical area it serves. For example, newspapers in Pittsburgh, center of the coal and steel industry, print front-page banner stories about the United Mine Workers that hardly make the inside pages of Philadelphia newspapers a few hundred miles away. A rise in commodity wheat prices may be front-page news in the Dakotas, Nebraska, and Kansas; it may be recorded, if at all, in the financial department on page 26 of a newspaper in Tennessee or Georgia. Interests vary from town to town and from region to region, and the deskman who changes his job may have to change his news values at the same time.

Even for newspapers published in the same city there are differences in news evaluations. The New York *Times* and the *Herald Tribune* agree fairly consistently in the play they give stories, but their values are not those of the *Daily News* and the *Journal-American*. The first two papers, though published in the same city, are hardly competitors of the latter two, for they appeal to an almost entirely different segment of the population. The newspaper's policy is another and very important determinant of news value.

Finally, the selection of news is influenced by whether a paper is published in the morning or afternoon, by the edition, and by whether it depends on street sales or home delivery for the greater part of its circulation.

Morning newspapers tend to be less sensational than afternoon papers. There is less opportunity for the morning newspaper to increase its circulation by street sales of different editions. The afternoon sheets may issue edition after edition. The deskmen constantly shift stories and replace them with reports of later happenings to make each succeeding edition like an entirely different newspaper. These street editions may play up lurid stories that are subordinated in the home edition; the late street edition generally puts sports and markets on the front page. On the other hand, workers on morning papers have fewer editions to get out. By the time the desk starts to work, the day's developments are in state of suspension. Most government offices are closed; congress and the legislature have recessed; business has stopped for the day; and there will be no further developments in many events the newspaper covers. Thus the morning newspaper puts the previous day's happenings in perspective. Stories chosen for the front page of the early edition are likely to stand up during the night.

Many of the larger newspapers get out different editions for different groups of readers. The state edition of a morning newspaper plays up important happenings that are of state-wide, national, and international interest. Its home edition may give priority to local news. Separate editions may be printed for distribution in a specific geographical area. A St. Louis newspaper, for example, may contain in its Missouri edition a great deal of Missouri news that is killed in the edition circulated in Illinois.

So many are the conditions that influence it that news can never be given absolute values. If it could be charted and diagramed, it would be like a weather map—out of date before it could be drawn, an abstraction rather than a reality.

CHAPTER **18**

Publicity and Propaganda

HANDOUTS SWAMP THE DESK

The mail addressed to the city desk is unusually heavy. Dumped on the desk with each delivery is a big stack of communications—typewritten, mimeographed, and printed offerings from advertising agencies, public relations offices, and publicity departments of institutions and business organizations.

The experienced deskman goes through this stack of releases, handouts, blurbs, puffs, and boosts with the quickness and efficiency of an automatic card-sorting machine in a business office. He is dealing with the problem of publicity at an elementary level, and his decisions as to which material should go into his oversize wastebasket and which should be dropped in his copy basket as news are almost reflex.

Some of the envelopes contain large sheets on which are articles printed in newspaper style with headlines. These are clipsheets. They come from such organizations as the National Cotton Council, the Women's Christian Temperance Union, the National Association of Manufacturers, the national committees of the Republican and Democratic parties, and the American Legion. The stories are usually well written and frequently informative, but the deskman ordinarily drops them into the wastebasket. He knows that the articles were not prepared to give necessary and objective information but instead were written to present a one-sided viewpoint or to acquaint readers with a slanted set of facts.

Many of the envelopes contain photographic mats with headlines and cutlines and proofs. They deal with a wide variety of subjects—a new model of an automobile; bathing beauties in Miami Beach; mannequins wearing new winter dresses made of woolens; a new, easy-to-make dessert; a Hollywood starlet with fine, long legs whom the boys at Polytechnic Institute have voted the girl with the most beautiful smile; a desk and chair showing how easy it is to make old furniture like new. Most of these follow the clipsheets into the wastebasket. The deskman realizes that they are cleverly disguised plugs for commercial products. Some of them, however, may be saved if they don't mention a trade name in the copy or show an identifiable packaged product in the illustration. They may be used by a small newspaper, for it often has difficulty getting illustrations for the Friday food page and the women's page.

Other envelopes contain long mimeographed stories that are often interesting reading. From a railroad may come a report of how it has replaced coal-burning engines with Diesels. A utility firm may send in an article about how farm life and farm work have been transformed by electrical appliances and machinery. A manufacturing firm reports on experiments showing new uses for plastics and tells how man-made products are superior to those found in nature. These releases, although factual and informative, also find their way into the wastebasket. They are too long, and the newspaper doesn't have space to print them.

Many of the releases come from colleges and universities and from such organizations as the Red Cross, the National Safety Council, the Salvation Army, and the Crippled Children's Society. The deskman looks these over more carefully than the handouts from what he knows are purely commercial sources. If the material is from a local educational or welfare group, he is quite likely to put it in his copy basket instead of the wastebasket. He realizes that it is designed to promote a good cause. Though it may not be the most interesting information in the world, his newspaper's policy is to promote programs carried on by such organizations and he prints the handouts if they are remotely newsworthy.

And finally there are a great many releases from public officials and departments and agencies of the state and federal government. The deskman carefully examines these for items that may be given a local angle. For example, the state tax commission reports on the quarterly sales tax collections from each county, listing them alphabetically. This can be made into a local story by playing up the newspaper's home county collection in the lead. Or the state highway commission releases a list of projects for which bids are being advertised. Projects in the paper's circulation area can form the basis for a news story. Government handouts and reports are among the most fruitful sources of tips for news stories. No matter how long and how jammed with figures, they should not be discarded until they have been examined for possible local interest news. Though the regional service of the newspaper's press association is on the lookout for such stories, it has so many clients that it frequently misses some or fails to report on others in the belief that they are trivial.

As has been indicated, the publicity problem faced by the deskman who sorts out the press releases mailed into the newspaper office is fairly elementary. Yet it is difficult because of the sheer quantity of material he must handle. A survey conducted by the University of Miami Journalism Department indicated that the number of handouts received by newspapers, both large and small, ranged from 10 to 500 daily. The average for all newspapers in the survey was 77.

Some editors with a strong antipathy to free publicity never open these stories. Most, however, have found that in this mountain of handouts there usually is a molehill of real news. The Miami survey indicated that an average of 6 percent of the unsolicited handouts was publishable. The common reasons for rejecting them were limited local interest, no reader interest, poorly written stories, reasons of policy, disguised advertising, obviously faked material, apparent inaccuracies in stories, release duplicated, and story stretched too thin.

In most newspaper offices the city desk sorts out the mimeographed handouts, printed clipsheets, and picture mats. Some are assigned to a reporter for rewriting, but many are passed on to the copy desk, often with only casual inspection by the city editor. The copyreader is expected to edit the material to winnow the grains of legitimate news from the chaff of free advertising and promotion.

SOME GUIDING PRINCIPLES

In handling material that he knows to be free publicity the deskman should be guided by a fundamental philosophy of news presentation and by an awareness of the devices employed by space grabbers.

The fundamental principles that he should keep in mind regarding publicity include the following:

1. The object of the newspaper is to print news for the benefit of the public, not for the benefit of the individuals and organizations creating the news.

2. News emanating from a publicity director is slanted. It may be interesting, important, and factual, but nevertheless it does not tell the full story. A disinterested person—a reporter—should have access to the facts and should be permitted to choose those he wants to write up.

3. The newspaper has advertising columns for persons and organizations that wish to get a special and selfish message before the public. To give away space reduces the value of the advertising columns.

4. The source of information must be known and preferably stated in the story. If the reader knows the origin of information, he can make up his own mind about whether to accept or reject it.

Broadly speaking, the acceptability of publicity items is based on their news value or interest and whether printing them is to the benefit of the public. Items that meet such a test can be edited and printed, special care being given to delete material that is obviously puffery or a substitute for paid advertising.

Handouts are usually prepared by newspaper-trained publicity writers. They are written in proper newspaper style according to a recipe perfected by Ivy Lee at the beginning of this century, but buried in the stories are plugs for the product or service and puffs for the firm. Although publicity material gets only a small headline and goes on an inside page, it must be edited as carefully as page-1 stories. Certain types of copy—in particular, recipes and features for the food page, articles on fashions, and stories for the business page—must be scrutinized for the discovery and elimination of brand names and trademarks.

Newspaper avoidance of mentioning well-known advertised products, however, is sometimes carried to an extreme that is silly. Names of automobiles usually are not mentioned in accident stories, though it is hard to see how a statement that a man was killed when his Chevrolet crashed into a tree will help General Motors sell more cars. Worse is the patent evasion in the statement that the bandits escaped in "a black sedan with out-of-state license plates" when the name of the car is needed for identification. If the brand name is an essential part of the story, it should be given.

On the other hand, newspapers sometimes omit the name of a store, hotel, café, or tavern because mentioning it would be "bad" advertising, as when an elevator falls and injures passengers, a building is cited as unsafe by a fire inspector, a café is declared unsanitary, a firm is charged with violation of the Pure Food and Drug Act. This, of course, is news suppression, fortunately of a type that is rare nowadays.

While newspapers are constantly on guard against individuals and concerns that seek free advertising, they unashamedly open their columns to stories that promote the welfare, education, and enlightenment of the public. Churches, schools, museums, libraries, hospitals, civic organizations, and many other institutions and groups are given space generously for activities whose news value may be slight. Likewise, newspapers publicize welfare and charity campaigns put on by the Red Cross, Community Chest, Salvation Army, and other agencies as part of their duty as quasi-public institutions.

The rule-of-thumb testing of publicity releases by their interest or value to the reader is described by Herbert Brucker of the Hartford (Connecticut) *Courant* as "an eminently sensible conclusion on how to handle most day-to-day issues." No advocate of printing advertising as news, Brucker nevertheless declares that "as long as our newspapers and other media of information devote their editorial space to matters of honest interest to their readers, it does not matter much whether commercial or political purpose is also served in the process."[1] An editor unable to accept this compromise would find it impossible to stay in newspaper work.

SOME SPECIFIC PROBLEMS

Though it is easy to set up general rules for handling publicity handouts, their application in specific instances is often difficult. Moreover, newspaper practices vary. Metropolitan papers generally maintain a tighter curb on publicity than do smaller publications; many weeklies unblushingly publish stories directing attention to sales announced in the advertising columns. Events that quite clearly are commercial in nature or constitute advertising for an individual or firm often at the same time have local news interest, and it is hard to weigh their value as news for the public against their value as publicity for the sponsor.

Competing newspapers in a city and also state press associations from time to time have attempted to establish codes regulating publicity, but even these have loopholes which leave specific problems to the discretion of the individual editor.

The widespread differences in what is acceptable as news are indicated by the lack of uniformity among newspapers throughout the nation in treating the following:

1. Recitals by pupils of dance, violin, piano, and voice teachers.
2. Flower shows, fashion shows, cooking schools, garden schools, and other events sponsored by local organizations but having commercial tie-ups.
3. Promotions and transfers of executives in local business and industrial establishments.
4. Construction of new buildings, expansion, or remodeling by stores and other firms.

[1] Herbert Brucker, *Freedom of Information,* The Macmillan Company, 1949, p. 142.

5. Company-sponsored teams in sand-lot baseball, softball, basketball, bowling, and other sports.

6. Social events such as picnics and banquets held by employees of local concerns.

7. The entertainment of prominent persons by department stores, bookstores, and other firms.

8. Contests conducted by business establishments.

9. Trips to market centers made by the buyers for department stores.

10. Sales contests won by local insurance agents and local representatives of nationally distributed products.

11. Trade conventions and meetings of salesmen or representatives of large local concerns.

12. Store promotions for special occasions and holidays.

13. Trick promotions—a free performance by a "human fly," an elaborately decorated show window for Easter or Christmas, a parade.

14. Stories and mats of new motion pictures, entertainers at night clubs and cabarets, professional lecturers, stage shows.

15. Special trains and buses to carry local sports fans to out-of-town athletic contests.

This list could be greatly enlarged, for there is almost no end to the ideas for promotion disguised as news that imaginative publicity men seek to get by both city desk and copy desk. In the absence of a specific policy laid down by their newspaper, city editors and deskmen must make their own decision about whether to print or not to print on the individual merits of each item.

THE PRIME EVIL OF PUBLICITY

There are few truly new problems in journalism. Today's editor who bewails the proliferation of public information bureaus in government and condemns the rise of the highly lucrative "profession" of public relations counseling had his earlier counterpart in the editor who guarded against the hoaxes of press agents and, somewhat later, in the editor who fended off publicity men.

Free publicity has been a problem ever since newspapers ceased to be primarily media for the dissemination of commercial intelligence. As early as 1809 Washington Irving got the New York *Evening Post* to print an item reporting the disappearance of one Diedrich Knickerbocker from his lodgings. Later it developed that Knickerbocker had left behind a curious manuscript, and soon a news story reported that it would be published as a book. Thus did Irving build up interest for his *Knickerbocker's History of New York.*

Editors ever since then have been plagued by such hoaxed news. Phineas T. Barnum's daring in using publicity stunts was largely responsible for his fame as a showman. Publicity stunts patterned after his exploits became the stock in trade of theatrical press agents. Some were used so often that only a very naïve editor would bite. At one time no city editor would print a story about an actress being robbed of her jewels; it was almost always a fake.

After the press agent—whose clientele was chiefly among theatrical people, although hotels, railroads, and other agencies hired people to get things into the newspapers—came the publicity man. He expanded publicity to include business organizations and their leaders, churches, universities, and public officials. Before long the publicity man evolved into the public relations director or counsel—the dignified-sounding title he prefers to be known by today.

Public relations counsel, public information director, publicity man, press agent—under any name his goal is free and profitable advertising for his employer and the good will of the public. It is a profitable profession, drawing most of its practitioners from the ranks of experienced newspapermen; and it is an artful one, using the techniques learned by editors for gaining public interest, the findings of psychologists, and the methods developed by public opinion experts. So entrenched has it become that it is an integral part of the machinery for gathering and disseminating news. The president of the United States employs a press secretary to act as liaison with the newspapers. Most of the departments of the federal government employ information assistants to feed news material to reporters. And so it goes down the hierarchy of government, with state, county, and city officials designating assistants to deal with the press. Large business firms, institutions, welfare organizations, and prominent individuals—all have their press and radio representatives.

The publicity profession could never have reached its important status today if its members had restricted themselves to the puffs and boosts of the old-time press agents. Much of their "public information" is news—news that could not be gathered by newspapers and press associations without great cost because they would have to employ extra reporters to get it. But it is always censored news; no publicity man is going to volunteer "bad" news in the sense of news that will reflect against his employer. Therein lies its prime evil.

The publicity problem is truly a major problem for newspapers—not the abolition of publicity, for that is impossible, but its curbing so that papers can continue to give full and impartial reports of the day's happenings.

At the local level the individual newspaper can guard against being imposed upon by publicity seekers by carefully scrutinizing the unsolicited releases that come in and by discouraging their senders. It can inform publicity departments and advertising agencies that it does not want their material by refusing to accept delivery and directing the post office to return it to the sender, by asking to be removed from their mailing lists, or by returning publicity material with a printed sticker or letter suggesting that it be incorporated in paid advertising. Another possible step is to lay down a stringent rule against the "business office must"—a story sent to the editorial office by the advertising department with a request that it be printed to please an advertiser or make it easier to sell an account.

Today the handouts and releases that come by mail are a comparatively minor part of the total publicity output. This route to the news columns is ignored by many of the more expert public relations men. They prefer to work through reporters on both newspapers and press services, for they know that their material is more likely to get into print if it is written by staff members.

Protecting the objectivity of the news columns by weeding out press releases is but one aspect of a much broader problem. Press associations and syndicates must also be watched, as George Olds, managing editor of the Springfield (Missouri) Newspapers, pointed out in an article in the November 16, 1946, issue of *Editor & Publisher*.

Skeptical of a friend's remark that 75 percent of the copy received via press association wires was originated by press agents, Olds made a check and came to the following conclusion:

> When you count the Washington report—which dominates the news these days and which largely is based on departmental handouts—and the politicians' statements and the business news and the sports report, both amateur and professional, and the movie and radio news and the odds and ends from conventions, "institutes" and haberdashers, you blushingly must concede most of the field to the press agents.

Some of the material sent out by press services actually is the type of free advertising that any deskman would quickly throw into the wastebasket if it came to him as a publicity release. Olds wrote:

PUBLICITY AND PROPAGANDA

The mailed feature services and picture pages are little heavens for press agents—particularly because few editors bother to read the stories and captions before they toss the stuff into the copy basket. One entire page—and it was fairly representative—of one news association's feature service was made up of press agents' contributions, dominated by a tempting piece from the Singer Sewing Machine Company. But in no instance was the source indicated. If you want to print press agents' stories, that's all right—but if you don't, you have to be awfully alert.

The man on the copy desk can't do much about the publicity in a press association story that is based on a release thoughtfully delivered to the news agency's office or in a story turned in by one of his paper's own reporters who got his information carefully screened by a press secretary. The problem requires coördinated action by state press associations, national editors' and publishers' groups, and press services and syndicates. But the individual deskman must be cognizant of the problem and constantly on the alert so as not to be deceived by publicity-slanted stories whatever their source.

FROM PRODUCTS TO IDEAS

Free publicity and propaganda, in the sense the word is commonly used in today, are closely related, differing only in quality. Free publicity springs primarily from a commercial motive; it seeks to sell a product. The motive of propaganda may also be economic, but its aim is chiefly ideological. It seeks to sell ideas.

The origin of the word "propaganda" is perfectly respectable. It made its appearance in 1622 with Pope Gregory's establishment of the Sacra Congregatio de Propaganda Fide, or Sacred Congregation for the Propagation of the Faith. The next year the College of Propaganda was formed for the education of missionary priests. The term was extended in meaning from the religious sense to the propagation of any doctrine.

The word acquired a derogatory connotation in America after World War I largely as the result of a series of debunking books purporting to show that the United States was duped into entering the European conflict. Among the propaganda devices exposed were the atrocity stories carried in the American press as reports of true incidents. Further evidence of the power of propaganda was revealed by the exposure of the machinations of big business, the utilities, and the "merchants of death" in congressional hearings and in books and magazines. Soon we began reading about the way totalitarian governments employed propaganda to enslave whole peoples. Propaganda became identified in the public mind with such agencies as the Nazi Ministry of Propaganda and Popular Enlightenment.

The dictionary definitions of propaganda have not caught up with the popular meaning of the word. The definition given by William Albig in his *Public Opinion* more nearly coincides with our ordinary use of the word than do those in the lexicons: "Propaganda is a special term referring to the intentional dissemination of conclusions from concealed sources by interested individuals and groups." The sources, of course, are not always concealed; nevertheless, disguised propaganda is one of the most effective methods of putting ideas across.

Besides concealment, the fine art of propaganda employs appeal to the emotions, lying and fabrication, exaggeration, distortion by selection, repetition, and the manipulation of symbols. Straightforward propaganda from a known source presents no particular danger. The reader can make allowances if he knows who is advocating the ideas and why. It is when propaganda is presented covertly that he—and the newspaperman—must be on guard.

Editors are faced with the same problem in dealing with propaganda as with publicity: much that they recognize as propaganda they also recognize as news. The president's message to congress, a speech by the Secretary of State on the foreign situation, a white paper issued by a government—these may be propaganda in the good and bad meanings of the term. They are also news, and a newspaper cannot refuse to print reports of them even when it recognizes them as obvious special pleading. To cope with the propaganda problem, the newspaperman must understand the techniques of the propagandist and the effects of propaganda on people's thinking.

TECHNIQUES OF PROPAGANDA

The methods of propagandists have been analyzed so well that any person can apply to statements and information a few simple tests to determine their nature. Although considerably oversimplified, the following devices listed by the Institute for Propaganda Analysis are worth consideration:

1. Name Calling. Name calling is used to build up prejudice against persons, organizations, policies, beliefs, and practices by means of a disparaging label. The American Medical Association, for example, fought President Truman's efforts to establish a compulsory health insurance program by calling it "socialized medicine." Labor unions sought to arouse prejudice against the Taft-Hartley Act by labeling it a "slav

PUBLICITY AND PROPAGANDA

labor" act. Words likely to appeal to our fears, hates, and biases include Red, Communist, Tory, Wall Street, Fascist, dictatorship, bureaucracy, and capitalist, among others. The choice of an adjective can condition our attitude toward the thing described. There is a big difference between saying that a person is thrifty and saying he is miserly, or between describing a book as scholarly and describing it as pedantic.

2. Glittering Generalities. The opposite of name calling is glittering generalities. The device asks for a favorable judgment or attitude by appealing to what we look upon as good, noble, or just. Thus the propagandist opposing government regulation of business malpractices declares that such legislation interferes with the American tradition of free enterprise. By means of glittering generalities the propagandist identifies his campaign with such ideals as patriotism, liberty, truth, freedom, social justice, progress, and the American way.

3. Transfer. By transfer the propagandist seeks to shift "the authority, sanction and prestige of something we respect and revere to something he would have us accept." A candidate for mayor, for example, may conduct a campaign promising a cleanup of the city's vice dens. If he can get the endorsement of the town's ministers, he will have the sanction of the church. Huey Long was cognizant of the power of this device when he said that if Fascism ever came to America it would come under the guise of 100 percent Americanism.

4. Testimonial. Testimonial is a familiar advertising device. The famous movie star says that she uses an advertised brand of soap; the athlete, that he eats an advertised brand of breakfast cereal; a "man of distinction," that he drinks an advertised brand of whiskey. The implication is that to be like them the reader must buy and use the same products. The same method is employed by the propagandist. A candidate for the U.S. senate gets the endorsement of the president; many of the city's prominent men support a campaign to raise funds for a new Y.M.C.A. building; the nation's educational leaders are sought out for opinions favoring federal funds for education. These are common examples of the use of testimonials to support a cause.

5. Plain Folks. By pretending to be people like ourselves—"just plain folks"—individuals seek to win our confidence. This device was employed by Ivy Lee, one of the most famous publicity experts, to change the public's picture of John D. Rockefeller from a ruthless monopolist to a kindly old man with a penchant for giving away shiny new dimes. Well-educated politicians when electioneering in backwoods regions speak ungrammatically and wear sloppy clothes to make themselves appear no different from their constituents.

6. Card Stacking. Card stacking is the familiar red-herring technique in which the propagandist diverts attention from propositions dangerous to his cause by creating a new issue. In the words of the Institute for Propaganda Analysis: "He stacks the cards against the truth. He uses under-emphasis and over-emphasis to dodge issues and evade facts. He resorts to lies, censorship, and distortion. He omits facts. He offers false testimony. He creates a smoke screen of clamor by raising a new issue when he wants an embarrassing matter forgotten." Political candidates avoid issues by putting on a "circus"; an employer may seek to divert attention from low wages as a strike issue to "red agitators" among workmen; the national administration may seek to draw attention from the failure of its domestic policies by "creating" a new crisis in foreign relations.

7. Band Wagon. The propagandist seeks by the band-wagon device to obtain acceptance of his ideas or program by appealing to the individual not to be left out when "everybody's doing it." If everyone else believes it, it must be so. All candidates for public office, for example, make exaggerated claims of how many votes they will get at the polls—a device that fools nobody any more. Variations of the formula are reiterations of the idea that it's "smart" to do this or that, or that the "best" people believe it.

COMBATING THE PROPAGANDIST

The newspaper cannot reject all propaganda, but by careful editing and evaluation of the news it can check the propagation of ideas not in the public interest and expose the hidden sources of information designed to mislead.

One method of putting readers on guard against propaganda was employed by newspapers before and during World War II. These papers ran an editor's note above news reports of official pronouncements and communiqués from the belligerent countries warning readers against accepting the information as truth.

Perhaps this device could be used more often. For example, in its fight against government-sponsored health insurance, the American Medical Association assessed special fees on doctors for a campaign to "educate" the public regarding the dangers of "socialized medicine." The campaign was put in the hands of publicity experts. They prepared news releases containing arguments, statistics, and other data that revealed organized medicine's point of view. These releases, issued to the press directly as handouts or indirectly through spokesmen, were news. But they were also special pleading. An editor's note—"This article is printed as a public service to give the American Medical Association's views on government-sponsored health insurance. This newspaper does not vouch for the truth or accuracy of the statements contained therein"—would put the reader on guard, and he could then decide whether to believe the article.

Newspapers sometimes do use such a device. During a political campaign or a live local controversy, editors set aside space in which both sides can have their say without restriction except for the libel laws.

A warning over stories, however, could be used only on exceptional occasions. No deskman would like to take the responsibility, for instance, of labeling as propaganda a speech by the president or a diplomatic note issued by the State Department. He has no way of determining the motives behind the speech or the note in such circumstances.

But though unable to use such forthright treatment of propaganda as a note of warning, newspapers can at least name and identify the source of all stories known or thought to be special pleading. As a matter of fact, it is a fundamental journalistic rule that the source of all news reports must be given. Press associations consider this so important for some stories that they insist the source be put at the start of the story. The Associated Press tells its staff: "Don't be afraid to begin a story by naming the source. It is awkward sometimes, but also it sometimes is the best and most direct way to put the story in proper perspective and balance, when the source must be established in the reader's mind if he is properly to understand the story." The chief deficiency of newspapers and press associations in respect to stating the source is sometimes the failure to *identify* the source adequately or to give an explanation which will enable the unthinking reader clearly to grasp the propagandistic significance of the information.

Some of the covert methods propagandists use to slip their special pleading into the news columns should be mentioned. Among them are the following:

1. Press Releases and Handouts. The usefulness and danger of these were indicated in the discussion of free publicity. If such material is not rewritten before publication, it should be edited carefully to remove offensive propaganda, and if the source is omitted it should be stated.

2. Essay Contests and Competitions. When a business firm or trade association sets aside sums of money for prizes to high-school students for the best essay on an assigned topic, it can be assumed that other motives are at work than just wanting to assist young writers. The selection of a Cotton Queen, an Apple Queen, or a Sweet Potato Queen obviously is a promotional enterprise. A publicity man for a soap manufacturer is said to have inspired the once-popular fad of soap sculpture by means of a nation-wide exhibit and prizes.

3. Camouflaged Committees and Organizations. These often have a high-sounding name, but their outward activities and pronouncements may conceal ulterior motives. A Good Government League may not be interested in good government so much as in fighting corporation taxes. A Committee for Progressive Democracy may have the discrediting of organized labor as its chief but not publicly stated aim. Industrialists were shown to have given money to pro-Fascist groups in this country, and most newspapers are familiar with the "Communist front" organizations revealed by the attorney general's list of subversive groups. Newspapers should ferret out the financial backers of such organizations and write them up for what they are, not for what they profess to be.

4. Letters to the Editor. Readership surveys have shown that "vox pop" departments are the best-read feature on the editorial page. They are not overlooked by propagandists. A New York newspaper, investigating the flood of similar letters objecting to rent controls after World War II, discovered that the persons supposed to have written them did not exist. The letters were planted by propagandists for the real estate interests.

5. Conventions and Meetings. Much of the news emanating from meetings of trade, professional, political, racial, religious, labor, and other groups is tinged with propaganda. Some conferences are organized for the chief purpose of serving as a sounding board for propagandists. Reports of such conventions should contain adequate identification of the organizations and the nature of their membership.

6. Subsidized Speakers. Reports about speeches before civic organizations and schools provide much of the local news. Often these outside speakers are in the employ of an organization, and their purpose in giving their time and talent to informing the public is less altruistic than propagandistic.

7. Free Editorial and Feature Material. There is no end to the amount of editorials, feature articles, illustrations, and other materials made available to editors. They are often attractive to the small-town editor who lacks time to write his own editorials or money to pay for syndicated features. One of the best-known and oldest of these "free" services is the Manufacturer and Industrial News Bureau of E. Hofer and Sons of Portland, Oregon. Its activities and phenomenal success in getting its propaganda printed were revealed by the Federal Trade Commission's investigation of publicity and propaganda in the electric power and gas industries. The Hofer Bureau is able to carry on its nation-wide program of course only through grants from utility firms. Nevertheless, newspapers in every state in the Union continue to be vehicles for its propaganda.

8. Seduction and Purchase. Since newspapers have improved their financial standing, instances of a "bought" press are comparatively rare. Yet in 1949 the St. Louis *Post-Dispatch* and the Chicago *Daily News* revealed that editors and staff members of 33 Illinois newspapers were on the state payroll, most of them having no legitimate duties. They were paid to see that the governor got a good "press." There are dishonest newspapermen just as there are quack doctors and ambulance-chasing lawyers. Many newspapermen who would indignantly reject a bribe permit themselves to be influenced by small favors or friendship. Public relations firms, publicity directors, utility firms, and other groups generally have expense accounts for entertaining reporters. A man who has been wined and dined is less likely to write a story unfavorable to his host than one not thus entertained.

Much of the propaganda brought to newspapers is part of a conspiracy to influence legislation. The press as a molder of public opinion and disseminator of information is but one target of attack. Another target is the legislators themselves, who must be strong indeed to resist lobbyists and pressure groups. Edward L. Bernays, one of the most successful public relations counsels and propagandists, has said of propaganda: "Whatever of social importance is done today, whether in politics, finance, manufacture, agriculture, charity, education, or other fields, must be done with the help of propaganda. Propaganda is the executive arm of the invisible government." Bernays has given us a good term for propaganda—"invisible government." To continue the well-known analogy of journalism as the fourth estate, we might consider propaganda the fifth estate.

CHAPTER 19

Ethical Problems of the News

VIOLATIONS OF PERSONAL PRIVACY

Increasingly in recent years newspapers have been criticized for invading the individual's right of privacy—his right to be let alone to carry on his affairs without having them displayed in print for the public gaze.

As a legal right, personal privacy is a comparatively recent concept, but so is the situation that has brought about the need for recognition of the right. Until newspapers saw the circulation-building power of human interest stories, the person who kept out of politics, did not make his living entertaining the public, and avoided arrest was not likely to attract the attention of the press. But after human interest became news, almost no one was exempt from finding himself in the public eye.

Legal safeguards against violations of the right of privacy were first advocated by Louis D. Brandeis and Samuel N. Warren in a famous article in the *Harvard Law Review* in 1890. They wrote:

> Of the desirability—indeed of the necessity—of some such protection, there can, it is believed, be no doubt. The press is overstepping in every direction the obvious bounds of propriety and decency. Gossip is no longer the resource of the idle and of the vicious, but has become a trade, which is pursued with industry as well as effrontery. To satisfy a prurient taste, the details of sexual relations are spread broadcast in the columns of the daily papers. To occupy the indolent, column upon column is filled with idle gossip, which can only be procured by intrusion upon the domestic circle.

The doctrine has been slow to receive legal recognition, primarily because the courts believed that any restrictions imposed would violate the constitutional safeguard of freedom of the press. Several states have passed legislation protecting individuals from having their names or pictures used without permission for advertising, and the courts have concurred in considering this an interference with the right of privacy. For example, the Supreme Court of Michigan in 1948 upheld the right of privacy in a case involving the unauthorized use of a model's picture in a department-store advertisement of perfume. The opinion distinguished between "a person's photographic likeness in connection with or as part of a legitimate news item in a newspaper" and its "commercial use in an advertisement for the pecuniary benefit of the user," and stated:

> The weight of authority recognized in other jurisdictions is that under many circumstances the law will consider the unauthorized publication of a photograph of a person as an invasion of such person's right of privacy and as a tort.

On the other hand, in several decisions courts have ruled that an individual's right to be free from unwanted publicity must yield in cases when news events are of public interest or the information is of public benefit. Most often cited is the case of Boris Sidis against *The New Yorker* for an article advertised in the New York *World-Telegram* as follows: "Out Today, Harvard Prodigy. Biography of the Man Who Astonished Harvard at Age 11." In upholding the right of the magazine to print the article, the court observed:

> Regrettable or not the misfortunes and frailties of neighbors and "public figures" are subjects of considerable interest and discussion to the rest of the public. And when such are the mores of the community it would be unwise for a court to bar their expression in the newspapers, books and magazines of the day.

A similar decision was rendered by the Alabama Supreme Court in a suit brought by two sisters over a radio program about their deceased father, in which they alleged invasion of family privacy. Upholding the broadcast as of "legitimate public interest," the court said:

> Frequently the public has an interest in an individual which transcends his right to be let alone, and freedom of speech in broadcasting, like freedom of the press, among other things, is to preserve untrammeled a vital source of public information.

The court rulings make it clear that the right of privacy, if there is such a right, is an ethical not a legal matter. Such a concept gives the newspaper practically unlimited freedom, subject almost only to its moral sense of what should be printed or not printed. Newspapers have often been flagrantly culpable in invading personal privacy, yet at the same time they have almost universally given lip service to codes respecting the rights of the individual.

One type of news treatment in which newspapers are often at fault is the publication of material about relatives of persons who have been arrested for crimes or otherwise have appeared in scandalous situations. The parents, wife or husband, and children are often hounded for interviews and pictures to be used in connection with proceedings against the accused.

Even in these circumstances the innocent victim has no legal redress. A 1949 decision of a federal court apparently settled this question in favor of the newspapers. The case involved an action against the Minneapolis *Star* and *Tribune*. During the recess of a court proceeding to determine the custody of two children of divorced parents, a photographer took pictures of the litigants and their children. These were printed with the captions, "Mrs. Berg, 36, comforts youngsters during break in trial," and "Bewildered, Charleen, 7, and Charles, 3½, stick close to mother." The father sued the newspapers, alleging invasion of the right of privacy of the subjects of the photographs. The federal court, affirming the judgment of the trial court in favor of the newspapers, said:

If Berg by his litigation with his wife and the proceedings to retain the custody of his children made himself a legitimate item of news, it would seem that the personal appearance of the participants by way of photographs is a matter in which the public would have a legitimate interest.

Since the courts will not intervene to protect an individual's privacy, the press must set its own standards. The statement on the question in the Canons of Journalism, the code of ethics of the American Society of Newspaper Editors, is so elastic that the individual editor can interpret the rule almost as he sees fit: "A newspaper should not invade private rights or feelings without sure warrant of public right as distinguished from public curiosity."

Thus it is the editor's own sense of decency that must be invoked when it comes to questions like printing pictures of the children in a divorce case or of relatives of individuals charged with heinous crimes. Prominent persons especially are often made to suffer from the misdeeds of relatives. A black-sheep son, brother, or second cousin may make the headlines for an act that if done by an individual with no famous connections would hardly rate any mention.

Despite these instances when the innocent are made to suffer publicity for the guilt of others, there are cases in which newspapers protect an innocent victim. Many papers have a rule that the names of women subjected to rape or attempted rape are not to be printed, even though the matter is privileged when the criminal is prosecuted. Newspapers often protect the employer of a person charged with a crime if the place of employment is not essential to the story. Names of hotels and similar places where a suicide or a crime occurs are often omitted. The latter cases, however, reflect not so much a high moral code perhaps as the view that business is sacrosanct even if the individual is not.

The culpable at times are even protected from having their misdoings publicized. Except in major felonies, newspapers suppress the names of juvenile first offenders, because it is felt that they are capable of reformation. A few editors, especially those in small towns, have a rule that the names of adults arrested for a misdemeanor shall not be printed if it is their first transgression.

One of the sacrifices people must make for fame is the giving up of their private life. It is impossible for them to conceal their intimate affairs, and when they object to being hounded by reporters they get unfavorable mention in the papers. The attitude of many reporters and editors is that newspaper publicity is what made them famous, and now they must put up with it. The incident that has been most widely discussed among editors was Charles A. Lindbergh's decision to live in England after years of indignities at the hands of newspapers.

Does a public figure have a right to a private life? The question was dramatized in 1949 when newspapers reported the romances of Vice-President Alben W. Barkley and Mayor William O'Dwyer of New York.

Barkley's courtship of Mrs. Carleton Hadley of St. Louis was covered by the press in great detail—sometimes to the point of vulgarity. Yet during it all, he was affable toward reporters and seemed to delight in the stories about him. After the wedding ceremony, which was private, the new Mrs. Barkley was reported to have said to her husband, before emerging from the chapel to meet reporters, that she "hated to face that mess." The vice-president answered: "That's no mess; that's the American public."

In sharp contrast was O'Dwyer's attitude when, after winning a hard-fought mayoralty election despite sniping by the majority of New York newspapers, he retired to Saratoga Springs to visit friends. Among the guests was Miss Sloan Simpson, whom it was rumored that the mayor would marry. O'Dwyer was belligerent toward reporters who sought to find out his matrimonial intentions, and he was pursued by automobile when he sought to escape from them.

The vice-president got a good "press"; the mayor, a bad one. O'Dwyer's experience was not unusual. Any attempt by a public figure to shun publicity merely causes reporters to redouble their efforts. The famous cannot court the press one day, and decide it is a nuisance the next.

The marriage of a vice-president or a mayor is undoubtedly a matter of legitimate public interest, but there is a point beyond which the interest becomes poor taste and downright bad manners. The love affairs, pregnancies, assignations, domestic quarrels, and divorces of film stars, radio personalities, and sports heroes are of public concern only if we admit that the press should pander to people's interest in vulgar gossip.

THE OBLIGATION OF FAIR PLAY

The individual whose good name is harmed by a newspaper story has no means of defending himself unless the matter printed about him is libelous; but even if he sues and wins his case, the damages he is awarded may not clear the blot from his reputation. Consequently, responsible newspapers have recognized the necessity for fair play—for checking carefully the accuracy of any defamatory information and giving the individual concerned a chance to present his side of the matter. This principle is stated in the Canons of Journalism: "A newspaper should not publish unofficial charges affecting reputation or moral character without opportunity given to the accused to be heard; right practice demands the giving of such opportunity in all cases of serious accusation outside judicial proceedings."

One of the duties of the deskman should be to check stories to see that this requirement of fair play has been met. All too often it has not. Because of the deadline, the reporter may not have had time to ask the accused individual for his answer to the charges against him. Too many newspapers go ahead and print the story anyway, with the idea that the person can have his say the next day. Under a competitive situation this is almost inevitable. The chances are, however, that the follow-up will not be given a display equal to that given the original story, and it is likely, too, that many who read the story about the charges will not see the story answering them.

Perhaps nothing has damaged the reputation of the press as regards accuracy and fair play as much as the publication in recent years of unsubstantiated charges brought out in hearings of the House Committee on Un-American Activities and in the unevaluated reports by agents of the Federal Bureau of Investigation in trials or congressional hearings. Many individuals without means of proving or protesting their innocence have had their reputations blackened by newspaper publication of what all too often has been gossip or lies.

Bernard DeVoto protested against such misrepresentations in an angry article in *Harper's Magazine*:

> The Committee on Un-American Activities blasts several score reputations by releasing a new batch of gossip. Or a senator emits some hearsay and officially unaccused persons lose their jobs without recourse. Or another senator blackens the name of a dead man and then rejoices in his good deed, though the people he claimed to be quoting announce that they didn't say what he said they did. Or some atrocious indignity inflicted on a government employee by a loyalty board comes to light. Or we find out that the FBI has put at the disposal of this or that body a hash of gossip, rumor, slander, backbiting, malice, and drunken invention which, when it makes the headlines, shatters the reputations of innocent and harmless people and of people who our laws say are innocent until someone proves them guilty in court.

Of the scores of incidents of the type denounced by DeVoto, one that was of special interest to journalists involved Dr. Edward U. Condon, director of the National Bureau of Standards. His martyrdom at the hands of the House Committee on Un-American Activities and the press was the subject of a study made by the Columbia University Bureau of Applied Social Research. The results were printed in "Trial by Newspaper" in the February, 1949, issue of *Scientific American*.

On March 1, 1948, a subcommittee of the House Committee on Un-American Activities headed by J. Parnell Thomas (later tried and found guilty of defrauding the government) issued a report stating, among other things, that Condon "appears" to be "one of the weakest links in our atomic security." Because of Condon's prominence, the story received a big headline play throughout the country, although the only evidence brought forth by the committee was that he "knowingly or unknowingly entertained and associated with persons who are alleged Soviet espionage agents, and persons now reported to be under investigation by a federal grand jury."

The Department of Commerce announced that Condon had been unanimously cleared by a loyalty board five days before the house committee's accusation. But the damage to his reputation had already been done. Despite the fact that the committee never sought to prove its charges and that Condon was subsequently cleared by the Atomic Energy Commission, he is still known to his countrymen chiefly by his repeated identification in newspapers as the man who was branded "one of the weakest links in our atomic security."

The *Scientific American's* report of the press handling of the case was confined to an analysis of the accounts in the nine New York newspapers of general circulation. The papers showed wide variations in their treatment of the same news story, the study indicated, but the conclusion was that "the reporting techniques employed by the papers served to inflate the case against Dr. Condon far beyond its native size" and "the case against Dr. Condon as presented in the newspapers may well have raised a question in careful readers' minds as to whether there was any case at all."

The report said that of 3909 statements examined, 19 percent were unsympathetic to Condon, 24 percent were sympathetic, and 57 percent were neutral. It pointed out, however, that these percentages were not "particularly meaningful," because few persons "would consistently have read all nine papers and been exposed to this comprehensive coverage."

Especially damaging to the newspapers' reputation for fair play was their choice of background material for the running news stories, since a newspaper, the report said, "obviously exercises more selective judgment" in handling background than it can with respect to new material. Regarding the choice of background information the report said: "The background material revived for use in the running news stories had the effect of building up the case against Dr. Condon but did not build up his defense to anywhere near the same degree. All the papers reported the committee's promise to give Dr. Condon a hearing far more often than they reported its failure to do so."

Perhaps some of this bias against Condon was unconscious. Newspaper practice is to identify a person by the label by which he is best known to the public. The tieback, "named by the House Committee on Un-American Activities as one of the weakest links in atomic security," was the best one for recalling Condon to the readers' minds. Its repetition was clearly damaging to him. If it had to be used, reporters and deskmen should have inserted somewhere in it a statement that the accusation was unproved.

The case involving Condon has been described in detail because it illustrates the need for carefully qualifying all stories of this type. The problem is not confined to Washington news. The same thing may occur at a city council meeting, in a local election campaign, or at a session of the board of education.

The solution is not the newspaper's refusal to print such defamatory material. They could not suppress the information if they wanted to.

Yet it is not sufficient for them merely to publish an accurate account of what was brought out, and to disclaim responsibility for any damage because they were being objective and reporting only what they were told by others. As the Condon study showed, much of the harm resulted from what the papers chose to use again and again as background in the running stories. Public officials and witnesses at formal hearings have immunity against libel suits for their remarks. They can repeat gossip, express conclusions and interpretations, even lie, because there are no rules regarding the admissibility of evidence as there are in courts of law. A fair and impartial account of a congressional hearing conducted by headline-seeking senators and representatives may be manifestly unfair to the hapless victim of adverse testimony, especially since he may not be given an opportunity to defend himself.

To avoid smearing individuals by so-called "impartial" reporting, newspapers should if possible indicate the credibility of witnesses, be careful not to sensationalize unsupported accusations, and play the story under qualified headlines.

NEWS SUPPRESSION

In making decisions about what to print or not to print in respect to protecting personal privacy, the editor exercises his right to determine what will go into his newspaper. The right to reject goes along with the right to publish. News made available to the editor may be rejected for a number of reasons. One of the most important determinants is space. More stories reach the editor's desk than can be printed. He decides which ones to publish by estimating their importance and interest to his readers. He may eliminate others as violating canons of taste, decency, and fairness.

The rejection of news for these reasons does not constitute suppression in the evil sense of the word. Rather, suppression connotes omission of news which is of legitimate public concern and which the newspaper is in duty bound to print. If an editor fails to use it because of pressure by individuals or groups whom it would hurt or because of economic or political bias, he is guilty of cowardly or venal suppression. Omitting a story may be as great a journalistic sin as distorting or coloring facts or knowingly printing untruths.

The omission of news that encroaches on an individual's right of privacy, harms an innocent victim, or would do irreparable damage to the young if the facts were broadcast is considered legitimate suppression.

What about other types of stories whose publication would do harm? The question concerns an ethical rather than a legal matter, except when libel is involved.

Occasions when an editor may be asked to suppress news include the following: the facts in a suicide; escapades and scandals involving prominent or "respectable" citizens; stories that will hurt the town; stories that will hurt business; stories not in the interest of public welfare; stories that will endanger national security.

Editors are frequently asked by the surviving kin of a suicide not to reveal that the individual took his own life. The grounds for this request usually are that publication of that fact will unnecessarily embarrass the grief-stricken family. Editors often comply with the request, yet it is likely that they actually harm the family by doing so. Most stories which seek to veil the cause of death have a suspicious ring. They produce conjectures as to motive and method, and in the long run this gossip is more damaging than publication of the facts. The newspaper, moreover, harms its own reputation as an impartial recorder of local events, because the facts about a suicide are hard to keep secret.

Omission of the word suicide in a story also has legal grounds. Until the coroner has pronounced a verdict of suicide, a newspaper cannot properly label the death as such. This legal formality explains the hesitancy with which many reports of suicides are written. The details of the death are stated, but the word suicide does not appear because the coroner's verdict may not yet have been given.

Despite the fact that tuberculosis and cancer no longer have an objectionable connotation for most people, newspapers are still asked not to mention these afflictions as the cause of death. There seems to be no reason for refusing to comply with the request if it is made by the family.

The problem of what to do about publicizing the peccadilloes of prominent and respected members of the community is annoying, especially in a small city. Many newspapers refuse to print stories on misdemeanors handled in police courts and by justices of the peace on the grounds that, if routine, they are not worth making enemies for the paper. If, however, a newspaper makes a practice of reporting traffic offenses, disorderly conduct charges, drunkenness charges, and so forth, it should not have a double standard—one for the poor and unknown and one for the rich and prominent. If John Rich is arrested for being inebriated and engaging in mischievous pranks, he should receive the same treatment as John Poor. The word "same" should be stressed. The John Rich story should not be suppressed because Rich is influential, nor should it be given a bigger play.

When the offense is serious, the person's position in the community affects the news value of the story. If John Poor gets drunk and is involved in an automobile smash-up, the item may be worth a paragraph or two. If John Rich, president of the First National Bank and a director of the Chamber of Commerce, is involved in a similar accident, the story is bigger and better. It may not be fair to John Rich, but unhappily that is the nature of news. This conclusion, of course, will not be accepted by all editors. The question will be hotly debated at any conference of newspapermen, and good reasons will be advanced for not emblazoning John Rich's misfortune in the headlines. Yet by the standards of news values—prominence being a principal determinant—the John Rich story deserves a bigger play than the John Poor story.

Most newspapers are in the forefront of any movement to boost their community. When residents desire a new library, a new reservoir, or additions to the sewage disposal system, they first enlist the support of the newspaper publisher, knowing that the publicity he can give the project is almost essential for its success. It is to the newspaper's self-interest for the community to be known as a good place to live in, a city of fine churches and schools, and a well-governed municipality. Consequently, there is a tendency for publishers to soft-pedal news that will give the city a bad name. This inclination grows stronger when they are approached by civic and business leaders and asked not to air scandals and corruption.

There can be no question that such news is of public concern. It is the newspaper's responsibility to inform the people about how their local government is operated, how well the police enforce the law, and how honestly the courts uphold justice. Editors who have insisted on publishing unfavorable news have often done so despite pressure and even threats from individuals and groups whose objections were based on the grounds that the stories would harm the town or be bad for business. Suppression of this kind of news is never warranted. To clean out a political ring by throwing a light on its activities does not injure a city's reputation. Rather, it improves the city's standing and strengthens the newspaper that fearlessly prints the truth.

Closely related to the suppression of news that will harm a community's reputation is the suppression of news that will injure business. The charge is frequently made, and proved, that newspapers protect business interests and advertisers by killing stories. George Seldes, for example, in issue after issue of his publication *In Fact,* which was devoted wholeheartedly to exposing the misdeeds of the press, accused newspapers of ignoring Federal Trade Commission action against firms charged with fraud and unfair practices and similar action brought by the Pure Food and Drug Administration against violators of the pure food and drug law. Certainly this information is newsworthy from the standpoint of interest and importance to the reader. It is not true, as Seldes said, that newspapers do not print this news. They do, occasionally, but it is seldom played up prominently.

One of the best-known examples of alleged suppression of information that would harm business was the failure of Chicago newspapers to carry stories about the outbreak of amoebic dysentery during that city's Century of Progress exposition. It was charged—a charge that was denied by Chicago newspapers—that the press refused to print news of the epidemic because the broadcasting of such information would have kept visitors away. The fact that there was such an epidemic and that several persons died came out only after the exposition closed. The remissness of the Chicago press in either covering up the epidemic or not finding out about it until too late to warn the public was editorially condemned by many newspapers throughout the country.

In any community where an epidemic breaks out, the editor is likely to be approached by friends or fellow members of the Chamber of Commerce about playing down the news. Actually, soft-pedaling such news is not necessarily venal. To sensationalize it would unnecessarily terrorize the public. Public health knowledge has advanced sufficiently in recent years so that city officials can act quickly and efficiently to control epidemics. An epidemic is news that should not be suppressed; but scare headlines tending to throw the public into a panic may interfere with the work of health officials and make people lose confidence in them.

Situations in which the publication of news would not be in the best interests of the public are comparatively rare. Such a situation would be one in which the people might be thrown into needless and dangerous panic or in which the revelation might touch off a riot or incite mob action.

When there is tension between races or between union workers and strikebreakers, certain stories might inflame tempers already at the breaking point and lead to violence. For example, a newspaper report that a Negro had molested a white woman in an office building elevator—of all unlikely places—was the spark that started a race riot in one city. This irresponsible journalism had fatal results; open warfare was declared by whites and Negroes, and before peace was restored several persons had been killed and wounded.

The American Civil Liberties Union in 1949 blamed a local newspaper for the outbreak of violence near Peekskill, New York, over a concert by Paul Robeson, Negro singer, at a Communist rally. Local veterans' organizations protested the rally, and there resulted what Roger N. Baldwin, director of the American Civil Liberties Union, termed the "most shocking single incident of mob violence in the north in recent years." That organization's report on the affair declared: "The local press bears the main responsibility for inflaming, possibly through sheer irresponsibility, Peekskill residents to a mood of violence." It cited as examples of "provocation by the press" three items from the Peekskill *Evening Star*—a news report, an editorial, and a letter to the editor. Donald F. Ikeler, business manager of the newspaper, denied the charge and cited an editorial in which the paper urged local people to stay away from the concert "as the most effective way to wither its purpose on the vine."

Whatever the truth regarding the Peekskill riot, the incident emphasizes the care a newspaper must exercise when tensions mount in a community. It takes very little to incite a mob to violence. A carelessly written headline or even a phrase in the body of the story may be the spark.

Newspapers sometimes have been urged to suppress "bad news" or at least to soft-pedal it when the psychological effect on the public would be adverse. The question was often discussed during the business depression of the 1930's, and it was raised again in 1949 when there was fear that the postwar boom was about to burst. During that summer, the Bureau of the Census issued a report showing an increase in unemployment. This, together with other signs of a downward trend in business, led to newspaper scareheads about a recession.

In his "Shop Talk at Thirty" column in *Editor & Publisher*, Robert U. Brown took issue with the press treatment of the Census Bureau report, maintaining that the increase in unemployment had been overemphasized and a concurrent increase in total employment had been underplayed. The result was that the news stories tended "to scare the American people without reason." "Newspaper writers by factual analysis of economic conditions," Brown continued, "can do a lot to restore optimism and confidence to areas where there is now predominantly pessimism. Fear is destructive."

Brown of course did not advocate the suppression of news regarding the economic situation. It is a newspaper's responsibility to print the truth, so far as the truth can be determined. People cannot gird themselves to fight a condition if they are not informed about the facts. But a completely black picture and a deëmphasis on hopeful trends when they appear may produce despair and fear that will prolong a bad situation.

During wartime, in the interest of national security, newspapers uniformly give up many of their rights to print news, even in areas of information not subject to official censorship. With almost no exceptions newspapers during World War II carefully cooperated with the Office of Censorship. A proper military censorship during war was projected by *Fortune* in June, 1941, as follows:

> Inept and shortsighted censorship at the source can, of course, frustrate completely the efforts of a free and critical press to keep the public properly informed. Military censorship, by a law as forceful as that of gravitation, tends toward political censorship, becoming a means for stifling criticism of official ineptness and incompetence. The principle that must be established and adhered to strictly is that military censorship is confined to military secrets. Censorship for other reasons—"public interest," for instance, or that easy out, "national morale"—is a direct and intolerable interference with a free press.

The principle was good in theory. It did not stand up in practice, because modern warfare is psychological as well as military. World War II was fought with propaganda as well as bombs. Moreover, there is no way of determining what is a military secret and what is not, for with today's all-out methods of warfare everything is military.

NEWS ABOUT MINORITIES

Under the heading, "A Correction," on the editorial page the New York *Times* printed an apology for a derogatory reference to Roman Catholics in an article in its book review section. The correction said in part: "Every reviewer has the right to express his opinion and that opinion is his rather than the opinion of the *Times*. The editor, however, has the responsibility to delete statements that are inaccurate or offensive. That responsibility should have been exercised in this case. Unfortunately, it was not, and the offending sentence was not detected until after the press run of the book section had been completed."

The reference to which the editor took exception was a single sentence in a long book review in which the author was expressing his own opinion. In its context the sentence probably would not have been noticed by even Catholic readers. Nevertheless, the *Times* as a highly conscientious newspaper felt that the aspersion against followers of a religion was of such a nature as to call for a disclaimer of intent and an apology for remissness.

The incident illustrates the care with which deskmen must scrutinize copy to delete matter that unjustly reflects on the character of a religion, a racial or national group, or a professional or cultural unit of the population.

The responsibility of the newspaper is to avoid publishing material that would in any way contribute to the establishment of prejudice. The problem has received attention in recent years because of the ideological conflict between democracy and communism. Americans have realized that inequalities in our system arising from racial and religious bias not only give ammunition to our enemies but are dangerously evil in themselves. The issue has been thrown into relief by the debates in state legislatures and congress over fair employment practices laws and by a series of notable Supreme Court decisions knocking down racial bars against Negroes.

Newspaper practice in stories about crime is to omit mentioning the culprit's race, nationality, or religion unless it is essential to the story. Even in the South, where anti-Negro bias is strong, several papers have dropped racial identifications in order not to emphasize any differences between white and colored people. Newspapers also are wary of stories about the activities of hate groups like the Ku Klux Klan and about narrow religious orders whose leaders appeal to the prejudices of their followers. News reports concerning such groups should be edited so as not to indicate approval or acceptance of their doctrines. Many editors do not consider newsworthy the intemperate spoutings and appeals to prejudice of demagogues.

There is another reason why editors do not like to offend minority groups. These groups are organized to combat prejudice, and they are quick to bring pressure on publications that offend. They sometimes exercise censorship that is undesirable, especially in the means by which it is enforced. No publisher wishes his newspaper to be the object of a boycott, of mass demonstrations and picketing, and of protests registered in personal visits, telephone calls, and letters.

The extremes to which some groups go in suppressing what they consider undesirable manifestations of prejudice can be indicated by several examples. Negroes have opposed the presentation of *Uncle Tom's Cabin* and *The Green Pastures* because they felt that these plays ridicule their race and their history. Jews boycotted presentations of *The Merchant of Venice* and *Oliver Twist* in the belief that Shylock and Fagin malign their religion. Catholics succeeded in getting the *Nation* banned from New York City schools because of a series of articles against the church. Even American Indians have organized to protest against the portrayal of the red man in motion-picture horse operas.

Racial and religious minorities, however, are not the only groups that exercise censorship in journalism. Wherever there's an organization there's a pressure group that tries to make the rest of the people conform to its ideas. Organizations like the American Legion, the Veterans of Foreign Wars, the Daughters of the American Revolution, the W.C.T.U., and the Chamber of Commerce are less than reluctant to protest about what an editor chose to print or let slip past his guard, as are such professional and trade groups as doctors, lawyers, labor unions, farmers, bankers, teachers, chiropractors, osteopaths, and almost any other that we might mention.

MAINTAINING THE PROPRIETIES

Because newspapers are printed for all ages and groups of people, editors have for long been sticklers for the sternest proprieties in language and details of sex. Even before the age of Victorian squeamishness, James Gordon Bennett of the New York *Herald* was the victim of a "moral war" by ministers and his journalistic competitors. He was assailed because he insisted upon calling a leg a leg and not a limb and because he spoke in print of such unmentionable articles of clothing as pants, trousers, and petticoats. Our standards of propriety have changed, yet newspaper prudishness persists.

Two reporters who protested—in books—against copy desk conceptions of proper and improper language were Joseph Mitchell in *My Ears Are Bent* and H. Allen Smith in *Low Man on a Totem Pole*. Mitchell wrote:

> I admire the imagery in vulgar conversation. I wish newspapers had courage enough to print conversation just as it issues forth, relevant obscenity and all. Some of Mayor La Guardia's most apt epigrams, for example, cannot be printed in any New York newspaper. If a reporter tries to get anything unusually hearty in a story some copyreader or other will trim it out. There are scores of admirable copyreaders on New York newspapers, but most of them seem to be too bored to give much of a damn about anything. They don't have to be censored; they willingly censor themselves. They appear to prefer the nasty genteelism to the exact word; they will cut the word "belly" out of your copy and write in the nauseating word "tummy." I have seen a pimp referred to as "a representative of the vice ring." On the newspaper for which I work the reporters write "raped" and it always comes out "criminally attacked." Also, copyreaders appear to like tinsel words, words such as "petite." Day after day

in one newspaper I have seen Lottie Coll referred to as "the petite gun-girl," and Lottie is as big as Jack Dempsey and twice as tough. A good copyreader would rip a word like "petite" off a sheet of copy just on general principles.[1]

Smith had this experience:

> For the last five years I have been trying to get "stink bomb" past the copy desk. I write it "stink bomb," and it comes out in the paper as "stench bomb." I have squawked and bellyached about it, but to no avail. I once went so far as to confront my boss and demand to know if he had ever heard of anyone going out and getting stenching drunk. I got nowhere.[2]

In recent years, however, there has been a tendency toward accepting more plain-spoken language. The expressions "social diseases" (it would seem more accurate to use "antisocial diseases") and "vice diseases" are no longer used by many newspapers for syphilis and gonorrhea, although the latter word is rarely encountered. The acceptance of these words is largely due to the public health movement. The public must certainly have ceased to be shocked by these medical terms during World War II when civilians encountered them frequently on placards telling soldiers how to avoid infection.

But despite the growing laxness in observing the Victorian taboos, many newspapers still abide by them. Lawbooks are not so nice, and deskmen on some papers must translate, if the reporter did not, such words as "rape" into "statutory crime" or "assault" or "attack"; "fornication" into "intimate relations"; "abortion" into "criminal operation"; and "sodomy" into "perversion" or "unnatural act" or "morals offense."

Discussing attitudes toward forbidden words in *The American Language: Supplement I*, H. L. Mencken comments that newspaper prissiness is sometimes highly amusing. He cites an example from a New York newspaper in 1943 in which a "fiend" was said to have struck a girl, "dragged her down the cellar-steps, beat her with an iron pipe, and then assaulted her"!

Newspapers also avoid printing profanity. Mencken told of an experience of his own in 1939, when in a lecture delivered at Cooper Union in New York he said: "American grammar is fast going to hell, which is where all grammars will land, I hope and pray, soon or late." The New York *Journal-American's* report of the lecture the next morning printed "hell" as "h–l." But ten years later, in 1949, newspapers had little hesitancy in printing even in headlines the epithet "S.O.B." which President

---

[1] Joseph Mitchell, *My Ears Are Bent*, Sheridan House, 1938, p. 22.
[2] H. Allen Smith, *Low Man on a Totem Pole*, Doubleday, Doran & Company, 1941, p. 252.

Harry S. Truman applied to the syndicated columnist, Drew Pearson.

Mencken also mentioned a Chattanooga newspaper that made journalistic history by reporting that a man in that city had been arrested for "walking the streets accompanied by a woman." And *Time* related that in a story for the Houston *Post* the reporter told how a woman ran down the street screaming, "He's trying to rape me!" The paper's prim copyreader changed the quote to read: "He's trying to criminally assault me! Help!"

How far newspapers should or can go in printing details of sex and crime is a matter of policy. Newspapers are much bolder now than they used to be. Even the New York *Times*, whose slogan is "All the news that's fit to print," may publish as many details as a sensational tabloid. In a speech in 1947, Lester Markel, Sunday editor, said that he once asked Adolph S. Ochs, the publisher, how the *Times*, with that slogan, justified printing columns about a lovers' lane murder story. He quoted Ochs as answering: "If a tabloid prints it, it is smut; if the *Times* prints it, it is sociology."

The pros and cons of publishing details about sex were debated in 1949 over press association handling of a murder trial in Cedar Rapids, Iowa. The Associated Press received complaints that its coverage had been "entirely too lurid, dirty, and smutty" and "a primer of seduction." Thomas R. Waring of the Charleston (South Carolina) *News and Courier* declared:

> Details of seduction and other quotes in the testimony in my opinion were unnecessarily explicit. Press associations must and do observe some rules of good taste and also exercise judgment on newsworthiness. Our newspaper does not carry such lurid material, and my observation is that many others share our sentiments. Why waste wire time supplying pornography for the few who publish it?

From the other side of the fence came this from another publisher:

> For better or for worse, American newspapers are enormously franker about sex and sex relations than ever before. This tendency is far wider than the tabloids. If the opposition paper prints a spicy story that pleases the reading public here, I want to have had the opportunity to have printed a similar story. If we lose circulation because of conservatism I want it to be our own conservatism and not that of AP. Within limits of reason and decency, I want AP to furnish me what my competitor has available and then let me use my judgment.

The publication of the lurid details was defended by another editor on the grounds that they were essential to understanding the story:

The whole defense in this case was based on the alleged seduction of Mrs. ———, so I do not see how that portion of the testimony could have been suppressed or changed since it constituted the very foundation of the defense. It is unfortunate a few people were offended by the frankness of the news report of this trial, but I think a greater offense would have been done by its suppression or softening.

A newspaper which sensationalizes crime and sex news will always find critics of its policy. Yet such stories are undeniably widely read. Even those who profess to be shocked by them must have read them in the first place. It must be assumed that there is considerable hypocrisy in the expressions of condemnation. Such stories do not have to be splashed under big headlines to attract readers. *The Continuing Study of Newspaper Reading* cites many examples of off-color stories buried obscurely in the inside under inconspicuous captions which received high readership scores.

CHAPTER **20**

Press Law and the Copy Desk

CURBS ON THE PRESS

The Constitution of the United States in the first amendment and the various state constitutions guarantee the individual the right to speak, write, and publish his sentiments on all subjects. It is a right, however, that has strings attached. Under both statutory law and court rulings an individual can be brought to account for abusing the right of free speech.

As interpreted in statutes and court opinions, the right of free speech is abused when a person's reputation is harmed, when the administration of justice is interfered with, when the safety of the nation is endangered, and when society itself is harmed. In terms of the law, these abuses concern the following: defamation of character or libel, contempt of court, sedition and treason, and offenses against public morality and welfare. For violating laws governing any of these abuses a newspaper and its owners and editors must answer in the courts the civil or criminal actions brought against them.

Legal action against a newspaper or its personnel can be taken only after publication. Hence every editorial employee must have a basic knowledge of law in order to guard against printing material that might make the newspaper liable. Editors in authoritative positions and copyreaders as the principal wardens of a newspaper's content especially must be familiar with statutes and court rulings.

While newspapers employ attorneys to whom questions of law can be submitted, it is not feasible to present all such problems to a legal expert. He would have to sit on the rim of the copy desk with the copyreaders if he were to be available for advice on all such matters. The copyreader must be his own lawyer most of the time.

PRESS LAW AND THE COPY DESK

To be a competent judge of what should or should not be printed in accordance with the law, the copyreader should know the following:

1. The general principles of the law of libel, contempt of court, and the federal statutes. These will be covered briefly in this chapter.

2. The special statutes and court rulings of the state in which his paper is published. The statutory provisions are accessible in the compiled statutes of the state to be found in almost every newspaper office. Many of the state press associations have published both these and important judicial rulings in a newspaper code.

3. New developments in laws affecting the press and the upsetting of old judicial precedents and the adoption of new interpretations by the courts. These are reported in *Editor & Publisher* and other journalistic publications. An indispensable survey of new legislation, new trends in judicial rulings, and suits against newspapers appears annually in the *Editor & Publisher Yearbook*.

ON GUARD AGAINST LIBEL

One of the most cherished possessions of individuals is a good name. To protect the individual in his good name, the states have set up laws of defamation. Defamation may be briefly defined as any utterance tending to detract from the reputation of a person or to injure him in his profession or business. It has two main aspects—libel and slander. Libel is any defamation made by means of writing, printing, pictures, effigies, moving pictures, or any other permanent visual expression. Slander is spoken or oral defamation.

The law does not make a newspaper liable in the publication of all defamatory material. To be actionable, a defamation generally must meet these requirements: It must be false; it must be malicious; it must be unprivileged.

These three requirements are not set forth specifically in the definitions of libel in most state statutes. They are covered, however, in special articles of the law that deal with defamation and in the rulings of the courts. An excellent concise definition of libel is that in the laws of South Dakota:

> Libel is a false and unprivileged publication by writing, printing, picture, effigy or other fixed representation to the eye which exposes any person to hatred, contempt, ridicule or obloquy, or which causes him to be shunned or avoided, or which has a tendency to injure him in his occupation.

The deskman every day handles stories that contain material damaging to reputations. He must have a highly developed sense of danger in regard to certain types of material, so that he almost subconsciously pauses to change, correct, or verify copy that might unfairly and wrongfully do irreparable harm to a person's good name. The following four classifications include most of the statements that naturally tend to make readers think less of a person:

1. A statement that a person is guilty of crime, fraud, dishonesty, immorality, vice, or dishonorable conduct, or a statement implying lack of chastity in a woman.

All stories imputing commission of a crime are libelous if the published information should prove false. Hence in handling reports of arrests and convictions, the copyreader must verify names and identifications so far as he is able. It is not only libelous to say falsely that a person is guilty of a crime, it is libelous to say that one is suspected of or arrested for a crime. An arrest does not necessarily imply guilt. A person accused and brought to trial may be found innocent, and if a newspaper has called him a murderer when he has only been accused of murder, he may later have grounds for a suit. A statement not libelous in itself may be libelous because of its implications. Ordinarily, to print that a woman was divorced by her husband might not be the same thing as bringing a charge of immorality against her. But it would be in New York, because adultery is the only grounds for divorce in that state.

2. A statement that a person is insane or mentally defective or is afflicted by a loathsome or contagious disease.

Imputation that a person is feeble-minded or that he suffers from syphilis, smallpox, leprosy, or any other infectious disease may result in that person's being shunned by society or injure him in his business, trade, or profession. Consequently, the courts have held that such false publications are injurious and therefore libelous. It is particularly dangerous to say that a person has a venereal disease, since these diseases ordinarily are contracted in ways or as the outcome of actions that the public regards as censurable.

3. A statement that holds a person up to public ridicule or scorn in such a way that he may be deprived of the favor and esteem of his friends or the public.

Ridicule is not necessarily libelous, but it is considered so when it interferes with a person's right to enjoy social relations. To write that a man is married when he is a bachelor may expose him to jokes and banter, but it is ordinarily not injurious to his reputation. But it might be considered damaging to say that a woman was left at the altar or that a man has been sued for breach of promise, or to compare a person's social habits or manners to those of a repulsive animal.

4. A statement that might adversely affect a person in his profession, calling, office, business, or trade.

The courts have ruled that it is libelous to make statements that might create doubt as to a person's fitness to carry on his occupation or way of making a living. It might not be damaging to his good name to say that he is financially embarrassed, for that might excite only pity and sympathy; but such a statement could nevertheless be considered libelous if it affected people's confidence in him as a businessman or damaged his credit. A newspaper could not without great risk call a doctor a butcher, a lawyer an ambulance chaser, a teacher an ignoramus, a merchant a profiteer, or a skilled mechanic a blacksmith.

Certain words are generally recognized as libelous *per se*, or defamatory in themselves because of their interpretation by society at large. A person so libeled does not have to prove damages in court. The law presumes the damage. The words in the following five categories are some considered libelous *per se* over whose use newspapers have been sued:

1. Words imputing crimes: abduction, abortion, adultery, arson, bestiality, bigamy, blackmailing, bribery, burglary, conspiracy, counterfeiting, criminal operation, deserting, embezzlement, embracery, extortion, false pretenses, forgery, fornication, fraud, gambling, homicide, incest, indecent exposure, kidnaping, larceny, malicious mischief, manslaughter, murder, perjury, rape, robbery, sedition, seduction, smuggling, sodomy, swindling, treason.

2. Words imputing dishonorable conduct or moral vice: blackguard, boodler, common drunk, communist, crook, deadbeat, degenerate, drug addict, drunkard, grafter, humbug, hypocrite, liar, libertine, mistress, perjured villain, pettifogger, professional love-maker, profiteer, quack, rascal, scandalmonger, shyster, slacker.

3. Words imputing mental illness or contagious disease: afflicted with leprosy, feeble-minded, fit person to be sent to a lunatic asylum, having brainstorms, insane, lunatic, mental incompetent.

4. Expressions holding a person up to public ridicule: he is thought of no more than a horse thief; miserable specimen of humanity; you can't get him down any lower than he is—he is low enough—you can't spoil a rotten egg; he turned into an enormous swine, which lives on lame horses, will probably remain a swine to the end of his days; an egotistical, over-

estimated, self-conceited jackass; he is a liar and deadbeat of the first order; venomous incompetent.

5. Words damaging to one's trade, profession, or way of making a living: of a writer, that he is a plagiarist; of an artist, that he is a swindler and humbug; of a minister, that he is unmannerly, discourteous, and ignorant and a member of the Ku Klux Klan; of a lawyer, that he is a pettifogging shyster, a jack-leg lawyer, a disgrace to his profession as a lawyer, a street demagogue, a crooked mouthpiece; of a physician, that he is a quack, a manufacturer of vaccine, a jackass disguised as a doctor, a ghoul; of a businessman that he is a sharp-dealing shopkeeper, a profiteer, a business racketeer.

Yet while certain words may apparently be libelous in themselves, no one can ever be sure how a jury will interpret them. For example, it has been held libelous to call a man an "arch hypocrite" but not libelous to call him a "political hypocrite." In some cases a person was able to collect for defamation in one court, but in another court a jury refused to award damages when the same words were used.

Moreover, word values change with time, place, and association. Knowledge of definitions given in previous cases is not an adequate criterion. Words once held nonlibelous may with a change of place or a lapse of time be considered libelous. The word "Communist" once carried no opprobrium, but in 1947 and 1948 several persons sued because of being called a Communist, and they collected. To say in Harlem that a person is a "friend of the Negro" would bring no disrepute, but it might in Mississippi or Georgia. The designation "corespondent" in a divorce suit would not be considered derogatory in some states, but it might in others where adultery is the only grounds. As Associate Justice Oliver Wendell Holmes said: "A word is not a crystal, transparent and unchanged; it is the skin of a living thought and may vary greatly in color and content according to circumstances and the time in which it is used."

Occasionally, words not in themselves defamatory may be libelous because of extrinsic factors or innuendo. Such defamation is known as libel *per quod*. The courts require proof that words or expressions not libelous in themselves were injurious in character or in effect.

To say that a person has tuberculosis would not be libel *per se*, because no particular stigma is attached to the disease; but to say that a cook in a restaurant has tuberculosis might be construed as libel *per quod*, because the employment of such a diseased person might harm the restaurant's business and the cook himself might lose his job. A newspaper story which referred to a dress designer as a "chief seamstress" was held actionable by a court because proof was presented that the woman had suffered professional damage.

Writers on the law of libel recognize four absolute defenses in a suit, and several partial defenses that may reduce damages or avert punitive or exemplary damages. The absolute defenses are: (1) proof that the statement was true; (2) proof that the statement was privileged; (3) proof that the statement was fair comment or criticism; (4) proof that the statement was consented to in defense or in reply to an accusation. The partial defenses are proof of lack of malice and the publication of a correction or retraction.

Truth as a Defense. In common law the ability to prove the truth of a statement is held as a complete defense in a libel suit. The principle of truth as a defense is written into the laws of all except eleven states. The theory is that society's interest in the truth outweighs any interest it has in protecting reputations and that if a person does something that might injure his good name he may forfeit his right to that name. The difficulty with truth as a defense is that the newspaper must be able to prove the truth. In the states in which truth is not a complete defense, the defendant in a suit must also show that the publication was made with good motives and for justifiable ends. This, in general, involves the question of public interest—a matter to be interpreted by the jury.

Privilege as a Defense. In the public interest newspapers may print "fair and true" reports of certain proceedings. As defined in a Montana statute covering most of the points of privilege, a privileged publication is one made:

1. In the proper discharge of an official duty.

2. In any legislative or judicial proceeding, or in any other official proceeding authorized by law.

3. In a fair and true report, without malice, of a judicial, legislative, or other public official proceeding, or anything said in the course thereof.

The contents of public records generally are considered privileged. These include police blotters (in most states), court appearance dockets, marriage license records, records of the county register of deeds, records of the county commissioners, and county treasurers' records.

In some instances, the privilege of making fair and true reports of proceedings applies to such quasi-official bodies as bar associations, church boards, and medical societies.

Privilege is important because the newspaper does not need to concern itself with proving the defamation. Provided the report is accurate, fair and impartial, and not motivated by malice, the paper is not likely to lose a suit that is brought against it.

Fair Comment and Criticism as a Defense. Of utmost importance to a newspaper in its function of protecting society against corrupt practices of public officials and institutions is the freedom given it to criticize and condemn without incurring danger of libel. Thus, in what it honestly believes to be true and "in good faith and on reasonable grounds," the paper has great latitude in what it can say about candidates for public office and incumbent officials.

The rule of fair comment and criticism applies to public officers and candidates for public office; political parties and organizations; public institutions such as universities, hospitals, and asylums; and official agencies such as legislatures, county boards, city councils, and the courts.

The newspaper's right to criticize also covers comment on books, plays, musical and dramatic performances, public buildings, sports events, motion pictures, and radio and television programs. Here it is presumed that the author, actor, artist, architect, or athlete invites any criticism, either deprecatory or approbatory, when he asks the public to view his efforts. The right of criticism, however, does not extend to the personal character or private life of an individual. The critic may write, for example, that a highly sexed novel is "perverting and decadent," but he cannot say that its author is a "pervert and a decadent character" unless he is prepared to go into court to prove it.

In everything that comes under the right of fair comment and criticism, the deskman should keep these essentials in mind: the subject of comment must be one that invites public attention; the criticism must be made with a good motive and for a justifiable end and not be actuated by malice; the comment should be based upon fact; any attacks on moral character must have a bearing on the individual's qualifications to hold office or do his work.

The Right of Reply and Consent as a Defense. Of growing importance but still fairly rare is the privilege of reply and consent as a defense. A victim of a defamatory attack has a right to defend his character. This privilege has been upheld in several court rulings. "The importance of the defense," Harold L. Cross wrote about a case in the 1947 *Editor & Publisher Yearbook*, "is that where the necessary facts are shown, newspapers and other defendants have a complete defense for the publication of matter which is libelous, is not true, and is not a report of proceedings."

Similarly, E. Douglas Hamilton, counsel for the New York *Herald*

Tribune, said in *Late City Edition:* "Frequently, someone who has been charged with dishonorable conduct will issue a statement to the newspaper and will directly or inferentially consent to the publication of the libelous matter in order to get his denials and his side of the controversy published. Consent is a complete defense."

Partial Defenses. A partial defense in a libel suit is proof of lack of malice. It does not have any bearing on the actual damages that a libeled person may win, but it may serve to reduce or prevent exemplary or punitive damages. The newspaperman must understand the legal definition of malice. There are two types: (1) malice in fact, or express malice; and (2) malice in law. Malice in fact corresponds to the popular meaning of the word, that is, publication actuated by ill will, evil intent, hatred, or deliberate intent to injure. Malice in law is interpreted as disregard of the rights of the individual about whom a libelous statement is published. Hence intent is not in question, and malice is presumed in a libel published accidentally through error.

Publication of a retraction or correction is an important defense in a libel suit, because it can be submitted as proof of absence of malice. A retraction cannot prevent a suit, although it often does. Many persons are satisfied by a newspaper's "Beg your pardon."

A recent trend in legislation is the "honest mistake" libel law. Several states have passed laws freeing a newspaper of liability for exemplary damages when a libel is committed as the result of an error, provided that an adequate retraction is published.

A retraction should be published as soon as the newspaper learns of the libel, and it should be conspicuously displayed and be given approximately the same prominence as the libel. The Tennessee Court of Appeals, upholding a libel award against a newspaper which had published a retraction, declared that the retraction should be "frank, fair and unequivocal and unmixed with any attempted justification" and "should admit the defamation in language free from ambiguity, admit it was unfounded, made without proper information and offer the regrets and apologies of the publisher."

Newspapermen unfamiliar with libel laws occasionally follow practices that are not a legal defense in a suit. Among these practices are the following:

1. Such expressions as "alleged," "it was charged," "police said," or "it was reported" offer little protection. Their value—a dubious one—is that their use may show absence of malice or intent to libel. They are important as qualifications indicating doubt as to the truth of the informa-

tion or placing responsibility on persons other than the newspaper. The fact that they are not valid defense in a libel suit does not necessarily mean that they should not be employed.

2. Absence of intent to libel is not a defense. The fact that a reporter made a mistake in his identification or in an address does not protect the newspaper.

3. Use of a fictitious name or omission of a name is not a defense if readers of the article understand that a certain individual is meant or if the injured person can prove that they identified him as the individual in the story though in fact he may not have been referred to at all.

4. It is not a defense to print a prefatory disclaimer, as do most books and motion pictures, that the persons mentioned are the mental creations of the writer and that "any similarity to actual persons is purely coincidental."

5. It is not a defense to say that the libel was uttered by a third person, as in the news report of a speech, or that it is a republication of a statement printed elsewhere.

6. The fact that the article or story was supplied by a press association or syndicate does not relieve the newspaper of responsibility for a libel.

Besides libels reflecting upon the character of an individual, there is another type of libel for injury to society or the state. Criminal libel, as it is called, differs from civil libel in that the defamation is considered actionable if it tends to lead to breach of the peace or to violent disturbance. It is prosecuted by the state, and the person found guilty may be fined or imprisoned.

THE COPYREADER'S PROBLEM

The task of the deskman in protecting his newspaper against libel i difficult and onerous. He cannot perform it merely by memorizing the law, because newspapers do not adhere strictly to what statutes an court rulings permit them to print. They often exceed their privilege. Th deskman must not only know the law, he must know when it can safel be flouted in the interests of a good story. American and British libel law basically, are very similar; yet there is a world of difference betwee what American newspapers can print safely and what British newspape can print safely.

The potentially libelous material the deskman handles may be divide into two broad classifications.

1. Stories originating at the police station and in the courts or obtaine from public records. These include arrests, charges of crimes, civil sui

for fraud, divorce suits, accidents, and reports and actions of public officials and bodies that discredit individuals.

2. Stories attacking or criticizing individuals. These include the newspaper's own editorials and exposés, attacks by other persons in speeches and publications, and criticisms coming to the editorial offices in public statements and letters to the editor.

Newspapers today engage less in character assassination than did those of an earlier period of personal journalism. Nowadays few libel suits result from an intentional attack against an individual. Before publishing such articles, editors clear them with the newspaper's legal counsel. The most serious danger of libel is found in routine news reports whose nature tends to discredit the persons involved—crime and court news.

Most libel suits resulting from this type of news are caused by carelessness in reporting facts. Because many crime stories are of only minor news interest and may be worth only a paragraph or two and because the reporter may handle a large number of such items, he has many opportunities for making mistakes. If he is careless in taking notes, he may transpose the name of the person making the complaint and that of the person arrested. Because of carelessness in making identifications, he may confuse persons of the same or similar names. In writing down the address where police made a raid he may write "100 East First Street," when it should have been "2100 East First Street."

These errors, of course, are extremely difficult for the copyreader to catch. He is told to verify names, but that advice is easier to give than to follow. Most people arrested for such crimes as larceny, burglary, or assault and battery just don't seem to get into telephone and city directories. Moreover, there is no way of making sure that the person in the directory is the one listed on the police blotter. Every city has many persons with the same or similar names.

Fortunately for the newspaper, most persons arrested for crimes are not in a position to sue it. It is hard to carry on a libel suit from a jail cell. The paper can be thankful that the police are more often right than wrong when they make arrests.

Libel in crime and court news is likely to take one of the following forms: (1) errors in names and identifications; (2) careless wording implying guilt; and (3) exceeding privilege.

In checking stories for accuracy, the deskman should be especially watchful in cases involving persons whose profession makes them extremely sensitive about their reputations. Something in a story that might not seem offensive to a tavernkeeper or truck driver would outrage a doctor, minister, schoolteacher, or lawyer. Inaccuracy is inexcusable in any story no matter what the rank or status of the individual, but it doesn't hurt to take extra precautions with stories concerning the white-collar groups.

In all crime and court stories, the deskman must see that explicit identifications are used. An adequate identification includes the full name, the address, and the age. This detail is necessary to avoid confusion with another person with the same or a similar name. If the reporter gives more than one source in the story, the deskman may feel greater confidence in the accuracy of the story. There is less chance for a reporter to err if in addition to consulting the documents in a case he also interviews the police officer, the prosecuting attorney, and the individual involved.

In the phraseology of the stories he edits and the headlines he writes, the deskman must avoid expressions implying guilt prior to a conviction in court. Thus it is imprecise for a story to state that a person "was arrested for embezzling $10,000." A person may be arrested and charged with a crime, or he may be arrested on a warrant accusing him of a crime. Until he has been convicted, he should not be referred to in news stories as an embezzler, burglar, or robber. To use these terms properly, the deskman must know their legal meaning. Even after he admits to a homicide, a person is not legally a murderer. He must be so adjudged by a jury, and murder is difficult to prove in court for by definition it is a matter of intent.

In stories about automobile accidents, danger lies in statements that fix responsibility for a crash. A statement that two automobiles "collided" is safe, because it is easy to prove that a collision took place. But a statement that one car crashed into another might be difficult to prove. Similarly, stories saying that a driver was speeding, that he was intoxicated, that he was on the wrong side of the street, that he failed to stop at traffic signal—all of these are extremely dangerous unless accompanied b reliable evidence or unless an arrest has been made.

The newspaper's greatest protection against libel suits arising fror crime and court news is the privilege of printing accurate and imparti: reports of judicial proceedings. The question that the newspaperma must answer is: What is a judicial proceeding? Does it begin with th arrest? With the filing of an information or an indictment in a crimin: case? With the filing of a petition or complaint in a civil case? Or do the judicial proceeding begin only when the case comes up for trial open court to which the public is admitted? The answers to these que tions are not the same in all states.

One confusion in reporting crime and court news that similarly arises from vagueness of definition and different state rulings concerns the privilege extending to public records. A newspaper is privileged to print fair and accurate reports of the contents of public records, even though they contain libelous matter. But in many states there is a question as to what constitutes a public record in the absence of specific statutes. For example, only two states have statutes declaring the police blotter a public record. In other states its status is determined by advisory opinions of the attorney general, by decisions of city officials, or by rulings of the courts. Three states hold that the blotter is not a public record.

In civil actions most newspapers operate on the rule of thumb that privilege begins when a case is called to the attention of a judge, as when he rules on a motion. The court clerk's docket is considered a public record, and the inception of a case may be taken as the filing of a petition or complaint. But the petition or complaint itself is not considered privileged until the judge is brought into the action.

Thus in a divorce action a newspaper, on information from a docket, may print that Mary Doe filed suit for divorce alleging cruelty. This is privileged, because the docket is a public record. But the contents of the pleading are not privileged at this stage. Details obtained from the petition—that John Doe was a drunkard, beat his wife, and mauled his children—are not privileged. A newspaper publishes such information on its own responsibility. Such material is always dangerous, because the petition may be withdrawn before it comes before the judge.

Similarly, in criminal prosecutions, the newspaper is usually safe in printing such facts as are recorded on the police blotter, when it is held to be a public record, but not additional information obtained from policemen, detectives, and complaining witnesses. An accused person's confession to police or the district attorney is not privileged. Confessions should be handled cautiously, especially if they implicate other people, because the accused may later repudiate them or they may not be admitted as evidence in a trial. Written reports of policemen and detectives, though they may be accessible to the press, are no more privileged than the information obtained orally from such officials.

Police court trials and hearings before magistrates and justices of the peace are privileged on the grounds of being judicial proceedings, though in the inferior courts no record is kept of testimony.

In covering trials the news report must be accurate and fair. Privilege extends only to matter contained in the record. Any matter that the judge orders stricken from the record is published at the paper's risk.

Though they may realize these severe limitations upon privilege, newspaper frequently print all the details they can obtain in especially newsworthy cases. The desk must exercise considerable judgment when it decides to exceed legal privilege. In the first place the story must be of overwhelming public interest. Run-of-the-mill suits and crimes are not worth the risk. In the second place the newspaper must have adequate assurance that the information is substantially true. In this the desk must rely to a large extent upon the good sense and experience of the reporter covering the story. A potentially libelous story written by a cub and containing material that is not privileged should not be printed unless it has been verified.

In editing articles attacking or criticizing individuals, the copyreader must consider the following points: whether it is legitimately fair comment and criticism; whether it is true; whether it is privileged; and whether it is malicious.

The greatest risk of libel lies in reporting speeches of political candidates and attacks by such individuals as ministers and reformists on graft and corruption in public office. In the heat of a campaign speakers make all sorts of slanderous allegations—sometimes true, sometimes partly true, sometimes false. These speeches are not privileged. The newspaper has no defense in a libel suit other than truth and fair comment and criticism. The truth, it should be emphasized, does not lie in the report's being an accurate account of a speech. The copyreader should delete defamatory matter referring to an individual's private life and matter imputing criminality or corrupt motives.

Many reporters do not understand that statements by public officials not made in line of duty are not privileged. A police commissioner, for example, may dismiss or demote a policeman, giving incompetence or acceptance of a bribe as the reason. His statement is privileged. But such a statement in a political speech is not privileged. A newspaper that prints it does so at its own risk.

Failure to take this into consideration may explain a typical complaint by reporters about copyreaders. In *My Ears Are Bent*, his book of newspaper anecdotes, Joseph Mitchell, condemning namby-pamby deskmen, told of a political rally at which a tipsy statesman flayed his opponent with fifteen minutes of vigorous and varied profanity. Mitchell said he put some of the milder remarks in his story, but they were cut out by a copyreader. "There is no fury which can equal the black fury which bubbles up in a reporter when he sees his name signed to a story which has been castrated by a copyreader or one of the officials on the city desk," Mitchell moaned. He apparently overlooked the copy desk's responsibility for eliminating libel from stories.

CONTEMPT OF COURT

The privilege given newspapers to print fair and true accounts of judicial proceedings is a recognition of the public's right to know how such proceedings are conducted and the details of the cases being tried. But abuse of the privilege under certain conditions may result in a citation of contempt of court, known as contempt by publication.

In general, a newspaper may be in contempt of court if its reporting of a case or comment delays or interferes with the administration of justice. Specifically, contempt proceedings may result from any of the following: news stories or editorials that tend to prejudice the jury, intimidate either party to a suit or the judge, impute corruption or prejudice to a judge, discredit attorneys in a case, or prevent parties to a suit from getting a fair hearing.

The freedom with which a newspaper may comment on court cases varies with whether a case is pending or has been completed. After a case has been disposed of, there is obviously little possibility of interfering with the administration of justice. In pending cases the rule of law is that there shall be no restrictions except where there is "a clear and present danger" to the administration of justice.

The tenor of recent U.S. Supreme Court opinions on contempt cases is that judges cannot stop criticism of their acts, even unfair and vindictive criticism, by the summary contempt method of suppression. Contempt, the Court ruled in Craig v. Harney, is "not made for the protection of judges who may be sensitive to the winds of public opinion," and judges "are supposed to be men of fortitude, able to thrive in a hardy climate."

The test applied in determining contempt based on the concept of clear and present danger was set forth in Bridges v. California and Pennekamp v. Florida. The opinions held that the effect of editorials and articles must be appraised in the setting of the news article and in light of the community environment. The question of contempt depends upon the court's interpretation of what constitutes clear and present danger.

The Florida case involved the Miami *Herald*, which attacked a judge's conduct in extremely unfavorable terms. The Supreme Court's majority opinion stated:

Free discussion of the problems of society is a cardinal principle of Americanism—a principle which all are zealous to preserve. Discussion that follows the termination of a case may be inadequate to emphasize the danger to public welfare or supposedly wrongful judicial conduct. It does not follow that public comment of every character upon pending trials or legal proceedings may be as free as a similar comment after complete disposal of the litigation. Between the extremes there are areas of discussion which an understanding writer will appraise in the light of the effect on himself and on the public of creating a clear and present danger to the fair and orderly judicial administration.

Courts must have power to protect the interests of prisoners and litigants before them from unseemly efforts to pervert judicial action. In the borderline instances where it is difficult to say upon which side the alleged offense falls, we think the specific freedom of public comment should weigh heavily against a possible tendency to influence pending cases. Freedom of discussion should be given the widest range compatible with the essential requirement of the fair and orderly administration of justice.

An interesting aside on newspaper coverage of law cases was contained in a concurring opinion in the same case by Justice Rutledge. He wrote:

But if every newspaper which prints critical comment about courts without justifiable basis in fact, or withholds the full truth in reporting their proceedings or decisions, or even goes further and misstates what they have done, were subject on these accounts to punishment for contempt, there would be few not frequently involved in such proceedings.

There is perhaps no area of news more inaccurately reported factually, on the whole, though with some notable exceptions, than legal news.

Some part of this is due to carelessness, often induced by the haste with which the news is gathered and published, a smaller portion to bias or more blameworthy causes. But a great deal of it must be attributed, in candor, to ignorance which frequently is not at all blameworthy.

For newspapers are conducted by men who are laymen to the law. With too rare exceptions their capacity for misunderstanding the significance of legal events and procedures, not to speak of opinions, is great. But this is neither remarkable nor peculiar to newsmen. For the law, as lawyers best know, is full of perplexities.

Despite the liberal rulings of the U.S. Supreme Court, newspapers do not attack courts or judges indiscriminately. When the issue is considered vital to the protection of society, a newspaper may lay itself open to contempt proceedings by adverse comment. If the issue is a minor one, the paper may seek to avoid becoming involved in a troublesome and expensive defense by refraining from sharp criticisms.

Of more importance to the copy desk than criticism of the courts is the possibility of contempt in publishing details about pending cases

By printing information that reporters obtain from witnesses and principals in a case, by quoting remarks of the prosecuting attorney and the defense counsel, and by describing all the circumstances in highly colored prose, newspapers may make it difficult to obtain unprejudiced jurors and an atmosphere of judicial calmness and detachment during the trial. This process is known as "trial by newspaper."

Though trial by newspaper is condemned by many in the legal profession and by responsible editors, it is sanctioned by custom and often has the active coöperation of prosecuting attorneys and judges not averse to the wide publicity a sensational case receives.

As a matter of fact, there is a growing sentiment against restricting newspapers regarding the information they can print about a pending case. In the March, 1950, issue, the editors of the *Yale University Law Journal* urged the Supreme Court to outlaw contempt by publication. They attacked as "dangerously vague" any rule that allows a judge to restrict press comment whenever he believes it might affect the outcome of a case and asserted that such a rule forces a publisher to guess whether or not his story will "bring down the wrath of the court." The law journal statement continued:

> The rule harms the public no less than the press. A general inhibition on criminal reporting would keep from circulation some material vitally needed by an informed electorate. Political and economic issues raised by national defense, securities, and anti-trust laws are now commonly involved in criminal cases.
>
> Impartial verdicts formed only on the basis of courtroom evidence are supposedly assured by examination of jurors, instructions from the judge, and, in the last resort, power to declare a mistrial. If devices such as these fail to neutralize the predisposition of jurors, the fault lies not with the press but with the system as a whole. . . .
>
> Viewed in this light, the suppression of news reporting during a trial cannot eliminate prejudice or even substantially reduce it. Instead, it represents a futile effort to insulate the jury from the prevailing climate of opinion.

In handling news stories dealing with pending court cases, the role of the copyreader is to see that they conform to journalistic standards of fairness and accuracy. They should not be of such a nature as to inflame the public against an accused person or give the impression that the court or the prosecution will not conduct a fair trial. The story should be objective and factual. Comment and criticism are problems for the newspaper's executives, who consult with their legal counsel before embarking on a campaign or crusade.

MISCELLANEOUS RESTRICTIONS

State statutes as well as federal legislation contain bans against the publication of certain types of material that might harm the nation or society.

The states have criminal syndicalism laws against publications that advocate violence or the overthrow of the government by force, and the United States penal code contains similar provisions regarding the advocacy of or incitement to treason and sedition.

The printing of obscene, lewd, lascivious, or pornographic matter is forbidden by many municipal ordinances and state laws, and the sending of such material through the mails is a federal offense.

Other miscellaneous bans imposed by federal statutes include the faking of weather forecasts and the reproduction of certificates of citizenship and of paper money.

Of the miscellaneous restrictions on what a newspaper may print, the one that the average copyreader encounters most often is the one prohibiting the publication of information concerning lotteries. Many state statutes forbid news stories and advertisements of lotteries, and sending newspapers containing such matter through the mails is a federal offense.

A lottery is defined by the courts as a scheme wherein something of value is exacted from participants for the chance of winning a prize, and wherein there are present the three necessary elements of a lottery—consideration, chance, and prize.

According to an outline of interpretations prepared by the office of the solicitor of the U.S. Post Office Department, the following have been held to be lotteries by the courts:

The awarding of a prize to the first fifty women visiting a department store on a certain day.

The awarding of prizes to persons whose names are selected from the telephone directory and published in the classified advertisements of a newspaper.

The announcement that a home in a city will be selected at random and visited during the day and that the housewife will be given a prize if she has a certain food product on hand.

Contests in which the prize depends upon the number of persons participating.

A promotion in which balloons are released over a city at a certain

PRESS LAW AND THE COPY DESK

time and the prizes attached to them, or for which they may be redeemed, are of unequal value.

The game known variously as "Bingo," "Bunco," and "Keno," especially popular with church and civic organizations.

A contest that consists of guessing the number of beans in a glass jar.

Football score contests which require entries to be submitted on a blank published in a newspaper.

All drawings for prizes and raffles.

The Post Office Department regards any article concerning a lottery as against the law, even though details of the scheme are omitted, and it considers that newspapers containing stories about the winners are not mailable.

Nevertheless, many of the lotteries in the above list are frequently publicized in newspapers. The reason is the considerable laxness on the part of local postal officials in cracking down on papers for violations of the law. Many newspapers take the precaution of eliminating from mail editions all stories and promotions about lotteries. This, however, is a dubious procedure because according to second-class mailing regulations the mail edition must be substantially the same as editions distributed through other channels.

State laws often exempt civic, fraternal, and religious organizations from the ban against conducting lotteries to raise funds. News items about these or references to them are likely to turn up in club notices, and the copy desk must be on the alert to delete them to avoid violating the postal laws.

The solicitor's office of the Post Office Department does not regard as a violation of the law mentioning a lottery that is incidental to a news story. This interpretation was given in 1948 when the St. Louis *Star-Times* was cited for violating the postal regulation by printing a story of national interest concerning a lottery winner, a Negro, who was denied his prize by the white sponsors of the event. The solicitor's office conceded that despite its literal wording the law was not intended to exclude from the mails publications which are of value in their own right and in which the lottery is only incidental to a newsworthy event.

PROPERTY RIGHTS IN NEWS

Many newspaper stories are obtained from published material—magazine articles, books, pamphlets, and reports, as well as from other newspapers. If this material is copyrighted, a newspaper may not reproduce it without permission of the copyright holder.

Copyright protects only the literary form of the material, not the facts or ideas it contains. So long as the newspaper does not employ the same phraseology as the copyrighted matter, it can make any use of printed material it wants to. The only exception to the ban on exact quotation is the "fair use" of copyrighted material by critics and reviewers. A book reviewer is thus permitted to use direct quotations in describing the contents of a book or illustrating the author's style.

Giving the source of the material does not protect the newspaper against infringement of copyright. A newspaper may not rewrite an article from another newspaper even though it states that it is quoting from a copyrighted article. It can print the information but must take care to avoid using the expressions that appeared in the original article. A wire service that picks up an exclusive story from a newspaper can send out its rewrite only because it has obtained permission to quote from the copyrighted article.

It is common practice for newspapers to rewrite stories appearing in other papers. The afternoon paper rewrites the morning paper, and vice versa. It is not considered illegal or ethically wrong. Only when the lifting of news becomes a systematic unfair practice and interferes with its sale or circulation does a newspaper take action against a competitor. In this case it is not a matter of copyright violation but an unfair trade practice that comes under state laws or under the jurisdiction of the Federal Trade Commission.

CHAPTER 21

Pictures and the News

THE PLACE OF PICTORIAL JOURNALISM

The setting up of leased wire circuits in 1935 for the wire transmission of pictures evoked enthusiastic response from advocates of pictorial journalism. With illustrations available almost as quickly as a verbal account of an event, forward-looking editors predicted drastic changes in the treatment of news and in the format and appearance of newspapers.

The far-reaching changes expected have not come about. Newspapers use more pictures than formerly, to be sure, but inspection of them before and after wire photography shows no radical alterations. Commenting on the failure of the new devices to produce fundamental changes in journalistic techniques, Basil L. Walters, executive editor of the Knight Newspapers, said:

> The machine that transports pictures with the speed of light is the outstanding journalistic development of our day. Wirephoto, or telephoto, or call it what you may, should produce as revolutionary a change in newspapers as did the invention of the linotype. We have failed dismally, however, to take advantage of this machine. Newspaper editors and publishers take an entirely different attitude toward the cost of getting good pictures to put on that machine than they do toward getting the type story that goes on to the automatic printer. The machine will not and cannot improve the original copy.

Walters blamed the failure to make full use of the new photographic devices on older "type-minded" editors who were unable to become "picture-minded" and on World War II with its drain on young men and its newsprint shortages.

There are other and more fundamental reasons, however, why newspapers have not made greater use of the techniques of pictorial journalism exploited in the popular weekly picture magazines. Consciously or subconsciously, editors have realized that pictures can seldom be more than an adjunct to the conventional reporting of news by words because of inherent limitations in the ability of photographs to tell a story.

Proponents of pictorial journalism argue that a picture is worth a thousand words—or is it ten thousand? This is a widespread fallacy. Only occasionally can a picture succeed where words fail. Photographs give the newspaper reader a report of the appearance of a person or scene better than words. But they require captions to tell who the person is or what the scene represents. A photograph of Einstein snapped at a certain instant tells nothing about his mind or character. A picture of a flaming building or the debris of an airplane crash reveals little. What caused the disaster? How many were killed or injured? Where is the building? Where did the plane crash take place? A picture may evoke dozens of questions which the picture—a mute visual representation—is powerless to answer.

Another great weakness of the camera as a reporter is that it is seldom focused on the event at the exact instant it happens. Once in a great while a moment in history is caught pictorially, but these times are so few that the great news shots number only a few score. Most pictures must be taken after the event.

A popular fallacy about photography is that the camera does not lie. It records only what is before it—but is the picture one of the event itself or one which the photographer got the principals to reenact? Was President Franklin D. Roosevelt actually looking harried and worried over problems of state, or was his facial expression caused by his being partly blinded by flash bulbs? Was it really a picture of the famous movie actress smiling at her newborn baby, or was it a photograph of an entirely different mother and baby with the actress' face superimposed on that of the real mother?

And there are stories that the camera cannot tell at all—perhaps the bulk of the events that the daily newspaper records. A photograph of the president signing a new law does not tell what the law is, does not explain its significance, does not give its history. A photograph of a congressional hearing can portray the official inquisitors and the persons on the witness stand, but that is all. Who they are, what questions are asked, what answers are given—all must be told by words.

The picture magazine—often held up as a model for newspapers to copy in utilizing pictorial techniques—must limit the number of stories it tells by pictures to a half dozen or so. A newspaper in the same space

PICTURES AND THE NEWS   **341**

can report dozens in type. If the paper attempted to illustrate even partly all the news it prints, it would have to be many times its already too bulky size. For a pictorial representation of anything—though it may give more visual detail and have a greater impact on the observer than a written article—requires much more space than the same story told in words.

These remarks are not made with the purpose of belittling photography. Newspapers should use more and better pictures, but not with the false idea of usurping the place of words and type. Because of their instant appeal and popularity with all kinds of readers, pictures are an asset to a newspaper—but chiefly as adjuncts to or illustrations for the text. They increase readership and they make the paper more attractive and interesting. They succeed where words may fail in describing persons, places, and scenes. They have an intrinsic interest even when what they portray is of no great news significance. On occasion they can be used in sequence to tell a story. For all these reasons present-day journalism should make use of pictorial techniques. The editor who is not picture-minded cannot get out a newspaper that will compete successfully with magazines, radio, television, and other agencies, both communicative and recreational, for the attention of the people.

Knowledge of how to handle pictures is necessary for all deskmen. They may have to order pictures and engravings, and they need to develop standards of judgment in deciding on what photographs to use and what size cuts should be made. Frequently also their duty is the writing of captions or legends for engravings.

SOURCES OF NEWSPAPER PICTURES

Newspaper systems for handling pictures and photographic assignments vary. Only the larger ones employ a picture editor for this work. The tendency has been for newspapers to integrate the photography department into the regular news-gathering setup, with the city desk acting as the central agency for all local picture assignments. The photographers get their assignments and instructions from the city desk, the sports, society, and other departments channeling their requests for photographers to the city editor.

There is sound reason for the popularity of this system. If photographs are considered an essential part of news coverage, the staff member with the greatest knowledge of what is going on can best explain the picture needs to photographers. Time necessarily will be wasted and exactitude of instructions lost if the city editor has to relay his desires through a picture editor.

The Bulletin of the American Society of Newspaper Editors in its issue of September 1, 1949, printed a roundup of methods used by editors in handling picture assignments. Typical of the systems described was that used by Roger A. Connolly, managing editor of the New Haven (Connecticut) *Register*. He explained it as follows:

> Our cameramen are controlled by the city desk. On spot news, where circumstances cannot be anticipated, they are given verbal instructions, told to use their own judgment or advised to check with our reporter on the scene as to best shots. Later information may be relayed to them by radio phone to our emergency car, and this also enables us to find out what we are getting before the man returns to the office.
>
> All other pictures are taken on the basis of assignment cards made out by the news editor or department heads and filed with the city desk which schedules the work day for each photographer. These cards must contain time, place, subject, person or publicity man to consult, and number and type of pictures wanted. They must note whether they are to be interior or outside shots, groups, individuals and whether prints will be used in a layout or one or two selected from the lot. If a writer is to accompany the cameraman, place of meeting is stated.
>
> The desk is expected to be insistent that all this information be on the card or otherwise return it for clarification. Photographers are also encouraged to demand clear and full instructions before accepting assignments. This reduces uncertainty in advance and limits alibis when results are not satisfactory.
>
> The photographer enters his assignments before leaving the office in our photographers' daybook and completes the record as to films, bulbs, and paper drawn and used when the job is completed. Assignment cards are turned in with the prints and must contain caption information by numbers for each print.

Fortunately editors have dropped the idea that all reporters can be equipped with cameras and take time out from gathering news to take pictures. The system was tried out by some managing editors during the candid camera fad of the 1930's. Editors found that no reporter could cover a story and take pictures and do good work in both fields. There is a place for the combination reporter-photographer, particularly on small newspapers and for special assignments and features, but for general purposes writing the news and photographing the news belong in different departments.

The newspaper receives many usable local pictures from sources other than its own staff. Photography is a popular hobby, and amateurs who have been on the spot when something momentous happens

PICTURES AND THE NEWS

have supplied newspapers and press associations with prize-winning shots. Other pictures may be purchased from professional free lances. Commercial studios furnish pictures for the society pages and portraits of people not in the newspaper morgue. The subject of a story may prefer to supply a photograph which he thinks is a good (usually this means flattering) likeness. The studio portrait, however, is often poor photography from the newspaper standpoint. A picture showing the head and bust of a person with hair meticulously combed and features set in a stiff smile or an expression of earnest concentration has little human appeal.

A useful and inexpensive source of local pictures is the publicity or public relations office of firms, institutions, and organizations. Since public relations staffs are usually manned by persons with newspaper training, they supply pictures of their firm's officials in active poses or interesting surroundings. Often this art is available in the form of mats ready for casting so that the newspaper does not have to bear the cost of engraving.

Nonlocal pictures are obtained from special picture services of the press association to which the newspaper belongs, other picture services, and feature syndicates. The type of service—wired pictures or mats—and the quantity depend on the paper's size and needs.

The small newspaper with no engraving plant of its own can obtain mats by mail within 24 to 48 hours after an event. Many of these have captions and hence the paper does not have to set them in its own plant. But since the cutlines may not conform to its style and since they do not print as sharply as type set in its own plant, the overlines and underlines are frequently sawed off the casting and reset. Press services regularly provide mats of prominent persons which can be filed in the morgue for use when needed. The small paper with its limited facilities may not have a picture of the president giving his inaugural address, for example, but from its morgue it can obtain a suitable mat to run with the story of the speech.

The distribution of important news pictures over the country and around the world has been enormously speeded up by radio and wire transmission of photographs. Only the metropolitan newspapers could afford wired photographs when introduced in 1935. But as the facilities for transmission expanded, the cost decreased and many small-city publications now have equipment for receiving pictures from distant points. Even small papers benefit from the speed-up system. Instead of pictures or mats being sent from such remote distribution points as

New York, Chicago, or Kansas City, they come in by mail from cities nearer home to which they have been transmitted by wire. Thus the small daily may be only 24 hours behind its big-city competitor in receiving important news pictures. Often the small publication gets several shots of a big news event, among which may be one or two not

Fig. 66. One 9 x 12-inch picture or several smaller pictures on a sheet that size can be transmitted on the Telephoto transceiver. Here an operator is loading a five-picture layout on the cylinder in preparation for transmitting them.

already used in the big-city paper that comes into the community. Since prepublication has not killed their value, the readers of the small newspaper find such photographs as interesting as if they had been available 24 hours earlier.

Several services use networks of leased wires for the transmission of photographs. These include Wirephoto of the Associated Press,

PICTURES AND THE NEWS

Telephoto of the United Press, and Soundphoto of the International News Service.

The transmission of pictures by electrical signals was accomplished experimentally as early as 1891, but the development of the photoelectric cell in the 1920's made telephotography feasible for the first time. Practical demonstrations of sending pictures by wire were given in 1924 by the American Telephone and Telegraph Company. By 1934 the New York *Times,* the Associated Press, and other agencies had started the construction of transmitting and receiving sets throughout the country. Regular transmission of news pictures began the next year.

A telephotography transmitter consists of a revolving metal drum on which a picture is placed. A light focused on the print is reflected into a photoelectric cell unit which converts it into an electrical current composed of impulses of varying intensity proportionate to the gradations of light reflected. The electrical current is carried by wire to the receiving units which contain a cylinder to which a film is attached. As the drum revolves, the film is exposed to a beam of light whose intensity is regulated by signals from the transmitter. In a few minutes the complete negative is exposed and is ready for the development of positive prints.

Picture coverage of events was subsequently speeded up by the development of portable transmitting and receiving units which are only slightly bulkier and heavier than an ordinary suitcase. Photographs can now be sent from any place where there is a telephone outlet.

WHAT PICTURES TO PUBLISH

"Anyone with two dimly functioning eyes can be—and is—a fairly sound judge of pictures," said Vincent S. Jones, executive editor of the Utica (New York) *Daily Press* and *Observer-Dispatch,* in a brochure published by Gannett Newspapers, Inc. The experts may argue over such esoteric matters as composition, tone quality, and focus, he said, but with the newspaper reader the picture either clicks or it doesn't.

So it is also with most newspapermen, but the culling-out process involves many factors that the picture editor must consider. He may know immediately that the shot of the dirigible *Hindenburg* bursting into flames, a bandit falling to the ground from a policeman's bullet, or a woman hurtling to death from a flaming building is a good news picture. But such historic seconds caught forever by the camera are rare. Most of the pictures the editor considers are only run of the darkroom, and he must choose from them a few for publication, weighing one against another and deciding if any are indispensable in terms of the news situation at the moment.

The two fundamental factors influencing the picture editor's choice of a photograph are its content or storytelling value and its reproduction value—how well it will come out on newsprint after going through the engraving and stereotyping process. A third factor is policy. This includes good taste and ethical considerations, as well as the paper's policy—whether the picture is a "must," as when a newspaper makes a practice of printing pictures of officers of civic organizations or photographs to aid a Community Fund or Red Cross drive.

The criteria for judging news pictures for content are approximately the same as those for evaluating news stories. They include timeliness, propinquity, importance of the persons, significance of the event, and human interest. A picture that reaches the desk in time to be used with a story rates high, whatever its other defects. After interest in the event dies down, the picture illustrating it may have little news value. Local art has greater reader appeal than pictures of remote persons and places, and photographs of prominent people are more newsworthy than those of obscure ones. The magnitude and significance of the event obviously are important factors that lead to the publication of photographs which otherwise may have little appeal. Under human interest come pictures that appeal to our elemental concerns—home, food, clothing, shelter, love, ambition.

Since the picture editor cannot use all the photographs available, he must attempt to choose those that will interest the greatest number of readers. A guide to this choice is given in *The Continuing Study of Newspaper Reading*. Bert W. Woodburn, special projects director of the Publication Research Service in Chicago, tabulated readers' choices in an article in the September, 1947, issue of *Journalism Quarterly*. His analysis of pictures in the first 100 studies of *The Continuing Study* indicated that newspaper readers "seem to read what interests them and what touches upon their daily lives."

Classified by subject matter, 698 two-column photographs ranked as follows among men and women readers:

Men Readers

Human interest 67%
National defense 67
Crime 66
Servicemen's news 64

Foreign war news 62%
Science and oddities 62
Children and babies 59
International and national general news 58
Beauty queens and glamour girls 58
Accidents and disasters 58
Sports 57
National politics 55
Local civic and political groups 47
Local general news 43
Weddings and engagements 36
Theater, movie, and radio celebrities 34
Women's, society, and club news 33
Fashions 13
Food and table decorations 5

Women Readers

Weddings and engagements 79%
Children and babies 77
Women's, society, and club news 76
Crime 72
Servicemen's news 71
Human interest 70
Science and oddities 70
Beauty queens and glamour girls 69
Accidents and disasters 69
Fashions 66
Local civic and political groups 61
National defense 61
International and national general news 60
Foreign war news 57
Theater, movie, and radio celebrities 54
Local general news 52
National politics 50
Food and table decorations 49
Sports 20

Generalizations about the value of news pictures and tabulations of "best-read" photographs on the basis of subject matter, however, do not give a final answer to whether a picture is good or bad. The immediate impact is the thing. This important quality can be described in the word "action." A picture of an event of the utmost significance is not good from a news standpoint if it has no action. A photograph of the greatest man in the world is dull if there is no action.

Action in one sense connotes physical or bodily motion—a runner breaking the tape, a football player plunging through a line for a touchdown, a policeman dragging a recalcitrant robber to jail. Another kind of action is facial expression—an enraptured child looking at Christmas toys, a political candidate smiling in victory, a football coach on the bench grimacing over a play poorly executed by his team.

Most photographs of people in the news cannot show them in violent bodily movement. Action—the impression of life—is caught in their facial expressions and by picturing them in appropriate surroundings. Among the dullest pictures are the single-column "mug" shots of individuals and group photographs in which the members are lined up in front of a wall.

Kent Cooper, executive director of the Associated Press, inveighed against these poses in a memorandum to staff members:

> Pictures of people, individually or in groups, ought to be among the most interesting of our spot news pictures. Too often they are the worst—because they are posed. Sometimes this is because the photographer seeks to instruct his subjects where to look, whether to smile, whether to sit, or whether to stand. The result is that most pictures of people, in groups or individually, have taken on a definite, glassy form, without distinction or personality. . . . I earnestly ask you to put a premium on the natural, unposed pictures of people. . . . I would like to see more closeup portraits. Let them show the imperfections of warts on the face and everything else because such markings often indicate character. It is the one kind of picture intended to serve a basic purpose—to show what a person actually looks like when one talks to him, closeup.

In addition to choosing a picture—if one is available—that shows a natural, lifelike expression, the photo editor should try to find one that portrays the individual in his customary surroundings. A scholar in a commonplace studio portrait might not be distinguishable from a banker or a merchant; his character and interests are shown immediately if he is pictured poring over a manuscript in his library.

And, unless he can find no other pictures, the editor should eliminate all hackneyed and obviously posed shots—girls clad only in bathing suits frolicking in the snow; persons supposedly caught unawares and intent on their own affairs but with faces and eyes cocked toward the camera; people reading a newspaper and holding it so that the name plate is the first thing noticed.

If photographs could be reproduced with all the clarity of detail and gradations of tone in the original print, the picture editor would not have to concern himself with certain technical niceties. But many photographic values are lost in transforming a picture into an engraving from which a mat can be rolled and a stereotype cast for the press. A picture that rates high in news value and human interest may not

PICTURES AND THE NEWS

be usable because it will be only a smudge of black and gray in the newspaper.

For making half-tones newspapers insist upon photographs printed

Fig. 67. The first decision about a news picture is made in the darkroom. Here a photographer examines several negatives to choose the one that looks best and tells most. (Washington *Post* photo.)

on white glossy paper. Engravings can be made from pictures on rough-textured or matte paper, but they do not reproduce well unless the engraver takes extra pains with them. A photograph larger than the size to be used in the paper is preferable. If the original has to be "blown up" in rephotographing it for engraving, some of the detail is lost; the image becomes sharper when the picture is reduced. Newspapers prefer prints measuring 8 by 10 inches or larger.

In judging a print for reproduction qualities, the picture editor considers the following: (1) sharp focus; (2) good detail; (3) contrast in tones.

A picture is in focus when the outlines are clear and sharp. When the image is blurred in the photograph, the fault is intensified in the engraving process so that the image is almost unrecognizable in the newspaper. Good detail shows best in the smaller objects in a picture —the pupil of the eye, a button on a shirt, wrinkles in the sleeves of a coat. When the print is so poor that it does not show adequate detail, the reproduction in the newspaper will be indistinct. Sharp contrast in tones is a requisite for newspaper photographs because it is impossible to show the subtler gradations from gray to black in the engraving and mat. Thus the face of a person in a picture usually stands out more if it is against a dark background. A print that has an overall gray appearance will reproduce indistinctly; one that is mostly dark will appear as a smudgy expanse of black. While sharp contrast— black against white—is needed for newspaper photographs, there must also be the intervening shades of gray. The contrast is too startling if there are only the two colors—black and white—and the picture may seem artificial and exaggerated.

Because a photograph has so much greater impact than a written description, the picture editor must guard against art that may offend his paper's readers. Many publications have absolute bans against photographs of dead bodies and those that show physical injuries and wounds in gruesome detail. The degree of offensiveness is a relative matter. Readers might not object to such pictures if they portray persons in a distant place, but they may be outraged at similar photographs of people well known in the community.

Cheesecake and leg art—pictures of lovely woman in scanty attire— are a staple of newspapers, usually being sent in by theatrical and motion-picture press agents and publicity men for beach resorts. These pictures do not rank high in newspaper readership studies, although the statistics cannot be taken at face value because many persons may be reluctant to say they enjoy looking at such art. Vincent S. Jones of the Utica (New York) *Daily Press* and *Observer-Dispatch* commented that a reasonable amount of cheesecake hurts no paper. "There's no reason," he said, "to apologize for printing a picture of a pretty face, a bright

PICTURES AND THE NEWS

smile, or a general view of any natural, clean-cut female who is not showing more than, say, 85 per cent of her hide." But Jones objected—as do many editors—to most of the "stunts" dreamed up to justify such pictures.

While photographers are urged to snap lifelike shots and to avoid posed pictures, so-called candid photographs must be carefully scrutinized to avoid using any that might hold the subject to ridicule. Anyone in an unguarded moment may scratch himself, pick his nose, or make odd grimaces, and a picture under such circumstances would embarrass him if published. If through his own actions, such as committing a crime, he has not lost the respect of the people, the newspaper should picture him as he would like to be seen by the public. This does not mean that candid shots should not be used; it merely means that the picture editor must exercise careful judgment, weighing the individual's right of privacy against the right of the public to see.

EDITING THE PICTURE

The picture print received from the darkroom often requires some alterations to make it suitable for reproduction in a newspaper. If the print is poor—that is, if it is grainy, not sharply focused, or lacking in detail and contrast—it may require retouching. This is ordinarily a job for a specialist with art training, though the deskman can do a few things with a copy pencil to sharpen outlines or tone down white areas. When the picture editor wants to use only a portion of a photograph, he indicates to the engraver the part he wants by means of crop marks.

On large newspapers that have specialized retouchers in the art department even very poor prints can be altered so as to be suitable for an engraving. On smaller publications that do not have this talent available, picture editors must limit their selection of photographs primarily to those with good copy value. Unless they have had training in retouching, their amateurish efforts will result in botched pictures that show plainly that they have been "doctored up." Commercial engravers have artists available for retouching.

Except for the few improvements the picture editor can make with a copy pencil, retouching is the process of painting over a print with black, white, and gray water-soluble colors. The paint is applied with a camel's-hair brush or an air brush. Indistinct outlines can be sharpened by being painted over with narrow brush strokes, by darkening or lightening the background so that figure shows up in bolder relief, or by toning the figure to a lighter or darker shade. If a picture lacks con-

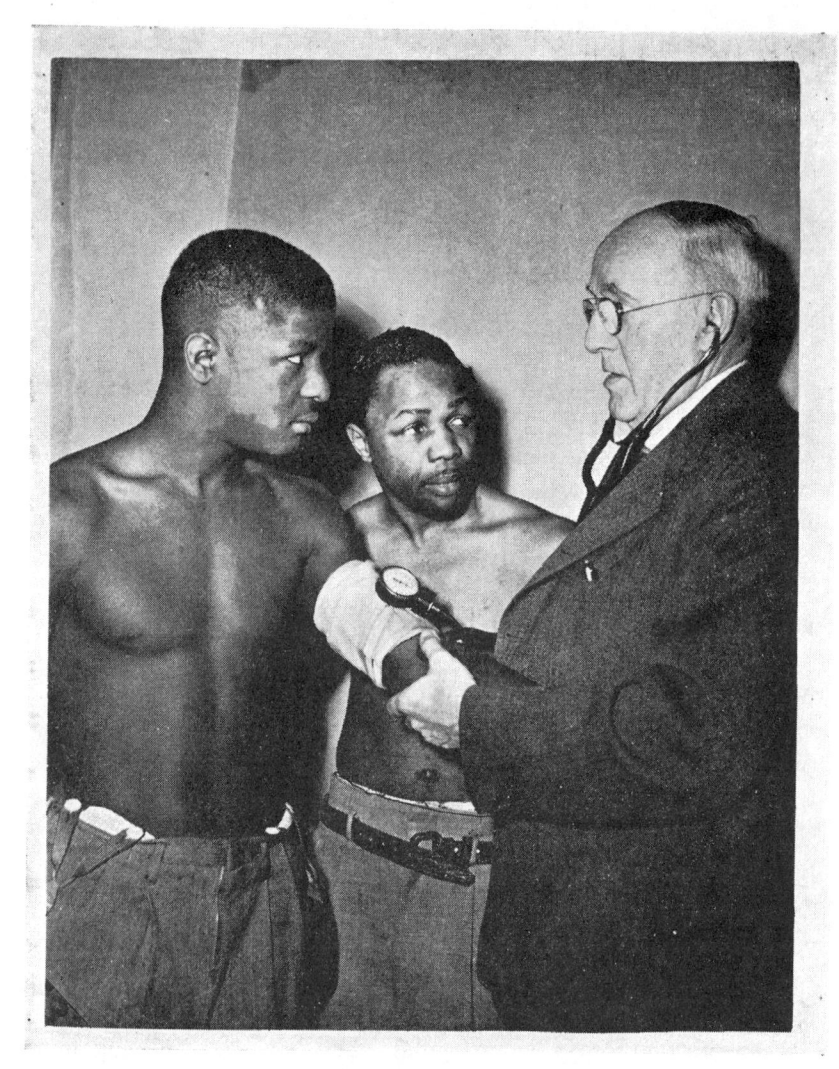

Fig. 68. Here is the print, received from the photographer, of Boxer Percy Bassett having his blood pressure checked and Boxer Harold Dade awaiting his turn. The same print retouched and cropped is shown in Fig. 69. (Philadelphia *Inquirer* photo.)

trast, certain areas may be given heavier or deeper shades. Details such as eyes, lips, ears, and other physical features may be fuzzy or blurred and require sharpening by outlining or the application of lighter or darker paint.

Retouching is defended on the grounds that it makes possible the

PICTURES AND THE NEWS 353

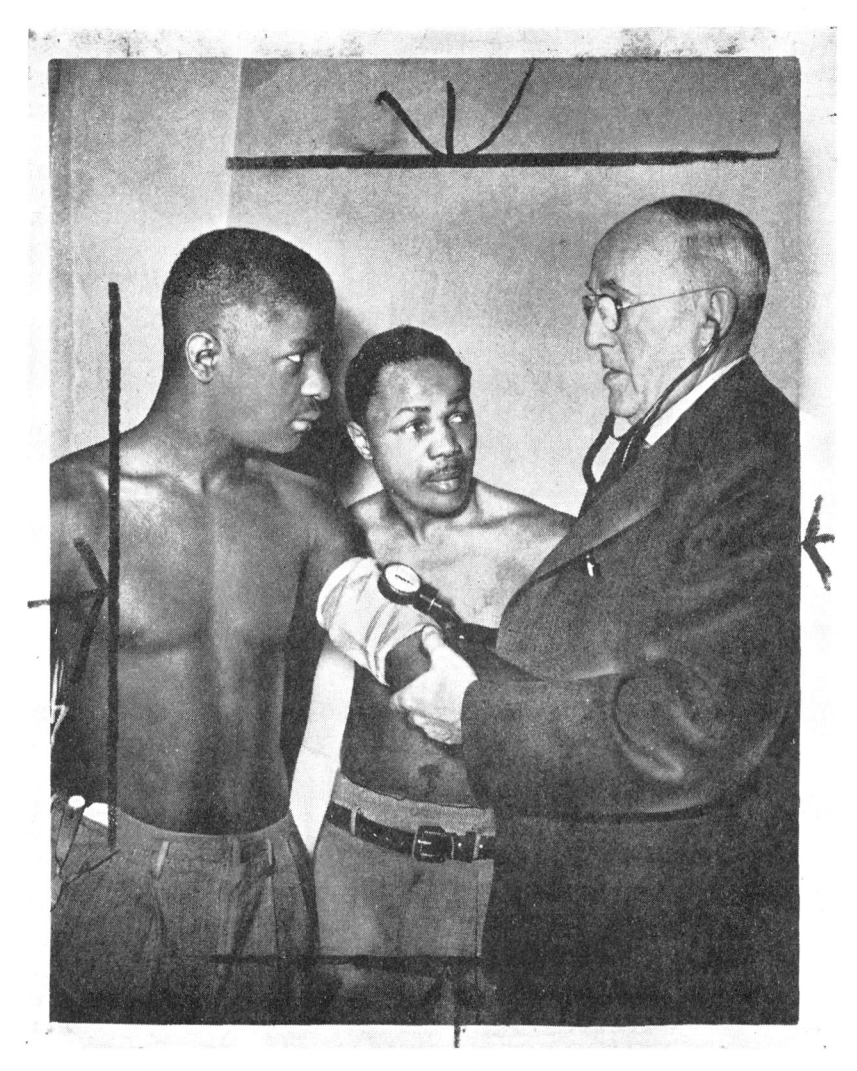

Fig. 69. The photoengraving will include only the portion of the picture within the crop marks. The retoucher outlined more clearly the body of the fighter on the left and painted out the men's underwear. (Philadelphia *Inquirer* photo.)

use of photographs that would otherwise have to be discarded. Photographers often must make news shots under adverse conditions, and many pictures are poor in quality from the standpoint of print and development. Skillful retouching here and there does not necessarily falsify the picture. If possible, the picture editor should provide the retoucher with an enlarged print, because retouching is less likely to be apparent when the picture is reduced for the engraving.

Before sending a print to the engraver, the picture editor indicates by crop marks the portion he wants made into a cut. Cropping is needed when there are large areas of uninteresting background and when the center of interest is in only one section of the print. By omitting the uninteresting areas, the important detail can be blown up into a larger engraving. Cropping makes it possible to pick out one individual in a group photograph for an engraving when the picture editor does not want to include the other persons.

A simple device to aid him in deciding where to put his crop marks consists of two L-shaped pieces of cardboard. The arms should be about 10 inches long and one or two inches wide. These pieces can be moved over the picture to frame the area of greatest interest. When the frame encloses all that is most interesting and vital and shuts out all the uninteresting parts, the editor knows exactly where to place his crop marks. This aid to visualization is not necessary for experienced picture editors, but it helps a beginner to develop pictorial judgment.

The quickest method of indicating crop marks is to draw lines or arrows in the margin of the photograph with a grease pencil or soft lead pencil. A box is sometimes drawn on the print around the area to be used, but many editors avoid it because, unless a grease pencil is used, the markings ruin the photograph for other purposes. Another method, used primarily when a print is to be returned to its owner, is to reverse it against a windowpane or on a tracing table and draw in the crop lines on the back. Care must be taken not to press so heavily that the lines come through on the emulsion side of the photograph.

Occasionally an uninteresting corner of a picture may be utilized by sawing out the area, leaving an irregularly shaped picture. The space can be used for a caption. It is also possible to mortise out a portion of the engraving and fill the opening with type.

Several pictures may be used in combination in a layout. When the layout is simple and only two or three pictures are used, good effects can be obtained with separate cuts. For more complicated layouts the pastedown system is used. The photographs are trimmed to the desired size and fastened to a sheet of cardboard with rubber cement—not glue or paste because these may make the print wrinkle or curl up at the edges. In the engraving process, the pastedown is photographed as though it were a single print, and it can be enlarged or reduced.

A more complicated and more finished type of layout is the photomontage, in which the separate pictures are blended so that all of them seem to have been developed from a single photographic negative. There are several methods of making photomontages, all of which require elaborate darkroom processes.

Since picture layouts and photomontages require extra time to prepare, they are more useful for feature art than for spot news illustrations. When a newspaper wants to carry several photographs of a news event, it usually has separate engravings made.

Present-day practice in newspaper illustrations is to use engravings without borders or fancy decorations and ornaments. If borders are used, they should be a single black line. Occasionally an outlined picture or silhouette may be used. The vignette, in which part of the background is eliminated, leaving an irregular patch that shades off around the edges of the figure, is another method of using engravings.

DETERMINING THE SIZE OF THE CUT

Factors influencing the size of the cut are the picture's newsworthiness and its subject matter. Mug shots, especially those in which the person is posing formally, are seldom worth more than a single column in the news section. The women's departments of many newspapers, however, are addicted to multi-column portraits of socially prominent brides and leaders of the local *haut monde*. Also fairly popular are half-column or thumbnail cuts, useful for short items about individuals and for pictures of the authors of columns and by-line stories.

Few pictures showing two or more persons, a scene, or action of any sort can be made into cuts less than two columns wide. And even a two-column cut is small for many, because the figures and details are so reduced that it is difficult to make them out clearly. If space is at a premium, it may be better to leave out a picture entirely than to run it too small. By expert cropping, however, a photograph that ordinarily requires three columns can often be made just as effective for two columns.

The Continuing Study of Newspaper Reading indicates that the percentage of readership increases with the size of the picture. For men, the scores in the 100-study summary were: one-column pictures, 37 percent; two-column, 49 percent; three-column, 64 percent; four-column, 64 percent. For women, the scores were: one-column pictures, 45 percent; two-column, 61 percent; three-column, 67 percent; four-column, 73 percent.

The scores are about what we would expect. A larger picture naturally attracts more attention than a small one. Furthermore, one-column pictures ordinarily are inherently less interesting than larger ones containing action.

Newspaper cuts are ordered by the column measure, the width of the cut being determined by the column width. If the column is 12 picas wide, the cut ordered will be 11 or 11½ picas so that it does not come flush to the column rules. For cuts wider than one column, the picture editor must include the space taken by the column rules to avoid having too much white space at the sides. A two-column cut for a 12-pica column would probably be 23½ picas; a three-column cut, 35 picas. On a large paper that has its own engraving plant, these measurements will be known to the engravers; hence the editor will need only to mark on the picture the desired number of columns. But if the cuts are made by a commercial engraver, the widths should be indicated by picas and not by columns, since he has no way of knowing the width of the paper's columns.

The column width determines the depth of the cut. When a picture is enlarged in the photoengraving process, the depth becomes greater in proportion; when a picture is reduced, there is a corresponding reduction in depth. If the picture editor does not take this change in depth into consideration, he may find himself with an outsize cut much larger than the space he had allotted for it or a minuscule one that takes up only a fraction of the space he had planned to use. An engraving twice the width of the photograph has a total area four times the size of the picture; and an engraving half the width has only one-fourth the area of the photograph.

A quick method of scaling a picture to determine the size of the engraving is to place the picture on a newspaper page so that the left side is lined up with a column rule. Then lay a ruler diagonally across the print from the upper left-hand corner to the lower right-hand corner. The depth of the cut will be the point, down from the top, where the ruler crosses the right-hand column rule that indicates the width of the engraving.

If the picture editor is mathematically inclined, he can figure the depth by an algebraic formula. Suppose the area of the print to be included in the engraving measures 7 by 9 inches, and the editor wants a three-column engraving, the column measuring 12 picas or approximately 2 inches. He uses the following formula: $7:6::9:x$. Multiplying the means and extremes gives: $7x = 54$. The unknown quantity x

(which represents the depth), is obtained by dividing 54 by 7. The depth thus would be 7.7 inches.

Other methods of finding the depth of engravings quickly involve the use of specially prepared logarithmic tables obtainable by newspapers, engraver's slide rules which can be purchased cheaply, and patented expanding rulers advertised in trade journals.

ORDERING ENGRAVINGS

Newspaper illustrations are of two general types: (1) line engravings or zinc etchings and (2) half-tones. Line engravings reproduce a picture only in black and white; half-tones reproduce the tonal values and shadings of photographs.

Line engravings are used for maps, diagrams, cartoons, and black-and-white drawings found chiefly in advertisements. Half-tones are used for photographic illustrations.

Both types of engravings are used in relief or letterpress printing, that is, the process in which paper is pressed against inked surfaces that stand out in relief against a base. Ordinary type, linotype slugs, stereotype plates, and woodcuts are also used in this method of printing.

Drawings carved on blocks of wood or chalk-coated steel plates were used in newspapers until the development of the zinc etching in 1872. Half-tones made by a photographic engraving process (photoengraving) made their appearance in the 1880's.

Photoengraving consists of transferring by an involved photographic process a picture to a sensitized plate. The image on the plate is inked with a special ink and then coated with a red topping powder known as Dragon's Blood. The Dragon's Blood forms an acid-proof coating over the image. The plate is then dipped in an acid bath which eats away all the portions not protected by the Dragon's Blood, leaving the lines of the illustration in relief on the surface.

The same process is used for making line etchings and half-tones, except that the copy for a half-tone is photographed through a screen consisting of a double thickness of glass with ruled intersecting lines. Filtering the light through these apertures produces a picture made up of a multitude of tiny dots of varying sizes. These dots survive the acid bath and make it possible to reproduce the photograph's gradations in tone from gray to black in the printing plate used by the newspaper.

The fineness of the screen used in the rephotographing process deter-

Fig. 70. The first step in making an engraving is rephotographing the picture through a glass "screen." Here a photoengraver focuses his big lens on a piece of copy. (Washington *Post* photo.)

mines the fidelity with which the original picture will be reproduced. Newspapers are forced to use fairly coarse screens. The necessity of making a mat from the engraving for the stereotype plate, the high-speed rotary presses, and the soft newsprint on which papers are printed do not permit a fine screen. Newspapers printed on rotary presses use screens of 60 or 65 lines an inch. Smaller newspapers which print direct from the engravings on a flatbed press can use a finer screen; 85 lines is often ordered. The screen sizes in most commercial engraving plants are 60, 65, 85, 100, 120, 133, and 150. Magazines printed on a hard-finish coated paper can use screens as fine as 150 lines.

PICTURES AND THE NEWS

Each print that the picture editor sends the engraver must contain complete instructions. In addition to crop marks, the editor must indicate the width of the cut in columns or picas, the screen (if a photograph), and the type of border if any. This information may be penciled lightly on the back of the photograph, or written on a piece of paper and pasted—not clipped, because a paper clip will mar the print or make it crack—to the reverse side.

Fig. 71. The Fairchild Scan-a-graver takes up less room in the plant than a desk. On the drum at the right is the photograph. It is reproduced in minuscule dots on a plastic plate attached to the drum at the left. (Photo by Richard O. Byers.)

In 1948 the Fairchild Camera and Instrument Corporation introduced a revolutionary new engraving process for making half-tones. It involves the use of an electromechanical device, called a Scan-a-graver, that produces engravings on plastic material by a direct process without photography or chemicals. Unlike the photochemical process of making engravings—etching zinc or copper plates with an acid—the Fairchild engraver burns away the surface of the plastic and produces the same result. This is accomplished by means of a heated pyramid-shaped stylus on an engraving assembly which penetrates the plastic to varying depths according to the impulses transmitted from a photoelectric cell. The unburned surface forms the dot pattern of the half-tone; the more deeply burned portions produce the highlight areas and those of shallower depth the darker tones.

The advantage of the Scan-a-graver is that it makes engravings in a few minutes at a low cost. The equipment is leased, not sold to newspapers, and hence there is no heavy investment for it. A person can learn to operate it in a few hours, and thus it requires no high-salaried personnel. The machine is fast—a two-column cut can be produced in 12 minutes, and a five-column one in 30 minutes. But the maximum size of engravings is 8 x 10 inches. Two types of the engraver are available—one makes 65-screen half-tones and the other makes 85-screen.

The plastic engravings can be used for rolling mats for casting stereotypes, or they can be printed from directly by letterpress printing. The plastic is flexible and can be attached to a curved stereotype plate by double Scotch tape or other adhesive. This is an advantage, since none of the quality of the engraving is lost in the matting and stereotyping processes.

Photogravure or gravure plates use the intaglio process of printing. Intaglio printing differs from letterpress in that the image to be reproduced is sunk on a plate instead of being in relief. The ink penetrates the depressions, the nonprinting surfaces are wiped clean, and a paper pressed over the engraving absorbs the ink. Gravure or photogravure engravings are known popularly as rotogravure, the prefix indicating that they are printed on a rotary press. Rotogravure requires a special press, and newspapers use it only in pictorial sections, usually in a brown or sepia monochrome.

WRITING CUTLINES

The effectiveness of a photograph does not depend alone on its subject matter, its size, or its clarity of outline and detail. The text that accompanies it is also important. This fact was brought home early to the picture magazines established in the 1930's. At first they relied primarily on photographs to tell the story; the text was held to a minimum. But the editors soon realized that good pictures were not enough, that their intrinsic interest was enhanced by adequate captions; and consequently the reading content of the magazines was increased.

Newspaper editors also recognize the importance of captions. The Associated Press Managing Editors Association, after an analysis of Wirephoto, placed near the top of its recommendations "the training of caption writers to the end that captions shall be terse, informative, specific, and, above all, accurate."

Analysis of reports of *The Continuing Study of Newspaper Reading* indicates that the readership scores for captions is only a few percentage points below those for the photographs themselves. A compilation of readership scores for about 500 pictures and captions in 25 post-World War II studies showed the following:

Photograph Size	Photograph Men	Photograph Women	Cutlines Men	Cutlines Women
1 column	35%	39%	31%	37%
2 column	49	59	47	53
3 column	56	60	52	54
4 column	53	49	49	40
5 column	49	58	42	53

Newspaper practice in writing captions varies. If the reporter who covered the assignment with a photographer is in the office, he writes the caption. If not, the job may be given to a rewrite man, who gets his information from the reporter and his identifications from the photographer. But the job is just as likely to be handled by a copyreader, especially if the newspaper's style calls for an overline, because the content of the caption underneath should not duplicate information in the overline.

The typography of the captions and the placing of the cut in the story govern the content of the caption. When a picture is "floated," that is, printed without an accompanying story, the caption must give full details and identifications of the persons or place depicted. A cut that is sunk in a story or run under a headline may require only the briefest of captions; in the case of an individual, the name suffices.

Popular methods of handling captions include the following:

1. A single-line overline centered or set flush left above the cut; the legend below it gives the identification and explanatory matter needed to understand the picture.

2. A single-line heading in smaller type than that used for an overline, set immediately below the cut and above the legend.

3. A run-in sidehead in all-caps or boldface that takes up part of the line on which the legend begins. Sometimes the sidehead is set in larger type than the legend and must be mortised into it.

4. The first three or four words of the legend set in all-caps or boldface.

The rules for writing overlines and underlines are flexible. The overline does not necessarily tell the whole story as does an ordinary headline; it may be merely a catchy phrase, especially with feature pictures, that will

Fig. 72. Some typographical styles for picture captions.

attract the reader's attention. The underlines should be brief, but they must contain sufficient detail to explain the picture fully. The present tense or historical present is used by most newspapers for captions. Some use present participles instead of complete sentences.

The people in pictures must be clearly identified. If more than one individual is shown, each must be identified in terms of his position in the photograph. Position is usually expressed in terms of left, center, and right. If there are only two persons, the position of only one is of course sufficient. When the individuals are so grouped that the left-right designation is meaningless, other expressions may be used, such as: in the foreground, nearest the camera, wearing a sweater, seated, and standing. Progression from left to right is the natural order to follow, but it is not absolute. Thus, if the person on the right is the most prominent and most newsworthy, he may be mentioned first in the caption.

As in writing the lead for a news story, the caption writer should emphasize the most important or most interesting information in the first part of his sentence. He should not waste words on the obvious: "The picture above portrays . . ."; "Shown above is . . ."; "Shown reading (or studying, looking at, standing by) is . . ." It is silly to describe a woman in a picture as "pretty" or "beautiful." If she is, the picture will show it; if she isn't, the caption is a lie.

Picture editors should conquer the temptation to use a morgue or file picture as a photograph of a current scene. A picture taken last year when the president read a message to congress may be no different from one taken of him today; but it would be fraudulent to say or imply strongly that it is a new photograph. The small-city editor desperately looking for some live front-page art is of course most strongly tempted to resort to this subterfuge. There should be no faking of captions, just as there should be no faking of pictures.

Picture syndicates require that a legend or credit line give the source of their pictures. This usually appears inconspicuously in the lower corner of a print or mat, but often it is lost in cropping. Most credit lines are put in small type just below the picture. Pictures obtained from commercial photographers for newspaper use often have a provision that they carry a credit line naming the studio. A growing tendency of newspapers is to recognize the work of staff photographers by giving them a credit line.

Guidelines for pictures are put on the back of the photographs with the instructions about size. The same guidelines are put on the copy for the picture captions and overlines, and on the dummy in the space reserved for the pictures. Care must be taken to use the same guidelines in all three places.

Newspapers follow different practices in handling cuts received from the engravers. On larger publications that use many pictures, the original photograph, the cut, and the proof may go to a cut bank in the composing room where a printer assembles the captions and engravings. Often, however, the captions and overlines are put in the make-up forms in which bases have already been placed for mounting the engravings. This practice makes it necessary for the depth of the cut to be determined before the picture is sent to the engraver. In other offices the engraving together with the photograph and proof goes to the copy desk. The guideline is then written on back of the engraving which is sent to the composing room.

The copy for the captions must instruct the printer as to how wide it is to be set and what size of type is to be used. To insure the best appearance typographically, the underlines should be set the same width as the cut. The cutlines for engravings two or three columns wide should be set in 9- or 10-point type. The cutlines for wider cuts—those three columns or more—should be broken up into shorter units. A three-column cut, for example, might have a caption set in two columns 18 picas wide; a four-column cut, a caption set in two columns 24 picas wide.

CHAPTER **22**

Trade Area News

A GAP IN NEWS COVERAGE

The daily newspaper's problem of coverage on the local level and on national and international levels has been fairly well solved. A local staff under the city editor gets news about the immediate vicinity; the wire services provide coverage of national and international events of importance.

But there is a broad field between that poses problems which are not the same for all publications. It consists of what may be termed "trade area news." For the small-town daily the trade area is likely to be countywide, especially if the paper is published in the county seat. The whole state may be considered the news beat for large-city publications such as the Des Moines *Register* and *Tribune*. A few newspapers, like the Denver *Post*, consider themselves the organ for an entire region that may take in parts of several states.

The wire press associations to some extent provide newspapers with extensive budgets of state and regional news, and in recent years they have expanded these services. In New York City, for example, the papers have dropped their suburban correspondents; instead, they rely heavily on press associations for spot news coverage. The associations, especially Associated Press and United Press, operate on a state and regional network plan.

But the wire services do not supply the needs of newspapers that want intensive coverage of a county or several counties, or of a metropolitan paper whose requirements for state news are greater than those of the smaller-city newspapers served by the same organization. To fill this gap in news coverage, newspapers have developed various systems according to their individual needs.

Most publications keep themselves supplied with news of their trade areas by means of part-time correspondents. A few correspondents who send in a steady volume of news are paid a monthly or weekly salary, but most of them are paid by space rates—that is, so much an inch or column for stories that are printed. They clip their articles and send them in to the newspaper each month for payment. The pasted-up clippings are called "strings," and the correspondents usually are spoken of as "stringers."

The methods of handling correspondence vary according to its volume. A newspaper with state-wide circulation that carries a large amount of news from other towns usually finds it feasible to employ a state editor to direct coverage by its correspondents and to edit and headline the copy. Metropolitan newspapers that have bureaus and correspondents in nearby communities have suburban desks and editors. Smaller dailies with correspondents in the surrounding trade area may assign a county editor to handle the correspondence. On other publications where the volume of correspondence is small, it is handled by the city editor and the copy clears through him on the way to the copy desk. Sports editors generally have their own setup for covering athletics, and society editors handle such stories as engagement announcements and weddings.

One of the major problems of state and county editors is to secure capable correspondents—no easy matter considering the limited budget on which they are usually expected to operate and the protests they are likely to hear from the business office about excessive telephone and telegraph charges.

HANDLING STATE CORRESPONDENTS

The task of getting correspondents is in some respects easier for the state editor than for the county editor. Often the state editor can secure the services of a staff member of the local newspaper—by far the best type of correspondent. The local newsman knows immediately when anything of state-wide interest happens in his community and he does not have to spend extra time gathering the information. Consequently, for the few extra dollars a month his string brings in, he is willing to telephone a good spot news story to the state editor or put in half an hour at the end of his day's work writing a condensed version of his stories for his own newspaper and mailing them to the state editor.

Most publishers do not object to having a member of their staff serve as correspondent for a larger newspaper. Some consider it a kind of bonus for the reporter in lieu of a higher salary they might have to pay to keep him. Others regard it as good publicity for the town to get frequent mention in the metropolitan newspaper.

But some publishers will not permit their reporters to serve as correspondents. They look upon a big-city paper that comes into the community as direct competition, and they want the local news gathered by their employees to appear exclusively in their own papers. Some permit their reporters to serve as correspondents with the provision that the news will be made available to a metropolitan newspaper only after it has appeared in the local paper.

When a local newsman is not available to serve as correspondent, the state editor looks for someone else with journalistic experience. Often available are former newspaperwomen who have quit work on being married but still find reporting interesting and can use the "pin money" they earn by a few hours' work a week.

The best way of securing the loyalty and coöperation of correspondents of course is to make it financially worth while for them to send in items. Within his budget limitations, the state editor should use as much contributed material as possible. At a trade area news clinic at Northwestern University's Medill School of Journalism the manager of the Consolidated News Service of the Rockford (Illinois) newspapers said that reporters and rewrite men who take spot telephone calls from correspondents often discourage them by gruff treatment. Instead of having correspondents turned over to whatever rewrite man is available, some state editors insist that all such calls go to them personally.

SOME STATE DESK PROBLEMS

The qualifications of a good state editor, other than those common to all newspapermen, include an especially broad knowledge of the state and its people. The state editor selects and edits the news on the basis of two standards of judgment—what will be of general interest and what will interest the people in the town where the news originated.

One of the purposes of carrying state correspondence is to win readers in smaller towns and cities, and a state editor who is ignorant of the communities his correspondents write about can lose good will and circulation by poor judgment. For example, if he consistently plays up news about crime and scandal in a town and gives only an inch or two to items that show it to be a progressive, law-abiding place, the readers may object. Big black headlines about the city treasurer's defalcations and only a paragraph about the completion of a new high-school building will strike the readers as prejudiced or perverted news. With or without justification, local readers often say that the big-city newspaper always gives the high-school football team a big write-up when it loses but that they can hardly find the story when the team defeats its bitterest rival in the biggest game of the year.

An aid to the state editor in judging the value of news sent in by correspondents is an up-to-date list of towns with his newspaper's circulation in each. When he has stories of about the same intrinsic interest from two different towns, it is only sensible for him to give the bigger play to the one from the town with the greater number of readers.

The state editor should keep as careful a check on the paper's circulation in the various towns in which he has correspondents as the circulation manager. When the circulation starts dropping in a town, the state editor should find out why. And the best and quickest way is to consult the circulation manager, who has probably already been given the reason by the local agent. If the circulation manager wants to expand the newspaper's coverage into a new area, the state editor coöperates by running more news from that region.

One fault common to almost all the copy sent in by stringers is verbosity —for the obvious reason that correspondents are paid by space rates. The longer the story, the bigger the figure on their monthly check. Hence the state editor must edit their copy carefully to trim it down to what the articles are worth. This is not always an easy job. Some stringers have an ability approaching sheer genius for putting words together so that it is hard to shorten a story without rewriting it.

An almost daily problem for most state editors is what to do with two stories about the same event—one from the paper's correspondent and one from the wire service. With his mind intent on his budget as well as on the duplicated stories, the editor may be inclined to use the press association article. It won't cost extra. But such an automatic decision is manifestly unfair to the stringer. Unless the wire story is clearly better and contains later information, the state editor should hesitate before depriving the correspondent of money he has really earned.

When the two stories differ as to facts, the immense prestige of the wire service should not becloud the state editor's judgment and make him think that the correspondent is necessarily wrong. Confronted with contradictory information, the obvious thing to do is to obtain verification—from either press association or correspondent, or both.

The volume and quality of the stories received often have no relationship to the size of the town. An ambitious correspondent in a small place may send in dozens of stories to the one or two written by the correspondent in a larger town. Perhaps the first stringer writes a lot of copy because he has hopes of being hired by the city paper, or perhaps he just needs the extra cash. Not all his stories are usable; but rather than kill them day after day without explanation the state editor should write him and tell him why everything he submits can't be printed. Certainly a correspondent who sends in 50 stories in a month but who has only 25 of them printed is not being paid a high rate for his production. Unless he is told why the others aren't used, he may get the idea that the newspaper doesn't want any material and stop sending it.

COVERAGE BY STAFF MEMBERS

Instead of relying on stringers and part-time correspondents for coverage, some newspapers in thickly populated areas find it feasible to assign a full-time staff member in key towns; in larger places they establish a bureau with several reporters.

For example, to provide full coverage of Rhode Island, the Providence *Journal, Evening Bulletin,* and *Sunday Journal* maintain a state staff of 48 full-time reporters, including 14 bureau managers who work out of 14 suburban offices. The staff covers all the thirty-eight Rhode Island cities and towns outside Providence, as well as Fall River, Massachusetts, and Stonington, Connecticut. It is augmented by stringers who cover less important news in small towns. Wherever a story happens in Rhode Island, a staff man can be on the scene in only a short time.

As reported in the April 19, 1947, issue of *Editor & Publisher,* these papers' state staff offices are under the general supervision of the state editor, whose headquarters are in Providence. However, he spends part of his time in the field working with the men on developing important stories and assisting in training the new men.

Under the Providence plan, the state staff is used as a training ground for reporters and a proving ground for newcomers. It is also used for the placing of school of journalism graduates and reporters hired from smaller newspapers. State staff reporters are assigned to the city staff for one or two weeks to acquaint them with the newspaper's practices and policies.

The spot news written by state staff members is transmitted to Providence by telephone and teletype. Feature and time stories are sent by mail or bus. The newsroom has separate copy desks to handle the state staff copy. They have their own battery of teletypewriters and their own dictation banks. Each of the desks is manned by an editor and two assistants.

DISPLAY OF AREA NEWS

Editors differ as to whether state news should be segregated in departments or pages or given the run of the paper. The decision as to which plan to follow depends upon local conditions and the volume of the material. One consideration that the state editor should keep in mind is that the space given to news from a smaller town usually cannot compete on the same level with the local newspaper unless the latter does an outstandingly poor job of covering the community or unless the community is served only by a weekly.

Following are some typical situations in the handling of state and area news:

1. The newspaper is a morning publication that is printed in a central location in the state's biggest city. Its bulldog edition, off the press at 9 P.M., reaches every part of the state on its own fleet of delivery trucks before subscribers sit down to breakfast. The paper is almost truly a statewide newspaper. It carries more national and international news than do any of the smaller-city publications. It also carries a large amount of state news selected on the basis of its general appeal. This news is played on the basis of its newsworthiness against that of all the other news available, and there is no departmentalization or segregation exception for a column of minor stuff carried under the heading "State Briefs."

2. The newspaper is a morning publication published in a city in the northeastern part of the state. Its policy is the same as that of the preceding paper, except that it concentrates on news about the immediate area and makes no attempt to cover lesser news in other parts of the state where it does not circulate.

3. The newspaper is a morning publication printed in a big city in one corner of the state. Its editions include three published for special circulation areas: (a) the state edition; (b) an edition for the state bordering on the north; and (c) an edition for the state bordering on the east. The area news for each edition is concentrated on one or two pages in the main news section.

4. The newspaper maintains bureaus or full-time correspondents in several towns within the nearby trading area. The news is printed in separate departments, with the name of the town and the local correspondent, and his office address and telephone number, as a standing heading.

5. The newspaper concentrates all area and state news in one or two pages near the front of the main news section. Eight-column lines across the top of the page indicate that all the items on that page are regional.

The departmentalization of state and area news just described applies only to items of a local and routine nature. Stories of real importance and general interest, judged in relation to wire and city news, are given page-1 spots. If the newspaper regularly segregates state and area news, all items

Fig. 73. The *Herald-Journal* of Spartanburg, South Carolina, gets out a lively-looking page of correspondence from the local trade area. (Reproduced by permission of the Spartanburg *Herald-Journal.*)

other than those worth the first page should go on the special page where the readers customarily find them.

Much of the regional correspondence is killed for the newspaper's home edition, but it is a mistake to eliminate all the stories even if space for important local and wire stories is at a premium. Every city draws large numbers of its population from smaller towns in the state, and most of these people still have an interest in what happens "back home." To serve these readers, many of the stories sent in by correspondents can be trimmed for filler or short items for the inside pages or made up into a column of state briefs.

COUNTRY CORRESPONDENCE

Country correspondence is usually thought of in connection with a weekly newspaper, but it is equally a commodity of a small-city daily. Berated by many small-town editors, country correspondence nevertheless is one of the departments that help most to keep a paper going. Many an editor with big-time ideas has angrily cut out the country correspondence because of its apparent triviality, only to find that, as a result, a great many "stops" are reported by the circulation manager.

The appeal of country correspondence lies in the almost universal interest of people in other people. This interest is manifested in metropolitan newspapers especially in gossip columns and human interest stories and in the society page. In smaller newspapers, the news printed under such headings as "Prairie Grove" and "Happy Dale" satisfies the readers' interest in other people's affairs, and it has an added attraction in that it concerns people the readers know.

Metropolitan newspapers, with their speedy delivery systems, can bring a bigger and brighter package of news into the homes than a small-town publication usually can; radio is now omnipresent, and television is rapidly becoming so. But none of these media can compete with the local newspaper in its own territory; none of them is ever likely to find the news about Prairie Grove and Happy Dale worth broadcasting. Country correspondence, together with local city news, is the life preserver that keeps the small-town newspaper afloat, despite the efforts of metropolitan press, radio, and other media to swamp it.

Townspeople as well as the residents of Prairie Grove are interested in Prairie Grove items. "Jasper Rodgers has been on the sick list with the flu this week," the Prairie Grove correspondent writes. And the manager of the farm equipment firm in town reads it and says to himself, "So that's the reason Jasper didn't come in this week to get that new part he ordered for his cultivator." "Mr. and Mrs. J. T. Grimes are being visited this week by their daughter Alice, who is employed as a secretary in the capital city," another item reports. And the women in town who know Alice will speculate as to why she hasn't come to see them, and why is she taking a vacation this time of year anyway? Almost every item in the country correspondence arouses some sort of reaction in at least a few readers in town. This is one reason why country correspondence ranks high on readership surveys.

Country correspondence is a liaison between town and rural districts. It enables the newspaper to extend its circulation and influence, and it makes it a better advertising medium for local merchants. In this era of good highways and motor cars, farmers aren't limited to the nearest town for their buying and banking. They take their business where it is to their best advantage and where it seems most appreciated. By printing rural news, the newspaper gives country people a bond with the town.

SELECTING CORRESPONDENTS

The newspaper gets most of its news of general county interest from local sources—the county building or courthouse; district offices of the United States Department of Agriculture; grain, produce, and livestock dealers; warehouses and elevators; creameries and canneries; and officers of farm organizations. This type of news is handled routinely by the local staff. Special efforts, however, are necessary to get the personal, intimate news of Prairie Grove, Happy Dale, and other neighborhood communities in the county.

Newspapers employ several methods in obtaining county news. Some hire a field representative who acts as both reporter and subscription agent. Others assign someone in the office to get the news by calling everyone, or certain persons, on the rural telephone. But by far the most common method is the employment of part-time correspondents. The first two methods have serious handicaps. The coverage by both is likely to be sketchy. Bad weather and bad roads interfere with the traveling reporter. Telephone calls mount up in expense, and many farm homes don't have telephones.

But despite the popularity of employing correspondents, most editors admit that this method also has its disadvantages—in fact, it may be a big, continuous headache. The greatest difficulty is to find suitable correspondents in every community; this is often particularly hard because there are no trained persons for the job and the rate of pay is small.

Some of the faults found with the correspondents are:

1. They don't know what news is.
2. Even if they do know, they can't write it in proper journalistic style.
3. What is worse, their copy is ungrammatical and their spelling mostly phonetic.
4. They don't supply all the details, particularly full names and identifications.
5. Their facts are often inaccurate.
6. They write too many items about their own families, relatives and friends.
7. Their handwriting is often illegible.
8. They are undependable and don't get their copy in on time.

A major problem of the staff member who handles country correspondence is securing faithful news gatherers who are willing to serve for low pay. Surveys indicate that about 85 percent of the rural correspondents are women, selected largely because they are most available, are reliable, and do not expect high pay. Editors who have employed men as correspondents have found their work satisfactory, but such men are difficult to find because they are too busy to devote much time to writing news letters. According to a poll of editors conducted by *Folks*, a magazine devoted to the work of rural correspondents, the order of preference for correspondents is: housewives, schoolteachers, telephone operators, store clerks, school children, preachers, and farmers.

The correspondence editor must give his writers a continuing course of instruction if he expects to receive competently written articles. Manuals of instruction for correspondents are available—many newspapers publish their own—and every writer should be supplied with one. Some editors use periodic meetings, with a luncheon or dinner thrown in, to develop job enthusiasm among correspondents and to instruct them in gathering information and writing their material. Other editors manage to call on them at their homes. Random meetings, telephone calls, and letters can be utilized for explaining the newspaper's needs to the rural writers. A house organ—perhaps only a mimeographed letter—issued at intervals is another possibility.

Since the pay is small, the editor must take advantage of other than financial appeals to get his rural writers to do good work. One appeal is the correspondent's prestige in the community because of his association with the newspaper. If he is given a by-line and a thumbnail cut goes with his column, he is more willing to exert himself than if his copy is anonymous. Promotional stories directing attention to the correspondents —perhaps a series of biographical sketches that run throughout the year—

is one way of rewarding the writers. The editor should show personal interest in their work and praise them when their stories or columns are better than usual. Many correspondents enjoy contributing to a newspaper because of pride in their community, and this can be appealed to by attractive display of columns and stories.

While the correspondence editor should accept spot news whenever his rural reporters have items, he can best manage the large volume of material if writers are instructed to send in their columns on specific days. By such an arrangement, the correspondence can be fairly evenly distributed throughout the week, instead of piling up on one day, most likely toward the end of the week. The editor should list the names of the communities, the date, and the day of the week each correspondent is supposed to get his column in. By keeping such a record, he will know approximately how much space he will need each day for letters and he can quickly spot the writers who are off-schedule.

The quality of the correspondence depends upon the editor's efforts to train his writers. If he does not try to instruct them and to inspire them to do their best, he will get a column of items that is hardly worth printing. If he devotes himself to a program of whole-hearted aid for his correspondents, he will develop a department that may prove to be one of his paper's outstanding services and features.

EDITING AND DISPLAY

All correspondence should be carefully edited and preferably retyped before being sent to the composing room. While the aim should be to make the copy conform as closely as possible to the best journalistic practices, some latitude may be allowed rural writers. Most persons who are going to read the items will do so regardless of the way they are written. Therefore, it does not matter so much if the writer buries his lead or puts the most interesting details last. But there should be no compromising on grammar, sentence construction, and spelling; absolutely worthless items should be deleted; and every effort should be made to check the accuracy of information.

One of the most frequent faults in country copy is the absence of full names. Occasionally when a writer sends in an item about "Mrs. Peyton" or "Grandpa Smithers," it does not hurt to let it stand if the story seems important enough. But the publication of that item should be followed with a note to the correspondent telling him to give complete names in the future. The copyreader should resist the temptation to change the spelling of first names. If a correspondent regularly writes "Jonny Smith" and

Fig. 74. The line across the top directs attention to "interesting news," but many readers won't stop to find out because of the page's dull appearance. (Reproduced by permission of the Altoona *Mirror*.)

Park Crest News
MRS. EDNA M. KESSLER
Phone Lakewood 42-R-4

DAY OF PRAYER SERVICE

The annual World Day of Prayer service will be held in St. Peter's church, Locust Valley, on Friday, February 9, at 7:30 P. M. The theme for this year's service is "Perfect Love Casts Out Fear."

Mrs. Arthur Knoebel, Mrs. Vernon Miller, Mrs. Eltur Purnell and Mrs. James Stein, presidents of the four local Missionary Societies, will be the leaders, assisted by other members of the societies. The choir of Bethany Evangelical United Brethren church, Barnesville, will snig several selections with Miss Carol Hughes as accompanist. Mrs. Ronald Shafer will be pianist for the service.

GIRL SCOUT MEETING

A meeting of the Girl Scouts of Grier City was held recently at the home of Mr. and Mrs. Herbert Purnell. The girls are learning "The Girl Scout Laws" and "How to Display the Flag." Following the business session, a delicious luncheon was served on a table decorated with a valentine motif.

The next meeting will be held Wednesday, February 14, at 6:00 P. M. at the home of Mrs. Isaac Christ. Mrs. John Kleinginna, of Tamaqua, who served as a missionary in the Near East countries, will

BIRTHDAY GREETINGS TO

Herbert Purnell, secretary and general manager of the Park Crest Builders and Supply Company, who will observe his natal anniversary Friday.

WAYNESBURG
Tickets On Sale For Greene Fox Chasers' Dinners

WAYNESBURG — Tickets are on sale for the annual George Washington's Birthday dinner of the Greene County Red Fox Chasers association the evening of February 22 in the East Franklin Grange hall at Morrisville.

The dinner is held annually on that date in recognition that Washington is generally regarded as the patron of American fox hunters, inasmuch as he introduced fox hunting in the United States.

O. J. Shriver, president of the

Frackville News
Phone Frackville 183-J
MRS. HILBERT D. BANKES
145 North Centre Street

Retired Frackville School Teacher Dies

Miss Jane Dingle, a retired Frackville school teacher, died unexpectedly early this morning at her home at 143 South Nice street, Frackville.

Born in Stockton, Luzerne County, she was a daughter of the late Henry and Jane Dingle.

She spent the greater part of her life at Frackville and was graduated from the high school there and Kutztown State Teachers' College. Until her retirement seven years ago, she taught in the Frackville schools, first as a grade school

DELRAY BEACH
* * *
CECIL S. FARRAR, Correspondent
Phone 4962

$1,802.20 Is Total For Yule Seal Sale

DELRAY BEACH—Mrs. Robert L. Britt, Christmas Seal Sale chairman, has announced that $1,802.20 was realized in the recent sale. This is an increase of $81.35 over the 1949 sale. A total of 847 persons contributed by mail. Boca Raton residents subscribed $220.18.

Junior Women Are Told Of General Federation

DELRAY BEACH — Mrs. N. A. Benevento, State Junior Woman's Clubs chairman, spoke on the Gen-

Boyertown
EARL S. BENFIELD, Representative   Phone 7-9546
129 Walnut St.

Eugene Rothenberger and Jean Grim Are Crowned King, Queen of Hearts

Crowning of the King and Queen of Hearts by the past year's king and queen, highlighted the annual Valentine dance by the High school students in the gymnasium Saturday night.

Jean Grim, daughter of Postmaster and Mrs. Harry E. Grim, 395 West Philadelphia avenue, was crowned Queen of Hearts.

Eugene Rothenberger, son of Mr. and Mrs. Stuart H. Rothenberger, 128 North Walnut street, was crowned King of Hearts.

Miss Grim, a commercial student, is a member of the business staff of the 1951 Bear yearbook, president of the Senior Tri-Hi-Y club, manager of the girls' hockey team, and a member of the drill team.

Rothenberger, an academic student, is a mainstay of the varsity football team, is a hurdler on the track team, played basketball until

an ankle injury forced him to retire, and is a member of the varsity letterman's club.

Miss Grim and Rothenberger were crowned by 1950's king and queen, David Steltz and Nancy Renninger. A record attendance witnessed the crowning, with most of the parents of the court in attendance.

* * *

OTHER MEMBERS of the court included: Ethel Aston, Joan Hartline, Sylvia Miller, Gladys Renninger, Janice Seasholtz, Janet Reigner, Laverne Gresh, Lamar Hartline, Willis Kulp, Robert Magee,

MINERSVILLE

Amvets Auxiliary to Meet

Minersville, Feb. 7.—The regularly scheduled meeting of the Auxiliary of the Minersville Amvets is scheduled for the post home tomorrow evening at 8 o'clock. At this time plans will be completed for their coming game party. All members are urged to be in attendance.

School Board to Meet

The regular monthly meeting of the Minersville School Board will be held Wednesday evening in the office of Supt. Edward A. Brady in the high school building.

H. S. Play Try-outs

Tryout for the annual play to be produced in the Minersville High School auditorium prior to Easter, were held during the past several days. The play will be under the

Fig. 75. Live headings combined with standing headings are used by many newspapers to attract attention to columns of country correspondence.

"Lauran Jones," the chances are that those are the real names, not "Johnny Smith" and "Laura Jones." Many parents like to use their imagination in naming their children; hence the odd spelling may not be just a peculiarity of the correspondent.

In arranging material, the editor should lead off the column with the longest and most important item, following this with other items in order of descending importance, with the two- and three-line personals at the end. Occasionally he may feel that an item is of such general interest that it is worth pulling out of the column and giving page-1 display. Some editors do this regularly, paying the correspondent a higher rate than usual for the story.

The editor should dress up the column to make it attractive typographically. The longer items leading off the column may have individual headlines, and the stories may be separated by star or jim dashes. The first lines of shorter items not worth a head may be set in boldface, or the first two or three words may be put in all-caps. While such display takes up space, it can be used if the stories are trimmed carefully to eliminate verbiage.

Live headings should be written for correspondence from villages and towns where longer stories such as reports of school board meetings, town council meetings, and other community affairs may originate. A "town line" in the form of an eyebrow or the name centered above the heading may be used to distinguish the column as correspondence, or a standing department heading may be used, with live headings beneath. If no standing head or identification line is used with a live head, the heading of the column should contain the name of the town so that readers can easily find the news they are in the habit of reading. Additional identification can be given by using a date line for the first item in the column.

Correspondence from tiny crossroads settlements or other neighborhood units often does not produce much news beyond personal items, except occasionally a death, a serious illness, or an accident. Since it is often difficult to get a headline from this material, the column can be carried under a standing head.

The size of town in which the newspaper is published usually sets the standard of quality for the country correspondence. A daily brought out in a town of from 5000 to 10,000 may publish rural news that differs little from that in a country weekly, and even neighborhood visits and shopping trips may be considered worth mention. The larger the town of publication, the more selective the editor will be in what he considers worth publication.

CHAPTER 23

The Sports Section

A HIGH-PRESSURE JOB

Editing the sports page or sports section of a daily newspaper requires not only a thorough understanding of sports but good grounding in desk practices and print-shop procedures as well. Mere interest in sports, as many sports editors have pointed out to young applicants for jobs, is insufficient qualification for this specialized reportorial and editing field. Almost unanimously they recommend general experience on the city staff before shifting to the sports staff.

The young person planning to specialize in sports is all too likely to look upon a newspaper job as a means of gratifying his liking for athletic events by providing free admission to games. Actually, he will find that sports writing itself requires a burst of speed seldom demanded of other reporters and that holding down the sports desk, especially on Saturday nights during the football season, is one of the toughest editing assignments.

Stanley Woodward, former sports editor of the New York *Herald Tribune*, several times emphasized the need for general newspaper experience before specializing in sports. Of his method of training men for the *Herald Tribune* sports staff, he wrote:

> Most of the bad sports writing of the present day is contributed by people who have never had any experience outside of sports. I have hired inexperienced men, but always at the first opportunity I have detached them from the sports staff temporarily and sent them over to work on the general staff under the city editor. Wherever possible I have given the neophyte another preliminary course on the sports copy desk. Experience there is almost identical with that which a man would get on the main copy desk. The stylebook is the same, the heads are the same and the need for speed is even greater.[1]

[1] Stanley Woodward, *Sports Page*, Simon and Schuster, 1949, p. 26.

There is little likelihood of the college journalism graduate's getting a job on a metropolitan sports staff—the goal of most of those who are "interested in sports" and have perhaps covered athletic events or edited the sports page for their campus newspaper. Before the student can break into the big time, he usually must get some experience on a small-city daily. On such a publication he may have the title of sports editor. Often this work is merely additional to other assignments, for many smaller newspapers cannot afford a full-time sports editor.

The title of sports editor is anomalous, on either a metropolitan daily or a small-city publication, for the work combines both writing and editing. The sports editor of a big-city newspaper is likely to prefer covering important athletic contests to turning them over to a staff man, and almost invariably he does a column—one of the perquisites of his position. The small-city sports editor finds that his job includes editing and headlining the wire copy and covering such local sports events as he can find time for. Since column writing is endemic for sports writers, he may also have his say under a standing head such as "Sports Scoreboard" or "The Sports Trail."

From the viewpoint of the man on the desk, getting out a sports page or section requires the exercise of spontaneous judgment and demands the utmost in speed and efficiency. There is no place in the sports department for the slowpoke, either writer or copyreader.

The sports editorship of a newspaper is usually a daytime job except for coverage of night events, for most newspapers are afternoon publications—there are 329 morning dailies to 1451 evening dailies in the United States. Since morning publications get the breaks on nearly all sports events, the afternoon sports editor usually finds that his news consists of rehashes and feature angles of the previous day's events. His page ordinarily is one of the first made up. The sports editor on a small-city publication finds that he must edit and head the wire copy, write his local stories, and do his column by 9 or 10 A.M. After that he may be assigned to do general reporting under the city editor. On an afternoon metropolitan newspaper the sports staff gets the breaks only in daytime sports like golf and tennis and occasionally baseball, and these frequently are incomplete reports that appear only in the late editions.

The situation the small-city sports editor faces is fairly well disclosed in a survey of the sports pages of Michigan newspapers conducted at Albion College. The sports editors of 51 of the state's 54 dailies responded to a questionnaire. Of these newspapers, 47 were evening publications, and 42 had copy deadlines at 10 A.M. or earlier. Many had one-man

Fig. 76. The sports editor frequently has his say in a personal column. Illustrated are some typical column headings.

sports departments, the sports editor being called upon for other editorial duties after meeting the early deadline for his page.

Because the sports of national interest are covered by the morning newspaper, the editor of an afternoon paper likes to emphasize local news. The practice generally followed, therefore, is to use all the local sports news first and then devote the remaining space to wire copy. But the Michigan study indicated that because of small staffs and time limitations sports editors were forced to use much more wire copy than their paper's actual policy called for.

From this it can be seen that the sports editor of a small daily almost invariably falls into the habit of railroading through copy—not only the wire stuff that he handles but also his own stories. Such a habit of course is bad for him if he expects to work later on a metropolitan paper where stories are more carefully edited, or to join the league of literary sports writers like the late Ring Lardner, Westbrook Pegler, Paul Gallico, and Red Smith.

The situation is not much different for the sports writer and the deskman on the metropolitan newspaper. Speed is what counts—in getting the running account of a game or a fight on paper, in turning out a lead after an event, and in revising stories from edition to edition. The deskman's job is especially trying. The reporter covering a football game or a prize fight writes his story under difficult conditions. After he completes his lead or first page of copy he is likely not to waste time correcting it before putting it on the telegraph wire, leaving the job of finding inconsistencies and errors to the copyreader. The stories that reach the desk in takes must be assembled. The box scores and summaries must be checked to make sure that the figures jibe. Finally the headlines must be written. Newspapermen who have worked on both a general copy desk and a sports desk say that the latter is by far the more strenuous and nerve-shattering.

SPACE AND COVERAGE

A major problem of the sports editor—as with most departmental editors—is space. In exercising his news judgment he realizes that there are certain "must" stories for the page. During the baseball season required items include at least roundup stories each day on the major league games no matter what the size of his paper's city or its geographical location. Another baseball must is such tabular matter as league standings, game results, and the next games scheduled. Furthermore, a newspaper is usually published in an area where there is local interest in a minor league, and the sports editor must find space for reports of its games. Similarly,

THE SPORTS SECTION

coverage of nearby collegiate and high-school athletic competitions is a requisite for a complete sports page. National coverage—at least an agate column of results—is necessary on Sunday for college football games. Certain national and international events must be reported when they occur—the Olympics, the Kentucky Derby, a championship prize fight, the Davis Cup matches, the National Open Golf Tournament, and other headline competitions.

For coverage of these sports events the editors of the majority of newspapers rely upon their press association wires. Only metropolitan publications have the manpower and expense accounts to assign a staff writer to report them. Major sports news is carried on the general news wire of the press associations. For metropolitan dailies that want more details and more complete coverage of all sports there is a special sports wire.

Finding space for all the local sports news that must be printed is an equal problem. The sports editor of a small-city publication, realizing that he cannot compete with a metropolitan newspaper in completeness of covering the national sports scene, ordinarily cuts the wire report down to the barest essentials and emphasizes local happenings—high-school competitions, sand-lot baseball, softball, bowling, and so forth. But so popular are sports and so numerous are the local events—amateur and semiprofessional—that few papers have enough staff members to cover them first-hand or the space to print the stories. Many communities may have a half dozen or more sand-lot baseball or softball games every evening. Obviously a sports staff of one to three men cannot go to all these games.

The solution is for the sports editor to depend upon voluntary contributors—the coach or a team member or a rabid supporter. As a matter of fact, every sports editor in the country—from the big-city newspaper down to the small-town daily—makes use of amateur and part-time correspondents, especially for high-school and prep-school sports. The paper usually supplies these correspondents with printed score sheets and has them telephone in the results or bring the sheets to the office. All that the regular staff has to do is write a lead for the box score and summary, which often are sent to the composing room without being copied.

But even these telescoped reports require more space than many newspapers can spare. Some editors have abruptly cut out covering such sports as sand-lot baseball, softball, and bowling—against the vociferous protests of the players and their followers. Others, realizing that these loyal adherents of small-time sport are important readers of newspapers, have solved the space problem by running a column once or twice a week in which individual players are given recognition and team standings and achievements are mentioned. These columns often have as large a following as any sports feature on the page. If nothing else, they help quell the objections when a newspaper which formerly carried stories on all these events eliminates them because of lack of space.

NEWS ABOUT PARTICIPANT SPORTS

The question of what to do about sand-lot baseball, softball, bowling, and other such popular sports is but one aspect of a broader problem of the sports editor—that of spectator vs. participant sports. It should be obvious that the number of persons who participate in a sport is no indication of the interest in reading about it. Fifty men take part in a World Series game; a hundred million people are interested in the outcome. Nevertheless, in recent years a conscious effort has been made to print news about the less dramatic participant sports, though this is not so true of metropolitan as of small-city editors.

The metropolitan editor's attitude is summed up by Stanley Woodward in *Sports Page*: "The sports editor should not care how many people play a game or how loud are its disciples. The question he must answer is: How many readers of his newspaper are interested; or—how many of them in a pinch can be made interested?"

The small-city sports editor realizes that names of local people make news. Thus, space permitting, he is not only willing but eager to print stories about the country-club golf tournament, the city's bowling leagues, its softball leagues, and other participant sports.

But even metropolitan publications have recently realized that a weekend column or, in a few instances, an entire page devoted to fishing and hunting pulls readers. Both sports are favorite American pastimes. Almost 30,000,000 hunting and fishing licenses are sold each year, and the money spent for equipment, including licenses and gasoline and other incidentals, would make a good down payment on the national debt. Any sport that interests so many people or looms so large in the national economy is worth the attention of newspapers.

In a talk before the Pennsylvania Newspaper Publishers Association, Al Clark, executive sports editor of the Harrisburg *Patriot* and *News*, told about the following situation at Dayton, Ohio:

On a Sunday in early April 90,000 people were checked in at Indian Lake, forty-five miles north of Dayton. On that same Sunday we found 9,000 people attending the second Sunday game of the season played at Cincinnati. On that very Sunday 65,000 people fished at Lake St. Mary's, 32,000 were at Kiser

Lake, and 48,000 at Lake Loramie. These figures did not include hundreds of bank fishermen who fished five streams which flow through Dayton.

All these people were fishing within a sixty-mile area of Dayton. The important point, I believe, is this: the 9,000 at the ball game read a two-column-length story of that game. But not one word was devoted to the luck of the thousands of anglers.

The sports staff of the Dayton *Journal-Herald* began to print hunting and fishing news, and the readership of the sports page jumped. A public meeting sponsored by the newspaper to arrange a program for wildlife conservation, improvement of recreational areas, and promotion of participant sports facilities, was attended by 25,000 persons.

Other newspapers have found that a week-end column or page devoted to hunting and fishing results in reader response. Pertinent information obtained from authoritative sources such as fish and game wardens includes the best places for fishing and hunting and directions for getting to them, weather reports, the condition and temperature of streams and lakes, the type of fish biting, the bait and equipment needed—anything that helps the outdoorsman plan for a successful outing.

There is a strong probability that sports editors who are ignoring participant sports are overlooking a type of coverage that would win extra readers and provide service to subscribers. Books and magazines are published to tell people how to become proficient in sports, what equipment to buy, and how to construct home game facilities. The big sales of these publications indicate a demand for this type of information that newspapers have signally failed to satisfy.

SPORTS—RACKET OR RECREATION

One of the frequent criticisms of our sports pages is their soft-pedaling of the commercial aspects of sports. "By the magic of the sports writers' high-powered writing, crooked fight promoters often become masterminds," said a group of Nieman Fellows at Harvard University, "professional athletes become the embodiment of all that is brave and honorable in the human spirit, and the commercial sports industry becomes a noble expression of selfless public service."[2]

There have been exceptions to the willingness of sports editors to overlook the fact that professional athletes may not be good models for Boy Scouts or Sunday-School classes. In the main, however, the victorious athlete is depicted as a hero whatever his real character. Midge Kelly, the prize fighter in Ring Lardner's story, "Champion," was a bum and a bully

[2] Leon Svirsky (ed.), *Your Newspaper,* The Macmillan Company, 1947, p. 115.

in private life and a fair-haired hero in the sports pages. At the end Lardner made it clear that an exposure of Midge Kelly would never pass the sports editor: " 'Suppose you can prove it,' that gentleman would have said. 'It wouldn't get us anything but abuse to print it. The people don't want to see him knocked. He's champion.' " If the truth were known, the same could probably be said of many a sports hero in fact as well as fiction.

Recent sports history contains repeated examples of sports-page ballyhoo about prize fighters, to cite but one field, in which readers were led to expect a match between Titans. Stanley Walker[3] cites the billing of the Dempsey-Carpentier fight as "the battle of the century," though nearly "every observer of prize-fighting knew beforehand that, barring accident or the collapse of Dempsey by poison or gunfire, Carpentier had no chance." Woodward mentioned the ballyhoo for Primo Carnera despite the fact that "he looked as if he couldn't break a pane of glass." And the build-up for the Joe Louis-Billy Conn fight in 1946 led Warren Brown of the Chicago *Sun* to comment on the perspicuity of his sports-writing confreres: "Anyone who . . . gave Conn any sort of chance, much less selected him to win, either must have been actuated by ulterior motives, or was utterly lacking in common sense. The ballyhoo exceeded all previous bounds of good taste. Its tom-toms from the beginning beat out a rhythm of the public be damned."

It is to the interest of boxing promoters to secure a good build-up for a fight. Why sports writers coöperate by falsifying the fighting fitness and power of the contenders is hard to see. A political news writer who accepted a campaign manager's claims as to the number of votes his candidate would get would be laughed out of the newspaper business. There are sports writers whose predictions and estimates of a title contender's chances flop completely but whose reputation for acumen is about as great after a match as before. Sports editors whose writers pull such boners should curtail the enthusiasm of their reporters, and hinterland editors who rely on syndicate or press association copy should process it skeptically.

The creation of synthetic heroes and the heralding of gigantic battles, however, are not the worst effects of the overcommercialization of sports. It is well known—at least outside the sports pages—that professional sports are linked closely with gambling syndicates and that the rackets have extended to collegiate football and basketball games. Some light on the attitude of sports editors toward gambling was thrown in a survey in

[3] Stanley Walker, *City Editor*, Frederick A. Stokes Company, 1934.

THE SPORTS SECTION

1947 made by Leo H. Petersen, sports editor of the United Press. His questions and the answers he received follow:

1. Do you favor publishing odds on athletic contests? 51.8% no; 48.2% yes.
2. Do you think that gambling on athletic contests would be curbed to some extent by not publishing the odds? 51.4% yes; 48.6% no.
3. Do you believe that odds form an important part of the story on a forthcoming contest or should be bracketed in so sports editors could eliminate them without changing the body of the story? 55.3% no; 44.7% yes.
4. Are you in favor of publishing the probable pitchers? 84.2% yes; 15.8% no.
4-A. If the major leagues should formally ask the newspapers not to publish the probable pitchers would you accede to their request? 66.4% yes; 33.6% no.
5. Do you believe that the anti-gambling crusade of the NCAA will tend to curb gambling? 55% yes; 45% no.
6. Has there been a notable increase in gambling on athletic contests in your area? 57.4% yes; 38.4% no.
6-A. Has there been a decrease? 4.2% yes.
7. Do you feel that the gambling evil is serious enough to threaten the future of intercollegiate athletics? 55% yes; 45% no.
8. Do you feel that confining college contests to their own grounds rather than neutral courts and gridirons in large cities would help to curb gambling? 54.3% yes; 45.7% no.
9. Do you favor a national lottery and, if so, do you believe it would lessen gambling? 63.3% no; 36.7% yes; it would increase gambling.
10. What measures do you suggest for curbing gambling? First, a high commissioner to rule all sports with authority beyond appeal; second, stricter laws on sports gambling and their strict enforcement.

The sports editor's attitude toward printing information that will facilitate gambling (especially in horse racing, the sport that is carried on almost entirely for those who want to bet) depends largely on the local situation. As to the ponies, about half the states have legalized betting, and around the tracks in such cities as Miami, New York, Washington, Chicago, and Los Angeles handicaps are usually a sports page feature. The newspapers in these places are likely also to accept the reality of gambling in other sports. The papers in states where gambling is forbidden by law are less inclined to regard betting odds as news. Many sports editors limit the printing of betting odds to major professional sports. When odds are carried they should be genuine and not suppositional. In an advance story the sports editor or writer should not use the word "odds" as a figure of speech in predicting what he considers a team's chances of winning.

Commercialism, gambling, and other off-color aspects of sports, tacitly accepted by newspapers, have resulted in a hypocritical attitude toward amateurism. No one is naïve enough nowadays to maintain that there is complete bona-fide amateurism in many American sports. Newspapers have published exposés of commercialism in college athletics, but these have been rare in recent years because they are old stuff. The acceptance of the situation by institutions of higher learning, sports editors, and others who should have upheld the integrity of amateurism is partly to blame for the basketball scandals of 1950 and 1951. Youngsters receiving "scholarships" and other emoluments from colleges were easy prey to gamblers who bribed them to throw games. Sports editors, because of the power they have in wielding publicity, are in a position to help maintain high standards of sportsmanship.

Many sports editors themselves are part of the commercialized system and are powerless to write objectively and honestly. It has for long been the policy of the baseball clubs, both major and minor leagues, to defray the traveling expenses of reporters for the spring training trips and for out-of-town games. In many a city the sports editor is on the payroll as official scorer for baseball games and he receives a regular stipend from boxing and wrestling promoters for publicity and promotion.

The ramifications of the commercialism of sports are extensive and hardly bear investigation, so culpable are many sports editors and writers. The sports page has had honest debunkers—W. O. McGeehan, who emphasized the professional character of almost all sports, and John R. Tunis, who pointed out the dominating influence of the gate receipts, to name but two—but there is a tendency, it seems, for the majority of the sports writers to accept commercialism without criticism and ignore the realities. Critics and commentators in other fields—motion pictures, drama, and music—don't treat the performers so gently or portray them falsely to the public. The objectivity of the straight news reporter and the judiciousness of the critic of the arts are needed on the sports page.

COLLEGE PUBLICITY HANDOUTS

Though a respectable sports editor refuses to write or print the more blatant publicity that is paid for by a promoter or the owner of an arena, he nevertheless is part of a great sports promotion scheme. Press agentry does not seem to have flowered so riotously in sports as in some other fields, however, perhaps because promoters have found sports editors willing to coöperate.

So far as handouts are concerned, the sports department receives the bulk of its mimeographed ballyhoo from schools and colleges. These publicity releases are frequently useful, especially during the week when the staff does not have time to cover team practice for all the schools in the vicinity. A college publicity man can be depended upon for adequate reports of injuries and ailments of athletes, the type of workout the coach is concentrating on, any probable shifts in line-up, and statistics on the records and previous encounters of the opposing teams. The preseason background material about individual players and their athletic past is also useful, and should be kept on file for reference during the year.

In two respects, however, the publicity releases should be taken skeptically. One is the customary gloomy attitude shown by all coaches toward forthcoming games. Practically no coach ever says his team will win; the most optimistic one may grudgingly say that his boys will put up a good fight or that their chances are fair if nothing goes wrong. The astute coach uses publicity as a psychological device for developing what he conceives to be the proper morale; ordinarily he doesn't like his players to go into a game with a bad case of overconfidence. Moreover, he will look bad to the fans and the alumni—especially the alumni—if the victory he predicted turns out to be a rout. If his players go in as underdogs, a victory will enhance his prestige.

The other grounds for skepticism in much collegiate publicity copy is that it may be a build-up for an individual player with a popular following whom the publicity man is promoting for one of the several all-American ratings or some other athletic trophy. Stanley Woodward says that even in the press box reporters have to guard against the overzealous publicity man:

> In quest of an honor or trinket, a press agent is apt to station himself at a vantage point, generally close to the press announcer, and loudly call attention to the real or fancied exploits of a boostee.
> He will say, "Smithers made the tackle," when Smithy is twenty feet away on the seat of his pants. He will point out that Goldberg made the big hole through which the touchdown was scored, when the truth is that the runner went through the other side of the line.[4]

THE STRANGE WORLD OF SPORTS

The copyreader on the sports desk has all the headaches of the men on the general news desk plus several others created by the sports writers or scribes—they almost never call themselves reporters as ordinary newspapermen do—and by the nature of the news they cover. In addition to such usual problems as trimming for space, checking for grammar and spelling, and correcting errors and inconsistencies, the sports copyreader is confronted by the following: the use of meaningless jargon, overwriting

[4] Stanley Woodward, *op. cit.*, p. 161.

in an attempt at drama and color, hurriedly written running stories, and box scores and summaries which must appear in a prescribed form.

Nearly everyone who has written about sports journalism has commented on the excessive mauling given the English language on the sports pages. Much of the jargon is but the natural extension of the vocabulary created by people in any specialized field to what is written about the field. Many sports terms are thoroughly familiar to the public, and there is of course no reason for excluding them from the news because of difficulty of understanding.

Many others, however, are spurious coinages made by sports reporters to brighten their writing and avoid stereotyped expressions. Some critics assert that the reason so many sports writers don't call things by their right names is the inherent sameness of the subject matter. Thus Stanley Walker in *City Editor*:

> After all, the subject matter of sports is pretty much the same. Almost every suicide, murder, shipwreck and train collision is cut on a different pattern, and the reporter does not have to search for outlandish substitutes for common terms. One baseball game, however, is pretty much the same as another. The few standard nouns and verbs which may be used in writing of baseball, football, boxing and rowing become tiresome. . . .[5]

And A. J. Liebling in *The Wayward Pressman*:

> The scribe is expected to be entertaining when there's nothing to be entertaining about, and whereas the City Hall man or the police reporter doesn't have to write anything unless something is happening, the sports writer has to burn the old adverbs across every day.[6]

Red Smith, the New York *Herald Tribune* columnist, denies that games are pretty much alike. According to him, every ball game is different from every other ball game if a reporter has the knowledge and wit to discern the difference:

> If he can report the difference intelligently, every story will have a freshness without labored groping for an "angle." He ought to get the score right, describe the play simply, and make it clear why one team beat the other team. He should remind himself frequently that it's only a game, and that the natural habitat of the tongue is the left cheek. And he must shun the frumious cliché.[7]

Perhaps the sports writer's biggest motive in seeking to make his copy sound different by frequent coinages and other verbal inventions is to

---

[5] Stanley Walker, *op. cit.*, p. 119.
[6] A. J. Liebling, *The Wayward Pressman*, Doubleday & Company, Inc., 1947, p. 196.
[7] Joseph G. Herzberg (ed.), *Late City Edition*, Henry Holt and Company, 1947, p. 113.

establish a reputation as an original and amusing writer. Only with this type of showmanship, he believes, will his by-line become well enough known for him eventually to be invited to do a column.

At any rate, it should be one of the jobs of the copy desk to weed out the wilder flights of fancy, to eliminate the shopworn clichés and untangle the mixed figures of speech—in short, to make the story understandable to the reader and at the same time preserve the writer's originality and flavor if they are worth preserving.

Thus the copyreader should not hesitate to replace such terms as "apple," "tomato," "pellet," "spheroid," or "horsehide" with the word "baseball." He should do his best to halt the practice of transplanting terms from one sport to another, as when a pitcher is called a bowler or an inning a chukker. He should let an athlete be called by his own name occasionally, not always by nicknames coined by reporters. One New York reporter called Joe DiMaggio by name only once in his story—the first time he was mentioned, subsequent references in order being Joltin' Joe, DiMag, the illustrious Clipper, the Jolter, and back again to DiMag, the reporter's inventive powers apparently then having been depleted. The copyreader should try to find better expressions for such bromides as "sea of mud," "inspired effort," "crucial game," "Jupiter Pluvius," "King Football," and "circuit clout."

Some expressions coined by sports writers have been truly happy inventions—"daisy-cutter," "skimmer," "lawn mower," and "grass-cutter" for a grounder; "cloud-buster" for a high fly; and "clothesline hit" for a line drive. The sports editor or copyreader should not develop an antipathy for originality just because he encounters so many coinages that have a leaden ring. The good ones should be treasured, at least as long as they have some of the original luster of the mint.

Another major fault of sports copy is the exaggeration of athletic exploits by comparison with great deeds of the past. This tendency is found in writers for whom Grantland Rice ranks with Shakespeare and who accordingly imitate his style. A football game is merely a football game; it does not warrant comparison with Thermopylae or the Alamo. A fighter may have a lot of force behind his right arm, but the blow it delivers is hardly to be compared with Thor's thunderbolts. This type of writing was considered the acme of literary style for the sports pages some years ago. Happily there is less of it today, but it is still found, as when an enthusiastic sports writer described Bitsy Grant as "a new mighty atom of the tennis courts" and another called Tami Mauriello "the Bronx Boy of Destiny" before he got knocked out by Joe Louis.

The world of sports, as portrayed by many writers, is a wonderland peopled by superhumans. The best sports reporter, to judge from the anthologies of "best" stories of the year, is the one who can by overwrought prose transform the sweat and grime of the boxing and wrestling arena, a dusty baseball diamond, or a cold and windy stadium into something marvelous. Here, for example, are leads on two successive days of the race for the American League championship; the paper in which they appeared is considered to have a literate sports page:

Recovering from the shock of last night's sudden, stunning, ninth-inning defeat, the Yankees took advantage of 12 bases on balls and 2 errors and put the Indians back in their tepee this afternoon to brood over a 10-to-3 rout.

(The literary allusion here is a sports page stand-by; many reporters who use it don't know its Homeric origin.)

From the death-trap that is Fenway Park, the Yankees barely escaped with their lives this afternoon. Lingering where even angels fear to tarry, the Bombers absorbed their second straight defeat from the awesome Red Sox, 10 to 8, and in so doing showed signs of coming apart at the seams.

(A 10-to-8 score hardly seems a wide margin of victory for an "awesome" team.)

The editor who has some respect both for the language and for sports should see that his reporters eschew such fancies, and he should complain to the press association if it wastes wire time with such verbiage. People read the sports page to find out who won, what the score was, and how it was made—not to lose themselves in prose that sounds as if it were written by someone under the influence of marijuana.

THE DESKMAN AT WORK

The usual small-city newspaper gets out only one edition each day. If it is a morning newspaper, the deadline will be late enough to include complete reports of all night sports events. An afternoon paper in a small town goes to press so early—by 2:30 or 3 P.M.—that it makes no attempt to cover any afternoon games. Its sports page carries stories of the previous day's or night's events. Thus the editing task is relatively simple, except that ordinarily one or two men do everything.

The metropolitan newspaper, however, with its several editions during the day or night, has the problem of keeping up with sports events while they are happening. The score when the paper goes to press must be included in the story. This makes reporting a game or match and handling the story on the desk complex operations.

THE SPORTS SECTION

Covering an event under such conditions has become fairly well standardized. For the early edition the reporter writes what is called a "bunk" lead; this says that the two teams are playing at a certain place and uses any feature angle that seems advisable. Immediately after the bunk lead space is left (usually three lines, indicated by a turn rule) for a flashed score at the end of the period just before the deadline for copy. The story then continues with reporter's play-by-play account phoned or telegraphed to the office.

A typical bunk lead and the midgame score are shown in the following from the New York *Herald Tribune*:

PHILADELPHIA, Sept. 7.—Jubilant over the fact that their double-barreled victory the night previous had lopped two full games off the Phillies' league-leading margin, reducing it to five and one-half games, the Dodgers sent Carl Erskine against Philadelphia's right-handed star, Robin Roberts, in the third of a crucial Shibe Park four-game series before 30,000.

Tempering this enthusiasm somewhat was the announcement that Brooklyn's all-star catcher, Roy Campanella, would be out for a period ranging between a week and ten days. Campanella suffered a dislocation of his right thumb in the second game last night.

The Dodgers led, 3 to 2, in the eighth inning when this edition went to press.

Both Erskine and Roberts were going with a two-day rest. Erskine was seeking his first victory over the Phils this year. . . .

The *Herald Tribune* always includes the phrase "when this edition went press," so that the reader will understand why the final score was not given. Many newspapers do not explain the use of a midgame score; hence a person who has an early edition may be perplexed by the incompleteness of the story, especially if he is an out-of-town subscriber and doesn't get his copy of the paper until hours after the game is over.

The foregoing procedure makes it possible to get into type a large part of the story before the event is over. For the next edition the reporter writes a new lead based on the final outcome. This is marked new lead and the bunk lead is killed. Box scores and summaries are sent to the composing room as adds.

Metropolitan afternoon newspapers have long carried accounts of sports events—chiefly baseball and racing—on the front page of the last street edition. Even after the paper has gone to press scores can be brought up to date without replating by means of special "baseball matrices" or a "fudge box." The matrices provide white figures on black squares and black squares into which later scores are punched by hand. The fudge box is a device that holds slugs or hand type and that can be inserted in a blocked-out portion of the stereotype plate. Scores can be brought up to the minute by either of these devices with only a momentary stopping of the presses.

An important feature of the sports page is the statistical material—box scores and summaries, team standings, individual records, line-ups, and so forth. To save space, these are ordinarily set in agate or 6-point type. Though they have been fairly well standardized over the country, there are minor individual differences among newspapers.

The complete box score for major league baseball used by the Chicago *Tribune*, the New Orleans *Times-Picayune*, and other newspapers consists of seven columns after the name of the player and his position: at bat, runs, hits, runs batted in, put-outs, assists, and errors. The New York *Times*, the St. Louis *Post-Dispatch*, the San Francisco *Chronicle*, and other papers have only six columns, the runs batted in being part of the summary below. Many newspapers—probably the majority of them—have only five columns, both the runs batted in and the errors being included in the summary.

A box score consisting of five or more columns even in agate usually is set full measure, though the New York *Times* gets six columns in half measure and the New York *Herald Tribune* five. Most sports editors use full measure only for the bigger games and those played on home grounds; to conserve space the other box scores are printed side by side half measure. Half measure ordinarily allows for only three or four columns of statistics; hence the sports editor must decide on what he wants to print in the box and what is to go in the summary. Probably the majority of newspapers have four columns for half-measure boxes—at bat, hits, put-outs, and assists. The St. Louis *Post-Dispatch* half-measure box has only three columns: at bat, runs, and hits.

In choosing the form for the box and statistical matter, the sports editor takes the line of least resistance by adopting the style used in his press association reports, unless he seriously objects to it. This at least reduces the amount of work for the desk.

Besides seeing that all the sports boxes and summaries are in the prescribed form, the copyreader has one other important task: to add up the figures to verify the totals.

Headline writing and make-up for the sports page are about the same as for any other department of a newspaper. The principal difficulty in writing heads is to find satisfactory short synonyms for defeat. Some commonly used are: beat, nip, rout, whip, crush, batter, down, humble, subdue, thwart, maul, topple, nick, rap, sink, shellac, blast, top, wallop, trounce, smash, drub, paste, trip, curb, slam, baffle, and hold. Occasionally

Fig. 77. Sports editors are addicted to lively make-up. Note the use of the "flag" to identify the page in the Appleton, Wisconsin, *Post-Crescent*. (Reproduced by permission of the Appleton *Post-Crescent*.)

a deskman can gain variety by having a team lose, yield, bow, or succumb to an opponent.

A livelier make-up is desirable for the sports page than for other inside pages. Usually the page or section is kept fairly free of advertising, and hence big headlines and a carefully designed arrangement of type masses and pictures can be employed. Following the general rule for inside-page make-up, the play position is the first column. If the sports editor writes a personal column, his by-line material frequently gets this favored spot—often in double-column measure. This means that the news stories must go in an inside column or the last column of the page. When sports news is put in a special section of several pages, the first page is considered the front page. Most newspapers identify the sports page with a special name plate or "flag." Many use just the word "Sports" in a special type or casting two or three columns wide which can be floated somewhere near the top of the page.

The maximum popularity of the sports page has not yet been reached. When big-time events were first broadcast by radio about twenty-five years ago, newspapermen feared that it would reduce interest in the sports page. Instead, the broadcasts have whetted people's appetite for sports. Similarly, television seems also to have increased popular interest in written accounts of sports events. The most notable evidence of this is the increased number of women sports-page readers. Women who had never seen a boxing or wrestling match and perhaps had gone to only one or two baseball games became quickly acquainted with the sports through telecasts. Now when the daily newspaper is divided among the members of the family, the wife or daughter is just as likely to grab for the sports page as for the women's page. This may make the men of the family unhappy, but it has increased the sports editor's opportunity to serve more readers.

As yet, neither radio nor television has brought about any marked change in the reporting and handling of sports events by the newspaper. The paper still tells about the event as if the reader hadn't heard or seen it and doesn't know the score. Maybe this practice is all wrong, but there is no indication that a proper sports page lead should not tell who won, by what score, and how. Television, however, permits the viewer of a game to check the sports writer's account against his memory of it. This means that the story must be more accurate than ever before and must give details that could once be ignored.

CHAPTER **24**

Business and Financial News

ROOM FOR IMPROVEMENT

Dissatisfaction with the business and financial pages of newspapers is frequently expressed by editors. They realize that of all classes of news the financial has about the lowest general readership. They want more stories that will interest more readers.

The following are typical statements from papers in all parts of the country who were covered in the Associated Press Managing Editors Association survey of the AP's business and financial reports:

There is romance in money, and the present-day American has his mind on money. Market coverage could tell the real story of what is going on. We need more stories of the business, banking, industrial and trade progress of leading American cities for determining comparative economic status. The AP should write of the human side of finance and industry in down-to-earth style.—Fort Worth *Star-Telegram*.

We want more stories on new products and interesting personalities. There are many good stories in small business and industries.—Hartford *Times*.

Business and financial news needs popularizing the way science news has been popularized. There is nothing more vital to the individual citizen than economic events.—Bangor *Daily News*.

We need more stories of personalities behind big business news. They should be more readable for the man on the street who is not an investor but who is affected.—Minneapolis *Times*.

There are not enough creative stories tied to everyday life. Sharper, brighter writing is needed to increase interest and draw the average reader to business news.—Louisville *Times*.

We need more stories on the man-in-the-street level.—San Francisco *Call-Bulletin*.

The need for more meaningful and interesting reporting of news of business, finance, industry, and agriculture is being increasingly realized by editors throughout the country. Yet, except for a few city newspapers and isolated instances of smaller-city publications, the financial pages present column after column of market quotations in agate type—information that only the relatively few investors in a community refer to. Mixed with this tabular material are a few stories written in a jargon almost as incomprehensible to most readers as the verse of an ultramodern poet.

Business—in an inclusive sense—impinges on our lives more frequently than anything else reported in the newspapers. We all use money and credit; we buy and sell; we are affected by higher and lower prices; we want to know about new products. But except for advertising, which newspapers are paid to publish, there is little in them that deals with our intimate daily concerns.

Perhaps no complete explanation of their failure in this respect is possible, but some of the following factors account for the neglect of business as news:

1. We all engage in business in one way or another, and our business occupies much of our conversation; but business, we think, is a dull affair. It isn't nearly so interesting as sports, crime, and catastrophes. Business has not been given an aura of glamour by our novelists and poets, and we tend to look down upon the businessman.

2. Newspapermen are excessively fearful of giving free publicity or free advertising to an individual or firm, and hence tend to treat business in generalities.

3. Businessmen themselves consider their personal and financial affairs as private and of no concern to the public; they are also fearful of giving out information that will be of value to a competitor.

4. Because of Wall Street's dominance in financial affairs, we look to New York as the center and source of business news, thus missing the importance of the local businessman in the national economy.

5. Editors, knowing that financial news is of limited interest, have not sought to develop the business news desk as they have the sports desk. Market reports are buried in the rear of the newspaper. Spot business news is given the run of the paper.

But our attitudes toward business news are changing. The depression of the 1930's, economic controls during World War II, and increasing governmental involvement in business have made us realize that better news coverage in this field is necessary. Public relations men have educated business leaders in the importance of informing the public. The weekly news magazines, with their lively reports on business and finance, have shown that this type of news can be interesting.

These tendencies have resulted in expanded business news departments on many newspapers; financial reports are still the core of the page but are relatively less dominant than they used to be.

THE BUSINESS PAGE EDITOR

Business news departments vary in scope according to the size of the newspaper and the prevailing interests of the region in which it is published. Metropolitan publications usually have a full-fledged department with an editor, reporters, and copyreaders; there may also be subeditors, such as a real estate editor, an automotive editor, and an industrial editor, who handle specialized aspects of business.

On other publications the business and financial editor himself may be the "department," editing wire and syndicate copy, covering local business news, and making up his page. On smaller newspapers, business and financial news is usually handled by a copyreader who has an understanding of such matters.

A newspaper published in a locality with a dominant industrial interest may devote a special page or department to that interest. For example, Oklahoma City and Tulsa newspapers have pages devoted to authoritative reports on oil news. Papers published in major seaports contain a page of shipping news. Many midwestern publications run a weekly page of agricultural news.

In printing business and financial news, the newspaper should strive to appeal to the general reader. In only a few areas, if any, can a daily newspaper successfully compete with the trade newspapers and magazines in specialized fields of industry and business. The businessman who seeks authoritative and complete information about his own field invariably subscribes to the specialized publications and the newsletters and bulletins in that field. There are more publications of this type than there are daily newspapers in this country. Many of them are themselves the source of newspaper stories, for they collect data that would otherwise not be available—figures on production, inventories, prices, sales, profits, trends. The newspaper business editor tries to select the news that affects people most directly and most generally and that helps give them an understanding of our complex economic system.

Some suggested rules for the business editor include the following:

1. Give comprehensive coverage to local news—banks, real estate concerns, department stores, retail credit associations, business associations, and so forth.

2. Watch the wire stories for legislative action and court decisions that affect business and for national developments that can be given a local angle.

3. Emphasize interpretive articles that make economics meaningful to the reader.

4. Spice the page with personality and feature articles and illustrations. A pictograph showing production levels will be studied by readers who will skip over a column of figures.

5. Regard news about labor as an essential part of news about the economic system.

6. Do not be afraid to publish "bad" news. Everyone would rather read that business is "good," but to suppress adverse information violates the newspaper principle of truthful reporting. When business is bad, publication of all the good news that the editor can find will not make it any better. This was tried during the depression of the 1930's—to no avail.

7. Beware of predictions and interpretations. Hardly ever do any two economists agree. Despite the claims of its practitioners, economics is not an exact science. The best that any economist can do is to make an informed guess.

8. Don't be afraid of trade names and prices. If you have a story about a new product, let the reader know what it's called, who makes it, and how much it costs. If you can't get over the idea that this is free advertising, don't use the story at all.

9. Choose wire and syndicate stories carefully with an eye to the interests of your readers. Try to apply the same standard of news judgments you would use on the general news desk.

10. Don't attach too much importance to Wall Street. The stock market is no longer a reliable barometer of business conditions. The Street's investment bankers no longer have a stranglehold on business expansion. In brief, Wall Street is now relatively unimportant in the nation's total economy.

LOCAL BUSINESS NEWS

Business is such a widespread and varied activity that it is often difficult to segregate it from the general run of news. Reporters often turn in to the city editor stories that should properly go to the business news editor, and much that the business editor puts on his page might be classified as

Fig. 78. A good local business page is this of the Johnstown, Pennsylvania, *Democrat*, devoted to the bituminous coal industry. (Reproduced by permission of the Johnstown *Democrat*.)

general news. The business editor, therefore, should consult with the city editor and reach a working agreement on the exchange of stories. If the business page is made popular so that readers will turn to it with the expectation of finding something interesting, there will be fewer occasions for stories of general appeal to go on the front page or elsewhere in the main news sections. But no business page or news department will ever become popular if it contains nothing but financial news.

Local business news coverage depends largely on the character of the dominating industry in the community. A paper in a port city has a large volume of shipping news; a mining town newspaper plays up the mineral industries; a publication in a milling town like St. Paul or Minneapolis gives liberal space to stories about wheat.

But certain areas of business and financial news are common to almost all cities. Among the possible topics for news stories in these fields are the following:

Banks—Periodical statements issued at least quarterly at the time of the federal bank call; annual meetings of stockholders in January; interviews, on occasion, regarding local business conditions.

Real estate—Sales and transfers of property; new construction; building permits; meetings of the local real estate association; action by the city's planning commission or council on building codes and zoning regulations.

Retail trade—Statistics on the volume of business; reports of the Retail Credit Association; news about individual stores, such as improvements in physical plant, personnel changes, and similar items.

Corporations—Earning reports, usually issued in the first month of a new quarter; new issues of stocks and bonds; annual meetings of stockholders.

Public utilities—Statistics on telephone connections and on gas, electric, and water meters; periodical statements and reports of the companies.

Transportation—Railroad carloadings; changes in rates and service; truck operations; passenger service.

Business organizations—Chamber of Commerce, Junior Chamber of Commerce, Better Business Bureau, Retail Merchants' Association.

Government agencies—Employment office, Production and Marketing Administration, and so forth.

Labor organizations—Meetings, conventions, and other activities; negotiations for contracts; employment situation.

Agriculture—Crop reports; farm coöperatives, local market prices—wheat, corn, poultry, eggs, livestock; local processing establishments—

canneries, dairies; local shipments of livestock, fruits, vegetables, and produce; cotton gins, grain elevators.

Much of the local business and financial news does not demand highly specialized knowledge from the editor. He must be able to interpret a bank statement and must understand the Federal Reserve System and other state and federal controls, and he must learn enough about corporate finance and structure to understand earnings reports and financial statements and explain about stock issues. Most of what he needs to know he can find in standard textbooks and manuals.

Until the editor has had some experience and has developed an ability to judge the significance of these intricate matters, he should avoid extensive interpretation, at least without checking his articles with a knowledgeable person in whom he has confidence. But if he wants his page to be read and understood by the man on the street, he should not hesitate to throw in plenty of *explanation*—especially of the terminology he uses.

THE WIRE NEWS REPORT

Financial and business pages conventionally devote most of their space to news originating outside the city of publication. The great bulk of this news comes from New York. Other news originates in Washington because of the increasingly large part the government is playing in economic affairs. A few other cities—the market centers for various commodity products—provide essential news. These include Chicago, Minneapolis, Kansas City, Omaha, Memphis, New Orleans, Pittsburgh, Des Moines, and Winnipeg.

Metropolitan newspapers which have detailed financial news coverage subscribe to a special wire service operated by the press associations that gives complete stock market quotations and a full report on commodity prices. The general news wire usually carries enough of this news for other newspapers, but those that find this inadequate arrange for supplementary special service. Smaller newspapers that are hooked up to a state or regional network obtain only a skeleton report of financial news.

The market news is extremely routinized, certain stories appearing every day and others recurring periodically.

Security Markets. Transactions on the New York Stock Exchange, the largest security market in the United States, have the most widespread interest for investors. Most metropolitan newspapers carry complete reports of transactions in tabular form, and smaller newspapers print information about leading stocks. In a complete report the tabular information, set in agate type, includes the following: the high and low price at which each issue sold during the current year; the name of the stock; the number of shares which changed hands; the price at which the day's first transaction was consummated; the day's high and low price; the closing price; and the net difference between the day's closing price and that of the previous day. Briefer reports give only the high, the low, and the closing price and the net change from the previous day's closing.

The most important news story that comes in over the wires is the stock market lead which gives a summary of the day's trading. This story, in the words of a New York *Times* booklet on financial page news, is the keynote of the entire section. The booklet continues:

> By emphasis placed on certain developments, the reader is informed of the points considered to be significant. In addition to a summation of the more important daily characteristics of the markets, an insight into market psychology and an appraisal of the temper of the trading community are afforded. In other words, effort is made to impart the "feel" of the markets.

The stock market lead is carried on the general news wires of the press associations. Even newspapers which have no other financial news generally print this market roundup.

In addition to the list of transactions on the exchange and the news story describing the general tenor of trading, the wire carries several summaries often printed under the heading, "Markets at a Glance." These summaries include a list of the ten leading stocks, total sales compared with those of the previous day, and composite averages and indexes based on representative groups of stocks.

The second largest security market in the country is the New York Curb Exchange. The bigger newspapers carry full reports of its activities just as they do for the New York Stock Exchange. Of only regional and local interest are the smaller stock exchanges in such cities as Chicago, Baltimore, Philadelphia, and San Francisco.

Bonds. Trading in bonds is less speculative than trading in stocks, and the market is relatively stable. Hence the bond market does not rank in news importance with the stock market. As distinguished from stocks, which represent a share in the ownership of a corporation, bonds are receipts for loans made by the bondholders to corporations or governments. The bondholder has no voice in the management of the enterprise. Bonds carry a definite interest rate and usually have a specific maturity date.

The newspaper's tabular reports on the trading in bonds usually classify bonds as corporation, government, and foreign. The information given in these reports includes the number of sales, the high and low price for the day, and the last sale price.

Since the bond markets are less active than the stock market, many newspapers do not print a daily lead story. But weekly summaries of new offerings and market transactions usually are carried.

Commodities. Trading in commodities is less concentrated than trading in stocks and bonds, and the important news originates in several cities throughout the country. "Commodity" as used on the financial pages means raw materials and provisions that are processed into food, clothing, and other finished goods. Commodities include wheat, cotton, wool, livestock, coffee, eggs, rubber, coal, iron, copper, and so forth.

New York's commodity markets of world importance handle cotton, coffee, sugar, cottonseed oil, cocoa, rubber, silk, hides, metals, and wool. Other cities may outrank New York in importance in some commodities. Chicago has the leading wheat market of the world. Memphis is important for cottonseed and cottonseed meal; St. Louis for millfeeds; and Kansas City, Omaha, and Chicago for livestock.

Because of the wide distribution of markets, commodity reports are more localized than the financial news. Thus a midwestern newspaper is likely to carry livestock reports from Chicago, Omaha, Des Moines, Kansas City, Fort Worth, and Oklahoma City.

Commodity news is of two types. In the contract markets, buyers make agreements to purchase a definite amount of a commodity deliverable during a specified future period. The tabular reports for such transactions give the month of delivery, the opening price per unit of measurement (pound, bushel, or bale, depending on the product), the high price, the low price, the closing price, and the previous day's closing price.

The second type of commodity news covers the actual selling and buying in the produce markets. Thus a livestock market report will include the total receipts for cattle, the types involved, and the prices paid. These produce market reports are usually of immediate interest to local persons. Thus farmers want to know the condition of the market so they can compare prices in determining the best time to sell their produce.

In addition to the daily market stories carried by the newspaper because of their probable interest for readers, other recurring stories appear weekly, monthly, and quarterly. These include the following:

Automobiles—Ward's figures on weekly production issued for Saturday release. The Automobile Manufacturers Association figures appear about the eighth of each month.

Bank debits—Federal Reserve System. Sundays.

Business failures—Dun and Bradstreet. Tuesdays.

Carloadings—Association of American Railroads. Fridays.

Copper production—Copper Institute figures on production, deliveries, and stock. About the fifteenth of each month.

Cost of living index—National Industrial Conference Board. Second week of the month.

Cotton consumption—Bureau of the Census. The sixteenth of each month.

Crop reports—First of each month by the Department of Agriculture. Cotton acreage and forecast on the ninth, and grain report on the tenth during the season.

Crude oil—Production and gasoline figures compiled by the American Petroleum Institute. Wednesday mornings. Monthly figures on production of crude and refined petroleum and the stock at the end of the month are published by the Bureau of Mines.

Department-store sales—Federal Reserve Banks. Nineteenth of each month.

Electric power production—Edison Electric Institute. Thursdays.

Employment—Department of Labor, twenty-third of each month. National Industrial Conference Board, third week of each month; gives estimates of the number of employed and unemployed. American Federation of Labor employment estimate middle of the month.

Foreign trade—Imports and exports from the Department of Commerce. After the twenty-sixth of each month, or later.

Iron and steel—American Iron and Steel Institute. Tuesdays for the rate at which the industry is operating. Output of steel ingots by tons on the ninth of each month. Pig-iron production estimates in *Iron Age* in the issue appearing on the second Thursday in the month. United States Steel Corporation monthly figures on shipments on the eleventh.

Lead—Figures released about the third week of the month by the American Bureau of Metal Statistics.

Life insurance—New life insurance underwritings about the seventeenth of every month.

Lumber—National Lumber Manufacturers Association. Fridays.

Payrolls—National Industrial Conference Board. At the end of each month.

Sugar—New York Coffee and Sugar Exchange publishes figures on production and consumption, usually the third week each month.

Tin—New York office of the International Tin Research and Development Council, statistics on tin exports by the five principal producing countries, consumption, and stock. Available the third week of the month.

Wholesale price index—Bureau of Labor index on Friday mornings. The Dun and Bradstreet wholesale food index about the middle of the month.

FINANCIAL PAGE JARGON

Language sets up a barrier that adds to the difficulties of making economics and business intelligible. Learning the vocabulary needed in the beginning course in economics is actually harder than learning the words in a foreign language. The beginning French student has no difficulty in comprehending *le livre,* nor does the student learning Spanish have trouble in comprehending *el libro.* But the economics student is faced with such abstractions as capital, marginal utility, credit, and cost, and with such finely drawn distinctions as inflation and reflation.

The initial difficulties with economic terminology are multiplied in financial writers' reports of stock exchange and commodity market operations and their articles on the state of business. Where we would least expect it in a newspaper we find the highest development of poetic and figurative language. Almost everything is said in metaphors. The language of the market place has been little studied, but a tentative treatment of it appears in "The Muse of Mammon," an article by Arthur Minton in *American Speech* for October, 1949.

According to Minton, the language of market commentators includes a formidable body of figurative expressions, relatively few of which are to be found in standard glossaries. But more revealing perhaps than the language is Minton's description of the attitude of which the language is an outward manifestation:

> Figurative language used to describe happenings in the markets illuminates certain attitudes toward these institutions. Fundamental to this language is the conception of the markets as independent systems of being—sometimes as organisms; sometimes, it would seem, as arenas for contending ethical forces. A source of this conception is the high degree of mystification on the part of market students about the causes of price movements. Because of the vast number of sales and the wide dispersion of customers, the factors influencing prices are difficult or impossible to obtain. . . . Commentators use figures of speech which seem to imply that the markets are independent entities obeying unspecified forces.

Minton classified this figurative language in five major groups:

1. Progression: "Corn prices inched upward today. . . ."
2. Kinetic phenomena: "The stock market steadied a bit yesterday after clearing away the wreckage of the two preceding days."

3. Tactile phenomena: "After irregularly higher prices in yesterday's stock market, the tone weakened."

4. Structure and form: "The bulge in Eastman Kodak . . ."

5. Organismal response: "Timidity of upswing in stocks at the year's end is linked to uncertainty."

These classes represent only a few of the figures of speech with which market stories are interlarded. A casual check of these stories reveals many such poetical devices.

Despite the tendency to personify the market and to use highly figurative language, much of the terminology is strongly conventional, and some of the figures are so well fixed in meaning as to be taken as exact quantities: "The outside market for government bonds was steady to a thirty-second higher."

The following list of stock market terms, by no means complete, indicates some of the conventional newspaper usages:

Steady. Prices generally stable.
Firm, hard, strong. No change in prices, but an upward tendency is suggested.
Shaded. A slight decline.
Whittled. A decline greater than *shaded* denotes.
Market easy or *gives ground.* A decline greater than *whittled.*
Dip. A decided decline.
Retreat, slump, break, plunge. A sharp and deep decline.
Fell out of bed. A bad break in prices.
Bulge or *lift.* A slight rise in prices.
Improvement. A general rise in prices.
Advance. Better than an improvement.
Breakthrough. A strong and sudden increase.
Goes through the roof. An extreme advance.
Spotty. Scattered lower prices.
Mixed or *irregular.* Good and bad prices combined over a considerable area.
Flash quotations. Used by the New York Stock Exchange when the tape lags as much as five minutes during heavy buying. Prices of 16 key stocks are reported simultaneously instead of being recorded on ticker tape in sequence.
Rally. A return to higher prices after a decline.

In commodity market reports the following terms are frequently used:

Market stronger. Prices going up.
Market firm. Prices about the same or a shade higher.
Market dull. Little trading.
Market weaker. Prices going down.
Demand slow. Buyers "just looking."
Supply light. The market could sell more of certain commodities.
Supply heavy. The market is oversupplied and prices are dropping.
Demand good. Buyers are buying at present prices.

BUSINESS AND FINANCIAL NEWS

The financial and business page, with its agate columns of cabalistic abbreviations and figures and its stories that for the most part are in a mysterious jargon, frightens the average newspaperman. To him, keeping his checkbook straight may be a financial feat of the first order. Yet, as the New York *Herald Tribune*'s Harvey E. Runner says in *Late City Edition*, there is a growing tendency for the business news departments to select men with city desk experience when filling vacancies or adding to their staffs.

To the uninitiated, reporting and editing financial and business news seem extremely hard. But it is no more difficult to master than it is to become an expert in sports or politics. Studying the business and financial pages, supplemented by reading books on economics, will give the neophyte a start. But experience is the only way he can become an authority.

The business and financial news department needs news writers and editors, especially people with the ability to present information so that the average reader can understand it. The recent shift in interest from financial to general business news really indicates a comparatively new field in journalism and it offers many opportunities for young people.

But a job of education will have to be done before the business news department has a staff as large as the sports staff and space equal to that allotted sports. Editors themselves must learn to recognize the possibilities in the field, and readers must be trained to look for interesting information on the back pages of the newspaper.

CHAPTER **25**

The Women's Department

NEW STYLES IN WOMEN'S PAGES

One of the discouraging prospects formerly faced by women entering journalism was writing society news. Prejudice in the city room barred general assignments; consequently women found themselves in the society department writing repetitive accounts, day after day, of engagements, weddings, luncheons, and parties, and checking long lists of those present.

Today the situation is changed. Having proved themselves good newspapermen, women now hold down such jobs as city editor, general assignments reporter, city-hall man, political writer, and war correspondent. "The 'for males only' city room is about as old-fashioned as giving a lady your seat on a street car, or taking your hat off in elevators, or giving her elbow room at the local bar," wrote Robert U. Brown in his "Shop Talk at Thirty" column in *Editor & Publisher*. "There may be a few such city rooms left, just as there most certainly must be some gentlemen with old-fashioned manners. But, generally speaking, the so-called fair sex has established itself in journalism."

And even those who are working in the women's departments of newspapers today are finding a variety of jobs that are intellectually stimulating and informatively worth while. Society news, which made little demand on writing skill and reportorial ingenuity, is slowly being relegated to secondary importance, and articles and features of greater significance and wider interest are replacing weddings and parties as subject matter.

An example of the new type of journalism designed for feminine readers is the women's department of the Detroit *News* today. Since the turn of the century the *News* had followed the general newspaper practice of devoting about 70 percent of its pages for women to stories and pictures about society. The new program shifted emphasis to features that were

THE WOMEN'S DEPARTMENT 411

thought to interest the majority of women readers instead of just the social elite. The emphasis was still on the "woman's angle," but the items dealt with events, conditions, and personalities affecting the average woman's own life, her family and her home. The reaction to the change was typified in the letter which one woman wrote to the newspaper: "Thank you for giving us something worth while on the women's pages. I am glad that at last a newspaper realizes that women are people, that they can read and even think a little."

The recognition that women are people as well as mothers, homemakers, and party-goers and party-givers is the dominant influence in the changing emphasis in the women's pages. The shift came about gradually on most newspapers; a few, such as the Detroit *News*, made a rapid change-over after conducting studies of what interests most women.

In an interview appearing in *Editor & Publisher*, Miss Mary Morris, the Detroit *News* women's editor, was asked what measuring stick she used in selecting features. She replied: "The same any editor uses—reader interest. Features are chosen which will be the most thought-provoking, entertaining, instructive, or helpful to the most people."

Even though the Detroit *News*, the Chicago newspapers, and others have found the subordination of social news a means of improving the women's page, it is not the answer for all newspapers. Generally it appeals to editors and managing editors; but they, it must be remembered, are men—and men escort their wives to dress-up society affairs with something less than alacrity. Answers to a questionnaire sent to society editors of daily newspapers favored the broadened conception of women's pages but pointed out that there is still reader interest in reports of weddings, receptions, parties, and showers. Some typical replies were:

My department is called "Society–Clubs," but it is of course a woman's page. When women do something of value they take precedence over mere party stuff. But the public will never fail to like to read about who is doing what at parties. The trend of throwing it into columns makes more space for the rest, but I think you'll find people reading the columnists first just because it is informal "society."—Santa Fe *New Mexican*.

I like the trend personally, but I do not believe that a town of 36,000 is ready for it. Our city is still small town when it comes to looking for names of friends in the paper, and I'm sure our personals are read by a greater number of readers than our fashion articles.—Eau Claire (Wisconsin) *Leader* and *Telegram*.

In these days of uncertainty I doubt if so-called society news is too important. However, the rank and file like to read about the doings of the upper crust and what now has come to be known as cafe society. Here, there is no indication of society news being on its way out.—Utica (New York) *Observer-Dispatch.*

The *Herald* is expanding news of general interest to women. "Society" news is confined to two social columns, with the exception of weddings and engagements.—Miami *Herald.*

I don't try to get bridge parties, private parties, etc. at all any more except when they're given for a special purpose: for instance, a birthday party, shower, farewell party, anniversary. Many readers have told me they like my hobby features and club activity features better than the old "society" type story. I still try to get visiting items, though, so that we can have more people's names in the paper. I do believe that the "high society" story is giving way to general interest stories.—Missoula (Montana) *Missoulian.*

I heartily endorse the move to subordinate "society" news to items of broader interest and significance to women. We try to have an equal amount of both types of news in our women's section.—Birmingham (Alabama) *News.*

I'd like to see this society business upset. It makes for a so-called "minority report" on the people living in a town. Who's to say that these minorities are the ones that should be given the most consideration? We use a great many more features now than we did when I came here seven years ago—a healthy trend, I'd say. I should still like to preserve, however, the personal note type of society items—visitors, luncheons, dinners, etc. Makes for a homey page.—Cedar Rapids (Iowa) *Gazette.*

Personally, I think the new trend's wonderful, but being in a community which is more or less still "small town," we have to adhere to society news and publish it. We are, however, supplementing it with features on fashions, beauty, food, and home furnishings.—Amarillo (Texas) *Globe-News.*

The new women's pages—those that play down society items and play up items of general significance and interest—are found chiefly among metropolitan newspapers. The smaller papers tend to cling to the traditional formula of news about parties, weddings, and clubs. This trend was noted in a conference of women's editors held by the Medill School of Journalism at Northwestern University and the Inland Daily Press Association.

What has happened is this: The metropolitan newspapers are tending to become more like the women's magazines, with authoritative and expertly written articles on health, homemaking, and feminine affairs. The old concept of society in the sense of the "four hundred" has been fading for many years. The elaborate parties—the exhibitions and shows—that the wealthy could afford fifty years ago are rare nowadays. And even if they were still being given they would be less interesting than the gossip-column reports about café society. In the large cities today it's hard to tell who belongs to society. The world pictured in the novels of Edith Wharton no longer exists. Mrs. Amy Birdsall of the St. Paul *Dis-*

Fig. 79. Social news is subordinated to items believed to be of more general interest to women in this page from the Pittsburgh *Press.* (Reproduced by permission of the Pittsburgh *Press.*)

patch and *Pioneer Press* gave this valedictory for the older conception of society: "I think society news as such is on its way out. In this democratic world (the war has changed many ideas) there is little place for so-called 'society' or the 'four hundred.'"

But in smaller cities, where everyone knows nearly everyone else, readers are still interested in weddings, parties, and club meetings. If a bride-to-be is given a shower, the women in the town want to know who gave it, what the hostess' house looked like, and who was invited. Even women who do not belong to that particular clique know some who do, and hence are interested in the details. *Their* particular clique will have its turn next. Moreover, society editors on small newspapers must rely for fashion, food, and other feature material upon syndicates whose stuff is often unsuitable locally. A society staff of one or two persons cannot write authoritatively every day on the subjects that can be handled by a newspaper with a large staff of experts in various fields.

THE EDITOR'S QUALIFICATIONS

The work of getting out the pages or section of the newspaper written and edited primarily for women has not become standardized in respect to titles and duties. On many papers the society page and the women's page are distinct departments, each with its own editor. On others one woman heads both departments; a society editor and other departmental editors—fashion, homemaking, foods—work under her. The small-city newspaper, however, generally retains the title of society editor, because this type of news is emphasized; general women's features are handled by this editor or her staff.

Until recent years women were not entrusted with responsibility for the layout and make-up of the women's pages, or even for the final editing and heading of the copy. The practice was—and still is on many newspapers—to send society and women's copy over the general copy desk. Today many women edit and make up the pages but are directly responsible to the feature editor, the Sunday editor, or some other male executive.

Women have been slow in assuming full responsibility for their pages because formerly a society editor was ordinarily not a trained newspaperwoman. Often she was a gentlewoman in reduced circumstances who was given the job because of her social entree and her acquaintance among the fashionable people of the community. She knew little about newsroom and print-shop practices when she started work—and not much more after years on the job.

THE WOMEN'S DEPARTMENT

Today the trend is to throw all responsibility for the women's pages on women. Now that girls are trained in journalism schools and women reporters are capable of competing with men on beats like the courts and the state capitol, it is no longer necessary for men to make a final check of the copy, write the headlines, and dummy the page. In one respect, however, many women are still unprepared to take over full control of a page or department. Many have not learned how to choose photographs suitable for engraving, how to mark them for cropping and retouching, and how to plan layouts. Since the women's pages, especially in the Sunday issue, make more extensive use of pictures than any other department of a newspaper, knowledge of newspaper illustrations is essential for the editor who wishes to free her department from male supervision.

Editing a society or a women's page is never an easy job. It is first complicated by the fact that on many newspapers the editor has to convince her employer that she can be relied upon to undertake full responsibility. Thus Mrs. J. Harold Brislin, women's editor of the *Scrantonian* and the Scranton *Tribune,* said at a meeting of Pennsylvania publishers:

> May I suggest that you allow your women's editor to be her own boss? Talk with her occasionally, passing along ideas and suggestions by way of the managing editor, but let her understand that you have as much faith in her evaluation of women's news as you have in the judgment of the city editor concerning local news.
>
> A comparison of papers where women editors handle all details of their department with those publications where women's page copy goes through a universal copy desk with men writing heads and dummying pages proves a far superior women's section is created by the woman editor who is her own boss.

Besides the problems created by her relationship with the paper's other departments, the women's editor must please an extremely critical reading public. "Women," says Miss Treva Davis of the Binghamton (New York) *Press,* "have long noses, big ears, green eyes, and fat curiosities." To please this creature, the women's editor must have tact, broad knowledge of the community, and, above all, intelligence. Only an extremely clever woman can manage such a department without making enemies, becoming involved in feminine feuds, and showing her personal likes and dislikes.

The successful women's page editor must have one other attribute: a sincere interest in the social doings of women, in fashions, in the home arts, and in children. This interest is often lacking in women who enter journalism. Many of them would rather talk with a murderer in Death Row than attend a tea. They may consider rankest flapdoodle a fashion writer's description of "a deliciously oversized stole," an interior decorator's whimsy of "a witty screen of drawings cadged from your artist friends," a cookery expert's "little tricks of garnishment," or a beauty

Fig. 80. Some typical departmental headings and "flags" used on women's and society pages.

writer's advice about exercises to reduce the hips while washing dishes. The woman with such a sardonic attitude toward the foibles of her sex can't write convincing copy, and if she does take over the editorship of a women's page she is likely to be unhappy in her work.

WHO IS SOCIETY?

Society news in our newspapers got its start when James Gordon Bennett began publishing in his New York *Herald* descriptions of the costly parties given by the city's oldest and wealthiest families. At first shocked by Bennett's presumptuousness in publicizing their affairs in the "cheap" or "penny" press, social leaders objected violently; but by the 1840's they generally accepted the publicity and some even sought it. Thus long, lush accounts of balls and soirees became commonplace in the New York newspapers of that period. Later the society reports were segregated, and became one of the first regular departments of the newspaper.

Generally speaking, society news has had as its basis snob appeal or class consciousness. In view of our lack of a titled aristocracy, what constitutes society in this country has been somewhat nebulous. In 1888 Ward McAllister superciliously remarked that there were only four hundred people in New York society, and that figure became a byword for the rarity of the socially elite.

Asked in a questionnaire what they thought were the chief qualifications for being considered as "in society," women editors almost universally throughout the country ranked family first. By "family" they meant being descended of the early settlers of the community. In the East and the South one's family can be traced back for many generations; in the comparatively new state of Oklahoma it dates only to 1889 when the Indian lands were opened to white settlement.

Though wealth does not necessarily give entree to society—a popular theme of novels in the latter part of the nineteenth century was the effort of the *nouveau riche* to be accepted socially—it is an important factor because, as one women's page editor put it, "running in social circles is an expensive proposition." Other criteria of social status include club memberships (country clubs and the Junior League are often mentioned), listing in the Social Register, location of residence, business and professional standing, and prominence in cultural activities.

In many of the older communities society is fairly well confined to families who have been prominent in town affairs over a period of years. Other cities have no fixed tradition as to who belongs to society. The papers in these cities tend to avoid the term and to call the department "women's world" or something similar. Society editors in smaller cities frequently make no social distinctions. "We do not discriminate, assuming that everyone is equal," said the women's editor of the Fort Madison

(Iowa) *Evening Democrat.* "We do not attempt to draw a line," said the women's editor of the Eau Claire (Wisconsin) *Leader* and *Telegram.* "Everyone is treated equally, whether their marriage took place in a dilapidated shack or our local cathedral."

SOCIAL NEWS PROBLEMS

Handling the society department, it is obvious, depends a great deal on the type of community. Whatever a woman's abilities in journalism, the first requirement for a good women's page editor is thorough familiarity with the people of the city in which she works. "No one should be employed as a society editor or in that department, no matter what it's called, who does not know people in her town," emphasized the women's editor of the Fort Worth (Texas) *Star-Telegram.* "She should not only know them by sight and sound, but should have a wide personal acquaintance—the wider the better."

Society news coverage is primarily telephonic; there are no regular beats like the city hall or county building. Much of the women's news is brought in or telephoned to the office. Today few women want to keep secret the fact that they are getting married, giving a party, or entertaining guests from out of town. But the society editor of course cannot depend solely on contributed news; she must dig for much of her news. Her first resource, perhaps, is a master telephone list containing the names of people generally in the know; they may be called on an average of once a week. Another essential aid to getting news is a file of yearbooks of clubs and organizations. Prepared a year in advance, these books give the dates of meetings and other events and the women who will serve as hostesses. The society editor's future book actually is an extensive calendar of club meetings and social events. Secondary sources of information for news tips include the daily record of marriage licenses, and caterers, florists, hotel and club stewards, and others whose business is to serve the needs of hostesses.

The most important editing task of a society editor is probably that of checking names. In preparing club yearbooks, members have a chummy practice of using first names. Hence the society editor must know whether the Kathy Smith who is to entertain the Jolly Twelve on Thursday is Mrs. Thomas Smith or Mrs. John Smith. She must not make the mistake of putting Mr. and Mrs. Oliver Jones in the reception line when Mr. Jones escaped the social whirl for the quiet of the cemetery ten years ago.

In verifying information there is one important, essential, unbreakable rule that must never be violated: Do not report a wedding announcement

THE WOMEN'S DEPARTMENT

received by mail or telephone from an unknown source without calling up to verify it. Practical jokesters consider it extremely hilarious to get a false report into the newspaper.

In straight society coverage most of the space is given over to announcements of engagements and weddings. The ritual of getting married gives the society editor her most important and most interesting

Fig. 81. "My Peggy is getting married Monday. How about a stick on the society page?" (Cartoon by W. P. Trent; reproduced by permission of *Editor & Publisher.*)

news, but at the same time creates problems that must be handled with extreme tactfulness.

The first problem is the allocation of space. Almost every girl wants "the works"—a picture of her in her wedding dress and a prominently played story that gives all the details. Yet space does not permit a picture or a top-of-the-column story for everyone. The bride-to-be whose photograph is only one column wide may feel hurt or discriminated against if other pictures are two-column. Certainly no society editor can afford to tell the truth—that some brides are socially more prominent or prettier than others.

To avoid the need for explanations some society editors have adopted a fairly well-defined policy. A few use only one-column cuts for all engagements and weddings. Some use this width for all engagement pictures but base the size of wedding pictures on such factors as the prominence or prettiness of the bride or the size and elaborateness of the ceremony. Others limit the size of cuts to one column in the weekday issues, but may use larger ones in the Sunday paper. Some give the girl a choice—a picture with the engagement story or the wedding story, but not both. Most society editors do not consider a head or bust picture worth more than two columns. Frequently the photographs of several brides are used in a picture layout, especially in the Sunday issue.

Stories of weddings and engagements generally follow a well-established formula, and little effort is made to vary it. Wedding leads—often long compared with those elsewhere in the paper because of the necessity of including the names and addresses not only of the principals but their parents as well—ordinarily take one of the following forms:

Miss Mary Smith, daughter of . . . , became the bride of . . .
Mr. and Mrs. John Smith . . . announce the marriage of their daughter, . . .
Miss Mary Smith, daughter of . . . , was married in St. Paul's Chapel today to . . .
In Christ's Church yesterday Miss Mary Smith, daughter of . . . , became the bride of . . .

To expedite gathering the information and writing the stories, most society departments have a printed form. The bride-to-be may be asked to fill it out and return it to the office, or the society reporter may use it to jot down information that is telephoned or brought to the office.

The form provides space for the following data: the bride's full name and her address; the full name of her parents and their address; the bridegroom's full name and his address; the full name of his parents and their address; the date, hour, and place of the wedding; the number of guests; the full name and title of the minister; the full names of the bride's attendants—the maid of honor and the bridesmaids—and the bridegroom's attendants—the best man and ushers; a description of the bride's bouquet and gown; a description of the bridesmaids' flowers and gowns; a description of the dress worn by the bride's mother; a description of the dress worn by the bridegroom's mother; the music, including the names of the musicians; the decorations for the wedding; the place and decorations for the luncheon, dinner, reception, or breakfast; guests at the reception; the wedding trip; when and where the newly married pair will be "at home"; the bride's schools, sorority, clubs, and occupation; the bridegroom's schools, fraternity, clubs, and occupation; the out-of-town guests.

Because of space limitations society editors usually restrict the list of guests to those from out of town. Information in the story announcing the engagement ordinarily is not repeated in the wedding story; this usually consists of biographical data on schools and club affiliations and employment. Incidentally, one of the most irritating aspects of society reporting is the writers' reluctance to recognize that people work for a living. A young man who has a job at a filling station, for example, may be described in the wedding story as "associated with the Standard Oil Company."

Another major society-page problem is handling news about organizations and clubs, many of which are not strictly society but are put in that department because the membership is primarily or entirely comprised of women. These include the women's auxiliaries or divisions of veterans' organizations, labor unions, and political parties; Parent-Teacher Associations; church circles; garden and flower clubs; and the League of Women Voters. Polled in a questionnaire on where news about these organizations belongs, society editors expressed divergent opinions. Most favored carrying it in their department on the grounds that it gave variety to the content and broadened the readership. Others said that whether it goes on the women's or society page or in the general news section should depend upon the type of activity reported. If an organization is of general interest or significance, they said, stories about it should go in the general news section; if its appeal is mostly to women, the stories should go in the women's department.

In almost any community the number of clubs and organizations is so great that carrying full reports of their activities is almost impossible. Most society editors simplify the problem of coverage by educating the members regarding the newspaper's needs and procedures so that they can take the responsibility of getting information to the newspaper.

Because of space limitations most society editors do not run a story on every club meeting. Advance notices of meetings may be handled in the club calendar, unless there is an important speaker or unless business of general interest is to be taken care of. Meetings at which nothing of interest happens are not reported. Meetings at which officers were elected, a speech of general interest was given, or plans were made for a definite program or project naturally are worth a story.

A few newspapers handle organizational news as a department under a heading like "Club Notes" or "P.-T. A. Activities" once or twice a week, but most society editors say that they prefer not to hold back news for such a column. They point out that, printed daily when the news is still timely, the brief items are extremely useful in make-up.

Though names make news, most society editors have eliminated long guest lists except for a truly important party such as an important debut or an event attended by a large number of notables. In the case of a small social gathering, however, not too much space is required for the listing of names. Attendance at club meetings is almost never reported, since this would result in repeating the names over and over during the year. Special or out-of-town guests at club functions are usually mentioned. Practically no society or women's page editor today would be guilty of the following: "James T. Smithers, winner of this year's Pulitzer Prize in history, spoke on 'Diplomacy and World Peace' before the Women's Athenaeum Club yesterday afternoon. Those present were . . ." The editor would realize that the speech is of more interest than the names of the persons who heard it.

The climax of the society editor's work week is preparing the Sunday section. Held down during the week to less than a page, for the Sunday issue she must fill a section or several pages. Naturally she does not wait until the day the Sunday section goes to press to get her copy ready. Most of it must be planned early in the week, and work on some features with numerous illustrations must be started weeks in advance. Because of the big press run on Saturday night, the society section is frequently printed on Thursday or Friday.

Besides such tasks as lining up picture layouts and getting feature articles together, the society editor has the additional problem of determining which material should go in the weekday paper and which should be held for the Sunday issue. When they send in items, many women express a preference for Sunday publication. Most engagements, for example, are for Sunday release. A few society editors try to follow this preference, if stated; but most regard the material as news and, so far as practicable, print it as soon as possible after the event has happened.

Some comments on the Sunday preference problem follow:

> Would that all papers could be Sunday editions—it's the bane of the society editor's existence. We run all club and party material which takes place prior to Thursday in the weekday editions. Weddings to get in the Sunday section must have happened within the week or at most ten days.—Amarillo (Texas) *Globe-News*.

The great urge of women to get into Sunday editions is amazing. My policy is to use stories there only if they belong there on a timely basis. If we're working for daily newspapers, events belong in them as they come along each day.—Santa Fe *New Mexican.*

We run our women's department just as a city room is run—on the philosophy that news is news when it happens. We do not hold back material for Sunday, but try to have special features that day. We show a predominance of engagements in our Sunday edition; there is a preference among readers that engagements run on that day.—Birmingham *News.*

FEATURE ARTICLES FOR WOMEN

In broadening the interest in her page, the editor of the women's department has such a wide field from which to choose that she finds it hard to determine what will appeal to the greatest number of readers. Despite the fact that feature material for the department is fairly well standardized—foods, fashions, household arts, beauty hints, and so forth—the readership of these items is highly variable.

Readership averages for the various classes of material on the women's pages as compiled in 25 recent reports of *The Continuing Study of Newspaper Reading* show the following ranges:

>   Personals, from 1 to 75 percent.
>   Club news, from 1 to 42 percent.
>   Lovelorn columns, from 13 to 61 percent.
>   Recipes, from 1 to 57 percent.
>   Wedding reports, from 1 to 68 percent.
>   Fashion, from 0 to 42 percent.
>   Food articles, from 1 to 54 percent.

Such averages of course are not accurate guides, because they do not take into consideration the size of headline, position on the page, and the quality of the material. Women's editors, when asked to rank the usual departmental features in importance, voted food and recipes first. Others, in the order assigned to them, were fashion, beauty, homemaking, child care, patterns, home decoration, etiquette, gardening, health, lovelorn column, Hollywood column, and New York column. The lovelorn column, which has the highest readership in *The Continuing Study* surveys, was ranked near the end by the society editors, because most of them apparently consider such material as suitable only for retarded intellects.

One of the most fully developed of these specialized women's departments is the one devoted to foods and cooking. Many metropolitan newspapers maintain a homemaking department with a test kitchen, and no recipes are printed without first being tried out by their own cooking experts. Trained persons for these departments are recruited from colleges with home economics-journalism programs whose graduates have a knowledge of foods, clothing and materials, and homemaking skills, and ability to write for publication.

On most newspapers food news is of greatest importance on Thursdays

Fig. 82. The food editor of a newspaper must be at home at the range as well as at the typewriter. Lucia Brown, food reporter for the Washington Post, is shown preparing food to be featured in a photograph. (Washington Post photo.)

and Fridays when the publications are fat with grocery advertising. The fact that so much information has to be crowded into these multiple-page sections is unfortunate. The tendency is to railroad copy through just to fill up the space, and much of what is printed is not judiciously chosen to serve the readers. Even worth-while items may be overlooked by busy housewives who don't have time to read such a large quantity of material at one time.

Food news—recipes, menus, new products, recommended ways of preparation, dietetics, seasonal suggestions, and so forth—is obtainable from many sources. Much of it comes from processing companies and is accompanied by either photographs or mats for illustrations. The syndicates supply material, especially in the form of signed columns. Publications of the United States Department of Agriculture are another source—more authoritative than most—that is often overlooked by women's page editors. Material can be obtained from local housewives if the newspaper conducts a regular department such as "Favorite Recipes of Middletown Housewives," and especially if it offers a prize for the best recipe or cooking hint each week.

In handling food news, recipes in particular, the editor must place a premium on accuracy if she does not want to bring down the wrath of her readers on her head. Hell hath no fury like that of the woman who faithfully follows a recipe and produces a failure because an essential ingredient has been omitted by the newspaper.

The recipes and stories that come in from food processors must often be rewritten because they are too long or do not conform to journalistic style. In rewriting and editing the trade names must be changed to generic terms to comply with newspaper restrictions against free advertising.

A good food news section is an aid to the newspaper's advertising department and has received careful study from agencies and other organizations. The Bureau of Advertising of the American Newspaper Publishers Association has issued a number of releases dealing with food news and advertising. A recent booklet, *Reader Interest in Food News*, suggested the following means of handling material to increase readership:

1. Pictures with appetite appeal.
2. Timeliness.
3. Popular rather than unfamiliar dishes.
4. Close-ups rather than distant spread-shots for illustrations.
5. Promise in headline rather than just the name of the recipe.
6. Informative rather than "cute" headlines.
7. Short copy with illustration.

In addition to publishing such conventional material as recipes and ways of cooking, the alert editor can improve her page or department by doing some straight reporting and interpretation. If the price of sugar or coffee suddenly goes up, the housewife will know about it from reading the advertisements or seeing the prices in the grocery; she will be interested in a background story explaining why. If in the canning season she finds that peaches are scarce, she will be interested in knowing that there is no home-grown fruit because of the late spring cold spell. Timeliness of information is always of first importance. When berries are extremely plentiful and cheap, an article advising the housewife to take advantage of the situation by canning, making jellies and jams, and stocking up the home-freezer will serve as a valuable reminder. New discoveries in nutrition and dietetics reported by home economics schools and college research institutes certainly belong on the women's page.

Possibly too many recipes are printed. A housewife who files all of them she reads in the newspapers and magazines for a few months, in addition to those in the cookbooks, would have to move everything but her files out of the kitchen. Moreover, cooking is not the passionate obsession for most women that some writers on the topic seem to think it is. Most dinners consist of dishes that can be prepared without referring to cookbooks; the novelties that brighten the magazines and newspapers have little or no appeal in most homes.

Clothes are of paramount interest in the women's pages, not only in the guise of fashion articles and patterns but as an incidental part of many news stories. At almost every major society affair the reporter takes notes on what the style leaders of the community are wearing, and these descriptions appear in the story about the event.

Pictures and descriptions of the extreme fashions conceived of by New York and Paris designers adorn the women's pages. It is not expected that local women will rush off to buy these high-priced creations; the fashion editors publish such items because they indicate trends in styles or because their bizarreness is interesting in itself.

For the most part, the editors attempt to localize the fashion news and to use suggestions that have some bearing on the stocks in community stores. For photographs the fashion editor gets local college girls and society women to model clothing from the stores. She covers a style show as a routine part of her job and frequently visits stores to inspect new stocks as they come in. Many newspapers send their fashion editor or women's editor to New York to attend the National Press Week held by the New York Dress Institute.

Fashion of course is a gigantic activity aimed at selling goods, and the editor has to be on guard against free advertising. The names of stores usually are given in a story about a style show, but they are ordinarily omitted in general articles about clothes available locally. Even when store names are used, few editors print the prices. Many newspaper stories carry a note saying that the article mentioned is available locally and that information can be obtained by telephoning the paper. Publicity releases from the fashion centers are often used by editors in smaller cities where first-hand fashion news is hard to obtain, and metropolitan fashion editors also find them helpful for background information.

Fashion writing, like other specialized writing, tends toward esoteric jargon—what Miss Treva Davis of the Binghamton (New York) *Press* calls "the rich, beautiful prose department." She says:

> Fashion writers can use adjectives, or they can use words with meaning. Most of them don't even realize there is a choice. They reach into their stock of plushy adjectives and pile them on, slowly smothering their readers. They particularly like a good resounding triple adjective, and they're nuts about hyphens. So you get a small-waisted, full-skirted, button-trimmed, long-sleeved, gold-embroidered, Victorian-inspired . . . gown. This kind of thing is, I think, a cover-up for sloppy writing. The only reason it gets by in the paper is that newspapermen don't have any idea what the fashion editor is talking about and assume that the jargon means something to women. Well, a lot of it has no meaning to women, either.

The other women's page features—etiquette columns, advice on child care, beauty and health articles, and so forth—do not ordinarily call for such extensive treatment as food and clothes. Most editors rely on syndicates for this material. The syndicate offerings, however, should be supplemented by locally written features. For example, the editor might interview local kindergarten teachers for suggestions to mothers on preparing a child for the first day of school. The home economics teacher or some other dietetics expert can offer tips for preparing food for people who take their lunch to work. The women's editor who organizes her work so that she has thirty minutes every day for listing such ideas or tips will never be at a loss for good local articles and features.

In addition to fashions, cookery, homemaking, and other topics considered primarily of interest to women, the society or women's editor on smaller-city publications frequently finds herself also covering music, art, and drama. A poll of editors showed them about evenly divided on whether to cover these fields in the women's section. Many of them said that more American women than men seem to be interested in culture and that the women's pages seem the logical place for such news. Others, especially those on metropolitan publications, maintained that news about the arts should appear as general news or be put in separate departments. Some said they liked to run this news because it gives variety to the women's pages; others urged shifting it to other departments because it often crowds out society and women's news.

WOMEN'S PAGE MAKE-UP

In line with the trend toward broadening the appeal of the society and women's pages, newspapers in recent years have striven for greater variety in make-up and a more extensive use of pictures.

The society or women's department, like most specialized departments, is designated by a special name plate. Rather than labeling the page merely "Society," the trend nowadays is to indicate its wider interest by such labels as "Women's World," "The Feminine Angle," "For and About Women," "Women's News and Views," or "Women in the News." Theoretically, at least, there is some objection to such labels, for they tend to make the page too exclusive and they frighten away men readers. Actually, of course, men do read the women's section, or at least glance at it casually for something that looks interesting. They are as likely to appreciate a picture of a pretty bride as much as a woman does—perhaps more.

The women's pages also may be set apart from the rest of the newspaper by a different headline type from that used for other headings. In the general news sections bold type faces are customarily used; on the women's pages a lighter and "more feminine" type is often used. All the standard typographical devices for brightening the page should be used—live headings instead of standing headings for columns, thumbnail cuts for by-line writers and columnists; subheads, boldface, indentions, and star dashes to break up long stories; double-column leads set in 10 point; and so forth.

The front page of the Sunday section ordinarily features a photographic layout that takes up all or most of the page. Typical front-page layouts include a group of the week's brides, the season's debutantes, a back-to-college feature, an Easter fashion display, women who have interesting jobs—any feature idea that the editor thinks will be of interest to her readers, both men and women.

APPENDIX A
Stylesheet

The stylesheet that follows is a composite of usages set forth in stylebooks issued by newspapers in all parts of the country. It is designed for use in classroom copyreading exercises. The student who masters it will have little difficulty in adapting to the stylebook of the newspaper on which he finds employment.

ABBREVIATIONS

Do not use abbreviations that the average newspaper reader will not grasp quickly. For many organizations it is best to use the full name the first time it is mentioned in a story, with an abbreviation or shortened version of the name thereafter. For example, make it *the Federal Communications Commission* the first time it appears. For subsequent references use *the FCC*, or preferably *the commission,* since there is a tendency to use the confusing initial abbreviations unnecessarily.

Titles. Use the following abbreviations for civilian and professional titles: *Mr., Mrs., Dr., Prof., Supt., Sen., Rep., Gov., Lt. Gov. Mr.* should be used for all local men of good repute. Do not use it in wire stories, or when the full name is given: *John A. Jones,* but *Mr. Jones.* Women's names should be preceded by *Miss* or *Mrs.* In society stories the plurals *Misses, Mmes., Messrs.* may be used.

Abbreviate junior and senior after a name but do not set it off by commas: *John Smith Jr., Alfred Adams Sr.*

Do not abbreviate the following: *president, vice president, congressman, principal, alderman, councilman, secretary, treasurer, attorney, manager, constable, sheriff, deputy, chairman, supervisor, director.*

Use the following abbreviations for military titles: *Gen., Lt. Gen., Maj. Gen., Brig. Gen., Col., Lt. Col., Maj., Capt., 1st Lt., 2nd Lt., Pvt., Pfc., Cpl., Sgt., Sgt. 1c, Staff Sgt., Tech. Sgt., Master Sgt., 1st Sgt.*

Use the following abbreviations for naval and coast guard titles: *Adm., Vice Adm., Rear Adm., Cdr., Lt. Cdr., Lt., Lt. (j.g.), Ens., Seaman 2c, Seaman 1c.* Do not abbreviate *Commodore.* Do not abbreviate petty officers' titles because many readers do not know them: *Chief Quartermaster John Smith, Fire Controlman 1c Alfred Adams.*

Use the following abbreviations in ecclesiastical titles: *the Rev., the Rev. Mr.*

(when the first name or initials are not used), *the Rev. Dr., the Right Rev., Msgr.*

Abbreviate only French titles among foreign titles: *M.* (monsieur), *MM.* (messieurs), *Mme.* (madame), *Mmes.* (mesdames), *Mlle.* (mademoiselle), *Mlles.* (mesdemoiselles).

Geographical Names. Abbreviate the names of states only when they follow the name of a city: *Tulsa, Okla.* Use the following forms: *Ala., Ariz., Ark., Cal., Colo., Conn., D. C., Del., Fla., Ga., Ill., Ind., Kan., Ky., La., Md., Mass., Mich., Minn., Miss., Mo., Mont., Neb., Nev., N. H., N. J., N. M., N. Y., N. C., N. D., Okla., Ore., Pa., R. I., S. C., S. D., Tenn., Tex., Vt., Va., Wash., W. Va., Wis., Wyo.* Do not abbreviate *Idaho, Iowa, Maine, Ohio, Utah.*

Use the above abbreviations when state names are inserted parenthetically in the names of periodicals, establishments, firms: *Springfield (Mass.) Republican.*

Omit the names of states with well-known cities. The state name is not needed with towns and cities in the state where a newspaper is published.

Do not abbreviate *United States* except when used as an adjective. Say *the people of the United States*, but *the U. S. army*. Omit the period in such designations as *USN, USA, USS Iowa.*

Do not abbreviate the names of U. S. possessions—*Hawaiian Islands*—or of such areas as *Canal Zone, Philippine Islands, Long Island.*

Do not abbreviate names of foreign countries; the only exception is the *USSR*, written without periods.

Organizations. If well known, the names of organizations, institutions, boards, commissions, agencies, and committees containing three or more words may be designated by initials, used without periods: *CIO, YMCA, FSA, IOOF.* Use periods for two-letter initials: *U. S., U. N.* Use periods also for names containing the words *of* or *and*: *A. and M., C. of C.*

Follow the preference of the particular firm in writing *company, corporation, limited,* and *incorporated* and in using the ampersand.

Do not use abbreviations for Greek letter fraternities and sororities in a general newspaper; their use is permissible, but not recommended, in a college publication.

Streets and Avenues. In addresses, abbreviate only the direction: *100 E. First Street, 220 N. W. Second Street, 800 S. Elm Avenue.*

Political Designations. Use the following form for political designations after a name: *Sen. John Smith (D.-Cal.), Rep. Adam Jones (R.-Grady County).*

Divisions of Time. Abbreviate the names of months only when used with dates: *Feb., 1950, Jan. 2, 1950.* Do not abbreviate *March, April, May, June, July.* Do not abbreviate the days of the week.

Miscellaneous. Lower-case *a. m.* and *p. m.* Write out *noon* and *midnight.* Use the form *per cent;* the sign % may be used in tabular matter.

Abbreviate weights, measurements, distances, and prices in sports and financial stories, listings, and tabular matter.

Avoid such colloquial abbreviations as *frat, exam, soph, frosh.*

Write radio station letters without periods: *WOR, KVOO.* Such abbreviations as *SOS, IOU, TNT, AWOL,* and naval craft abbreviations: *LCVP,* are written without periods.

APPENDIX A: STYLESHEET

CAPITALIZATION

Newspaper styles for capitalization call for upstyle, or frequent capitalization; downstyle, or minimum capitalization; or modified "up" or "down." This stylesheet is modified upstyle.

In general, capitalize all proper nouns. A proper noun is the name of an individual or object as distinguished from others of the same class: *John, London, Canada*. A common noun is the name an individual or object has in common with others of its class: *man, city, country*. Also capitalize adjectives derived from proper nouns: *Shakespearean, Parisian, Russian*. Do not capitalize proper names and derivatives whose origin has been obscured by long and common usage: *india rubber, pasteurize, guillotine, watt, brussels sprouts, chinaware*.

The names of many organizations, firms, institutions, clubs, and buildings, are made up of common nouns alone or combined with proper nouns. All such nouns should be capitalized: *Veterans of Foreign Wars, the Peerless Printing Company, the Pennsylvania State College, the International Relations Club, the Empire State Building*.

Titles. Capitalize recognized titles and offices when they precede a name: *Prof. T. R. Smith, Sen. Allan Brown, Coach John Jones, Secretary of State John Williams*.

Do not capitalize a word that precedes a name when it is used primarily as an adjective or, without commas, in close apposition with a name: *halfback John Smith, attorney John Brown*.

Do not capitalize *former, ex-*, and *-elect* in a title: *former President Herbert Hoover, ex-Sen. John Smith, Gov.-elect Robert Ames*.

Do not capitalize any title or office when it stands alone or is used as an identification following a name.

Government. Capitalize the names of national and state legislative bodies when referring to specific ones: *Congress, the Senate, the House of Representatives*. Do not capitalize the adjectives *congressional* and *senatorial*. Do not capitalize congressional and legislative committees, permanent or temporary.

Capitalize the full names, and reasonably exact designations, of federal and state governmental bodies, organizations, institutions, departments, commissions, boards, bureaus, services, offices, agencies, administrations, and so forth: *Department of Agriculture, Interstate Commerce Commission, National Resources Planning Board, Tennessee Valley Authority, Farm Security Administration*. Do not capitalize such terms as *department, commission, board*, and *administration* when they stand alone: *the Interstate Commerce Commission*, but in subsequent use *the commission*. Do not capitalize sections, divisions, or branches of a primary organization: *the procurement division of the Treasury Department, the wage and hour division of the Department of Labor*.

Capitalize the names of specific courts: *the Supreme Court, the Circuit Court of Appeals, the District Court*. Do not capitalize when referring to courts in a general sense: *an appellate court, a justice of the peace court, a police court*.

Capitalize political subdivisions such as *county, township, province, precinct,* and *ward* when used with a distinguishing name: *Fairfield County, First Ward, Owen Township, Precinct 2.*

Legislation. Do not capitalize the names of bills introduced in a legislature or of acts after their passage: *the fair trade and practices bill, the Taft-Hartley act.*

Political Parties. Capitalize nouns and adjectives designating organized political parties and members thereof: *Democratic party, Republican minority leader, a Communist, a Laborite.*

Educational Institutions. Capitalize the principal words in the names of all institutions of learning: *Iowa State College, Indiana University, the University of Missouri.* Do not capitalize the subdivisions or classes of such institutions: *the college of arts and sciences, the department of geology, the senior class.*

Capitalize collegiate degrees when abbreviated: *B. A., Ph. D.* Do not use capitals when they are written out: *bachelor of arts, doctor of philosophy.*

Military Organizations. Capitalize the names of military organizations, units, branches, services, and commands: *45th Division, First Army, Company D, the 12th Naval District.* Do not capitalize *army, navy, air force, marine corps* when used in a general sense: *the American army, navy enlistments.*

Capitalize all the letters in initial abbreviations of names of military or service organizations: *AAF, WAC, WAVES, USNR.* In referring to personnel, capitalize only the first letter of terms derived from these names: *a Wac, the Waves.*

Geographical Names. Capitalize only the identifying parts of the names of rivers, lakes, oceans, mountains, forests, and other natural features: *Red river, Grand lake, Pacific ocean, Green mountains, Black forest.* But if the generic or class term precedes the identifying name, it should also be capitalized: *Lake Erie, Gulf of Mexico.*

Capitalize terms used to designate definite geographical regions: *the East, the Midwest, Dixie, the Bible Belt, Back Bay, Outer Mongolia, Western Europe.* Capitalize also such words as *Easterner, Midwesterner, Southerner.* Do not capitalize descriptive or compass terms used to denote direction or position: *the southern part of Florida, the central regions of Pennsylvania.*

Capitalize fanciful appellations of places: *the Empire State, the Golden Triangle, the Oil Capital, the Crescent City.*

Holidays and Celebrations. Capitalize the names of holidays, expositions, celebrations, and special weeks: *Fourth of July, Labor Day, Pioneer Celebration, Homecoming Week.*

Historical Events. Capitalize geological and historical eras, important events, the notable documents and treaties: *the Cambrian Age, the Middle Ages, the Revolutionary War, the Renaissance, the Battle of Bunker Hill, the Mauve Decade, the Treaty of Versailles, the Declaration of Independence.* Do not capitalize such terms as *20th century.*

Organizations. Capitalize the full names of all civic, commercial, social, fraternal, and other organizations and associations: *Rotary Club, Chamber of Commerce, American Association of University Professors, American Feder-*

ation of Labor, the Eastern Star, the Rockefeller Foundation. Follow the organization's preference as to abbreviations and punctuation.

Names of Breeds and Flowers. Capitalize the identifying or designating parts of the names of breeds and flowers, but not the common nouns denoting class: *Barred Rocks, Shetland pony, Southdown sheep, Radiance rose, Elberta peaches.* In breeds of dogs capitalize words derived from proper names, but not common adjectives or common nouns designating class: *Afghan hound, Airedale, cocker spaniel, poodle, Irish setter.*

Book and Other Titles. Place in quotation marks and capitalize the principal words (all words except articles, prepositions, and conjunctions unless they begin the title) in the titles of books, songs, pictures, speeches, sermons: "*The Red Badge of Courage,*" "*Silver Threads among the Gold,*" "*September Morn,*" "*Acres of Diamonds.*" Capitalize but do not quote the designations of musical compositions that have no formal title: *Concerto in A Minor, the Fifth Symphony of Beethoven.* Do not capitalize or use quotation marks with a part or a movement: *the overture to "William Tell," the finale from Symphony No. 4 by Tchaikovsky.*

Capitalize the principal words in the names of newspapers and other periodicals; do not use quotation marks: *the New York Times, Harper's Magazine, the Bulletin of the American Society of Newspaper Editors.*

Use capitals in debate questions as follows: *Resolved: That Hawaii and Alaska should be admitted to statehood.*

Religious Terms. Capitalize the specific names of religious faiths, denominations, and bodies and their adherents: *Christianity, Catholicism, the Methodist church, a Presbyterian.* Capitalize the words *church* and *cathedral* when referring to specific buildings: *the First Baptist Church, St. Paul's Cathedral.*

Capitalize the names of sacred writings: *the Bible, the Talmud, the Koran.*

Capitalize religious feasts and observances: *the Feast of the Passover, Lent, Easter, Yom Kippur.*

Capitalize ecclesiastical titles, regardless of faith, only when they precede a name: *the Rev. Dr. John Smith, John J. Cardinal Jones, the Most Rev. John J. Jones, archbishop of Middletown.*

Buildings. Capitalize the names of buildings, hotels, bridges, and monuments: *Empire State Building, Roosevelt Hotel, Golden Gate Bridge, Washington Monument, Federal Building, City Hall.* Do not capitalize *county jail, city jail, city pound, Leavenworth prison,* and other such designations.

Streets and Avenues. Capitalize the names of streets, avenues, boulevards, highways: *E. First Street, Grand Avenue, MacArthur Boulevard, Lincoln Highway, Highway 40.*

Fanciful Appellations and Personifications. Capitalize such terms as *Old Sol, the Pirates, Old Glory, the Union, Mother Nature.*

Decorations, Orders. Capitalize the principal words in the names of decorations: *Congressional Medal of Honor, Purple Heart, Navy Cross, Croix de Guerre.* Do not capitalize *oak leaf cluster* or other terms denoting duplication of an award.

Capitalize the principal words in chivalric, fraternal, religious, and military orders: *Order of the Garter, Legion of Merit, Knights Templar.*

NUMERALS

Spell out cardinal and ordinal numbers up to 10; use figures for 10 and above: *two, second, 15, 15th.*

Dates, Measurements. Use figures in all the following:
Time of day: *8 a. m., 2 o'clock.*
Percentages: *1 per cent.*
Weights: *5 pounds, 7-pound baby.*
Measurements: *5 feet, 11 inches.*
Sums of money: *$5, 2 cents, 3-cent tax.*
Ages: *2 years old, 8-year-old boy.*
Calibers: *.22 rifle.*
Degrees of temperature: *80 degrees.*
Scores: *Missouri 20, Nebraska 14.*
Betting odds: *odds of 8 to 1.*
Dates: *Dec. 4, April 24.*
House, telephone, license numbers: *200 E. First Street, Circle 3-9802, license number 54-100.*
Latitude and longitude: *latitude 4 degrees 20 minutes north.*
Biblical references: *Genesis 1:10.*
Whole numbers followed by fractions: *3½, 10½.*

Punctuation of Numbers. Use commas with any number containing four or more digits except serial numbers, dates, and house and block numbers: *1,000; 5,223,100; license number 533-011; July, 1950; 5400 S. 15th Street.*

Miscellaneous. In compounds of exact numbers and measurement units, use figures: *5 yards, 6-inch pipe, 1-foot rule.* But write: *three-way switch, one-act play, three-story building,* because these do not indicate units of measurement.

Do not use *st, nd, rd,* and *th* after dates.

Do not use zeros for minutes or cents in stating hours and sums of money that are in round numbers: *8 a. m., $5.*

To prevent misreading of large figures write out *million* and *billion: 250 million, 2 billion, $40 million.*

Use an apostrophe to indicate the plurals of figures, letters, and words: *2's, 1890's.*

Use an apostrophe when the century designation is omitted in a date: *the class of '50.* Spell out *the nineties, the thirties* in referring to a particular decade.

Spell out numbers that begin a sentence: *Fifty persons signed the petition.*

Do not use constructions that throw two figures together: *Of the 300, 250 were present.* Recast to: *Of the 300 members, 250 were present.* It is permissible to break style rules to avoid such juxtapositions: *The ship carried 12 eight-inch guns.* In identifications, insert *of* between the age and a house number: *James Smith, 21, of 200 E. First Street.*

APPENDIX A: STYLESHEET

PUNCTUATION

Newspaper punctuation is based on the theory that marks should not be used unless they clarify a sentence. Avoid excessive punctuation. In general, newspaper prose is streamlined, and its uninvolved sentences and constructions simplify the problem of punctuation.

Period. Use a period after declarative and imperative sentences, after abbreviations unless otherwise specified (see pp. 429-430), between dollars and cents, and as a decimal point. Omissions in quoted matter are indicated by three periods or leaders.

Comma. Use a comma to set off identification elements such as age, occupation, and address after a name: *John Smith, 31, Valley Grove, was injured. James Jones, president of the Chamber of Commerce, spoke.* Do not use a comma with *of* in phrases indicating position, title, or place of residence: *John Smith of the Bureau of Vital Statistics; James Jones of Pittsburgh.* Do not use a comma when appositions are closely connected: *the poet Keats, the novel "Bleak House," the yacht Flying Arrow.*

Use a comma before *and* and *or* in a series: *Pencils, pen, and paper.*

Use a comma before coördinating conjunctions (*and, but, for, yet, or, neither, nor*) in compound sentences when the clauses are long: *The resolution was adopted by a big majority, but afterward many members said they thought the action was perhaps too hasty.*

Use a comma between two adjectives modifying the same noun if they are coördinate in thought: *A disagreeable, uncomfortable trip.* Do not use a comma if the two adjectives are closely joined in meaning: *The good old days.*

Use a comma to set off a long dependent clause that precedes the principal clause: *When the governor announced that he would be unable to attend, the committee voted to cancel the meeting.*

Use a comma to set off nonrestrictive clauses and phrases but not restrictive ones. A restrictive clause is necessary to the meaning of the sentence and cannot be omitted without changing the sense. A nonrestrictive clause is a parenthetical expression and hence can be omitted without affecting the meaning. *The workers who went on strike were not rehired.* The sense is that only the workers who struck were not rehired. Thus the "who" clause is restrictive; it could not be omitted without changing the meaning. *The workers, who voted the strike at a meeting last night, established picket lines this morning.* Here the dependent clause is nonrestrictive; it is a parenthetical explanation whose omission will not change the meaning.

Use commas to set off items in addresses and dates: *He was born in Springfield, Mo., on Feb. 20, 1915.*

Semicolon. Use a semicolon between the coördinate parts of a compound sentence when the conjunction is omitted or when there are commas within the coördinate elements. In newspaper writing, however, it is better to use two sentences.

Use a semicolon between items in a list in which commas are also used: *Officers are James Smith, president; Robert Jones, vice president; Andrew Johnson, secretary; and Alice Adams, treasurer.*

Colon. Use a colon after introductory words, phrases, or sentences when the words *the following* and *as follows* are expressed or implied. The material after the colon usually should begin a new paragraph:
> *The president named the following committees:*
> *Membership—James Smith, chairman; Arthur Jones, and P. L. Johnston.*
> *Finance—D. B. Adams, chairman; Paul R. Williams, and T. A. Andrews.*

Use a colon instead of a comma before direct quotations of more than one sentence and before any quoted matter that begins a new paragraph.

Use a colon in expressing clock time: *2:30 p. m.*

Use a colon between chapter and verse in Biblical references: *John 3:16.*

Parenthesis. Use parentheses around material inserted in a sentence when the material is independent in construction. Parentheses are also used for interpolations and explanations when brackets would be used in books and magazines: *He said that the new law (it went into effect July 1) would be enforced vigorously. "Many people oppose the law," he declared, "but they (the members of the legislature) knew this when they passed it."*

Use parentheses around the name of a state when it comes between the name of a city and of a publication or organization: *the Dallas (Tex.) News, the Lima (Ohio) Chamber of Commerce.*

Use parentheses for a political party designation after a name: *Sen. William Smith (D.-Md.).*

Dash. Use a dash to show hesitation or faltering in speech: *"Well, perhaps—oh, I'm not sure that I know."*

A dash may be used instead of parentheses for interpolations. *He spent 10 years in China—he went to Shanghai in 1930—as a press association correspondent.*

Use a dash in listings by subject matter:
> *The following committees were named:*
> *Membership—Mrs. T. R. Smith, chairman; Mrs. Albert Jones, and Mrs. Robert Adams.*

Apostrophe. Use an apostrophe to indicate contractions: *don't, it's* (it is). Some commonly used contractions do not require an apostrophe: *phone, bus.*

In forming possessives, use an apostrophe and *s* in the singular and the *s* and the apostrophe in the plural: *the governor's policy, the students' books.* For the possessive of words ending in *s*, use only the apostrophe: *Burns' poems.*

An apostrophe is never used in the possessive pronouns: *its, hers, theirs, ours.*

When names contain possessives, follow the practice of the particular firm or organization: *the American Newspaper Publishers Association, the Citizens National Bank, the Middletown Dads' Club.* Organization names that contain the words *man* or *woman*, or their plurals, usually retain the apostrophe: *Young Men's Christian Association, the Woman's Club.*

Omit the apostrophe in *Mothers Day, Fathers Day.*

Quotation Marks. Use quotation marks at the beginning and end of all direct quotations. When a quotation is more than one paragraph in length, use a quotation mark at the beginning of each paragraph, but only at the end of the

APPENDIX A: STYLESHEET

last paragraph.[1] Use single quotation marks for quotations within a quotation and in headlines.

Use quotation marks for the titles of books, plays, short stories, poems, musical compositions, sermons, and speeches.

Do not use quotation marks for debate questions, periodicals, ships, trains, airplanes, animals, or characters in literature or drama.

Use quotation marks for nicknames inserted between the first and last name of a person: *John T. "Spike" Smith*. Do not use the marks if only the nickname is used: *Babe Ruth*.

Hyphen. Use a hyphen in compound adjective modifiers that precede a noun: *up-to-date methods, English-speaking peoples*. Do not use a hyphen with modifiers that end in *-ly: badly chosen words, smoothly leveled surface*.

Use a hyphen in compounds denoting different occupations or duties: *soldier-statesman, secretary-treasurer*. Do not use a hyphen in *vice president, vice chairman, vice regent*.

Use a hyphen when numbers are spelled out: *twenty-eight, three-fourths*. Use a hyphen in adjectives consisting of a number and an object: *500-foot fence, 3-inch knife, one-act play*.

The hyphenation of word compounds cannot be discussed in this stylesheet because of lack of space. In general, words that have Latin or Greek suffixes and prefixes do not require a hyphen. But a hyphen is required when two vowels are thrown together or when it is necessary to distinguish between words that are spelled alike but have different meanings, as in *recreation* (diversion) and *re-creation* (act of creating again). No hyphen is required in frequently used words made by combining two other words: *bookcase, newspaperman, deathbed, theatergoer, textbook*.

[1] See Chapter 5 for the use of quotations in speech stories.

APPENDIX B

Words Frequently Misused

The following words are frequently misused because of similarity in pronunciation, spelling, or meaning.

Accept: to receive; **except:** to exclude.
Adopt: a resolution is *adopted*; **enact:** a law is *enacted*; **pass:** a measure or bill is *passed*.
Advice: a noun meaning counsel; **advise:** a verb meaning to counsel or inform.
Affect: a verb meaning to influence; **effect:** a verb meaning to bring about; a noun meaning the result brought about.
Allege: to assert to be true, but without proving; **assert:** to state positively.
All-round: an adjective meaning extending in many departments; **all around:** always two words; *around* is an adverb or a preposition meaning on all sides.
Allude: to make an indirect reference; **refer:** to make definite reference or mention.
Allusion: an indirect reference; **illusion:** an imagined appearance.
Alternative: a choice between two; **choice:** a selection from any number.
Amateur: a nonprofessional; **novice:** a beginner.
Ambassador: a diplomatic agent of the highest rank; **envoy:** a diplomatic agent below an ambassador; **minister:** the chief of an executive department of a government (called a **secretary** in the United States); **consul:** an officer appointed to reside in a foreign city chiefly as the representative of his country's commercial interests.
Among: used with more than two objects; **between:** used principally with only two objects.
Analyst: one who analyzes; **annalist:** a chronicler.
Anxious: worried; **eager:** excessively or impatiently desirous.
Average: the result obtained by dividing a sum by the number of its terms; **mean:** a quantity that has an intermediate value between two extremes or among several quantities; **median:** a middle quantity.
Balance: equilibrium; **remainder** or **rest:** what is left over or remains.
Bar: to hinder, exclude, prohibit; **ban:** to interdict.
Beside: next to, by the side of; **besides:** in addition to.
Better: the comparative of *good*; **bettor:** one who bets.
Burglar: one who breaks into or enters a premises with the intent of com-

APPENDIX B: WORDS FREQUENTLY MISUSED

mitting a felony; **robber:** one who takes another's property by intimidation or force; **thief:** one who steals furtively.

Canvas: a kind of cloth; **canvass:** a count or solicitation.

Capital: a city or seat of government; **capitol:** a government building.

Cinch: (noun) a sure thing; (verb) to get a tight grip on; **clinch:** (noun) a decisive argument; (verb) to confirm.

Complement: quota or supplement; **compliment:** praise.

Consensus: a collective opinion or general agreement; therefore *general consensus* and *consensus of opinion* are redundant expressions.

Continual: recurring; **continuous:** uninterrupted.

Corespondent: one who answers jointly with another in a suit; **correspondent:** one who communicates in writing.

Council: a deliberating body; **counsel:** (noun) advice, one who gives advice, as an attorney; (verb) to advise; **consul:** see **Ambassador**.

Creditable: worthy; **credible:** believable.

Disinterested: impartial, free from self-interest; **uninterested:** not interested, indifferent.

Each other: used of two persons; **one another:** used when more than two persons are involved.

Elicit: a verb meaning to draw out; **illicit:** an adjective meaning illegal.

Eminent: high in station, distinguished; **imminent:** impending in the near future.

Envelop: a verb meaning to surround or enclose in a wrapper; **envelope:** a noun meaning a wrapper.

Exceptional: unusual or superior; **exceptionable:** open to exception or objection.

Farther: more distant; **further:** additional.

Fewer: used with numbers; **less:** used with quantity.

Flaunt: to wave or display ostentatiously; **flout:** to ignore or scoff at.

Following: next in order, ensuing; **after:** next in time.

Hailed: called in greeting; **haled:** dragged by force.

Hanged: persons are *hanged*; **hung:** things are *hung*.

Happen: to occur by chance; **take place:** to occur by prearrangement.

Healthy: possessing good health; **healthful:** conducive to good health.

Hoard: something that is stored away; **horde:** a large number.

Imply: to intimate a meaning not expressed; **infer:** to deduce or accept on the basis of evidence.

Incredible: unbelievable; **incredulous:** unbelieving.

Indict: to charge with a crime; **indite:** to write or compose.

Ingenious: skillful, inventive; **ingenuous:** candid, frank, guileless.

Lady: a titled woman of the British aristocracy; **woman:** a person of the female sex.

Last: the end; **latest:** the most recent.

Lay: a transitive verb requiring an object; the past tense and past participle are *laid*; **lie:** an intransitive verb; the past is *lay* and the past participle is *lain*.

Luxuriant: having abundant growth; **luxurious:** characterized by luxury.

Majority: more than half a given number; in counting votes, the lead of one candidate over all the others; **plurality:** the lead of one candidate over the next highest.

Model: a miniature reproduction; **replica:** a duplicate exact in details and dimensions.

More than: in excess of; **over:** across, in a higher place.

Murder: in a legal sense, to kill a human being with malice aforethought; **kill or slay:** to take a life.

Notable: worthy of attention; **noted:** known by common report; **notorious:** widely known, especially unfavorably.

Oral: uttered by mouth; **verbal:** in words, either spoken or written.

Parties: participants in a legal action; **persons:** more than one individual; **people:** a group of persons united by race, government, or common characteristics.

Practicable: possible of being accomplished; **practical:** adapted to actual conditions.

Principal: the first or highest in rank; **principle:** a general truth or settled law or rule.

Prophecy: a prediction; **prophesy:** to predict.

Provided: on condition that; **providing:** the present participle of *provide*, meaning furnishing or supplying.

Raise: used for plants and animals; **rear:** used for children.

Raise: colloquialism for increase, as a *raise* in wages or prices; **rise:** preferred for advance or increase.

Rape: in a legal sense, forcible violation of a woman; **assault:** in a legal sense, a threat to do bodily harm; **attack:** to begin battle, to assail with speech or action. Newspapers incorrectly use *assault* and *attack* as euphemisms for *rape*.

Real estate man: one who deals in real estate; **realtor:** a term correctly applied only to a member of the National Association of Real Estate Boards.

Sanitarium: an institution for the treatment of disease or the care of invalids and the insane; **sanatorium:** has the same meaning as *sanitarium*, but through usage it is applied most often to an institution for the treatment of tuberculous people.

Serious: of grave import; **critical:** of or pertaining to a crisis; **dangerous:** attended with danger. These terms should be used discriminately in describing illnesses and injuries.

Set: a transitive verb requiring an object; the past tense and past participle are *set*; **sit:** an intransitive verb that does not require an object; the past tense and the past participle are *sat*.

Sewage: waste matter carried off in sewers; **sewerage:** a system of sewers.

Stationary: being in one place; **stationery:** writing paper, envelopes.

Suffer: to feel pain; **sustain:** to bear up under; **receive:** to get as a result of delivery.

Suit: a petition, clothing; **suite:** a series of rooms, furniture, dance movements.

Undetermined: not yet determined; **unknown;** not recognizable by anyone; **unidentified:** not yet identified.

Waive: to relinquish a right or claim; **wave:** to move something to and fro.

APPENDIX C

Newspaper Terms

Ad. Abbreviation for advertisement.
Add. New material added to an article; all pages of copy after page 1 are called *adds*.
Agate. The smallest type used by newspapers; it is 5½ points in depth. Agate lines, 14 of which equal one inch, are used to measure the depth of newspaper columns and advertisements.
Art. Any newspaper illustration—drawing, cartoon, photograph.
Attribution. Statement of the source of information; a speech tag like "he said."
Bank. A section of a headline, same as *deck*; a table on which type is kept.
Banner. A headline in large type that extends clear across the top of the page; also called a *streamer*.
Beat. A reporter's regular territory, also called a *run*; a story obtained first or exclusively by a reporter.
Beg your pardon. A newspaper's correction, printed as a separate item, of a mistake in an earlier story.
Blanket head. A headline more than one column wide that summarizes information given in two or more related stories.
Blow up. To enlarge a photograph.
Body type. The size of type used for most of the newspaper's content.
Boldface. A heavy black type, often abbreviated *bf*; the terms *fullface* and *ff* are also used.
Book. Assembled copy paper and carbon sheets ready for reporters to use; a story is frequently referred to as consisting of two or three *books* rather than two or three pages.
Border. A line or ornamental rule used to enclose a headline, story, or advertisement.
Box. A story or headline enclosed by a border.
Break. The point at which a story is continued from one page or column to another.
Bulldog. An early edition of a newspaper.
Bulletin. Last-minute important news covered in a paragraph or two. A press association *bulletin* consists of a lead paragraph that is followed by additional details as soon as information becomes available.

By-line. The line giving the name of the author of the news story or article.

Canned copy. Material purchased from syndicates or received from publicity agents.

Cap. Abbreviation for capital letter.

Caption. The explanatory material above or below a newspaper illustration; the cutline. See **Overline, Underline.**

Case. Cabinet for storing type.

Catchline. See **Guideline.**

Chase. A metal frame the size of a newspaper page in which the type is locked.

Cheesecake. Slang for photographs which emphasize the physical charms of women, especially legs; another term for the same is *leg art*.

Clips. Abbreviation for clippings, or stories cut from a newspaper and kept in the newspaper's library.

Clipsheet. Publicity material printed on one side of the sheet so that it can be easily cut out and used.

Column inch. A standard of measurement based on the newspaper column. An advertisement two columns wide and five inches deep is ten column inches.

Column rule. The rule that separates the columns of a newspaper.

Composing room. The department of the newspaper in which type is set.

Composition. The actual setting of type.

Compositor. A typesetter; the operator of a typesetting machine.

Copy. Manuscript from which type is set. A person who regularly does things that make news is spoken of as being *good copy*.

Copy boy. A boy who runs editorial room errands.

Copy cutter. The composing room employee who distributes copy among the compositors.

Copy desk. The desk where copy is edited and headlines are written.

Copyholder. The person who holds the manuscript while another person is reading proof for errors or deviations from it.

Copyreader. An editorial room employee who prepares copy for the composing room and writes the headlines for it.

Correction lines. Lines of type reset to correct errors.

Cover. To obtain information about an event for a story.

Credit line. The line acknowledging the source of a story, photograph, or engraving.

Crop. To indicate by marks the portion of a photograph to be included in an engraving.

Cub. A beginning reporter.

Cut. To delete or shorten. Any newspaper photograph or illustration; an engraving.

Cutline. The explanatory material above or below an illustration.

Cutoff rule. A rule used across columns to separate a headline, engraving, news article, or advertisement from other material.

Dash. A line less than a column wide that is used to separate stories, parts of stories, or divisions of a headline.

APPENDIX C: NEWSPAPER TERMS

Dash matter. Related material printed under a story but not part of the original story; it is separated from the story above by a dash.
Date line. The line at the beginning of a story that gives the place of origin, the date, and the source.
Dead. News copy or type that is no longer usable.
Deck. A section of a headline.
Double truck. The two facing pages at the center of a newspaper or section that are made up as one page.
Downstyle. A style which minimizes the use of capital letters, the preference being to lower-case letters on words that conventionally would be capitalized.
Dropline. A headline pattern in which lines are of the same length and are arranged to "step" or "drop" uniformly, as in the following:

―――――――――
 ―――――――――

Dummy. A small diagram of a newspaper page on which the editor marks instructions to the printer for placing type and illustrations.
Ears. Boxes at either side of the front-page name plate giving such information as the newspaper's circulation, the weather forecast, or a slogan.
Edition. All the copies of a newspaper printed at one time; regular editions are given such names as "Late Street" and "Final Home."
Editorialize. To write opinion rather than state facts in a news story or headline; to write an editorial.
Electrotype. A printing plate made by an electrochemical process.
Em. The square of the capital *M* in any size of type. It is used loosely as a unit of width based on 12-point type; for example, a newspaper column is 12 ems wide.
End dash. A dash used at the end of a story.
Face. The printing surface of type or of a plate.
Feature. To emphasize or give prominence to by placing first in a story or by using special typographical display; a special type of story written to entertain rather than inform; nonnews material such as comics, puzzles, and fiction.
Filler. Short items for plugging holes on the page; they often have no time limitations as to when they can be used.
Five W's. The main elements of news—who, what, when, where, and why.
Flag. The name of the newspaper on the front page.
Flash. Used by press associations for news of transcendent importance. A flash gives the gist of the news in a short sentence and it has priority on news wires.
Flimsy. A carbon copy of a news story, usually on onionskin or thin tissue paper.
Floorman. A printer.
Flush. Even with the column margin; a flush-left headline is one that aligns at the left with the left margin of the column and is irregular at the right-hand margin.
Follow or **follow-up.** A story giving new developments about one printed earlier.

Font. A complete assortment of type of one size and style.

Form. A page of type locked in a chase.

Fudge box. A device for clamping separate letters or figures to a stereotype plate; it is used primarily for getting late bulletins and sports results on the front pages of afternoon newspapers.

Fullface. Boldface type.

Future book. A record kept by the city desk of events that will take place in the future.

Galley. A shallow metal tray for holding type when it comes from the composing machine.

Galley proof. A proof pulled of type in a galley; this proof is read for errors and corrected before the type is put in the chase.

Glossy. A photograph with a hard, shiny finish.

Gothic. A type face that has strokes of the same width and without serifs.

Grapevine. Material set in type to be used at any time as needed to fill space.

Guideline. The label given a story and placed at the top of each page of copy for purposes of identification; also called a *slug*.

Half-tone. An engraving which duplicates the shadings and tones of a photograph by a multitude of small raised dots on the printing plate.

Handout. A publicity story or statement supplied by a press agent for publication.

Hanger. The part of a headline that descends from a banner or multiple-column deck.

Hanging indention. Copy or a headline with the first line set flush and subsequent lines evenly indented at the left.

Head count. The number of units—letters and spaces—in one line of a headline.

Headlinese. Jargon resulting from the necessity of using short words in a headline—such words as *rap, hit, solon.*

HTC or HTK. Head to come.

Human interest. A story interesting not for its significance but for its emotional appeal; it gives emphasis to people rather than the event.

Initial letter. A large display letter cut in at the beginning of a paragraph as an ornament to break up long stretches of body type.

Insert. Material to be incorporated in a story already sent to the composing room.

Intaglio. A method of printing by which ink is transferred to paper from areas sunk below the surface.

Inverted pyramid. A term used to describe the news story structure in which the most important information comes first, other information being given in order of decreasing interest. In headline patterns, a headline with the longest line at the top, succeeding lines being shorter and centered.

Italics. Slanting type.

Jim dash. A short dash used to separate the decks of a headline or unrelated short items in a column.

Jump. To continue a story from one page to another.

Jump head. The headline carried over the continued portion of a jumped story.

APPENDIX C: NEWSPAPER TERMS

Justify. To space out a line of type to full column width; to tighten the type in the chase by placing lead strips between the lines of type.
Kill. To delete from copy; to discard type.
Label head. A headline that states no action, such as "Mississippi Flood."
Layout. An arrangement of type and pictures for special display; a diagram of an advertisement to guide the printer.
Lead (pronounced lēed). The introductory summary of a news story, usually the first paragraph; the chief story, either of the day or on the page; a hint or tip that may be followed in getting information for a story.
Lead (pronounced lĕd). A thin metal strip inserted between lines of type to increase the space, especially in justifying a column in the chase.
Leaders. A row of dots or short dashes to direct the eye across an empty space in tabular matter.
Leased wire. A telephone wire over which a newspaper receives copy from a press association or a bureau maintained by the newspaper at a distant point.
Leg man. A reporter, especially one who merely gathers information and telephones it to a newspaper instead of writing his own stories.
Letterpress. A method of printing from a raised surface.
Lightface. A type design in which thin strokes form the letters.
Line engraving. A cut made from a black and white line drawing, such as a cartoon.
Locking up. Tightening the lines of type inside the chase so the form can be moved from the stone.
Logotype. A single piece of type containing two or more letters; a small reproduction of a name plate or store name.
Lower case. A small letter; often abbreviated *lc*.
Magazine. The part of a typesetting machine that holds the matrices.
Make over. To rearrange material on a page so as to improve the appearance or incorporate new stories.
Make-up. The arrangement of news stories, advertising, and other material on a page.
Masthead. An editorial page section listing the name of the newspaper, the publisher or business corporation, executives, membership in associations, telephone number, and other data.
Mat. Abbreviation of matrix.
Matrix. The impression of the page form on a cardboard for casting the stereotype or the printing plate; the brass mold for casting type in a typesetting machine.
Morgue. The newspaper's repository for files of engravings, pictures, and clippings needed for reference; the term is being replaced by *library*.
Mug shot. A photograph showing only the head and bust of a person.
Must. An instruction on copy indicating that it must be printed in the paper.
Name plate. The name of the newspaper that appears on the front page.
News hole. The space left for news and editorial matter after the advertising has been placed on the page.
Obit. Abbreviation of obituary; any news story reporting a death; also,

biographical information in the library or morgue about prominent persons.

Off the record. Information given a reporter that is not to be printed.

Overline. The heading over a cut.

Overset. Type set in excess of what is needed to fill the paper.

Personal. A short news item about an individual; it usually appears without a headline in a column with other such items.

Pi. Type that has been mixed or jumbled together.

Pica. Twelve-point type; the pica em is a standard measurement of width.

Pickup. Material already in type that is to be used with material sent later to the composing room, as when in revising a story part of the type matter is killed and the remainder is incorporated with the new information.

Pickup line. An instruction in a press association dispatch telling the desk where to insert or add material when a story is revised.

Play. The prominence given a story by the size of headline and position on the page.

Point. The unit of measurement of type; a point is 1/72 of an inch.

Precede. Material to be printed at the top of a news story, such as an editor's note or a bulletin.

Put to bed. To lock up the forms for an edition.

Railroad. To rush copy to the composing room without careful editing.

Read-out. See **Hanger.**

Retouch. To go over a photograph with pencil or brush to improve it for an engraving.

Revise. A new proof pulled after type has been corrected.

Rewrite. To revise a story in order to improve it, shorten it, or add new details; a story rewritten, without new information, from one in another paper.

Rewrite man. A staff member who receives telephoned information from reporters and writes the story.

Rim. The outer edge of the horseshoe-shaped copy desk.

Rim man. A copyreader.

Roman. A type face with pronounced differences in the weight of the strokes forming the letters and with serifs ending the strokes.

Rotogravure. A variety of intaglio printing adapted to a rotary press. Rotogravure sections of newspapers usually are pictorial sections in brown or sepia ink; the process is used on a few newspapers for the Sunday comics.

Rule. A metal strip that is type high and prints as a line.

Run. A particular territory, such as the city hall or capitol, to which a reporter is assigned to get news; same as a *beat*.

Running story. A story sent to the composing room in short sections to expedite setting it in type; a continuing news story, especially one about a rapidly changing situation.

Schedule. The city editor's record of assignments; the copy desk's record of stories sent to the composing room.

Screen. The cross-hatched glass through which pictures are rephotographed in making an engraving. The fineness or coarseness of the engraving is indicated by the number of lines to the inch; a 50-line screen is very coarse.

Series. The range of sizes in a type of one design.

APPENDIX C: NEWSPAPER TERMS

Serif. A small line at the end of the main strokes of a letter; most serifs are right-angled to the main strokes.
Slot. The inside of the horseshoe-shaped copy desk where the chief copyreader sits.
Slot man. The chief copyreader, the person sitting in the slot.
Slug. A guideline or label identifying a story; a single line of type from a typecasting machine.
Solid. Type set without spacing, or leading, between the lines.
Soundphoto. The name given by the International News Service to its system of transmitting photographs by wire.
Spot news. Unexpected happenings that furnish news for a paper; the news content of the paper as contrasted with the editorial and feature material.
Spread. A story that is prominently displayed, often over several columns, with accompanying art and subsidiary or "side" stories.
Star dash. A dash made up of a horizontal series of asterisks.
Step head. Same as *dropline head.*
Stet. Literally, let it stand. It is written above a change marked on copy or proof, and means do not make the change.
Stick. The holder used in setting type by hand. A stick holds about two inches of type; hence *stick* as a unit of measurement means about two inches.
Stone. A flat-topped table upon which forms are made up. Formerly it was of stone, but steel is now used.
Straight matter. Material set in body type, in contrast with headlines and advertisements set in display type.
Streamer. See **Banner.**
String. Pasted-up clippings turned in by a correspondent. The correspondent is paid "space" rates, the amount he receives depending on the length of his string.
Stringer. A correspondent paid space rates.
Subhead. A small headline, commonly one line in boldface, inserted in the body of a story to break up a long stretch of type.
Syndicate. A business organization engaged in buying news, feature, and art material for sale to newspapers.
Take. A section of a news story sent to the composing room before the complete story is written or edited. Takes may be as short as a single paragraph near deadline when maximum speed is necessary in getting a story in type.
Telephoto. The name given by the United Press to its system of transmitting photographs by wire.
Teletype. A typewriter operated by remote control via a telephone wire; often referred to as a *printer.* Press association news is received over a teletype.
Teletypesetter. A mechanical device attached to a typesetting machine so that the typesetting is controlled by a perforated tape instead of a person.
Thirty. The figure 30 used to indicate the end of a news story.
Thirty-dash. An end dash.
Thumbnail. A cut half a column wide.

Tieback. An explanatory clause, sentence, or paragraph in a news story that refreshes the reader's memory about earlier developments.

Tight paper. A paper so filled with advertising that little space is left for news.

Tombstone. Two or more headlines of the same type size and family placed side by side.

Trial by newspaper. Pre-trial publication of information and evidence that strongly influence the public regarding a person's guilt or innocence.

Trunk wire. The main news wire of a press association.

Turn rule. An instruction to the printer to turn a slug or rule upside down to indicate that a correction or alteration is to be made at that place.

Typo. A typographical error.

Undated. A press association story sent without a date line, because it was written in a bureau from stories originating at several different points.

Underline. The explanatory material under a cut.

Upstyle. Extensive use of capital or upper-case letters; the opposite of *downstyle*.

Widow. A short line of type that begins a page or column, or that ends a cut underline.

Wire filer. An employee in a press association bureau who arranges material for dispatching on the wire.

Wirephoto. The name given by the Associated Press to its system of transmitting photographs by wire. It is a trade name and not a generic term for any picture sent by wire.

Wrap around. To break a story from one column to another under a cut or under another story.

Wrap up. To cover all the angles of a story.

Wrong font. A notation on proof that the typesetter has used the wrong face or size of type; usually abbreviated to *wf*.

Zinc, zinc etching. A line engraving.

INDEX

Abbreviation, in headlines, 150-151
  stylesheet rules for, 429-430
Accuracy, checking for, 82-90
  newspaper regard for, 83-85
Action, in headlines, 143-146
  in pictures, 347-348
Adds, in wire report, 120
  marking copy for, 16
Advance stories, in wire report, 122-123
Advertising, free, 289-291
  inside-page make-up of, 238-243, 267-270
  ratio of news to, 248
Agate type, 13, 191
Albig, William, 296
Allen, John E., 134, 196, 203, 221
Altoona *Mirror*, 376
Amarillo *Globe-News*, 412, 422
A matter, 22
Ambiguities, 87-89
American Language, The, 153-154
American Language: Supplement I, The, 317
American Mercury, 44, 56-57
American Society of Newspaper Editors, 273, 304
American Speech, 407-408
American Type Founders Sales Corporation, 179
Anonymous sources, 63
Appleton *Post-Crescent*, 242, 395
Art of Plain Talk, The, 93
Art of Readable Writing, The, 93
Associated Press, 1, 51, 57, 64, 93, 94, 99, 103, 110, 114-116, 175, 318-319, 344, 348, 397
Associated Press Managing Editors Association, 51, 57, 359, 397
Attribution, 64-65, 75-76, 130
Authority, anonymous, 65

citing of, in news stories, 64-65
  in headlines, 155-156
Ayer, N. W., and Son, Inc., 201, 204

Balanced make-up, in inside pages, 239-240
  on page 1, 221, 222
Bangor *Daily News*, 397
Banks, in headlines, 137, 165-167
Banner headline, 137, 210-212, 261
Barksdale, W. D., 62
"Beg your pardon," 327
Bennett, James Gordon, 30, 39, 276-277, 316, 417
Bernays, Edward L., 301
Biglow Papers, The, 91
Binghamton *Press*, 415, 427
Birdsall, Amy, 412-413
Birmingham *News*, 412, 423
Black-letter type, 192
Blakeslee, Howard W., 100-101
Blanket headline, *see* Spread headline
Bleyer, Willard G., 276
Block-letter type, 194, 202-203
Body types, 12-13, 199-200
Boldface, marking copy for, 12-14
Boldface type, 192
Bookman, The, 40
Borders, 216
Boston *Post*, 227
Bovard, O. K., 31
Bowles, Samuel, 46
Boxed head, 138
Boxes, 215-216
Brace make-up, 224-225
Brandeis, Louis D., 302
Brislin, Mrs. J. Harold, 415
Broken page make-up, 224-231
Brown, Robert U., 283-284, 313, 410

449

450   INDEX

Brown, Warren, 386
Brucker, Herbert, 52, 85, 291
Bryant, William Cullen, 30, 37, 91-92
Budget, in wire report, 117-118
Bulletin of the American Society of Newspaper Editors, The, 69, 342
Bulletins, as precedes, 22
   in wire report, 121
   marking copy for, 22
Bumping headlines, 232-233
Business news, 397-409
   editing department of, 399-400
   improvement of, 397-399
   in wire report, 403-407
   local coverage of, 400-403
By-lines, marking copy for, 12

Canons of Journalism, The, 304, 306
Capitalization, 32
   in headlines, 152
   stylesheet rules for, 431-434
Capitals, marking copy for, 11, 14, 32
Captions, picture, 138, 360-364
Cedar Rapids *Gazette*, 412
Censorship, by minority groups, 315-316
   in war, 314
Chambers, Julius, 29
Changing American Newspaper, The, 52
Charleston (South Carolina) *News and Courier*, 318
Charnley, Mitchell V., 83-84
Chase, printer's, 187
Chase, Stuart, 107-108
Cheesecake, 350-351
Chicago *Daily News*, 95, 113, 301
Chicago *Sun*, 386
Chicago *Tribune*, 27, 31, 113, 394
Christian Science Monitor, 226, 236, 237
Cincinnati *Enquirer*, 27
Circulation, 4, 276 ff.
Circus make-up, 226
City Editor, 8, 30, 39, 386, 390
Clapper, Raymond, 89, 155
Clark, Al, 384-385
Cleveland *Plain Dealer*, 27
Clipsheets, 287, 289
Column rules, 196-197
Column widths, 199
Columns, country correspondence, 372-373, 375-378
   headings for, 175-177, 212-213
   sports, 380-381
Composing room, 15-19, 178-189
Connolly, Roger A., 342
Contempt of court, 333-335
Continuing Study of Newspaper Reading, The, 219, 236, 238, 278, 280, 319, 345-346, 355, 423
Contrast and balance make-up, 221-224
Contrast headlines, 212
Cooper, Kent, 348
Copy, editing tape report, 129
   headline, 159-160
   preparing for printer, 10-28
Copycutter, 18-19
Copyreaders, as guardians of accuracy, 82-83, 86-87
   duties of, 5-8
   faults of, 26-28
   need for, 3-5
   responsibility of, in libel, 320-321, 328-335
   role of, in evaluating news, 274-276
Copyreading, as art and science, 8-9
   in instructing printer, 12-14
   in marking wire copy, 14
   special problems of, in wire copy, 130-131
Copyreading symbols, 10-12
Copyright, 337-338
Corrections, in wire report, 121-122
Correspondents, country, 373-375
   state, 366-367
Counting out headlines, 138-142, 158
Country correspondence, 372-378
Craig v. Harney, 333
Credit lines for pictures, 363
Cropping pictures, 354
Crossline headline, 136
Cursive type, 193
Cutlines, 138, 360-364
Cutoff rules, 196-197
Cuts, *see* Engravings

Dashes, 197
Date-line, 215
Davis, Treva, 415, 427
Dayton *Journal-Herald*, 385
Decks, in headlines, 137, 165-167
Defense in libel, 325-328
Denver *Post*, 365
Department headings, 175-177
Descending order make-up, 240, 242
Design and Makeup of the Newspaper, 204
Des Moines *Register and Tribune*, 365
Detroit *Free Press*, 63
DeVoto, Bernard, 307
Disappearing Daily, The, 66
Downstyle, 32
Dropline headline, 136, 140, 142-143
Dummy, 252-256

INDEX

Early, Stephen, 1
Eau Claire *Leader* and *Telegram*, 411, 418
Editions, revision of stories for, 20-24
Editor & Publisher, 43, 235, 283, 294, 313, 321, 369, 410, 411, 419
Elrod caster, 189
Em, pica, 191
Engraving processes, 357
Engravings, determining size of, 355-357
  Fairchild Scan-a-graver, 359-360
  half-tone, 357
  line, 357
  ordering, 357-360
  See also Pictures
Errors, checking for, 82-90
  in grammar, 39-45
  in punctuation, 36-38
  in spelling, 33-36
  nature of newspaper, 83-85
  typographical, 33
Ethical problems, 302-319
  of fair play, 306-307
  of headlines, 155-157
  of maintaining proprieties, 316-319
  of news distortion, 66, 89-90
  of news of minorities, 314-316
  of news suppression, 309-314
  of personal privacy, 302-306
  of pictures, 346
Eyebrow headline, 137-138

Fadiman, Clifton, 96
Faherty, Robert, 95
Fairchild Scan-a-graver, 359-360
Fair comment and criticism, 326, 332
Families of type, 191-195
Fashion news, 426-427
Fat letters, in headlines, 138
Feature headlines, 138, 172-175
  nonnews, 175-177, 212-213
Figures, in headlines, 152
  stylesheet rules for, 434
Figures of speech, in headlines, 174
Fillers, headlines for, 204-205
  in make-up, 259
Financial news, 397-409
  jargon in, 407-409
  of bond markets, 404-405
  of commodity markets, 405-407
  of stock markets, 403-404
  wire report of, 403-407
Five W's, in headlines, 162-165
  in news story leads, 47, 67
Flash, in wire report, 121
Flat-serif type, 194
Flesch, Rudolf, 61, 93-94, 100, 103

Flush-left headline, 136-137, 140, 142-143
Focus make-up, 224-225
Folks, 374
Follett, Wilson, 40
Follow stories, 57
  headlines for, 171-172
Font of type, 195
Food news, 423-426
Forms, printer's, 187
Fort Madison *Evening Democrat*, 417-418
Fort Smith *Times-Record*, 62
Fortune, 314
Fort Worth *Star-Telegram*, 397, 418
Free advertising, 289-291
Freedom of Information, 85, 291
Freedom of press, 320-321
Front page, *see* Page 1 make-up
Fudge box, 393
Full-line headline, 136, 140, 143

Galley proofs, guideline system of marking, 25
  pulling, 186
Gothic type, 194, 202-203
Grammatical errors, 39-45
  conjunctions, 44
  number, 39-40
  participles, 42-43
  prepositions, 44
  relative pronouns, 41
  split infinitive, 44-45
  tense sequence, 41-42
Greeley, Horace, 29, 277
Guidelines, 15-20
  for pictures and captions, 363-364
  in wire report, 120
Gunning, Robert, 93

Half-tones, 357-360
Hamilton, E. Douglas, 326-327
Handouts, 267 ff.
Hanger headline, 137, 168-169, 259-260
Hanging indention headline, 137, 143
Harper's Magazine, 307
Harrisburg *Patriot* and *News*, 384
Harvard Law Review, 302
Headlines, 132-177
  abbreviation in, 150-151
  action in, 143-146
  appearance of, 142
  banks in, 137, 165-167
  banner, 137, 210-212, 261
  blind first lines in, 147-148
  boxed, 138
  condensing content for, 159-161

Headlines—*(Continued)*
 counting out, 138-142, 158
 crossline, 136
 decks in, 137, 165-167
 diction of, 151, 153-155
 drop-line, 136, 140, 142-143
 ethics of, 155-157
 evaluation of, 132
 eyebrow, 137-138
 feature, 138, 172-175
 flanking marks for, 160
 flush-left, 136, 137, 140, 142-143
 follow, 171-172
 full-line, 136, 140, 143
 functions of, 133-136
 hanger, 137, 168-169
 hanging indention, 137, 143
 headlinese in, 153-155
 identification in, 148-150
 inverted-pyramid, 137, 143
 jump, 138, 169-171
 label, 133
 marking copy for, 160
 multiple-deck, 165-167
 "must" elements in, 162-165
 nonnews, 175-177, 212-213
 omission of words in, 146-147
 patterns for, 136-138
 punctuation in, 151-152
 qualification in, 156-157
 rules for writing, 142-157
 schedules for, 141
 split, 147
 spread, 137, 168-169, 208-210, 259-260
 standing, 138, 175-177
 style in, 151-153
 subheads, 171, 213
 tense in, 143-144
 terminology of, 136-138
 top, 137, 208-209
 verb, 146-147
 voice in, 144-145
Headline type, 200-213
 banners, 210-211
 contrast, 212
 departmental, 212-213
 feature, 212-213
 fillers, 204-205
 flat-serif faces, 203
 gothic faces, 202-203
 patterns, 203-204
 roman faces, 201-202
 secondary stories, 206-207
 selection of, 203-204
 shorts, 204-205
 sizes used for, 204-212
 spread, 208-209
 subordinate stories, 205
 top-column, 208
Hearst, William Randolph, 116
Helter-skelter make-up, 226-227
Herbert, John R., 283
Hills, Lee, 63
Houston *Post,* 318
Howard, Roy W., 116
Human interest, 99-102, 346

Identification, in headlines, 148-150
 of events, 62-63
 of organizations, 60-61
 of persons, 58-60
 of places, 61-62
Illustrations, in make-up, 264-267
 See also Engravings; Pictures
Imagery, in headlines, 174
Indention, marking copy for, 13-14
Initial letters, 13-14, 215
Inland Daily Press Association, 204
Inserts, marking copy for, 21-22
Inside make-up, 238-243, 267-270
Institute of Propaganda Analysis, 296
International News Service, 1, 68, 77, 79, 110, 116-117, 345
Interpretation of news, 273-274
Intertype, 181
Inverted-pyramid headline, 137, 143
Inverted-pyramid news story structure, 46 ff.
Irving, Washington, 291-292
Italic type, 12, 13, 193

Jargon, 104-105
 fashion, 427
 federalese, 103
 financial, 407-409
 headline, 153-155
 legal, 104-105
 medical, 105
Jim dashes, 197-198
Johnson, Earl J., 93, 94-95
Johnstown *Democrat,* 241, 401
Jones, Jenkin Lloyd, 155-156
Jones, Vincent S., 281, 345, 350-351
Journalism Quarterly, 83-84, 133, 234, 345
Jump headlines, 138, 169-171
Jump stories, 233-238
Justification, of column, 195-196
 of line of type, 182

Kansas City *Star,* 26, 31
Keyboard, teletype, 123
Key words, in headlines, 162-165

INDEX

Kicker headline, 137-138
Kill, in wire report, 121-122

Label headline, 143
Laramie *Bulletin*, 235
Late City Edition, 327, 390, 409
Law, 320-338
    contempt of court, 333-334
    copyright, 337-338
    freedom of press, 320
    libel, 321-333
    lottery, 336
    restrictions on publication, 336-337
    trial by newspaper, 335
Layout, picture, 354-355
Leading of type, 13, 195-196
Leads, five W's in, 47
    in speech stories, 66-67
    in wire report, 120, 131
    minor details in, 50
    new, 20-21
    playing up the feature in, 50-51
    simplifying, 49-50
    slugging, 20-21, 22-23
Lee, Ivy, 290
Letterspacing, 143
Libel, 321-333
    copyreader's problem of, 328-333
    defenses in, 325-328
    defined, 321-325
    fair comment and criticism in, 326, 332
    "honest mistake," 327
    malice in, 327
    privilege in, 326-327, 330-332
    retraction for, 327
    right of reply and consent in, 326-327
    truth as defense in, 325
Libel *per quod*, 324
Libel *per se*, 323
Liebling, A. J., 89, 390
Lightface type, 192
Lindstrom, Carl E., 83-85
Line engravings, 357
Linotype, 181-185
Linotype News, 134
Lippmann, Walter, 272, 275, 283
Literary Digest, 87
Los Angeles *Times*, 26, 229
Louisville *Courier-Journal*, 278-279
Louisville *Times*, 397
Lowell, James Russell, 91
Low Man on a Totem Pole, 316-317
Ludlow Typograph, 184-185
Lundberg, Ferdinand, 282

McCormick, Robert M., 31
MacDougall, Curtis D., 276

Macfadden, Bernarr, 246
MacNeil, Neil, 9
Magazines, typecasting machine, 181-183
Make-up, 218-270
    checking errors in, 256-257
    determining space in, 248-249
    dummies for, 252-255
    for major news display, 260-263
    inside-page, 238-243, 267-270
    page 1, 220-238, 257-263
    position and rank of pages in, 218-220
    rules for, 231-238
    slugsheets and schedules in, 250-252
    tabloid, 243-246
    with pictures, 264-267
    See also Page 1 make-up
Malice, in libel, 327
Markel, Lester, 273, 318
Markets, news of, 403-409
Marks, copyreader's, 10-23
    proofreader's, 24-25
Markups and fixes, 23-24
Matrix, casting stereotype of, 189
    in typesetting machine, 181, 184-185
    rolling, 188
Meeman, J. Edward, 69
Memphis *Commercial Appeal*, 26
Memphis *Press-Scimitar*, 26, 69
Mencken, H. L., 153-154, 317-318
Mergenthaler, Ottmar, 180
Miami *Herald*, 333, 412
Mickelson, Paul R., 94, 100
Minneapolis *Star* and *Tribune*, 27, 304
Minneapolis *Times*, 397
Minton, Arthur, 407-408
Missoula *Missoulian*, 412
Mitchell, Joseph, 316-317, 332-333
Modern type, 194
Monotype, 185
More, 16, 19
Morris, Mary, 411
Morrison, Theodore, 54
Mortised cuts, 354
My Ears Are Bent, 316-317, 332-333

Name plate, 226
Nelson, William Rockhill, 31
New Haven *Register*, 342
New Orleans *Times-Picayune*, 394
New York *American*, 155
New York *Daily News*, 113, 243-244, 285
New York *Evening Post*, 291-292
New York *Herald*, 39, 316, 417

454 INDEX

New York *Herald Tribune*, 26, 53, 106, 107, 113, 201, 204, 225, 231, 285, 326, 379, 390, 393, 394, 409
New York *Journal-American*, 220, 285, 317
New York *Times*, 26, 52, 53, 59, 113, 204, 220, 222, 236, 239, 273, 285, 314, 318, 345, 394, 404
New York *Tribune*, 29
New York *World*, 155
New York *World-Telegram*, 303
New Yorker, The, 54-55, 87, 303
News, economic factors in, 276-278
   entertainment and, 281-284
   ethical problems of, 302-319
   evaluation of, 3-4, 274-276
   influenced by publication conditions, 284-286
   interpretation in, 273-274
   legal problems of, 320-338
   nature of, 271-274
   propaganda and publicity in, 287-301
   property rights in, 337-338
   readership polls of, 278-281
News distortion, 66, 89-90
   in headlines, 155-157
News Hunting on Three Continents, 29
Newspaper and the Historian, The, 85
Newspaper Designing, 196, 203, 221
Newspaper: Its Making and Its Meaning, The, 9
News services, *see* Press association news
News stories, attribution and authority in, 64-65
   coherence in, 52-54
   explanatory background in, 56 ff.
   handling revisions of, 20-24
   identifications in, 58-63
   inserts in, 21-22
   interpretation in, 57
   inverted-pyramid structure of, 46-48
   new leads for, 20-21
   opinion in, 78-79
   speech reports, 65-69
   tiebacks in, 63
   trimming, 70-81
News story structure, coherence in, 52-54
   inverted pyramid, 46 ff.
   leads, 47, 49-53
Newsweek, 226
Nieman Fellows, 385
Nieman Reports, 48
North American Newspaper Alliance, 113
Numerals, stylesheet rules for, 434

Oblique type, 193
Ochs, Adolph S., 318

Oklahoma City *Daily Oklahoman*, 262
Old style type, 194
Olds, George, 294-295
Olson, Kenneth E., 267
Overline, 138, 361-363
Oxford rule, 196, 216

Page 1 make-up, 220-231, 257-263
   brace or focus, 224-225
   broken page, 224-226
   contrast and balance, 221-224
   exact balance, 221-222
   experimental, 226, 231
   major news display in, 260-263
   special problems of, 257-260
   tabloid, 243-246
Paragraphs, marking for, 11
   length of, 99
Parallel rule, 196, 216
Patterson, Joseph Medill, 244, 245
Pearson, Drew, 318
Pennekamp *v.* Florida, 333
Peterson, Leo H., 387
Philadelphia *Evening Bulletin*, 27
Philadelphia *Inquirer*, 251, 352-353
Photoengraving, 357-358
Photogravure, 360
Pica, as measurement of width, 12-13, 191
Pickup lines, in wire report, 120-121
Pictorial journalism, 339-341
Picture editor, 341-342
Pictures, 339-364
   cropping, 354,
   cutlines for, 360-364
   editing, 351-355
   engravings of, 355-360
   handling assignments for, 341-342
   judging, 345-351
   layouts for, 351-355
   make-up with, 264-267
   mug shots, 348, 355
   reproduction qualities of, 350-353
   retouching, 351-354
   Soundphoto, 116, 344
   sources of, 341-345
   Telephoto, 117, 344-345
   typography of cutlines for, 264-267
   wired transmission of, 343-346
   Wirephoto, 116, 344, 359-360
Pittsburgh *Press*, 413
Pittsburgh *Sun-Telegraph*, 228
Poe, J. Charles, 273
Point measurement of type, 12, 189-191
Policy, *see* Ethical problems; Law; News; Propaganda; Publicity
Pope, James S., 278-279
Precedes, 22

INDEX

Press association news, 110-131
  adds, 120
  advance stories, 122-123
  assembly of stories, 124-128
  budget, 117-118
  bulletins, 121
  copyreading problems, 130-131
  corrections and revisions, 121-122
  day wire, 119
  end marks, 119-120
  flash, 121
  marking copy, 14
  night wire, 119
  95 slug, 121
  numbering dispatches, 119-120
  perforated tape operation, 128-130
  pickup lines, 120-121
  teletype code, 123
  teletypes, 110-111, 123
  world-wide networks, 110-114
Printing procedures, 180, 186, 187, 188, 189
Privacy, right of, 302-306
Privilege, in libel, 325, 331-332
Proofreader's marks, 24-25
Propaganda, 295-301
  definition of, 295-296
  techniques of, 296-298
Property rights in news, 337-338
Providence *Evening Bulletin* and *Journal*, 369
Publicity, 287-295
  clipsheets, 287
  guiding principles for printing, 289-291
  handouts, 287-289
Public Opinion, by William Albig, 296
Public Opinion, by Walter Lippmann, 272
Pulitzer, Joseph, 155
Punctuation, 36-38
  in headlines, 151-152
  stylesheet rules for, 435-437

Qualification, in headlines, 155-157
Quill, The, 83, 89, 155
Quincy *Patriot Ledger*, 283
Quotations, in headlines, 152
  in speech reports, 65-69
  stylesheet rules for, 436-437

Readability, Flesch test for, 94
  Gunning test for, 93-94
  in personal words and sentences, 100-102
  in sentences, 98-99
  measuring, 93-98
  paragraphing for, 99

Reader interest, in pictures, 346-347
Reader's Digest, 87
Readership studies, 5, 278-281, 346-347
Read-in headline, 137-138
Read-out headline, 137, 168-169, 259-260
Release dates, in wire report, 122-123
Reporters, need for copyreader to know, 83
  space-stealing, 80
Retouching photographs, 351-353
Retractions, 327
Right of privacy, 302-306
Ripley, George, 29
Roanoke *Times* and *World-News*, 27
Roman type, 193-194, 201-202
Roosevelt, Franklin D., 1-2, 150, 155
Rotogravure, 360
Runner, Harvey E., 409

Sacramento *Bee*, 31
St. Louis *Post-Dispatch*, 27, 31, 236, 301, 394
St. Louis *Star-Times*, 27, 337
St. Paul *Dispatch* and *Pioneer Press*, 27, 412
Salmon, Lucy Maynard, 85
San Francisco *Call-Bulletin*, 397
San Francisco *Chronicle*, 31, 43, 394
Sans-serif type, 194
Santa Fe *New Mexican*, 411, 423
Saturday Review of Literature, The, 95
Schedules, copy, 250-252
  headline, 141
Schramm, Wilbur, 234
Scientific American, 307-308
Scranton *Tribune*, 415
Screen, half-tone, 357-358, 360
Scripps, E. W., 116
Script type, 193
Secondary headlines, 206-207
Second-day headlines, 171-172
Semantics, 105-109
Sentences, personal, 100-102
  readability in, 93-96, 98-99
Shorts, headlines for, 204-205
Simplified spelling, 31, 36
Size of type, 12, 189-191
Slugs, *see* Guidelines
Smith, H. Allen, 316-317
Smith, Red, 390
Society news, *see* Women's department
Soundphoto, 116, 344
Space, estimating for news, 248-250
Spacebands, 181-182
Spartanburg *Herald-Journal*, 239, 371
Speech stories, editing of, 65-69
  faults in leads of, 66

INDEX

Speech tags, 65-69
Spelling, simplified, 31, 36
   words frequently misspelled, 33-36
Sport news, 379-396
   bunk leads in, 393
   college publicity and, 388-389
   columns, 380-381
   commercialism in, 385-388
   desk problems of, 392-396
   gambling problems of, 386-387
   jargon in, 389-392
   make-up, 395-396
   participant sports, 384-385
   space and coverage problems, 382-384
Sports Page, by Stanley Woodward, 379, 384, 389
Spread headline, 137, 168-169, 208-210, 259-260
Springfield (Massachusetts) *Republican*, 46
Square-serif type, 194, 203
Standing headline, 138, 175-177
State College (Pennsylvania) *Centre Times*, 5
State news, 365-372
   desk problems, 367-369
   directing correspondents for, 366-367
   placement and play of, 369-372
State wire, press association, 112-113
Steigleman, Walter A., 134-135
Step headline, 136, 140, 142-143
Stereotyping, 188-189
Stick, composing, 179
   Ludlow, 184-185
Straight matter, 12, 182-183
Streamer headline, 137, 210-212, 261
Style, down, 32
   in headlines, 151-153
   news and literary, 91-93
   special newspaper, 29-32
   up, 32
Stylesheet, newspaper use of, 29-32
   sample of, 429-437
Subheads, 171, 213
Subordinate headlines, 205-206
Sutton, Albert A., 204
Symbols, copyreader's, 10-12
   in wire report, 117 ff.
   proofreader's, 24-25

Tabloid make-up, 243-246
Takes, marking copy for, 19
Telephoto, 117, 344-345
Teletype, 110-111, 123
Teletype keyboard, 123
Teletypesetters, 127, 189
Tense, in headlines, 143-144
   sequence of, 41-42

Text type, 192-193
Thin letters, in headlines, 138
Thirty-dash, 197-198
Thumbnail cuts, 13
Tieback, 63
Time, 82, 226, 318
Titles, stylesheet rules for, 429, 431
Toledo *Blade*, 30
Tombstoning, 232
Top-column headlines, 137, 208-209
Trade area news, 365-378
Trade brands and names, 290
Transitions, 54, 74-75
Trimming news stories, by removing opinion, 77-79
   estimating length in type for, 71
   need for, 70-71
   of repetition, 77
   of unnecessary attributions, 75-76
   of unnecessary transitions, 74-75
   of unnecessary words, 71-72
   of wordy clauses, 74
   of wordy phrases, 72-74
Truman, Harry S., 2, 318
Trunk wires, 113-115
Truth, defense in libel, 325
Tulsa *Tribune*, 155
Turn rule, 16, 19
Type, body, 199-200
   designs of, 192-195
   foundry, 179-180
   headline, 200-203
   leading of, 195-196
   measurement of, 189-192
   parts of piece of, 179-180
   See also Headline type
Type-casting machines, 180-189
Typographical brighteners, 213-216
Typographical errors, 24, 33
Typography, principles of good, 216-217
Tyranny of Words, The, 107-108

Underlines, 138, 361-363
United Press, 2, 93, 94, 102, 110, 116, 345, 387
United States News, 226
Upstyle, 32
Utica *Observer-Dispatch* and *Press*, 281, 345, 350, 411-412

Verbiage, trimming, 72-75
Verbs, in headlines, 145-146
Villard, Oswald Garrison, 66

Walker, Stanley, 8, 30, 39, 386, 390
Walters, Basil L., 339

INDEX

Waring, Thomas R., 318
Warren, Samuel N., 302
Washington *Post,* 112, 349, 358, 424
Washington *Star,* 27, 223
Wayward Pressman, The, 89, 390
Weight, typographical, 192
Wheeler, Kittredge, 43
Wirephoto, 116, 344, 360
Women's department, 410-428
    club news, 421-422
    coverage of news, 418-419
    editor, 414-416
    fashion news, 426-427
    features, 423-427
    food news, 423-426
    make-up, 428
    shift from society news, 410-414
    society news problems, 417-423
    Sunday sections, 422-423
Woodburn, Bert W., 345

Woodward, Stanley, 379, 384, 386, 389
Words, commonly misused, 88-39, 438-440
    compounding of, 35-36
    definition of, in news stories, 63
    eliminating unnecessary, 71-75
    frequently misspelled, 33-36
    headline, 153-155
    jargon, *see* Jargon
    overuse of variants, 40-41
    readability of, 93 ff.
    semantics, 105-109
    smear, 156
Wrap around, 197, 243
Wrong font, 195

Yale University Law Journal, 335
York *Gazette and Daily,* 245
Your Newspaper, edited by Leon Svirsky, 385